A Full Hearing

A Full Hearing

Orality and Literacy in
the Malay World

Amin Sweeney

UNIVERSITY OF CALIFORNIA PRESS
Berkeley · Los Angeles · London

University of California Press
Berkeley and Los Angeles, California

University of California Press, Ltd.
London, England

© 1987 by
The Regents of the University of California

Library of Congress Cataloging-in-Publication Data

Sweeney, Amin.
  A full hearing.

  Bibliography: p.
  1. Malay literature—History and criticism.
  2. Oral tradition—Malaysia.   3. Oral tradition—
Indonesia.   I. Title.
PL5130.S94   1987   899'.28'09   86-25042
ISBN 0-520-05910-7 (alk. paper)

Printed in the United States of America

1 2 3 4 5 6 7 8 9

Contents

Preface

For many Westerners, a book dealing with Malay will immediately be associated with at best the exotic, at worst the obscure and peripheral. It is germane to mention at the outset, therefore, that in terms both of the number of people speaking it, and of its geographical distribution, Malay (now known as *Bahasa Indonesia, Bahasa Malaysia,* or still simply *Bahasa Melayu*) ranks no lower than sixth among the world's languages. More people speak Malay on a day-to-day basis than German, Japanese, French, or Arabic. Malay is spoken by more Muslims than any other language. Today, Malay is the national language of Indonesia, Malaysia, and Brunei; it is an official language of Singapore; it is the mother tongue of over two million people in South Thailand. The number of speakers is rapidly approaching the two hundred million mark.

A language spoken by such a sizable portion of humanity should surely attract more attention from those impressed by force of numbers. Yet officialdom in the United States often appears to equate its importance with the likes of Igbo and Ga. Furthermore, a language which has served as a vehicle of the four major world religions, and has been the major language of scholarship and trade in Southeast Asia for over a thousand years, is surely not peripheral. And a glance at the modern panoply of print and electronic media demonstrates that the Malay world is very much in the international mainstream.

While these remarks may incline the nonspecialist in Southeast

Asian studies to accept that what happens in the Malay world is worthy of his attention and even encourage him to read this book, they are not intended to imply that a study of orality and literacy in Malay is more worthwhile than would be one of a lesser-known language. Indeed, the danger of the "mainstream" argument is that it may lead the reader to equate literacy in Malay with his own brand of literacy, Western print literacy, which he may take entirely for granted. It is all too easy to perceive universals. The situation of the scholar is similar to that of E. H. Gombrich's artist, who is attracted by motifs which can be rendered in his idiom: "as he scans the landscape, the sights which can be matched successfully with the schemata he has learned to handle will leap forward as centers of attention." Yet, as Clifford Geertz emphasizes, our aim should be to make ourselves aware of the diversities of human culture, for "it may be in the cultural particularities of people—in their oddities—that some of the most instructive revelations of what it is to be generically human are to be found." And, often enough, those schemata may preclude a clear view even of one's own society, especially outside one's immediate milieu. An example is the notion of "Western print literacy." This term is acceptable when used to refer to the possibilities of print literacy which have been realized. However, the Western scholar of a Third World society who takes the standards of his academic coterie as the norm is likely to have a very idealized notion of Western literacy. A closer look at his own society may reveal to him many of the oral tendencies he had previously associated with cultures only recently introduced to mass literacy.

In traditional Malay society, the principles used to create both oral and written composition were essentially similar. The vital distinction to be made is rather between aural and visual consumption. Traditional Malay writing was intended to be heard, and this aurality continues to exert its influence even in this age of mass literacy. Paradoxically, a study of "orality" can only be undertaken by literates, and although we must attempt a "close hearing" in addition to our close reading, in the final analysis our work is visually based. We entertain the conceit of avoiding the term "text" for our oral materials; in fact, the moment we transcribe them, they become texts.

As I trust will become clear, the title of this book refers to the need to understand Malay tradition on its own terms. Only by subjecting our own givens—the assumptions of our predecessors—to a careful examination will it become possible to afford Malay tradition a full hearing. The present work is still but a modest step in this direction.

I wish to record my gratitude to the following persons for a variety of help and encouragement: Dato' Abdullah Mohamed, Alton Becker, William Collins, Robert Goldman, Ismail Hussein, Russell Jones, Ulrich Kratz, Campbell MacKnight, James Matisoff, Eric Oey, Nigel Phillips, William Roff, Frits Staal, and U. S. Wiradisastra. I am most grateful to the Malay students, storytellers, and other persons—too numerous to be cited individually—whose composition has formed the basis of much of my work.

For their helpful comments on an earlier stage of this work, I wish to thank A. H. Johns, B. Parnickel, J. J. Ras, C. Skinner, and C. W. Watson.

Much gratitude is due, as always, to Leonard Nathan for his helpful suggestions, for his friendship, and for suggesting the title of this book.

I am especially grateful to Sylvia Tiwon, my severest critic and major source of inspiration. If this book has any merit, much of the credit will be hers.

Berkeley
July 1985

Introduction

This book is concerned with oral and written composition in Malay. It is not an attempt to produce yet another "history" of Malay literature, nor is it an essay in literary criticism. It is rather an attempt to examine the relationships between oral and written traditions. Indeed, the basic argument is that only by studying their interaction can one begin to understand the workings of either, for, since the advent of writing in the Malay world, the development of neither tradition has been independent of or even parallel to the other. On the one hand, writing caused the displacement of large areas of the oral tradition and transformed much of what survived. On the other hand, oral habits persisted in written composition throughout the age of manuscript culture, and even in this age of print and mass literacy, many areas of Malay-speaking society still reveal a strongly oral orientation.

These traditions, however, are not merely objects of scrutiny placed in a state of suspended animation before the scholar. They are traditions of communication, shaped in the interaction between speakers and audiences: conventions that form and reinforce verbal communities. The basic premise of modern rhetorical analysis, which has been mainly concerned with written composition, is that a text constitutes a transaction between an author and an audience. This does not mean that we must know everything about the author of flesh and blood, or of the "real" audience who read the work. The author and audience are to be found within the text. By "author" we mean the implied author, the official or idealized projection of the author created in the text. The ethos of this implied author will vary, depending on the reactions the writer seeks to elicit from his audience. Similarly, by "audience," we mean the audience postulated by the writer, and which he hopes his reader may become. This audience implied in the text is also a creation of the writer and can only be discovered from a close reading of that text.[1]

In view of the oral roots of rhetoric, it is perhaps unnecessary to add that this rhetorical approach is equally valid for the study of oral composition. Although the performance is "live," the teller, no less than the writer, assumes an ethos, an official version of himself. Similarly, he, too, postulates an audience, with which he hopes his actual listeners may identify, and which he may adjust, depending upon the reactions he receives from those listeners.

It follows from this that in speaking of intentionality, we are concerned with the intentions of the author or teller implied in the text or telling. Indeed, the avowed intentions of the man who wrote the book or told the tale may be of interest to us only if they were not realized in his composition.

A composition, oral or written, is the result of a series of choices. By subjecting a text to a close reading,[2] one aims to discover why those particular choices were made. In other words, one seeks to establish what common ground the author or teller assumes of his audience, what role he requires them to play, what reactions he desires from them, and what methods he employs to achieve this. On the one hand, by insisting on a close reading of the text we avoid the temptation to regard that text as a series of cues which serve only to spark off all manner of unreined imaginings in the mind of the reader, or (producing much the same result), as a screen on which to project material extraneous to the text. On the other hand, by treating a text as an

1. The terms "implied author" and "postulated reader" were originated by Wayne C. Booth, 1961:70ff, 157. See further Sweeney, 1980:7, 29; 1980a:15ff.

2. A "close hearing" is also vital for understanding orally presented materials. It should be noted, however, that this is not the way a traditional audience would have heard such materials. Audience conditions were informal; the audience would not expect to catch every word. Both writer and teller responded to the needs of their listeners by unfolding the content of their tales slowly, spreading it thinly by the liberal use of repetition. (See further Sweeney, 1972, 1973, 1980.) Furthermore, while the scholar may devote much attention to the aural aspects, in the final analysis his approach will be visual. A successful interpretation will demand prior transcription, and he will presumably wish to write about his work. In studying oral tradition, our methods are not *of* oral tradition.

exchange or transaction, we do not allow ourselves to perceive it as an object, divorced completely from the idea of author or audience.

The basic prerequisite for an examination of the choices made by author or teller is a knowledge of the range of possibilities from which choices may be made. It is now a commonplace that any composition should be studied in its cultural context. It is rarely stressed, however, that such a contextual study must include an awareness of the constraints imposed and the scope offered by the medium of discourse employed, for the choices available in an oral culture are different from those in a society possessing writing, and within the latter the possibilities offered by a manuscript culture differ considerably from those in a print culture. The introduction of a new medium, furthermore, does not necessarily produce immediate cognizance in the recipient culture of a widened or transformed range of choices.

The fulfillment of this prerequisite creates no problem for the Western scholar who studies a contemporary work from his own tradition, for he does so contextually, whether consciously or otherwise. Even the most extreme of the New Critics who attempted to sequester literary works from life could not, of course, study a text in a vacuum. They naturally took for granted the knowledge, not merely of the literary background but also of their own society and history, required to understand that text. They also took for granted the conventions and possibilities of print, the medium they shared with the writers of the works they studied.

For the scholar of a culture not his own, such matters cannot be assumed, for otherwise, he will unwittingly study a composition in the context of his own culture, indeed of his own "Literature." His problem is further compounded when the composition he studies is the product of a medium not his own: he will tend to approach a composition of oral (i.e., nonliterate) or manuscript culture with the expectations of one who is to read a work produced by print culture. And in the Malay context, this tendency is reinforced by the fact that the traditional composition he reads—including both palace literature and oral performance adapted into written form—is likely to be in romanized Malay, produced with the format and employing the conventions of a modern printed work. For example, the use of repetition in the composition of an orally oriented society will reveal a different purpose from repetition in a printed work intended to be experienced visually. What might initially appear to the modern reader of such a text as a trope, only to be dismissed as mere redundancy, is likely to be neither. Rather it is an essential device for ensuring effective communication with a listening, nonliterate audience.

Unaware of the range of possibilities from which choices could be made in a medium very different from their own, scholars in the past were led to assume similarities with their own norms, particularly in the matter of intentionality, so that, for example, a composition concerned with perceptions of past events would be seen as the result of an attempt to write the scholar's idea of "history." The disparity between the two would then be taken as evidence that the Malay scribe was less than successful in his undertaking. More recently, it has become the fashion to insist on the need to avoid imposing one's own norms on a composition from a very different culture. This is an entirely laudable enterprise. But even given some knowledge of the contemporary culture, in the absence of an awareness of the constraints and scope of the medium, the scholar may tend merely to assume differences, and thus acquire the notion that Malay composition is everything his own is not. He is, in fact, still applying his own norms: he is perceiving reverse images. The result is that the Malay is turned into an alien being inhabiting another world. This impression may then be reinforced by the use of a "sympathetic" style, the underlying notion being apparently that to depict the exotic one must write exotically; to describe the alien, one's prose must acquire an alien flavor.

The current widespread interest in orality and literacy is clearly no accident: as is evidenced by the concerns of McLuhanism, the advent of the electronic age and the resulting concept of "media" have permitted us to begin to appreciate the workings of earlier media and the significance of the shifts therein.[3] Such an appreciation offers us the

---

3. One of the most striking features of the present technological age, moreover, is the electronic revival of sound, producing what Walter J. Ong has termed "secondary orality" (1971:20). It can hardly be coincidence, moreover, that the rehabilitation of "Rhetoric" occurred only after the appearance of this secondary orality of the modern age. I am not thinking merely of the fact that the human voice has never before been so widely used in the art of persuasion as in modern techniques of propagandizing and advertising; I would also suggest that the new understanding of earlier media of communication and of the interaction between them—an understanding made possible by the development of the electronic media—has engendered an awareness that the use of rhetoric is implicit in all human speech. While this observation is stimulated by the ideas of Ong, its emphasis is somewhat different. Ong (1971:vii–viii) considers that by the mid-twentieth century, the rhetorical tradition had become so remote that the very strangeness of the lifestyle it enfolded attracted scholars to the study of its history, and that the resulting understanding has "enabled us better to see the significance of the shifts in media and modes of knowledge, storage and retrieval."

possibility of liberating ourselves at least to some extent from the assumptions of a print-based society, and this is a vital prerequisite for an understanding of traditional Malay composition, both oral and written. An approach which takes into account the modes of composition, presentation, and consumption possible in a given medium opens up the way for us to battle down our presuppositions and preconceived criteria, and at least attempt to analyze and understand our material on its own terms. Seen from this viewpoint, the tired old accusations that such "relativism" erodes all standards of quality are simply irrelevant, and merely reflect the presupposition that the primary purpose of studying "Literature" is the dispensing of praise and blame according to some absolute yardstick. Our task is to understand, not to pass judgment. The corollary of this, of course, is that understanding the workings of oral tradition does not imply accepting its norms as our own or advocating a return to orality, as one or two of my students in California enthusiastically imagined. If that were so, one would certainly not be attempting to write a book about it. While our aim is to understand that tradition *on* its own terms, the elucidation of it is very much *in* our terms, for in an oral society—or one still revealing a strong oral orientation—the very concept of attempting to analyze one's orality is completely unfamiliar. Thus, for example, the scholar who teaches folklore to students from a strongly oral background may become aware that the task of turning those students into folklorists paradoxically involves weaning them away from oral habits: the very process of teaching them to analyze and articulate how the oral person operates will, if successful, ensure that they themselves no longer operate in that fashion. Similarly, the teacher of modern literature who presents Malaysian students with certain works of the Indonesian poet Chairil Anwar may have great difficulty persuading them to accept the poetry on its own terms. Yet this requirement is a relatively recent development even in Western literature—especially when the object of study is the product of a society not one's own.[4] And in Malay tradition, the communal (aural) consumption of oral

4. In the West, too, the subject of belief is highly relevant to the appreciation of literature, and the difference of attitude between Malay and Western society in this respect is one of degree, not of kind. We are not concerned with the author's personal beliefs, but with those of the implied author created in his work. For his writing to be effective, the writer must establish common ground between his implied author and his postulated audience. The reader, on his part, must be able to assume the role of the postulated reader. If the gap between norms is too great, this will seriously affect the reader's *literary* experience. For an incisive discussion of belief in literature, see Booth, 1961:119ff. See also Sweeney, 1980:29ff.

and written composition tended to limit its content to what was acceptable to the community as a whole and/or to those in a position of power. In such a milieu, the convention of consciously suspending one's own beliefs and seeking to understand something extraneous quite at odds with one's own norms on its own terms would have been quite alien. In other words, seeing things on others' terms was not part of one's own terms. The teacher of modern literary theory may justifiably wish to change this. However, an understanding of how the Malay student tends to evaluate extraneous material in the context of his own tradition will afford us an insight into the terms of that tradition, which is our present concern.

It should be clear from this that I do not wish to cast myself in the role of defender of traditional Malay literature, who, as a naturalized Malaysian, crusades with a patriot's zeal to replace the previously often negative evaluations of that literature with a correspondingly glowing appraisal, and in the process ends up seeming no less patronizing than his predecessors. Whether or not listening to a storyteller for seven hours at a stretch appeals to my personal taste should not be made a basis for evaluation. Rather than expending our energy on futile questions of what in oral or traditional written Malay composition is good or bad by Western or indeed modern Malaysian or Indonesian norms, we should be concerning ourselves with the whats, whys, and hows of traditional Malay composition.

In a recent study (*Authors and Audiences in Traditional Malay Literature*, 1980), I made a preliminary attempt to examine some of these questions in the areas of stylized oral and written composition. I had become aware that many of the formulary features so typical of oral composition were also to be found in works of traditional Malay literature. In the past, European scholars were almost entirely unfamiliar with the workings of oral composition or the distinctions to be made between stylized professional and nonstylized amateur storytelling, their acquaintance with "folk literature" being limited to materials which had been adapted under their aegis by Malay scribes into the literary *hikayat* Malay of the time, and which were thus well-nigh indistinguishable from other works of traditional *literature*. For these European scholars, who tended to contextualize works of traditional Malay literature in their own tradition, the formulary features of Malay writing were cast in a negative light, being described as "clichéd" and "hackneyed." Seen in the context of the distinction made by Hirsch (1967) between meaning and significance, these assessments constitute the significance of Malay literature for European scholars. They do not tell us about the *meaning* of such works in the sense of authorial intention as revealed in the text. It was the sum total of this significance which was bequeathed to the Malays in the guise of "literary criticism," a concept alien to Malay tradition. While the significance of traditional Malay literature for the modern Malay may differ from its meaning, that significance is again likely to be very different from its significance for Europeans. However, the fact that "Malay Studies" have, inevitably, been so cast in a Western mold means that Malays have been taught to see their own culture from a Western point of view, and to describe it using Western categories.[5] The result of this is that what the Malay "says" about his traditional literature often does not reflect what he "knows" but cannot articulate, and there tends to be a disparity, or indeed a tension, between the two. What he says is dictated by the terms available to him, and when he expresses himself on matters such as "literature," "literary criticism," or "literary history," these terms are culturally Western. The evaluations of the orientalists were seemingly confirmed for modern Malays who, after progressing to the study of their literature in college, were presented with "literary theory" such as the widely used Wellek and Warren, which purported to lay down universal principles, but which in fact merely set out in systematic fashion those same culture-bound values which underlay the orientalists' evaluations. In many instances, the application of such views to traditional Malay literature leads us into the realm of the absurd. For example, Wellek and Warren (1973:42) hold that the "total meaning" of a work of art is "the history of its criticism by its many readers in many ages," a view which, even in the context of Western literature, confuses meaning with significance. When such a notion is applied to traditional Malay literature, which had no tradition of "literary criticism" in the Western sense, one would have to accept that the total meaning of a work would reside in the orientalists' evaluation of it.

It became clear to me that an attempt to examine the meaning of traditional Malay literature as distinct from its significance for myself would entail knowing what tasks were faced by author and audience, and ascertaining the possibilities offered and constraints imposed by the medium. My investigations led me to an awareness of the aural

5. It may, of course, justifiably be argued that there were no other categories available for analysis. At that time, scholarship had not yet come to terms with the nature of orality.

nature of traditional Malay literature: presentation and consumption were in many ways similar to a performance of stylized oral composition; these similarities explained the presence in written works of many features which are normally associated with oral performance, and which would be out of place in material intended to be experienced visually.

While the palace scribe is no longer with us, it is still possible to observe the process of stylized oral composition. My research revealed that the teller depends upon the extensive use of formulas and patterns in every stage of his work. The term "oral formulaic composition" now has a rather specialized sense, being associated with the theories of Milman Parry and Albert Lord. Lord's concept of the "formula" concerns only one aspect of oral composition, which is of somewhat limited relevance to Malay composition. A rather broader framework was suggested by the ideas of Gombrich (1969) concerning the psychology of pictorial art, which emphasize the importance of the conceptual image or schema.[6] The idea of the schema or minimum stereotype seemed particularly well suited to the study of Malay composition, oral and written. Thus, the concept of schematic composition may be seen to underlie the patterns produced in the morphological and formulaic analyses of Vladimir Propp (1968) and Albert Lord (1976) respectively, for the writer and teller of traditional Malay composition relied upon schemata at every level of their work, from building the plot to choosing the actual words used. Scholars have tended to draw a sharp distinction between oral and literary techniques of composition. Lord, for example, contends that the introduction of writing will free the composer from the need of his formulas and well-established themes, and that the new reading public will demand new themes (1976:131). This contention assumes the creation of a reading public. Such formulas and themes would still be essential for effective communication with a listening audience familiar only with an oral/aural tradition. I submit that a vital distinction to be made is not merely that between oral and written composition, but also between aural and visual consumption. And indeed examination revealed that the same "literary grammar" was used to generate both oral and written composition schematically, although both traditions developed their own conventions in accordance with the different media involved. This reliance on schemata does

6. I was introduced to the idea of applying Gombrich's schemata to literature by Sylvia Tiwon.

not mean that traditional Malay literature was unable to deal with the specific. While the writer began with his given schemata, he might find that the need to achieve a certain purpose and elicit a certain response from his audience necessitated a process of correction and adjustment of the schemata. When the adjustment is found to achieve its purpose, the modified schema of one writer becomes the starting point for his emulators. When the latter are also motivated to make further adjustments, the process of schema and correction gathers momentum and, eventually, writers consciously struggle to abandon the methods of schematic composition and be "original," which only really occurs when a reading public appears.

In the present study, it is my intention to expand and develop some of these points raised in *Authors and Audiences*. In an examination of the relationships between oral and written traditions, however, we must cast our net much wider. A preliminary concern is delineating the materials which will provide the object of our study. In applying the term "literature" to traditional Malay writing, we should not lose sight of the fact that we are applying a Western concept alien to traditional Malay society, and that "Literature" is not a Platonic form possessing some universal, absolute attribute, the presence or absence of which enables us to determine what is "really" literature in the writings of any culture. Such a notion would lead one to identify as literature only that corpus of material in an alien culture which possessed some perceived similarity to what for the scholar is "literature." Traditional Malay society did not make a distinction between writing as an art and as a craft; the term "*sastra*" was semantically "refilled" during the post-print era to accommodate the European concept of "Literature"; previously it had signified "book of divination." In this study, therefore, the use of the term "literature" does not presuppose any process of evaluation; it is used to refer to all written materials.

What then of "oral literature"? This usage has been likened to always speaking of a horse as an automobile without wheels (Ong, 1971:291). This is no mere pedantic caviling: we are already conditioned to interpret all discourse according to the norms of our modern print-based culture. The use of the term "oral literature" cannot but further encourage us to view oral composition as a sort of unwritten writing, and this will create a formidable barrier to a valid interpretation. Indeed, in most studies of oral composition, by whatever term it is labeled, literary presuppositions generally tend to ensure that the body of material selected for study from the discourse of a culture is that which accords with the scholar's perception of "literature," the result being that oral composition is judged or even defined by the standards of what the scholar considers to be literary. For example, Archer Taylor (1965:39–40) attempts to distinguish between folklore and literature as follows: "An obvious difference is that folklore uses conventional themes and stylistic devices and makes no effort to disguise their conventional quality while the literary artist either divests his work of conventional quality by avoiding clichés of either form or matter or . . . charges them with new content."

"Folklore" is an equally unsatisfactory term for the orally produced materials with which we are concerned, particularly since the recent efforts of Dundes (Dundes and Pagter, 1975), which have convincingly demonstrated that the compass of folklore need not be confined to orally transmitted materials. This has, however, removed one of the few criteria upon which folklorists were able to reach some consensus in defining their field. Dundes's contention that his "urban paperwork" written materials are folklore, that is, traditional, insofar as they "exist in multiple versions and in more than one time or place"[7] (1975:xix) would force us to label all traditional Malay literature "folklore."[8] This in itself is not unacceptable. Indeed, I see no reason why the methods of folklore may not be applied to any written material. My point is that we can no longer use the term "folklore" to distinguish orally composed material.

Yet even if we adhere to the criterion of oral transmission, we find that folklorists, when they agree, are extremely arbitrary about what they accept as "folklore." As noted by Dundes (1965:1), "in a culture without writing, . . . almost everything is transmitted orally; and although *language,* hunting techniques and marriage rules are passed orally from one generation to another, few folklorists would say that these types of cultural materials are folklore" (my italics). Yet no

7. Dundes's definition clearly reflects the norms of a print-based society: writing which is folklore is defined by reference to and in terms of writing which is not, and in a modern society the most massive volume of that which is not thus folklore is material standardized by being published in mass printings. In pre-print Malay society, Dundes's definition would include almost all written composition.

8. It might seem that Archer Taylor would indeed have classed all traditional Malay literature as folklore, for he contends that the literature of some cultures is indistinguishable from folklore. But of course Archer Taylor was still using the criterion of oral transmission; the examples of Finnish tales noted by him are oral forms which have been written down. Traditional Malay literature, however, was composed *in* writing. He would then be forced to consider it as "sub-literary" (1965:37), a category which surely could be considered valid only in a society which possesses his notion of "literature" proper.

theoretical basis has been advanced to establish which oral materials may be included, and Dundes, for example, finds it necessary to give a definition of folklore "consisting of an itemized list of the forms of folklore . . ." (1965:3), which contains, in addition to legend, folktale, et cetera, such items of discourse as curses, taunts, greetings, and "folk metaphors." It is not made clear what areas of discourse are excluded and for what reason. Such an operational definition works in the Western print culture from which it originates because it is based upon unstated cultural assumptions shared by the members of that society.

We can explain the inclusion of "folk narrative" and "folk poetry" in that these are perceived to parallel literary forms. But what, then, of items such as taunts and greetings? The answer given by folklorists would be that they survive in tradition. I would argue that what is meant is that their distinctive form allows them to be *seen* to survive in tradition. They are seen to be formulas or formulaic; that is, expressions created upon the pattern of existing formulas. Yet no absolute criterion exists for determining what constitutes such a formula or formulaic pattern. In view of the patterns and substitutions necessary in speaking any language, discourse is by its very nature formulaic. In observing that an utterance is a formula or formulaic, we are merely perceiving that the utterance itself, or the pattern upon which it is based, is more fixed—that is, that the unit is larger—than is customary in the discourse of our print-based society. It would seem that it is this perception of schematic form which constitutes the criterion used by folklorists to distinguish all the forms of verbal folklore, including folk narrative and poetry, from the rest of spoken language; and, incidentally, it is this criterion which, in addition to that of oral transmission, is used to distinguish it from literature, as is clearly implied in the remarks of Archer Taylor quoted above.

The folklorist who undertakes the study of a non-Western culture and applies these criteria with the expectation of finding the various items of "folklore" may well be gratified to discover that they are all there in clearly distinguishable "genres," and this will reinforce his conviction that he is dealing with universal categories. It may be, however, that the tendency to see the unfamiliar (or the defamiliarized)[9] in terms of his familiar schemata will have led him to project these categories onto the screen of the culture he is observing. Thus, in applying the print-based implied criterion of schematic form to those

9. That is, for the Malay.

areas of Malay/Indonesian society which are still largely orally oriented, if we succeed in battling down the pull of our schemata, we
become aware that there are so many "formulary" features in everyday discourse, language would indeed have to be included within the
purview of folklore.

For these reasons, it is clear that we must commence our study of
oral Malay composition in the context of discourse as a whole, rather
than first allowing our presuppositions to make some arbitrary distinction between "oral literature" or "folklore" and other areas of
discourse. A failure to do this will lead to very distorted conclusions.
For example, the oral-formulaic theory of Milman Parry and Lord
has, in the hands of many of its "appliers," itself become a formula, to
be mechanically applied to a text: a reasonable percentage of formulas
detected is said to indicate oral composition, and it is felt that the
needs of rapid-fire composition are the only explanation necessary to
account for the presence of such formulas. While these formulas were
undoubtedly necessary for oral composition in performance, such a
view is unsatisfactory on two counts. On the one hand, it does not
take into account the process of communication and the needs of the
audience. I have argued with reference to schematic composition in
Malay that as long as the consumption of tales was aural, both teller
and writer employed a variety of schemata to handle every aspect of
composition, thus not merely on the level of word choice (1980). On
the other hand, an approach which is concerned only with detecting
the presence of oral-formulaic composition in the Lordian sense is
unlikely to reveal that this is but one facet of schematic composition,
designed to solve a specific problem which arises only where a stretch
of utterance and melody (or rigid rhythmical pattern) must coincide. It
is unlikely to reveal, moreover, that many of the features of schematic
composition are not peculiar to storytelling but may be an intrinsic
part of discourse as a whole. Such features are thus not merely an aid
to composition or necessary for communication; in an oral society
they are essential for the preservation and transmission of knowledge
in general.

At this point it is necessary to emphasize that the composition of an
orally oriented society does not differ in kind from that of a print
culture. The modern writer also comes to his task with a set of given
themes, schemata, or models, which allow him to bring some structure
to what would otherwise be meaningless chaos. Without such themes,
the historian, for example, would find it impossible to deal with

events. It would be a vain task to attempt to relate everything that "happened" even within the span of only five minutes in but one location. The use of such schemata or themes enables the historian to select for discussion what he considers significant and likely to be regarded as such by his readers. It is thus that a work of history may possess inner consistency and appear to be an autonomous whole. It is in this way, too, that history appears to repeat itself. In a print culture, however, the given schemata are vastly more numerous or more "fragmented" than in an orally oriented society. Furthermore, there is much more of a perceived need to adjust the schemata in order to handle the specific. In an oral society or radically oral manuscript culture such as traditional Malay society, while the schemata are fewer in number than in a print society, the schematic "chunks" are much bigger than those to which we are accustomed, and they possess a more distinctive form to facilitate memorization. Even though all human discourse is by nature formulaic, the fact that the units tend to be so much larger in an orally oriented culture leads us to see its literature and oral performance as schematically or formulaically composed. In such a society the need to correct and adjust the schemata in order to accomplish a particular purpose is much less than in a print culture. Even so, the need may well arise for a composer to grapple with (what *we* see as) the specific, which will entail using smaller chunks.

During the summer of 1980, I lectured on "oral literature" (*sastra lisan*) at the Universiti Sains Malaysia in Penang, after an absence of two years from Malaysia. As in the past, I noted the "uncritical" approach and loose argumentation of many of the essays submitted by my students. The quality of these essays could not be explained away as the result of "carelessness," for the students, many of whom were Malay school teachers enrolled as mature students, were extremely hard-working. After repeated readings of the more "uncritical" essays, it dawned upon me that they contained many of the formulary features normally associated with oral composition, and were assembled almost as schematically as the performances of storytellers which formed the topic of the essays. It became clear to me that a prerequisite for the valid interpretation of the oral composition and literature, traditional or modern, of a society is an awareness of the systems of preserving, retrieving, and transmitting knowledge operative in that society.

It was at this time that I became acquainted with the writings of Eric Havelock and Walter J. Ong, for whom such systems are a central concern. Havelock (1963, 1971) attempts to interpret the growth of the early Greek mind. In this effort, his focus is upon "the transition from the oral to the written and from the concrete to the abstract, and here the phenomena to be studied are precise, and are generated by changes in the technology of preserved communication which are also precise" (1963:xi). Ong's major concern (1967, 1971, 1977) is to explore and interpret "the evolution of modes of thought and verbal expression" from primary oral culture through writing and print to the electronic culture of modern times, which produces a "secondary orality" (1977:9). I was intrigued to note that my findings in *Authors and Audiences* concerning the traditional composition of Malay society appeared to support many of the conclusions drawn by Havelock and Ong from their study of the growth of Western literacy. However, a number of differences revealed themselves; for example, the very different environmental conditions in the Malay world and the implications for the development of literacy (Sweeney, 1980:68) underlined for me the danger of assuming that literacy must everywhere follow inexorably one universal pattern of development. Nevertheless, the work of Havelock and Ong has provided me with a broader perspective from which to view my own studies, and has suggested a number of new lines of inquiry.

In the West, the evolution from the oral/aural cultures of the ancient world to the visualist, type-centered, and electronic cultures of modernity spread out over many centuries. In many Third World countries a similar development has been compressed into little more than a hundred years. In the Malay world, the study of the way new media interact with the old is particularly complex, and the fairly recent introduction of typographic and electronic technologies has caused radical reorganizations of verbalization and thought. Even so, hardly surprisingly, there remains a strong oral orientation. An understanding of the extent and significance of this orality makes it possible to explain much in modern Malaysian and Indonesian society that may appear strange and exotic or simply dull to the Western observer, not merely in the realm of "literature," but also in other areas of communication such as news broadcasts, political speeches, propaganda, television dramas, university lectures, and their impact upon their audiences.

Ong's study of the development of media in the West is of relevance to our concerns for another reason: an awareness of the technological transformations of the word and the resulting changes in thought processes enables us to shed much light on the attitudes and assumptions of the scholars who pioneered the study of Malay language and literature in the West and who are responsible for creating the mold in which "Malay Studies" are cast today. Not infrequently, one hears from both Malays and Westerners the opinion that the old orientalists have nothing to teach us, that they can be safely forgotten, and that we should go straight to the Malay primary materials. My reply is that only by examining our predecessors' attitudes can we learn why we are doing what we are doing, for the terms employed, the categories perceived, the questions posed, the assumptions held—in a word, the "givens" of Malay/Indonesian studies—are inherited from those predecessors and reflect the concerns of Western society, which produced them. Paradoxically, therefore, an attempt to interpret Malay literature on its own terms must commence with an examination of Western writings. It is for this reason that the following two chapters deal with Western perceptions of Malay language and literature. It is possible that such an examination may lead some Western scholars to realize that certain of their unquestioned assumptions are unjustified, and Malay scholars to see that they have been taught to see their own literature through Western eyes. If this sentiment sounds arrogant, then I should emphasize that I myself have become aware in recent years that my failure to battle down the assumptions of one educated in a "mass-literate" print culture led me to perceive oral composition as some kind of unwritten writing, so that I was able to advance the outrageous notion that each rendering of the professional storyteller's tale might be likened to "a paraphrase of an imaginary 'master-copy' " (1973:20) without realizing that such a concept is alien to an oral person. And as recently as 1980, I still wrote blithely of "oral literature."

CHAPTER 1

Predecessors and Presuppositions

In the field of Malay literary studies, it would seem that we take our predecessors far too much for granted. True, it is regularly impressed upon students that "we stand upon the shoulders of our predecessors," yet such a seemingly obvious assertion may be interpreted in numerous ways, depending upon one's perceptions of one's studies. All too often, those "shoulders" have been seen to represent the solid base of "fact" provided for us by earlier studies. Our task has been to dig up new "facts" still waiting to be discovered, which, once unearthed, would speak for themselves.

It seems to me that the influence of these positivistic assumptions still tends to cloud our awareness of where we stand and what we are about. Criticism of our predecessors' work has thus tended to center upon errors of "fact," with the result that the process of revaluation has been carried out in a superficial and piecemeal fashion. For facts are the product of interpretation and it would seem advisable to examine first the basic assumptions underlying those interpretations. Often, however, we do not even seem to be aware of the existence of such assumptions and, in the words of Frederic Jameson (1972:7), "we are still caught up in all kinds of positivistic presuppositions, because the position of the observer is still being taken for granted and has not yet come to strike us as problematical."

Elsewhere (1980:25–26), I have drawn attention to the now generally accepted view that the writer or storyteller is the product of a society, and that literature is not purely a crystallization of private fantasy. His audience and conditioning ensure that he define himself by reference to the norms and values of that society. The writer or storyteller, like any other artist, is further bound by his medium and technique. He composes in terms of all the other compositions he has read or heard, for art owes more to art than to direct observation of "nature." Otherwise, as Gombrich (1969) repeatedly emphasizes, there could be no history of art: the artist has a stock of mental stereotypes, which he adapts to suit his needs. When the artist does not actively seek to overcome the natural pull toward the schematic by correcting his schema, his art will tend to return to the minimum stereotype of the conceptual image. He must be able to construct a schema before he can adjust and correct it to fulfill a specific purpose, and he will naturally see the unfamiliar in terms of familiar schemata.

These remarks concerning the author or teller are equally valid as a description of the position of the scholar who studies him. He cannot be an impartial and objective observer, for he, too, is subject to the same constraints. As he is the product of a certain society, his perceptions are necessarily structured by the norms and values which constitute the ideology of that society. He, too, sees the unfamiliar in terms of familiar schemata, and, depending upon how far he carries the process of schema and adjustment, he will unwittingly tell us more, or less, about himself and his own society than about the object of his study.

The scholars who performed the great pioneering work in the field of Malay studies were largely the product of the nineteenth and early twentieth centuries—the age of Romanticism.[1] In view of the considerations raised above, it seems worthwhile to examine briefly some of the attitudes of this period in the hope of recognizing the assumptions underlying the work of these pioneers, for this knowledge should help us to explain how and why the basic mold in which the study of Malay literature is cast today has been taken largely for granted.

During the nineteenth century, the Western world experienced a growth of knowledge of vast proportions, both in the field of science, with its practical application in technology, and in the humanities with the burgeoning of the Romanticist movement. The belief that Romanticism was the enemy of science would appear to be a late nineteenth- and early twentieth-century projection into the past.[2] Jacques Barzun

1. For delineations of the "period," see for example Barzun, 1975; Ong, 1971.
2. See, for example, Wordsworth's sonnet "Composed on Westminster Bridge."

argues convincingly that, on the contrary, the Romanticists generally held science in high esteem, and that "specialization had not gone so far that a man could not combine an intelligent interest in science with every other liberal pursuit" (1975:65). Barzun further emphasizes their scientific methods, their thirst for new experience, their pragmatic realism and enormous industry (1975:58ff). These were values shared by both bard and businessman of the period. The nineteenth century saw power residing firmly in the hands of the bourgeoisie, and bourgeois values reigned supreme.

The Romanticists saw themselves as reacting against the neo-classical tradition, with its conventional themes and abstractions, which seemed to them to have become worn threadbare by repetition and refinement. Walter J. Ong, however, places this reaction in a much wider context.[3] For him, an essential opposition to be considered is one between residual orality and fully interiorized print culture. The typographically based Romanticist movement dealt the final blow to the ancient rhetorical economy of thought and expression. Ong demonstrates how Learned Latin was permanently aligned with the orally based rhetorical tradition and "helped keep this tradition alive long past the development not only of writing but even of print." Yet paradoxically, because Learned Latin was chirographically controlled, it "built up an extreme deference for the written word" (1971:17). In a culture where knowledge is preserved orally, constant repetition is needed merely to ensure its survival. A major part of the old rhetorical tradition was the use of commonplaces, or *topoi*. These had survived the invention of writing, and were indeed codified by writing to form what Ong terms "rhetorical culture," which was "basically oral culture shrouded in writing" (1971:261). When the Romanticist movement began to stir, some three hundred years after the introduction of the letterpress, the full effects of typography had been felt. Vast amounts of knowledge had been stored securely in print, and made easily retrievable. For Ong, the appearance of modern technology and Romanticism at the same time is no coincidence: both were the beneficiaries of this unprecedented "noetic abundance" (1971:279). With this new intellectual security, the Romanticists were able to face into the unknown; the *topoi*, epithets, and other prefabricated expressions were no longer necessary and

3. The summary of Ong's ideas presented in the remainder of this paragraph is drawn from *The Presence of the Word*, 1967; *Romance, Rhetoric, and Technology*, 1971 (esp. pp. 255–83); and *Interfaces of the Word*, 1977.

could be abandoned. Thus we see the increasing depreciation of the formulary features of the old oral tradition, culminating in the anathema for the "cliché" shown by the New Critics, whose Romanticist roots ran deep.

Scholars have often emphasized the preoccupation of the Romanticist movement with "otherness," and this is usually interpreted as the mysterious, bizarre, and exotic. Yet I believe that this "otherness" should rather be seen in relation to the schemata of the existing tradition. In their efforts to avoid being pulled in by these schemata, the Romanticists opted for any subject that was not provided for by prefabricated expression. It was not essential that such a subject be alien to everyday existence. Wordsworth, for example, was particularly concerned with the mean and humble, which, however, certainly had the quality of otherness vis-à-vis the tradition. The same tendency is found in novel writing. Here again, the quality of otherness is paradoxically found in the humdrum details of "ordinary" middle-class people's lives, for the commonplace tradition had little to offer in this area.

Of course, the age of Romanticism is not some hermetically sealed Spenglerian entity. The first signs of the rejection of the Latin-based rhetorical tradition appeared much earlier, with the rise of the bourgeoisie and its alliance with the vernacular. Ong draws attention to the weakening of the old tradition from the seventeenth century on, with the growth of commercially oriented schools, which taught in the vernacular (1967:241; 1971:280). The Romanticists were firmly anchored in the vernaculars, and it is no coincidence—nor is it mere etymologizing to say—that the name of the movement derives from the "romance": a tale told in the Romance languages, the vernaculars of the Middle Ages. On the other hand, the Latin-based tradition did not die suddenly; it limped on throughout the nineteenth century, and we may note that the great majority of orientalist scholars received their basic education in this area.[4]

A notable feature of the nineteenth century was the preeminence of history in the sphere of the intellect. "As against the assumption that no civilization had existed since the fall of Rome, they [the Romanticists] rediscovered the Middle Ages and the sixteenth century and made history their dominant avocation" (Barzun, 1975:60). Of course, man's

---

4. Obituaries are a useful source of information in this area. A collection of them is presented in Maier and Teeuw (1976).

concern with his past was nothing new; his need to place himself in a historical framework is age-old, as is evidenced by the early appearance of the genealogy, which, as Ong points out, is one of the limited ways in which oral man succeeded in "lining up a sizable assortment of discreet [sic] elements" (1977:258).

The nineteenth century's enthusiasm for historical writing derives not merely from the concern with "otherness"; more importantly, it arose from the need to classify the vast amounts of knowledge which had recently become available. That "history" should have been an obvious model to accomplish this is not surprising, for "narrative is the primal way in which the human lifeworld is organized verbally and intellectually. All science itself is grounded somehow in narrative history . . . all knowledge is grounded in experience; experience is strung out in time; time sequence calls for narrative" (Ong, 1977:245).

Many new disciplines developed during the nineteenth century, and these thus tended to be organized according to the historical model. Examples in the field of the humanities are ethnology, art history, philology, literary criticism, and literary history.

Literary history—as distinct from the history of civilizations using literature as documentation, in the manner of Hippolyte Taine and Spengler, who sought to discern a total period style—consisted largely of a chronological listing of great, or at least significant, authors in print. Histories of literature thus tended to be rather histories of authors, which included impressions and evaluations of the authors' specific works, also arranged in chronological order. These were the historian's basic units, which he would then attempt to link, with remarks on sources and influences. In discussing the earliest literature, from the age of manuscript culture, where the "authors" were often unknown, he relied for his text on the "literary scholarship" of the philologist, and contented himself with remarks on the history of the manuscript, the age of the work, and a summary of the contents. Here, too, the historian, with supreme self-confidence and entirely lacking the acute self-consciousness of our modern age, did not flinch from delivering impressionistic judgments on the merits of the works. For example, George Saintsbury, a fairly representative English literary historian of his time, accompanies his remarks on Anglo-Saxon and early English writings with "the strictest criticism of intrinsic merit" (1898:6), and, when faced with a work that does not appeal to him, has no hesitation in delivering judgments such as "internal marks of absolute worthlessness as literature, if not of absolute worthlessness as history. . . . huge farragos of mere fairy tales" (1898:41). Other works have "not a little poetical merit" (1898:12), considering that "this literature is, after all, the literature of a childhood, the lispings of a people" (1898:9).

Literary criticism was still a relatively new art in the nineteenth century; in pedagogy, poetry had traditionally been regarded as a subsidiary of rhetoric, and pre-Romanticist criticism had consisted largely of prefaces and occasional essays. Although Coleridge is often described as the father of practical criticism, literary criticism on the whole continued to be an adjunct of literary history until the appearance of the New Critics and Russian Formalists, who insisted on a synchronic approach.

The purpose of this rather lengthy digression has been to focus upon some of the factors which contributed to the mental set of those European scholars who studied Malay literature.[5] The models available to them were the result of the process of schema and correction undertaken by Western man attempting to formulate his perceptions of the peculiar circumstances of his own culture.

The Dutch and British scholars who studied the Malay world differed somewhat in their practical approach: the British tended to be rather more "literary," the Dutch more "scientific," although neither held a monopoly on either aspect. However, they both shared the same assumptions and presuppositions, and a major feature of their mental set was an unquestioning acceptance of the diachronic as the only valid approach.

Almost all of these scholars had studied Latin and Greek in school. Awareness of the fact that this classical education was in the nineteenth century no more than a relic of the then almost defunct rhetorical tradition is reflected in the arguments used at the time to rationalize the teaching of Latin, as for example, the "Latin-toughens-the-mind" defense. In Britain, this system produced scholars in the "effortless amateur" tradition, and the majority of Malaici from Marsden and Raffles to Winstedt were of this type. In the Netherlands, the potential Indologist found that his classical education had some practical use: Latin and Greek were the stepping stones to the study of Sanskrit and Arabic, which were regarded

5. Those who imagine that the Dutch discovered Romanticism only in the 1880s (the period of the *Tachtigers,* or "Eightiers" generation of poets) forget that the Dutch are perhaps the most European of Europeans, and that they were closely attuned to Romanticist developments in Germany and France.

by the Indologists as the "classical languages" of the Malay world, based on the model of the "classics" for Europe. Ismail Hussein (1974:14ff) has provided some perceptive observations concerning flaws in this model. Suffice it to say here that the Dutch studies focused strongly upon the tracing of foreign elements in Malay, and Malay texts were treated to a large extent as source material for these historical and comparative philological studies. Similarly, Malay chronicles were studied primarily as providers of historical documentation.

The only reasonably comprehensive survey of Malay literature as such to appear during the nineteenth century was that of de Hollander, who included a section on literature in his *Handleiding bij de Beoefening der Maleische Taal en Letterkunde* (1845; 5th ed. 1882). Here again, the diachronic approach reigns supreme, with chapters on the history of the language, the history of the Malay people, and the periodization of Malay literature.

The more "literary" British revealed the same historical bent, although it manifested itself in a somewhat different way. Thus, the British revealed a propensity for writing "histories," which, in fact, often contained as much description of the contemporary scene as of the past—if not more.[6] Examples of such works are Marsden's *History of Sumatra* (1811) and Raffles's *History of Java* (1817). So strong was the pull of the historical schema for these writers that to describe the present they needed to understand it in terms of a projected past. This need to classify knowledge in terms of history was still felt in Malay studies well into the twentieth century, as evidenced by the approach used in works such as Winstedt's *The Malays: A Cultural History* (1950), which has been described as "a mere topical discussion of the various aspects of Malay cultural life" (Ismail Hussein, 1974:16).

The same susceptibility obtained in the field of Malay literary studies. The British scholars did not possess the years of training in Sanskrit, Arabic, Javanese, and so forth, that were considered essential prerequisites for the potential philologist who would study Malay texts, and they were justifiably somewhat chary of appearing to com-

---

6. And these would usually include "the branch of natural *history*" (my italics) as in Marsden (1811:viii). He emphasizes that his aim in collecting all manner of information is "more especially to furnish those philosophers, whose labours have been directed to the investigation of the history of Man, with facts to serve as *data* in their reasonings" (p. vii).

pete with the Dutch in this field.[7] Hardly surprisingly, therefore, their approach was more literary; and literary studies, as I have observed above, meant basically literary history, which consisted of a chronological ordering of great or significant authors and their published works.

By far the most influential work in the field of Malay literature has been Winstedt's "A History of Malay Literature" (1939). Winstedt was by no means the first scholar to concern himself with Malay literature, as distinct from "scholarship" or philology, as may be seen from the works of Wilkinson, Overbeck, and others; he was, however, the first to attempt a historical survey of the whole literature, and it is due to the ambitiousness and extensiveness of his undertaking that many of the presuppositions that were implicit in the writings of others stand out so sharply in Winstedt's work.

His first major presupposition was that it is possible to write a history of Malay literature. It was obviously clear to him that his initial schema, the contemporary Western idea of literary history based on known authors in print, was particularly unsuited to classify a manuscript literature lacking dates and names of authors. His classical education, which led him to see many aspects of Malay literature in terms of the Latin and Greek, was, moreover, of little help in enabling him to establish a typology for Malay, because the classics, although deriving from a manuscript culture, were the products of known authors. The texts, moreover, had largely been reconstructed and edited by the scholars, and their chronology established. It was clear that this work had yet to be done for Malay. A precedent was, however, offered by the treatment afforded to Anglo-Saxon and Old English texts in the literary histories of the time. Here there was so much vagueness regarding authors and dates, in spite of the efforts of the scholars, that literary historians were forced to limit themselves to a very loose chronological treatment, relying for the most part, as we have noted, upon perceived sources and influences. Apparent similarities between early English and Malay literature did not go unnoticed,

7. However, in the production of dictionaries (and let us not forget Marsden's [1812] or Winstedt's [1913] Malay grammars) the British certainly held their own. Wilkinson's dictionary (1932) is still unsurpassed for "Classical Malay." Yet predictably, the main criticism of it has been that "etymologies are its weakest point" (Teeuw, 1961:18). It is certainly not my intention to imply that the Dutch guarded a monopoly by attacking those who ventured into their field. On the contrary, they usually spare no pains to assist foreign colleagues. Scathing criticism has never been directed at foreigners *per se,* but at those perceived to be *slordig* (sloppy), as may be seen from the many pungent Dutch reviews of Dutch work which failed to meet required standards of rigor.

as we see from the parallels drawn by Winstedt with Beowulf and Tyndale (1958:145, 52) and the detailed comments of his mentor, Wilkinson, concerning similarities to "the tales that interested medieval Europe" (1924:9–10). But it was not yet evident to them that many of these similarities stemmed from the fact that both Old English and traditional Malay literature were the products of radically oral societies. The accepted view of the time was not that such literature was the product of a transition from a mature and adult oral mode of composition to a written one, but that it was, as Saintsbury contended, the childhood "lispings" of a people who were starting from scratch: "No vernacular writings other than their own can have been before these ancestors of ours, for none existed" (1898:9). There was thus no awareness of the desirability of a different approach to the study of a manuscript literature, and differences of treatment were rather the result of inadequate documentation. For nineteenth-century man, the idea of literature as spatially fixed print to be visually experienced was so interiorized that there was no awareness that many of the assumptions made about manuscript literature were not absolutes, but merely the presuppositions of a print culture.

As with historians of European literature, Winstedt was able to benefit from the labors of the philologist. An important difference, however, is that whereas the scholar of European literature was area centered, the Indologist, if only for the reason that he learned Sanskrit and Arabic before Malay, tended to see the latter as an extension of Indian and Arabic culture. Winstedt now made these two sources of influence the major categories of his typology: Hindu and Muslim (Malay) literature. This then made it possible to produce two more categories: pre-Hindu and transitional literature. The pull exerted by this schema of influence led him to create a further slot: Javanese influence. These were arranged chronologically: Hindu-Javanese-transitional-Muslim, and material which fitted none of these categories was then labeled "indigenous." While it might seem absurd in the field of English literature to speak of *Macbeth* mainly in terms of its origins in Holinshed's Scottish chronicles, *All's Well That Ends Well* in terms of Italian influence from Boccaccio, and to have to label even Cinderella and Snow-White "foreigners," such an approach would at least have provided one possible filing system if other documentation had been lacking.

This in itself, then, is no reason to reject Winstedt's typology. If his model fitted our present perceptions of Malay literature, we could at least accept it as a viable system of classification, albeit one that answered late nineteenth- and early twentieth-century European questions and needs, and did not throw much light on the internal system or makeup of Malay literature. The fact is, however, that the model is particularly unsuited to what we know of Malay literature.

The first problem is that there is no Hindu Malay literature.[8] It is true, of course, that there are Malay versions of the *Ramayana* and *Mahabharata*, but this in itself does not justify our classifying these works as literature of the Hindu period. For example, the *Hikayat Seri Rama* in its extant form is a Muslim work. This is not merely a matter of vocabulary and script: the work is the product of a Muslim, aimed at a Muslim audience or one receptive to Islam, concerning the breaking of a contract mediated by the prophet Adam between a Muslim king and the Muslim God. The argument that the majority of the motifs originate from India is irrelevant, and ignores the fact that traditional Malay composition, both oral and written, is schematic: it makes use of given patterns on every level of composition, from the plot framework down to the actual word choice. Thus, a *dalang* of the Malay shadow-play can produce in performance a play which, by Winstedt's standards, would be as "Hindu flavoured" as any of the versions of the *Hikayat Seri Rama* or other works assigned by him to the Hindu period. Yet such a play is undeniably a product of the *present*.

For the same reasons, two more of Winstedt's categories are seen to be invalid: the "Javanese element" and "From Hinduism to Islam." In the latter case, the criteria employed by Winstedt, such as Hindu names and "tags," and degrees of Hindu or Muslim "colouring," do not enable us to assign a work to a period of transition, for it is such formulas which formed part of the stock-in-trade of both writer and teller, and they are still used in oral performance today. Winstedt seemed somewhat aware of the problem, for he admits that "not always in time, because many belong to the Muslim period of Malay history, but at any rate in contents and in spirit most of them may be assigned to the era of transition between Hinduism and Islam" (1958:60). The argument thus becomes a vicious circle. Similarly, with the "Javanese element,"[9] while Winstedt is wary of calling it a histori-

8. There are, of course, a few dozen lines of inscriptions in Old Malay from the Hindu-Buddhist period, but these do not enter Winstedt's purview.

9. It seems that the *Hikayat Hang Tuah* is placed in the "Javanese Element" because of the presence of a Panji motif and a Majapahit episode. This is rather like classifying *Hamlet* as a Danish element because the hero is a prince of Denmark.

cal period, the implication is clear that the Javanese element came before the Muslim period, as, for example, in his remark that "neither of these reciters has a Muslim name" (1958:48). Yet how many Javanese *dalangs* have Muslim names even today? And his arguments for the great age of the *Syair Ken Tambuhan*[10]—inter alia Kawi words, Javanese forms, and a knowledge of Hindu mythology—reflect the same unawareness of the realities of schematic composition. Panji tales possessing these very features are still being composed in Kelantan.

A presupposition inherent in the arguments of Winstedt and his contemporaries concerns archetypes. It is not the Malay works as we have them but their presumed archetypes which are being historically classified. It is also still often taken for granted that our main task is to reconstruct these archetypes.[11] Indeed, one of the commonest criticisms of Winstedt's work is that it was premature, and that he should have waited until the chronology of Malay texts be established.

However, in view of the fact that both oral and written Malay composition was schematically created, the question of archetype becomes problematical. It is now a commonplace that every Malay copyist was a potential rewriter or a joint author.[12] There is, in fact, a notable exception to this: *Kitab* literature tended to be much less orally oriented, and indeed Voorhoeve (1964:262) has pointed out that the copyists of such religious treatises were often quite meticulous. It is in those works created with the schematic patterns of tradition that the copyist is afforded considerable freedom. Just as the storyteller regards the patterns and formulas he uses as common property, so the writer and copyist in traditional orally and aurally oriented Malay society could not conceive of the idea that these patterns could be the property of any one individual. This not only clarifies the vague concept of joint authorship but also helps to explain the anonymity of authorship so often noted in traditional Malay literature, although we should be aware that a writer's omission of his name in a manuscript does not mean that he was anonymous in his society. Especially in *silsilah* (royal genealogy) writing, it would seem that the writer's name was known by his con-

10. Teeuw, 1966:442; Sweeney, 1971:57.
11. For example, Ismail Hussein states, "By the philological work which I am proposing here, I mean largely textual reconstruction, interpretation and analysis. Each (of the) Malay text, by using all its available versions, must be reconstructed to its nearest original form" (1974:18). Out of fairness, however, it must be noted that earlier in the same paper (p. 16), he remarks that "one sometimes wonders whether there will ever be a chronology at all," a statement which appears to indicate that his own perceptions are engaged in a battle with his given schemata.
12. For example, see van Ronkel's remarks in 1900 (p. 309).

temporaries, for it is often included by a subsequent copyist, as in the case of Raja Culan of *Misa Melayu,* and Tun Seri Lanang of the *Sejarah Melayu.*[13] This did not, nevertheless, usually deter the copyist from recomposing, as is demonstrated by the various versions of the *Sejarah Melayu.* The copyist's task was to adjust his text to meet the needs of his postulated audience.

In Western society, works of literature are constantly reinterpreted and new readings perceived. In traditional Malay society one finds a similar process of reinterpretation. Here, however, it is performed by the copyist rather than by the audience. While Malay society had no tradition of "literary criticism," this process of reinterpretation by the many copyists of a "work" through many ages is another, but equally effective, way of ensuring that a text remains meaningful for its current audience. I would submit that this process is a valid subject of study, and equally important for the study of Malay literature as is the history of criticism in the West.

I am not, of course, suggesting that there was a body of written commentary in Malay tradition concerning this procedure of reinterpreting written compositions. On the contrary, there is little evidence of any more awareness than in oral tradition that such recomposition occurred. The ravages of climate and insect pests usually limited the life of a manuscript to little more than one or two generations, so that a "work" had to be continually copied merely to ensure its survival. Yet even had the original survived to bear witness against its copy, the fact that few people could read and that the consumption of literature was generally aural meant that the content of works was no more available for prolonged and intensive scrutiny by the audience or indeed by the reciter than in oral tradition (Sweeney, 1980:73). Furthermore, in such a strongly oral milieu, it would have been more important for a text to agree with what was *said* and *heard* than to agree with what was previously written. In such circumstances, one would rather expect "the unobtrusive adaptation of past tradition to present needs" (Goody, 1968:48) normally associated with nonliterate societies. And, indeed, the creative copying of the Malay scribe was intended to ensure this consistency between past and present. We should be aware, therefore, that the possibility of studying this process of

13. Note also the rhetorical games played by Amin, the author of the *Syair Perang Mengkasar* (Skinner, 1963). He does not include his name as author, but places himself as a character in the poem, and praises that character. One may speculate that this was calculated to elicit an amused reaction from his audience.

reinterpretation arises largely as a result of European activity in collecting manuscripts since the beginning of the seventeenth century. Manuscript collections such as those of Leiden and London, with works in numerous versions originating from different periods and areas, would have been an unfamiliar concept for a traditional Malay court, which had not sufficiently harnessed the environment to allow the development and maintenance of libraries. Yet here, too, an additional factor must be considered: it is likely that many of the Malay manuscripts preserved in museums and libraries were *not*, in fact, produced according to traditional norms. A large volume of those manuscripts were commissioned by Europeans.[14] It is very possible that many of those Europeans would have emphasized that great care should be taken in producing an exact copy. When such instructions were followed to the letter, the result would be much more similar to the original than would copies produced in the traditional context. And where the original of the copy has also been preserved, the close similarity may tend to obscure for us the reinterpretive function of the traditional scribe.[15]

The philologist who attempts to piece together an archetype from many manuscripts is thus in danger of casting aside what may be the most important material for the study of the development of a work. His undertaking, moreover, is an upstream battle to undo the efforts and thwart the intentions of generations of copyists. And while our proposal to study the process of reinterpretation may also be said not to be in accordance with the intentions of those copyists, our aim is to throw light upon those intentions, not to obliterate them. The presupposition underlying the undertaking of the reconstructive philologist, furthermore, is that the original author of the "work" possessed the same standards of what is "logical" and fitting as the Western philologist.[16] In actual fact, both author and copyist would be working with the schemata of tradition, and a variety of dynamic material

14. For example, many of the manuscripts collected by Raffles were copied on his instructions (Voorhoeve, 1964).

15. One well-documented case of copyists working under European supervision is that of the General Secretariat in Batavia (Voorhoeve, 1964), where copyists apparently had considerable freedom to make changes. However, it would be unwise to generalize about all European-inspired copying on the basis of this one instance.

16. I am not, however, proposing that we should accept what are obvious corruptions and attempt to interpret them as though they made perfect sense. A reading from another manuscript will often throw light on such problems, as with the beginning of the Bodleian *Hikayat Seri Rama* elucidated by Achadiati Ikram (1980:101). The important thing is not to discard such perceived corruptions, as those who follow us may find themselves able to interpret what we cannot.

would fit the same slots. And if, for the sake of argument, the philologist succeeded in reconstructing an archetype which corresponded to some text that actually existed, he would have just one more schematically composed text. Does he stop there, or does he continue his exercise in futility by trying to reconstruct the archetypes of the schemata employed? And this effort, moreover, is unlikely to be of much help in furthering his espoused cause of establishing the chronology of a work.

In a recent paper, Ulrich Kratz questions the relevance to Malay studies of the whole concept of archetype and Ur-text as understood in classical scholarship. He suggests, paradoxically, that the extant manuscripts are themselves archetypes in the sense that they were produced when the tradition was still alive, which is the period classical scholars are trying to reach with their archetypes. Kratz therefore contends that a manuscript merits attention "as a witness of its own time and place" (1981:238), and not merely as a bearer of variations.[17]

The morass in which an orthodox philologist may find himself when he rigidly applies his methods to a work in the schematically composed Malay tradition is seen in the study of the *Hikayat Seri Rama* carried out by Zieseniss (1963), whose conclusions are accepted by Winstedt. After comparing the Shellabear and Roorda van Eysinga versions, he becomes aware that the work will not yield to the tools of the philologist in search of an archetype. He notes a close relationship between the two versions, but is stymied by the contradictions and other differences, and is forced to conclude that the two versions "can only have arisen by means of oral tradition" from "the same original source" and that "this original Ro[orda] + Sh[ellabear] version cannot, as the contradictions show, have possessed a clearly defined form" (1963:180). However, a comparison of the many passages in the two versions with almost identical wording reveals that these similarities are typical of a written style, and that the relationship can only have been chirographically controlled. The two versions are the prod-

17. If it be thought that in arguing against "wanton interference" in manuscripts Kratz is building a straw man, one need turn only to Lode Brakel's answer (1980:128–30) to Russell Jones's review article (1980) of his *Hikayat Muhammad Hanafiyyah*. Here it is clear that for Brakel a "text" is "a rather abstract concept," and he apparently believes that this quasi-Platonic form—in fact the creation of a foreigner—is truer to Malay literature than the actual manuscripts: "the reader that I had in mind was someone whose primary interest would lie in Malay literature (as distinct from individual manuscripts!)" (Brakel's exclamation). The *langue/parole* parallel Brakel draws with text/manuscripts is telling: the *langue* would not be a text but merely a system of slots; the postulated original text would be only one more example of *parole*.

uct of schematically creative copying of an earlier version or versions, some of which is preserved in both versions. It is not necessary to resort to a primary oral tradition in order to find the causes of a lack of "clearly defined form."

In her recent study, Achadiati Ikram (1980:85) is still bound by the constraints of her discipline to speak in terms of archetypes. Her comparative work convinces her, however, that an essay in stemmatics would be a futile undertaking. She rejects Zieseniss's idea of an oral archetype—which in fact she attributes to Winstedt, who was merely following Zieseniss—although not entirely for the right reasons: a study of the texts of Maxwell (1886) and Sweeney (1972) leads her to believe that oral tales would show greater variation of content. I do not believe one can safely generalize on oral tradition in this way and consider that the determining factor is the undeniable presence of chirographic control in the texts.[18] Be that as it may, Ikram concludes that there were, at the very least, two (written) archetypes. One could almost say that each of the versions she distinguishes is an archetype in Kratz's terms. It is clear that the direction taken by these two scholars is evidence of the gradual moving away in Malay philology from the diachronic to the synchronic.

We see from Zieseniss's postulation to the effect that two manuscripts sharing many identical passages could have derived from an oral archetype that his understanding of "oral tradition" was extremely vague. As is natural for literate man in whose thought processes writing is fully interiorized, Zieseniss could only view oral composition in terms of writing. For him, the oral archetype was a sort of unwritten writing: it was fixed in form and clearly indistinguishable from written language. Yet in oral tradition, the idea of a fixed text of such length is alien; where relatively fixed passages occur, they are highly stylized, possessing strongly emphasized mnemonic patterns.[19] But, as noted in the introduction, this tendency to view oral composition in terms of our *literary* schemata is even reflected in our use of the term "oral literature."

18. Two oral versions need show no greater variation of content than two written versions. However, chirographic control permits much greater similarity of specific word choice. See also my comments on the law of self-correction in chapter 4.
19. A similar appeal to oral tradition is made by Teeuw (1964) in order to suggest a possible explanation of the similarity between parts of the *Hikayat Raja-raja Pasai* and the *Sejarah Melayu*. Yet these similarities can only be the result of chirographic control. The wording is too close—especially as the degree of mnemonic patterning is low—for such passages to have been transmitted orally. See also Sweeney (1967:94ff).

These considerations lead to a discussion of the treatment of folk or oral "literature" by our predecessors, and its inclusion in the rubric of literary history. The reaction of the Romanticists against the classical tradition was reflected in the new interest in "folk culture." In the field of scholarship this gave rise, predictably, to the historic-geographic method, which was mainly concerned with searching for origins and archetypes. Whether the folklorist's tales derived from oral or written sources mattered little; he employed the same philological method on both. Oral tales were thought of as latent written texts, and only when they had been written down did they become worthy objects of study; we thus learn nothing about *orality*. These developments are reflected in Malay Studies. Here again, the Dutch were the more "scientific," producing works such as those of de Vries (1925), Voorhoeve (1927), and Coster-Wijsman (1929),[20] which made use of the tale-type registers of Aarne and Bolte-Pavlika. British scholars such as Winstedt were apparently not familiar with these indexes and their implications regarding the spread of folktales, and tended to see everything in terms of *foreign* influence, so that Winstedt, for example, distinguishes quite arbitrarily between what he perceives to be indigenous and foreign farcical tales.

It is, however, the British studies, particularly those of Winstedt, which have had the most influence in shaping the present attitude toward Malay oral tradition, among both local and Western scholars. Winstedt certainly viewed folklore as consisting of latent written texts, though rather defective ones, formed of "shapeless colloquial passages," which had to be put into "grammatical prose" (1957a: flyleaf). The Malay scribes who were employed to turn these tales into "real" written texts, naturally, and quite rightly so, discarded the conventions of oral composition and employed literary style for a written medium, resulting in major changes of both form and content. The selection of tales for adaptation was unavoidably haphazard and took no account of differences between formal stylized and informal nonstylized performance, both being turned into the same, uniform literary style. These products are not Malay *folk*lore: they tell us almost nothing about the mechanics of the oral tradition.

Yet it is this material which continues to form the basis for scholarly observation on Malay "oral literature," and the fact that the

20. Although Voorhoeve and Coster-Wijsman were concerned primarily with Batak and Sundanese folklore respectively.

latter enjoys the dignity of print ensures that many Malays tend to regard these published tales as the standard versions, somehow more correct than those which issue from the mouths of men and women. And Western scholars whose knowledge of "oral literature" was based mainly on their reading of the printed tales would fail to realize that often, a "work" they regarded as a cornerstone of Malay folklore was merely one among hundreds, indeed thousands, of such tales. Thus, for example, the tale of *Pak Kaduk* does not appear to have been particularly well-known or widespread prior to its appearance in print. The fact that it was one of those tales which happened to drift into the tale catcher's net has resulted in its now being seen as one of the mainstays of Malay folklore.

The most problematic feature of the scholarly treatment of Malay folklore has been the attempt to place it in the framework of literary history. The fact that man spoke before he wrote led Winstedt, for example, to place folklore at the beginning of his history of literature, and thus to equate it with the pre-Hindu, "animistic" stage of development in his layer-cake model of Malay culture. Yet this reveals a lack of cognizance of the nature of oral composition. To say that oral predates written composition is very different from stating that the oral compositions we hear are older than the written works we read. It would be absurd to conclude that because the genre "novel" appeared before the invention of television, all novels are older than television dramas. Yet in a very real sense, the products of oral composition are much more contemporary than the latest novel, which after all is frozen in time, transfixed in print. The nature of human speech, however, ensures that oral composition can exist only in the immediate present: no sooner has a word been uttered than it has disappeared. Yet the contemporary nature of oral composition lies not merely in the transience of the spoken word: the concept of a fixed text of any considerable length is alien to oral tradition and can arise only when recourse may be had to a visual reference; that is to say, a written text. The oral composer works with the schemata of tradition; he thinks in terms of themes and formulas, and each new performance of a tale is a re-creation. Formulas may indeed agglomerate into relatively fixed passages, as in runs, incantations, fairly short poems, et cetera, but these are very far from the idea of a text fixed in writing. A teller operates in a society and is subject to its norms. Social, economic, and linguistic changes alter his schemata and are reflected in his performances, and material which is not relevant to the needs of the current

audience will disappear. Archaic language may survive in such performances, but its function will differ from when it was current usage.

In this sense, therefore, oral composition is much more contemporary and alive than written creations. It cannot be ordered chronologically in a history of literature. Not only can oral composition not be
considered as a corpus of material predating (written) literature; after
the introduction of writing, its development does not even parallel that
of literature.

In describing oral composition as "alive," I obviously implied that
written literature is somehow "dead." Ong has observed that "the
connection between writing and death is very deep" (1977:235). That
this is true of the Western mind at least is indicated by the fact that
literary references, open or veiled, associating writing or print with
death are legion. For oral composition to become "folk literature" and
be included in the rubric of literary history, it first had to die.

Another aspect of this connection made between literature and
death is reflected in the now-famous observation of Overbeck (1925)
that "Malay literature is dead,"[21] which has been accepted at face
value until the present day. It seems to me, however, that Overbeck's
comment tells us more about European society of his time than about
Malay literature. The association between a dead Malay literature and
the dead Latin and Greek classics is inescapable. Indeed, elsewhere
(1938:322) Overbeck is quite explicit about this, stating that he considers Malay literature to be as "*afgesloten*" (brought to an end, shut
down) as Roman and Greek classical literature.

On the one hand, Roman and Greek literature could indeed be said
to have died in a sense when they lost their vernaculars. But in this
sense, no analogy with Malay is possible, for the vernacular did not
disappear: it continued to be spoken both as a mother tongue in its
various dialects and as the lingua franca of the archipelago, and the
position of Indonesian-Malay as a chirographically controlled learned
language was a continuation on a much expanded level of the age-old
role of Malay in palaces throughout the archipelago.

On the other hand, the classical tradition did not die in Europe
after the appearance of the Romance languages, and the distinction
drawn by Overbeck (1938:316) between "Roman" and medieval

21. "Malaiische Literatur ist tot, dahingewelkt, seit der Glanz der malaiischen
Reiche verging." (Malay literature is dead, faded away, since the glory of the Malay
state has been eclipsed.) I am grateful to Ulrich Kratz for providing me with the reference to the original German of this.

Latin would have seemed highly arbitrary to the countless generations of Europeans who saw themselves as continuing the Roman tradition (see, e.g., Curtius, 1973:28). The tradition was kept alive by Latin, which, though used both orally and in writing throughout the European scholarly world, is, paradoxically, sometimes termed a "dead language" in the modern age. The reason for this is, of course, that it was chirographically controlled, yet another indication of the association made between writing and death.

In fact, it was only with the rise of the Romanticist movement, and its reaction against the rhetorical classical tradition, that Latin could really be said to have "died." It seems clear that Overbeck's views concerning the death of "Roman" literature are the perceptions of the age of Romanticism, for such perceptions were only possible when Europe had emerged from the classical tradition.

Vestiges of the old tradition lingered on into the early twentieth century, seen in the fact that the educated European still received his basic education in the classics. However, he belonged to an age that had rejected the rigid and standardized norms of that tradition as a basis for producing new works of literature. In perceiving Malay literature in terms of this schema, scholars were equating—whether consciously or not—that literature with a rejected tradition, and this, hardly surprisingly, militated against their appreciation of Malay literature. Thus, the label "classical" which the European scholar applied to traditional Malay literature did not indicate an appreciation of any "classical excellence" of that literature, but rather reflected the opposition to classicism of the Romanticist movement, and particularly the perception that the literature was dead.

This insistence on death has produced a somewhat hermetic approach to the study of Malay and Indonesian literature: the old one died; a new one began; and the study of each was compartmentalized. Moreover, although it can be said that the same urban, middle-class Western criteria were employed to judge both old and new, a major difference may be seen in the principles of selection used to determine what was worthy of study as literature. In studies of "classical" literature, there was clearly some awareness that no distinction could be made between writing as an art and as a craft, and thus all forms of composition were included, ranging from folktales to codes of law. In the study of the new literature, however, the purview of scholars has been limited to literature with a capital "L," thus excluding other forms of written discourse such as letters, newspaper reports, and fiction that was not thought to be up to the standard of "Literature." The result was that the old and the new have appeared quite remote from each other.

This compartmentalization has thus resulted from an arbitrary insistence on applying extraneous models of what constitutes literature. If we will only desist from caviling about what is "literature," and concentrate on examining Malay writing as a whole, we shall become aware that what Overbeck and his contemporaries saw as a death was in fact the most important development in Malay verbal communication since the introduction of writing, for they were witnessing the transmutation of a radically oral/aural manuscript culture into a print culture. While Hooykaas (1939), Teeuw (1967:6–7), Ismail Hussein (1970:220ff), and others have rightly emphasized the importance of the introduction of print in the development of the modern literature, there has yet been no concerted effort to examine the enormous implications of this "transformation of the word" in the context of the development of systems of shaping, storing, retrieving, and communicating knowledge in the Malay world. Ong has demonstrated how the introduction of typography causes man to "link visual perception to verbalization to a degree previously unknown" (1967:50). With print, knowledge is fastened down in visually processed space, locked into "exactly the same place upon the page in thousands of copies of the same book" (1971:277–78), and quickly retrieved by the use of the index. This development made possible thought processes inconceivable before: the printed surface enters the thought processes, producing new states of awareness, effecting a change in the psyche, and restructuring consciousness (1977:17, 46–47).

It would, of course, be anachronistic to criticize our predecessors for failing to appreciate the situation. Our present awareness of the development of various stages of verbalization (oral, chirographic, typographic, and electronic) is a product of our entering the electronic stage, for it was apparently not possible "for man to understand the psychological and cultural significance of writing and print and of oral expression itself, with which writing and print contrast, until he had moved beyond print into our present age of . . . electronic communication" (Ong, 1967:18).

The acute self-consciousness of the modern Western world resulting from the knowledge explosion of this electronic age has produced a heightened awareness of the problematic position of the observer in scholarship. It is this self-awareness which most distinguishes us from our predecessors, who were largely unaware that their confident value judgments were a reflection of the norms and values of a particular culture at a certain point in time rather than the expression of some universal and absolute truth. In the field of Malay scholarship, these evaluations tell us more about the reaction of the Romanticists against the old rhetorical tradition than about Malay literature *per se*. There is a certain irony in the fact that in their search for the fresh, the foreign, and the unknown, the Romanticists found in Malay literature a little too much that smacked of the old rhetorical commonplace tradition they had rejected in Europe. Indeed, the "stereotypes," "stock situations," and "clichés" which they eschewed were found in far greater abundance than in the European commonplace tradition, so that the pre-Romanticist, residually oral European literature must have suddenly appeared quite "fresh" in contrast with this still radically oral Malay manuscript literature. This is hardly surprising, for the shifts in European writing had been relatively small, involving mainly an increasing interiorization of print, and of course it has been the one class which has been setting the normative trends in Western literature for the past four hundred odd years: the urban middle class.

Predictably, Malay literature did not fare too well in the evaluations of the scholars. For example, Wilkinson (1924:6, 9) felt that Malay literature was "a very poor one indeed." The old Malay romances were "pompous, pretentious and verbose. They are full of digressions and repetitions. . . . Their moral tone is bad." Winstedt (1958:60) wrote that "The germ of every Malay romance is a folktale . . . manipulated by men wildly ignorant and intolerant of the unities of place and time and of historical truth." And Pijnappel, who felt that he did not dare to claim that the Malays had a literature and considered the *Hikayat Hang Tuah* to be "a nonsensical hodge-podge of all kinds of anecdotes" (1870:146), so well revealed the aspirations of the Romanticists in the following passage that it is worth quoting in translation at length:

> Yet I would suppose that the greatest part of the poetic products is original [i.e., not from foreign sources—AS]. The poetic products! One may well make a sacrifice to the Muses if one employs the word 'poetry' here. It is doggerel, which people collect as novelties or have preserved as curiosities. I have long attempted to defend the Malay pantuns, and wished to discover therein the stamp of unfalsified nature. But I have to give up. Not that unfalsified nature would be wanting in it; nature is never false, and it is wholly nature; but I had anticipated another nature, a nature such as that

of the uncontrived folk poetry of the folk of our stock, a nature to which our heart opens up, and we can feel sympathy. I had not considered the existence of another nature. I have sought, in a word, poetry, poetic feeling, be it in whatever form, but I have not found it in Malay poems.

(1870:145)

I referred above to the precedent offered by the treatment of Old English literature to the potential historian of Malay literature. Here, too, in the matter of evaluation, we find similarities, as a comparison of, say, Saintsbury with Winstedt reveals, both incidentally being fond of dismissing "farragos" of legends or folktales. Of course, to ridicule our predecessors for having such a normative approach would be absurd: we would merely be falling into the same pattern that they followed in their criticism of Malay literature. As I have already emphasized, only now are we able to see that the Malay (or indeed Old English) composer did not have some inherent weakness or was somehow "childish," but that his "style" is the result of the demands of schematic composition, be it written or oral, which is the hallmark of a radically oral society.

It should not be thought the Romanticists viewed Malay literature with unmitigated scorn. On the contrary, certain aspects of that literature were received with enthusiasm by some scholars. Yet even when something was found worthy of praise, its appeal tended to be extrinsic to the culture, so that the scholars often saw merit where a traditional Malay audience would have found none. To take an extreme example, de Hollander's version of the *Syair Ken Tambuhan*, translated into Dutch by Roorda van Eysinga in 1838, seems to have been favored chiefly because it ends with the death of Panji, appealing thus to the nineteenth-century European taste for the romantic and tragic.[22] Yet this ending results from the fact that the version is almost certainly incomplete: such a denouement for a Panji tale would have been quite unsatisfactory for a Malay audience, who would have demanded a happy ending, which indeed occurs in all the other versions of the tale.

Less obvious instances of extrinsic evaluation where the observer perceives the unfamiliar in terms of familiar schemata are found in the enthusiasm of some Western scholars for the *pantun* and the "rhythmical prose" of the "*penglipur lara*" storyteller. These genres, with their descriptions of and allusions to "nature," and their apparent "simplicity," were interpreted with the schemata of Romanticist poetry. Win-

22. See Teeuw (1966:430); also Sweeney (1980:1–2).

stedt, for example, speaks of "native woodnotes wild," indicating that he had found the "nature" which Pijnappel had sought in vain. In this rhythmical prose, according to Winstedt (1958:32), "we have the originality and sensitive fancy of genuine literature," and "with a few pantuns, it is the only genuine imaginative poetry . . . that Malay literature possesses" (1923:6). The *pantun* for Winstedt (1958:169) is "simple, sensuous and passionate," the aspirations par excellence of the Romanticist poet.[23] Here, for Winstedt and the Western middle-class audience he postulated, was poetry of the simple rustic, which had an additional appeal for that audience in that it was suitably remote and exotic. The association with Wordsworth and his language of the simple man is inescapable. Yet Wordsworth did not use the language of the simple peasant. As argued by Ong (1971:282), Wordsworth's style is a highly sophisticated, literate one, shorn of the typically oral features of the old tradition to which he objected. His poetry, moreover, was not a poetry of the rustic, nor was it intended for him. It was a private, isolated poetry intended for visual consumption by a middle-class audience. The concept of "pure poetry" is thus poles apart from schematic, oral Malay composition, which was intended to be heard by a live audience and which, particularly in the case of the *pantun*, was very much public poetry.

This schema for making evaluations, no less than the historical model in which it resides, has continued to limit our ability to perceive traditional Malay literature on its own terms. History is not some already fully formed entity waiting to be dug up. All historical writing is an attempt to answer contemporary needs. The history one produces depends upon the questions one asks. European historical writing developed within a tradition. Each new generation of historians came to its task with a number of given themes, which it adjusted to suit its needs. Historical writing thus tells us as much about the present of the writer via his perceptions of his past as it does of his past. A very different situation obtains when a historian looks at a cultural tradition entirely foreign to his own. Here, his given themes are not those of the tradition, and the questions he asks may not have any

23. The aptness of this description need not concern us, for what constitutes such qualities is determined by contemporary taste. The dictum quoted is in fact Milton's; "native woodnotes wild" is also from Milton ("L'Allegro": "Warble his native woodnotes wild"). Though the Romanticist perception of the "simple, sensuous and passionate" differed considerably from that of Milton, the Romanticists made much of him. His work was sufficiently remote for it to be intriguing in a way that the eighteenth-century neo-classical tradition was not.

significance in that tradition. An example we have noted in the field of
Malay literature is the wish to know the identities of authors and the
original forms of their creations, which were not at all matters for
concern in the Malay tradition. While such questions are entirely le-
gitimate, they do not enable the scholar to discover any inherent system in the object of his study.

The concept of the complete system is particularly associated with
the development of modern linguistics, where the perceived inadequacies of the historical and comparative methods of philology led to a
rejection of the diachronic for a synchronic approach, which involved
an attempt to articulate the grammatical system existing in the immediate experience of the native speaker. This shift to the synchronic
approach constituted the major intellectual development in the social
sciences and humanities during the early twentieth century. In literary
studies, a single-minded concern with the synchronic is manifest in
the work of the Russian Formalists and the New Critics. The corollary of all this is the perception that history is "ailing" or "dead."
Jacques Barzun (1974:3), for example, speaks of "the decline of a
true sense of history," and that "empirical observation also suggests
that History is sick, dying, dead." On the other hand, however, there
is a growing awareness, as evidenced by the work of scholars such as
Frederic Jameson (1972), of a need to reconcile the synchronic with
the diachronic.

Meanwhile, the study of traditional Malay literature is still, to no
small extent, bogged down in what is largely a nineteenth-century
approach, which, moreover, has been bequeathed to the Indonesians
and Malaysians.

The feeling still persists that Winstedt's work was premature, that
he attempted too much before scholarship had assembled adequate
data, and that such a literary history certainly ought to be written.
This attitude, I fear, will only lead us further into the morass. Not
only does the model we are still using hinder us from asking the
questions of the late twentieth century; too many of the questions it
does allow, indeed forces, us to ask simply cannot be answered. The
distinction may be seen in the treatment afforded modern Indonesian
and Malaysian literature. Here, the old historical model may be said
to fit, in the sense that questions concerning influences, chronology,
biographical data, and so forth, are answerable. That this model does
not enable us to answer questions of the modern age is clear from the
growing dissatisfaction with the process of neatly packaging and label-

ing *angkatan* ("generation") after *angkatan,* and from the present casting around for new approaches.

In the study of traditional Malay literature, the model simply does not fit. This has engendered a sense of frustration among scholars, giving rise to a feeling that there is something basically wrong with traditional Malay literature. The problem lies not with the material, however, but with the unsuitability of the model applied to study it. Unfortunately, scholars have so internalized this model that criticism of our predecessors is still being made within its framework, and few of its basic assumptions have been questioned. Thus, for example, while Liaw Yock Fang commences his *Sejarah Kesusasteraan Melayu Klassik* with the view that "Winstedt's greatest weakness is perhaps his fondness for foreign influences" (1975:ii), he proceeds to produce a "literary history" cast in exactly the same theoretical mold. And while certain scholars have become aware of the need for a synchronic approach, one may still observe the pull of the schemata of their diachronic model. And even in the paper of Ismail Hussein (1974), referred to above, where a clear awareness is manifest of the inadequacies of the model, we still observe a similar battle with the schemata.

It cannot be denied that the traditional historical model served us well. In particular, the manifestation of that model found in the work of Winstedt has provided us with a filing system, essential in any branch of scholarship, enabling us to bring some perception of order to our knowledge of Malay literature. Furthermore, no other model was available at the time. There were, of course, scholars who felt that knowledge of Malay literature was too scanty to permit Winstedt's brand of chronological ordering, and attempted to organize their writing according to a different pattern. Hooykaas's work *Perintis Sastra* (1961), for example, consists of a series of short paragraphs, each dealing with a separate topic. Yet the fact that Hooykaas and Winstedt shared the same presuppositions and were equally committed to the diachronic approach ensured that his apparent attempt to dispense with a chronological filing system only served to underline his concern with chronology and his commitment to the historical model. It also drew attention to the absence of an alternative system.

The developments of the electronic age have opened up new ways of looking at traditional Malay literature which were impossible for our predecessors. I am not thinking primarily of mere physical aids such as recording devices—audio and video—which can freeze certain aspects of oral performance. Rather I am referring to Ong's contention

referred to above, that the interiorization of new media of communication has had a radical effect upon our thought processes. While we
can never escape from "the prison-house of language," modern developments have provided us with a new perspective from which to view
"transformations of the word." We can now at least attempt to detach
ourselves from the assumptions of writing and print, and observe the
complex interaction between literacy and orality.

It is my conviction that, once we discard our antiquated historical
model for the study of traditional Malay written and oral composition, and attempt to study it in the context of systems of shaping,
storing, retrieving, and communicating knowledge, that literature will
appear much less remote. While certain aspects of oral composition
may be recorded, its performance exists only in the immediate present.
A study of the interaction between oral expression and writing and
print reveals the complexity of the relationships between those media,
and also enables us to throw light upon the development of written
composition. Our awareness of the schematic nature of much of
Malay written composition leads us to see each manuscript of a
"work" as a potential performance. The fact that the vast majority of
Malay manuscripts date from the nineteenth century brings these potential performances much closer to our own time.

My remarks should not be interpreted to mean that most of Malay
literature dates only from the nineteenth century, or be seen as an
attempt to belittle that tradition. On the contrary, the Malay literary
tradition is clearly very old, dating back at least to the seventh century
A.D. I am not saying that the Malay does not possess a "literary" past
to be proud of. I am saying, however, that that past cannot be cast in
the mold of a nineteenth-century European literary history, and that to
insist on the glories of traditional Malay literature in terms of the
norms and values of the nineteenth-century Western middle class is to
advertise the fact that one is still unconsciously enslaved by those
norms.

I have referred to the heightened awareness of the problems faced
by the scholar who studies a culture not his own. Without doubt, the
shrinking of the world by the communications explosion has produced a consciousness of the relativity of many of one's own norms
and values. This awareness of self in time and space has engendered
a sense of the need to rectify the distortions caused by the assumptions of our age, culture, and conditioning, and at least attempt to
perceive the object of our study on its own terms. This is very differ-

ent from creating an ethos as an impartial observer, which is merely self-deluding, for the modern scholar feels the difference between his own society and the one he is studying no less strongly than the earlier scholars, who had no qualms about giving vent to what they saw through their culture-colored spectacles. The scholar who adopts the posture of objectivity, using passive, mechanistic terminology in the belief that the categories he perceives become somehow more real, is still no less a slave of his own perceptions than were his predecessors. Rather we should accept the fact of our unavoidable subjectivity and indeed exploit it, for only thus may we consciously strive toward objectivity, which is still our goal. It should perhaps be stressed, therefore, that the point of our being self-aware is to monitor and correct our assumptions, and that our object of study is Malay literature, not ourselves. Otherwise, there is a temptation to make do with a rudimentary knowledge of one's subject and use it as a foil for at best an exposition of one's own cultural convictions and at worst an exercise in narcissism.

Two Eighteenth-Century Observers

In light of the observation that the negative reaction of Western scholars toward much of traditional Malay literature echoes the Romanticist rejection of the old rhetorical tradition in Europe, it might be expected that the pre-Romanticists would have found the formulary features and abundant repetition of Malay manuscript literature less oppressive, or even less noticeable, and that consequently their view of that literature might be rather different from that of our immediate predecessors.

Our next step, then, should be to examine the perceptions of Malay literature revealed in the writings of Europeans from the pre-Romanticist period, for this might not merely enable us to throw the assumptions of nineteenth-century scholars into sharper relief; the result of contrasting those attitudes might well be a clearer insight into the nature of the Malay manuscript literary tradition.

Two of the most useful sources for this purpose are François Valentijn's *Oud en Nieuw Oost-Indien* (1724) and George Hendrik Werndly's *Maleische Spraakkunst* (1736), which both provide a number of comments on specific works of Malay literature and the language in which they were written. Of course, an attempt to interpret the perceptions of eighteenth-century Europe—a period now quite remote from our own—concerning the literary products of a society very alien to it is not without its problems, for it is all too easy to naturalize those perceptions according to the mental set and historical perspective of the late twentieth century. We should therefore attempt to counter such tendencies by commencing with a brief examination of the context in which these two clergymen wrote.

Europe in the first half of the eighteenth century was still firmly entrenched in the old classical tradition. Three distinguishing features of this rhetorical culture, "which made a science or 'art' of its orality" (Ong, 1971:2), were the dominant position of Latin, dependence upon the *topos* or commonplace, and the use of *copia*. After vernacular Latin had developed into the various Romance languages, Latin as a learned language remained as the medium of scholarship throughout the Western world. Although used for oral as well as written communication, it was no longer used as a mother tongue. While a basic supposition of the tradition was that "the paradigm of all expression is the oration" (Ong 1971:3), Latin was chirographically controlled, and learning to speak it necessarily involved acquiring the patterns of writing. The residual orality of the rhetorical tradition is seen particularly in the need for *copia,* or abundance, which manifests itself *inter alia* in formulas, parallelisms, and repetition. Before the rise of the Romanticist movement, the writing of prose in the European vernaculars was governed to a large extent by the study of Latin, and this study favored the persistence of oral residue: "Latin sustained the rhetorical—which is basically oratorical and thus oral—cast of mind. The stress on *copia* which marked Latin teaching and which was closely associated with rhetorical invention and the oral performer's need for an uninterrupted supply of material favored exploitation of commonplaces," which were basic building blocks of composition.[1]

By these standards, the writings of Valentijn and Werndly are still very much products of the old rhetorical tradition. Of course, with the growth of the middle class and commercialism, the role of Learned Latin had become increasingly displaced by the vernaculars. Thus, the works of both Valentijn and Werndly are in Dutch, and Valentijn, in particular, was clearly writing for a commercially oriented audience. For him, trade not only produces riches; it furthers a knowledge of "history" and the spread of enlightenment. Yet both writers still regard Latin as the language of learning; indeed, the scholarly ethos is to be defined by a knowledge of Latin. Writing,

1. Ong, 1971:46. For detailed discussion of the role of Latin and *topoi,* see Curtius (1973, passim) and Ong (1967, 1971, 1977), to which this paragraph is not a little indebted.

furthermore—particularly that in Latin, but also, by way of emulation, that produced in the vernacular—is still to be at least nominally dedicated to oratory. For example, Valentijn's book opens with epideictic orations in Latin and Dutch. These are in poetic form and are the work of the publisher. One of these orations is an explanation of the suitably heroic frontispiece, and is a panegyric to trade and the Dutch East India Company (the V.O.C.). In this way, commerce, not usually felt to be an epic or heroic subject by modern norms, is placed firmly within the classical framework.

While the increasing interiorization of print produced a more visual experience of literature and led to the attenuation of orally derived features such as *copia* and *topoi,* prose written in the classical tradition often strikes the modern reader as repetitious, artificial, and verbose. In this respect, the writings of Valentijn and Werndly are no exception. For example, Werndly's introduction seems inordinately long-winded by the standards of the nineteenth and twentieth centuries, as may be appreciated from the excerpts translated below, particularly those concerned with the diligence of the Malays, and with the various levels of fluency attained by those who study Malay. Marsden (1812:xlii), who otherwise holds the work of Werndly in high regard, considers that "the fault of the work, a very pardonable one, is redundance." That Valentijn's writing leaves a similar impression on readers of the modern age is clear from the *Geïllustreerde Encyclopaedie van Nederlandsch-Indië* (Gonggryp, 1934:1455), which finds his style "boring."

In view of the above considerations, it should hardly come as a surprise to discover that eighteenth-century Europeans' perceptions of the role and nature of Malay language and literature were very different from our own. This is clearly brought home to us by the fact that Roolvink (1975:13–14) finds it necessary (and quite justifiably so) to point out that Malay literature was by no means the exclusive domain of the ethnic Malays. Such an observation would have seemed quaintly unnecessary to Valentijn and Werndly, rather akin to remarking that Latin was not the sole prerogative of ethnic Romans. The expectations produced by the mental set of pre-Romanticist Europe was that a language of scholarship would be a learned language in the tradition of Latin, Greek, and Hebrew. And in this respect, those Europeans who concerned themselves with the "East" were not disappointed: aside from Arabic and Persian, the learned language of scholarship throughout a vast area of the East was seen to be Malay.

I am not suggesting that such a perception was a misguided one. Indeed, Ong argues that "the establishment of special languages through chirographic distancing has been fairly widespread across the globe," and that these learned languages appeared "at roughly the same stage in the history of consciousness," when writing had been sufficiently interiorized to affect thought processes but before print had further affected those processes (1977:28). However, it seems to me that Ong's criteria for a learned language (see 1977:29) are overly narrow, being governed largely by his perception of the role of Learned Latin, which was the mother tongue of no one, and could be understood only by those who wrote it, a group which was almost exclusively male. With the possible exception of certain varieties of "*kitab* Malay," these criteria do not hold for written Malay composition, which was usually consumed aurally by a nonliterate audience. Indeed, it is worthy of note that eighteenth-century Europeans who concerned themselves with the Malay language soon decided that Malay did not entirely coincide with their understanding of what constituted a learned language. Certain earlier writers tended to perceive a simple parallel between Latin and Malay. Tavernier, writing in the latter part of the seventeenth century, includes Malay among thirteen languages spoken in Ispahan (in Persia), and goes on to say that it is "the language of the learned from the flow of the Indus, up to China and Japan, and in the greater portion of the Eastern islands, like the Latin in our Europe" (quoted by Werndly, xxxviii). Similarly, the French theologian Thomassin, writing in 1693, and probably influenced by Tavernier, whom he quotes elsewhere, saw Malay as "la language des sçavans dans toutes les Indes [elsewhere: tout l'Orient], comme la Latine dans l'Europe" (from excerpts in Gonda, 1940:105 & 107).

Of course, Malay, unlike the Latin of that time, was also a living mother tongue and the lingua franca of trade. It is not surprising, therefore, that van Linschoten (ed. Kern, 1910:74), a trader rather than a scholar, writing in the late seventeenth century, compared the role of Malay in the East with that of French in Europe. A growing awareness of the existence of various types of Malay is reflected in the writings of the eighteenth century. Valentijn certainly sees Malay as a learned language of scholars; indeed he quotes Tavernier almost verbatim (he adds Spanish) as "the language of the learned from the flow of the Indus to China and Japan" (vol. V, p. 206). Yet while he sees a parallel with Latin, he also compares Malay with French, and with the

"Lingua Franca in Italy or in the Levant" (V:310).[2] He attempts to
articulate the distinction he perceives between the scholarly and common languages in the following passages:

> The [Malay] language is . . . of two kinds: the high, which is the Malay
> used among the nobility at the Courts in matters concerning the Moham-
> medan religion, or the low which is the Pasar or market Malay which is
> used daily among the common people. The first Malay, called Bahasa
> Jawi,[3] mother and pure language by them, is incontestably the best, most
> correct, and the most grandiloquent Malay; but this language is understood
> by no others than the Mohammedan kings, rulers and priests, even on the
> Malay coast, not to mention Java or Sumatra, and even among these it is
> never used in daily intercourse but only in writings of the court or of
> religion. . . . Apart from this High Malay language there is also a Low one,
> which, because it has drawn something from many nations, each according
> to its own language and dialect, and also sometimes is mixed with various
> other words, be they from Portuguese, or be they from some other lan-
> guage, bears the name of Bahasa Kacukan, that is the mixed language, or
> of Bahasa Pasara, that is market language, in so far as it is the language in
> which the merchants, who deal with one another in the market, manage to
> understand one another.
>
> (II:244)

> Nowhere is this language spoken so properly and so purely as here,[4]
> though there is still a great difference between that which the courtiers use
> and that which the common folk use except that the former is also larded
> with an uncommonly large number of Arabic words which they usually do
> to show their great learning in this language over against the common
> people; this language is also so grandiloquent and differs so much from the
> common pure language (for this is impure) in that every people who speak
> this common Malay language, mix in something of their own language,
> that it shall not be understood by any of the common folk; just as it is to be
> noted that it is used by no others than the rulers, courtiers and priests, and
> therefore only as a language of scholars.
>
> (V:1, 310)

On reading the first passage, we may well wonder with de Hollander
(1882:290) what language then did the nobility use in daily inter-

2. Valentijn's section on Malacca, which contains this passage, is translated in
JSBRAS (Hervey, 1884).
3. Malay terms used by Valentijn and Werndly are reproduced here in their modern
spelling except in the passages on etymology.
4. That is, in Malacca. This passage also appears in the excerpt cited above (Hervey,
1884). The passage has been retranslated here, as the sense of Hervey's text seems
somewhat confused, the result of Valentijn's having apparently used the word *gemeen*
("common") in two different ways: "common" as in "common people," and "common" in the sense of "general," with which he clearly intends to indicate the "neutral"
state of the language before it has been "adulterated."

course.[5] It seems clear that the schemata and expectations Valentijn had inherited from earlier writers such as Tavernier, modified by his own experience of spoken Malay in the seaports and coastal areas he visited, and written Malay in the works he collected, led him to see Malay either as a learned language of scholarship or as a lingua franca of trade, which thus formed for him a convenient binary pair: high and low. It was then a major problem for him to fit the idea of Malay as a mother tongue into his schema. This mother tongue becomes for him an idealized notion of a pure, unadulterated language, which he first equates with the high language. But as is clear from the second passage translated, he perceives that this high language is just as "impure" as the low market language. While Valentijn is still clearly groping for an understanding of the various types of Malay, one point to emerge that will be of relevance to our discussion is that he perceives *Bahasa Jawi* to be the written Malay language of Muslims.[6]

It is in Werndly that we find the first systematic attempt to distinguish between the various types and functions of the Malay language:

This language may now further be considered as a mother tongue or as a learned language. Considered as a mother tongue it is excluded from the number of learned languages (by which one understands the languages which are foreign to us from infancy which, nevertheless, can be acquired by special diligence and labour, with the help of masters, books, reading, writing, etc.) and at the same time it is to be pointed out that it is known in its [own] land from the first tender years of infancy and motherly upbringing and the speaking of which becomes further consolidated with age, and is then given the best guidance of all when it obtains its properties from learning to read and write. Thus the Malay language is not a learned language in its land of birth in Zirbad of which Johor is now the main place, where the Persian and especially the Arabic languages are held to be the learned languages.

(Pp. xxxix–xl)

But secondly, the Malay language, in so far as it has spread beyond the motherland to other lands, may also be considered as a learned language, which must be made known to us by others, be they true Malays or those versed in the Malay language, since we, and so many others like us who are not original Malays, must first learn this language in the same way as other foreign languages by such means as are necessary for a true knowledge of the language, thereby to become versed in the language, and to be able to teach others; and these who are versed in the language are also still very diverse:

5. A problem with de Hollander's criticism, however, is that he, too, accepts the notion of there being a "pure" language.
6. Although, as de Hollander (1882:290) observes, the Malay histories and poems were certainly understood by others than rulers and "priests."

for some understand the language properly but do not have the capacity to be able to talk in it; others go one step further and can indeed speak the language but cannot read; then there is a third sort who indeed read the language but cannot yet write or cannot do so properly; and finally there are those who are truly knowledgeable in the language who can understand, speak, read and write this language. The first mentioned who can understand and speak the language are still but semi-skilled; but those who, over and above that, know how to read and write, are the trained people in accordance with the tuition of good masters.

(Pp. xliii–xliv)

In discussing the use of the term *Bahasa di bawah angin* (the language of below the wind) as applied to Malay, Werndly states that

In a narrow sense, it is the language of the people who live in Zirbad [by which he refers to the Malay Peninsula], that same Zirbad which has been described above at greater length as the Malay land. But taken in a wide sense, it is to be made known that it is the generally used language of the Eastern lands of India, for the Malays, being the most civilized of the eastern peoples of India, through their shipping and trade and especially by the propagation of the Mohammedan religion, have carried forth their language in such a way that it is accepted as a generally used language of all the lands that have been mentioned; so that all foreigners who come to this or that island or to this or that place need to speak the language in order to trade with the inhabitants.

Thus is this description of *Bahasa di bawah angin* based on the wide extent of its spread, and it is thereby distinguished from all the other languages in the eastern part of India, obtaining thereby a particular esteem, as it does in truth possess, for it is not only the proper or mother tongue of the Malay land, but it has, furthermore, by general consent been able to make entry and take up abode in almost innumerable places, above and beyond the mother tongue proper of the inhabitants.

We see this system clearly established on the island of Sumatra, where the Malay language was born, being a particular dialect of the common local language there, and still today it is considered the learned and most beautiful language, for which reason the most distinguished inhabitants make it their task to have their children given the necessary instruction, as is the case with what one experiences in Acheh, Jambi, Inderagiri, Palembang, and in many other places.

(Pp. xxxiv–xxxv)

It is clear that for Werndly, the importance of Malay does not reside in its being a narrowly defined, ethnically based language, or what he would call "a particular dialect [*spraakwyze*] of the common local [or country] language [*landtaal*]." For him, hardly surprisingly in view of his background, Malay merited its renown as a chirographically controlled learned language. Even as a mother tongue, it only acquired its true "properties" when one *learned* to read and write it. This is not to suggest, however, that Werndly assigns the Malays a merely passive role in the spread of their language, which was to be taken over and used by all and sundry. On the contrary, he gives them full credit, as becomes even clearer in his remarks on the etymology of the word "Malay." While these are linguistically absurd by our standards, Werndly's choices throw considerable light on his attitude toward the Malays. He equates the word *melaju* (from *laju,* "swift") with *Melayu,* and after considering Valentijn's statement that the Melayu river is also named the Melaju river, contends that the term *melaju*

> can refer only to the swiftness of the aforementioned flow or river, and if this meaning be applied to the Malay people, this will signify that they were quick and shrewd fellows, seeking their fortunes everywhere; in the same way they have been renowned as traders and travellers since ancient times; thereby they always exerted themselves, going from place to place in order to seek out or to visit other lands and thus to strive for profit in those places where they were foreigners.
>
> (P. xxi)

This leads Werndly to equate the term *Melayu* with *dagang,* "which properly means a foreigner; yet by which is often to be understood a foreign merchant." He thus contends that

> to this extent, the name Bahasa Malajuw [i.e., *Melayu*] gives us to understand that it was the traders' language or the language of the foreign merchants; or one could apply this word Malajuw to the Malay people on account of their diligence, industriousness, quickness and energy so that they are always busy with something; and the Malays generally express these qualities of diligence and quickness by the word Maladjuw [i.e. = *Melaju*]. Thus 'Awrang Malajuw' [i.e., *Orang Melayu*] would be a diligent, industrious, quick and energetic man, and then Bahasa Malajuw would be the language of the diligent, industrious, quick and energetic people.
>
> (P. xxii)

The point to be made is that while Werndly gives credit to the Malays (i.e., those for whom Malay is a mother tongue) for spreading their language, he does not see them as holding a monopoly on the Malay language any more than he would have viewed the Romans (even before the mutation of the Latin vernacular into the Romance languages) as possessing sole proprietary rights to Latin.

Roolvink (1975:13–14) has drawn attention to the tendency of both Western scholars such as Winstedt, and the "Malays" themselves to assume that Malay literature is the exclusive prerogative of the "Malays,"[7] with the outcome that Westerners have criticized Malay literature for being so full of foreign "influences," which in its turn has caused the Malays to feel defensive. For Werndly in the eighteenth century, when learned languages were still considered the normal, or at least, ideal, medium of scholarly discourse, such an assumption would have been incomprehensible. The irony of the Malay reaction to Winstedt's criticism is that both he and the Malays shared the same basic premise, which we can now see was an erroneous one. On the one hand, the demise of Latin as the learned language of scholarship in Winstedt's Europe led him to overlook the role of learned languages in the Malay archipelago—particularly as Malay was the mother tongue of the majority of the indigenous people in the areas under British rule where he served—so that he saw Malay literature rather as a product of a particular ethnic group, a perception of literatures which had become the custom in Romanticist Europe with the ascendancy of the vernaculars and the rise of nationalism. On the other hand, the Malays were at a disadvantage, for one of the hidden effects of colonialism is that the terms of the argument are usually dictated by the colonial power, and indeed the only terminology available for such argument is that bequeathed by that power; the stage is thus set by the latter, with the result that many of the "givens" of any argument are unwittingly accepted,[8] and not seen for what they are: the assumptions of an urbanized Western middle class.

In the Malay peninsula, furthermore, the twentieth-century appearance of nationalism—itself inherited from the West—fostered a new sense of "Malay" identity. The majority of the indigenous[9] people of the peninsula spoke Malay as their mother tongue; colonial rule had isolated them from the rest of the Malay world, where Malay, as the learned language of the archipelago, was to a considerable extent regarded as common property, regardless of ethnic origin. Ismail Hussein (1970:227) has argued that the power structure of colonial Malaya caused Malay nationalistic aspirations to be centered to a large extent on questions of language and culture, and he describes Malay

7. By which he is clearly referring to Malaysian "Malays." It cannot be denied, however, that a number of the more conservative Deli and Riau Malays still look to Malaysia as a source of inspiration, and may share such views.

8. An example of this in the context of racial difference is seen in the insistence by American blacks that "Black is Beautiful," which reveals, in fact, their unwitting acceptance of the racist premise that skin color is indeed a matter of importance.

9. That is, indigenous, at least, to the archipelago.

nationalism as a "linguistic nationalism." Furthermore, as Roff (1974:256) contends, the perceived threat to Malay interests from locally domiciled aliens, in particular the Chinese, and also the sensitivity within the Malayo-Muslim community itself to domination by those of Arab and Indian extraction led to the growth of ethnicism. On the other hand, in Indonesia, with its large number of indigenous ethnic groups, the concept of nationhood had to transcend ethnic loyalties, and the role of Malay as a learned language was to unite these diverse groups; even where it was the mother tongue, it did not serve to affirm an ethnic identity.

The notion of the Malays' possessing sole proprietary rights to all that was written in Malay, and the attempt to define what constituted a "Malay" in purely ethnic terms appeared only relatively recently, and were shared by both the Malays of the peninsula and the British, the latter being to no small extent indirectly responsible for the acceptance of such views by the former.

An examination of the works of Valentijn and Werndly reveals a very different view of the Malay language, literature, and people which, it would seem, was also to a large extent shared by, indeed derived from, the "Malays" themselves; a view which, on the literary level at least, emphasized the internationalistic rather than the ethnic aspects of being a Malay.

It is relevant to note that in recent years there has been a growing awareness among many Malaysian Malays that a Malay identity is to be sought not in a Western-style nationalism based on ethnicity; rather there is the perception that this identity is to be found in the supra-national tradition of Islam. This, of course, is not a new trend, but rather an articulation on the conscious level of what had traditionally been taken for granted. The fact that the concept of "Malay" has been regarded as synonymous with "Muslim" made it well-nigh impossible for Malaysia to define "Malay" in ethnic terms, as is seen from the constitution, where a Malay is one who is a Muslim, speaks Malay, and follows Malay custom. *Masuk Melayu* is the traditional way of referring to conversion to Islam; many Malays still regard Muslim societies outside the Malay world as "Malay." And in southern Thailand, where the Malay population is officially required to regard itself as Thai Muslim, people may refer to speaking Malay as "speaking Islam" (*kecek Selam*). Of course, it would be ludicrous to suggest that Malays are unable to distinguish between the various races professing Islam; I am arguing merely that the term "Malay" has traditionally carried too many religious connotations to serve as an adequate indicator of ethnicity without qualification.

We have seen from Werndly's general remarks on Malay that for him its importance lay in the fact that it was a learned language transcending ethnic and political boundaries. This view is amplified in his discussion of specific terms. Thus, for example, he considers it necessary to explain what might seem obvious to those with twentieth-century ideas of national languages, that "the Malay language is so named by reference to the land of its birth" (p. iii). The fact that "outside that land it is a learned language, just as is the case with Arabic and Persian, which are the commonly used languages in their birthplaces, but which are learned languages in other places" (p. iii) makes it necessary to identify the place of its origin.

Werndly's perceptions of the roles of the Malay language are further revealed in his comparison of the terms *Bahasa Jawi* and *Bahasa Melayu*. Although he quotes Guernier's dictionary to the effect that *Bahasa Jawi* signifies "the usual mother tongue" or "the usual, customary Malay language" (p. iii), his own comments clearly seem to imply that he perceives "*Jawi*" to refer to the learned, chirographically controlled, scholarly language, while "Malay" is seen to be more of an inclusive term which, nevertheless, carries the connotation of mother tongue.

Werndly (pp. xliv–xlviii) lists five types of Malay: *Bahasa Jawi, Bahasa Dalam, Bahasa Bangsawan, Bahasa Gunung,* and *Bahasa Kacukan. Bahasa Dalam* and *Bangsawan* refer to the speech of the court and aristocracy respectively; the *Bahasa Gunung* is the "peasant dialect, so-called because they live on the mountains,"[10] and the *Bahasa Kacukan* or *Bahasa Pasar/Bazar* is the "low speech," "street language," or "market language." *Bahasa Jawi,* however, is "the usual Malay language . . . as commonly understood and spoken and in which their books are written, so that it would not be improper to call it *a book language.*" A "book language" is, of course, a chirographically controlled language, which is a learned language, according to the definitions of both Werndly and Ong, and also in the sense that it is a learned dialect for those whose mother tongue is Malay.

The scholarly aspect of *Bahasa Jawi* for Werndly is again reflected in the observation at the beginning of his preface that "the language

10. This impression may have been gained from what he found in Padang, the first place he visited in the Indies (p. 256).

which we shall be dealing with is known among the savants as Bahasa
Jawi, the Jawi language, and among the common people as Bahasa
Melayu, the Malay language" (p. i). Werndly sees these terms as referring to two different aspects of the language, which can be revealed
only by examining them in context: "By the first name, the Malay
language is distinguished from Arabic and Persian, and at the same
time it is indicated that this language is the usual and customary
speech, whereas the other two languages are the province of the scholars. This distinction is placed before us in the Malay booklet entitled
Mir'ātu 'l-Mu'min. . ." (p. i). Here, Werndly is not attempting to discern some intrinsic meaning of "Jawi"; he is concerned with relationships: "*Jawi*" is to be defined by distinguishing it from other terms
occurring in the same context. It is clear that for him the Malay
language is *Bahasa Jawi* when placed in a Muslim scholarly context,
and this accords with Valentijn's view, referred to above, that *Bahasa
Jawi* was the written Malay language of Muslims. It is particularly
worthy of note that Werndly's observation is inspired by the distinctions made by the writers of Malay literature themselves. The passage
he quotes from the *Mir'ātu 'l-Mu'min* of Syamsuddin states that Syamsuddin wrote the work in *Bahasa Jawi* so that those seekers of
knowledge who did not understand Arabic and Persian might more
easily gain understanding (p. ii).[11]

Before the advent of modern linguistics, the primacy of the written
language over speech was taken for granted. As we have seen,
Werndly considers that a language acquires its true properties only
when it is written. In the case of a chirographically controlled language particularly, language was identified with writing, and for *Bahasa Jawi,* the Muslim identity of this "book language" was further
emphasized by the fact that it was written in the Perso-Arabic script.
The idea of considering *Bahasa Jawi* apart from *tulisan Jawi* (*Jawi*
writing) would have been an alien one indeed.[12] Only with the intro-

11. This had apparently become something of a formula by the time of Syamsuddin,
for the same remark is also found in the writings of Hamzah Fansuri (see the edition of
Doorenbos, 1933:176). However, there is no evidence to indicate that Hamzah was the
originator of the remark or that he was himself not using it as a given formula. Thus
al-Attas's (1968:44) citing it as evidence that Hamzah was the first to expound on
Sufism in Malay is unconvincing, for exactly the same contention could be made about
Syamsuddin.

12. Thus, while we may agree with Roolvink (1975:17) that *Bahasa Jawi* does not
refer exclusively to the script as al-Attas (1972:43) asserts, there is nevertheless much to
be said for al-Attas's view in the sense that the term *Bahasa Jawi* clearly referred to the
chirographically controlled language.

duction of romanized script (*Rumi*) did the term *"Jawi"* come to be used specifically for the script as a means of distinguishing it from the new script.[13]

Werndly's perception of two aspects of the Malay language referred to by the terms *Jawi* and *Melayu*, although not clearly articulated by our standards, is further revealed in his etymologizing: we have seen that with *Melayu/melaju* he refers us back to the place of origin of the Malay language; his first derivation of *"Jawi"* (equally absurd by modern standards), however, takes us outside the land of the Malays and refers us as far afield as Persian. He sees the origin of *"Jawi"* in the "Persian word *Dja* or *Djaj,* 'a place,' from which . . . the adjective *Djawij* derives, and signifies 'something that is placed' or 'has a place'; and this, applied to the Malay language, would carry with it the idea that thereby is to be understood 'a placed language,' or 'common language' " (p. iv). What is of significance here is Werndly's perception of Malay which leads him to such an explanation, for he tells us that "the Malay language bears this name on account of its extensiveness; namely, to signify thereby that it is the accepted and placed language in the eastern part of Asia, and in particular on the self same islands, which in truth it is" (p. iv). Although he also derives *"Jawi"* from *"Jawa"* and argues that *"Jawi"* may be "an old and general term" used to refer to both Malay and Javanese, he continues to derive the form *"Jawi"* from Persian (p. viii).

In referring us outside the area of Malay as a mother tongue for the provenance of the term *"Jawi,"* although his actual argument is incorrect, Werndly's general perception that the term originated in the Islamic tradition is not at fault; it is now a commonplace that *"Jawi"* derives from Arabic, being the adjectival form of *"Jawa,"* with which the Arabs designated both Java and Sumatra. Snouck Hurgronje noted that the Arabs use the term *"Jawi"* to refer to all the people of the Malay race in the widest sense, the geographical limits of their spread being the Malay peninsula and Siam in the west and New Guinea in the east, and that the whole area was referred to as Bilād el-Jāwah (1888:295–96; cited by Roolvink, 1975:17).

It is hardly surprising that the Arabs did not make detailed ethnic distinctions but rather applied the label *"Jawi"* to the peoples of the

---

13. We may note that in Indonesian the fact that *Jawi* signifies "Javanese" in Kromo meant that the term *Jawi* was unable to perform this distinguishing role when Indonesian Malay became the national language of the whole country, so that *Jawi* script is now referred to as *huruf Arab*.

Malay world in general: as traders, they would be most familiar with the coastal areas, where the lingua franca was Malay, and where the local Muslim population was likely to present considerable ethnic variety and intermixture. The tendency of the Arabs to see the inhabitants of the Malay world as one people was perhaps reinforced by the view of itself exhibited by the large "Jawi" community in Arabia, which perceived its identity as Muslim Malay in the widest sense, that is, *Jawi*, rather than emphasizing narrow ethnic loyalties; for it is natural that when thrown together in a society outside the Malay world, the various groups would become more conscious of their similarities than of the differences among themselves, over against the indigenous Arab population.

For the Arabs, the term *jawi* did not apparently carry any specific religious connotation, and was used generally to refer to that which originated from the Malay world; thus, Werndly, for example, notes the Arabic phrase *lubān jāwī* referring to "Malay" benzoin.[14] However, when the term "*jawi*" was adopted into Malay from Arabic, *the* language of Islam, it carried with it a Muslim connotation. This was especially the case when applied to language; thus *loghatu 'l-jāwiyyah* became *Bahasa Jawi* in translation and was used to denote Malay as a Muslim language in contradistinction to the other great languages of Islam: Arabic and Persian. Moreover, with the exception of Arabic terms containing the word "*jawi*" (e.g., *lubān jāwī*) taken over directly into Malay, "*jawi*" carries the connotation of "Islam" or "Muslim" in a variety of usages. Thus, in Malaysia, *Jawi peranakan* refers to Muslim Malays of Indian extraction; in Kelantan, *masuk jawi* ("enter *jawi*") is still used to refer to the circumcision of young boys, and also, but now less commonly, to the conversion of non-Muslims to Islam.

14. Roolvink (1975:2) uses the example of *lubān jāwī* in his contention that *Jawi* "means Sumatran, originating from Sumatra." In the absence of any evidence, I find this argument unconvincing. Roolvink does not examine the usage in context, but rather implies that "*Jawi*" has some intrinsic, absolute meaning. He does not appear to distinguish between the significance of "*Jawi*" in Arabic and in Malay. Although he cites the observations of Snouck Hurgronje (1888:295–96, referred to above) concerning the Arab's use of the term, he nevertheless contends that the Arabic term *lubān jāwī* means "Sumatran benzoin." Roolvink seems to imply that because the benzoin is found in Sumatra, "*Jawi*" must therefore mean "Sumatran." But in Arabic, the point of qualifying this *luban* with "*jawi*" is to distinguish it from other kinds of *luban*, such as *lubān shāmī* (pitch resin), not to make unneeded distinctions between places in the Malay world. Similarly, Roolvink argues that because Abdul Rauf of Singkel was an Achinese, his styling himself "al-Jāwī" is an indication that "*Jawi*" means "Sumatran." I find it inconceivable that this *kunwa* (by-name) would serve to distinguish him as a Sumatran as opposed to, say, a Patani Malay. Rather, it would, in a Muslim context, denote that he was a native of the Malay archipelago in contradistinction to other areas of the Islamic world.

Although Werndly is clearly aware of the Muslim flavor of Malay as a learned language of scholars, he certainly did not regard the Muslims, or indeed Malays, as having proprietary rights over the use of the language. And it is his emphasis upon the use of the language which should be stressed. Here was no Romanticist intent upon discovering the exotic. His concern with Malay language and literature was essentially a pragmatic one. His mission was to spread the Christian religion, and, for a man of his time and society, the obvious means to this end was to acquire a knowledge of the learned language of the area. It is thus that he perceives the Dutch involvement with the Malay language as merely following a pattern long established in the Malay world, and thus continuing a process that had led to the wide spread of the Malay language. For example, he remarks that "this language has penetrated even further into those islands and places possessed by the Netherlands East India Company, as a result of the propagation of the Christian religion, as can be heard daily in Ambon, Banda, Ternate, Makassar, Timor, etc." (p. xxxvi). Valentijn, moreover, finds it necessary to explain what might seem obvious to us now: that the "Moors" speak much better Malay than the Christians. The reason he gives is not that Malay is the "Moors" ' own language, but that they possess "reasonably good Malay books written by hand in Arabic letters," and that "this provides them . . . with more knowledge of the language" (vol. III, p. 26).

Perhaps the most revealing indication of eighteenth-century attitudes toward Malay language and literature is to be found in the presentation of Werndly's *Boekzaal,* which consists of two parts. The first part is clearly given priority; over one hundred pages in length, it is concerned with "Malay literature written by Europeans." The second part, consisting of only fourteen pages, deals with books written by the Malays "proper." Werndly and his contemporaries were not interested in Malay literature for the insight it might afford into the soul of a particular ethnic group. For them it was a practical vehicle, as it had been for the Muslims before them. Malay was the language of wisdom of the area, the language of religion and philosophy, the language it was essential to master if one were to produce scholarly work on these subjects. And indeed, it is clear that the main point of studying Malay literature written by the Malays "proper" is to improve one's ability in the language, and also to glean the *knowledge* contained in that literature which may be found useful.

It is germane at this point to consider what Werndly and Valentijn understood by Malays (*Malayers*) "proper." We have seen that

Werndly does attempt to distinguish what he calls "true Malays" as those for whom Malay is a mother tongue. Valentijn provides a similar description: they are the people of the "Malay coast," which he defines geographically, although in a more limited sense only the Malaccans are "*orang Melayu*"; while other people of the peninsula and Sumatra are also called "Malays," it is always with the addition of the country from which they originate, for example, Melayu-Johor, Melayu-Patani (vol. V, 1:317–18). This distinction is also taken over by Werndly (p. xxix).

In practice, however, both Werndly and Valentijn tend to use the term "Malay" in a much wider sense. In the context of Malay literature, for example, Werndly employs the category "books written by Malays" for all writings in Malay not produced by Europeans. In a number of places, Valentijn appears to use the term "Malay" as an equivalent of "Moor"[15] and "Mohammedan." This, of course, calls to mind the Arab's use of the term "Jawi." Roolvink (1975:17) considers this use of "Malay" an "appellation which gives rise to confusion," and cites Marsden's pronouncement that "it is not unusual with persons who have not resided in this part of the East, to call the inhabitants of the islands indiscriminately by the name of Malays. This is a . . . considerable error" (1811:40). I would argue, however, that the error lies in attempting to assign an absolute, "correct" meaning to a term taken out of its context, for it acquires meaning only by being distinguished from other terms, stated or implied. Indeed, while Marsden may have had the notion that he knew better, he nevertheless acknowledged that "Malay" usage itself does not coincide with his view:

> It must be observed, indeed, that in common speech the term *Malay,* like that of Moor in the continent of India, is almost synonymous with Mahometan; and when the natives of other parts learn to read the Arabic character, submit to circumcision, and practise the ceremonies of religion, they are often said *men-jadi Malāyo,* "to become Malays," instead of the more correct expression *sudah māsuk islām,* "have embraced the faith."
> (1811:42)

It is clear that this perception of what constitutes a Malay is not an erroneous assumption of foreigners who have not resided in the East, but reflects the view that "Malays" had of themselves. Without doubt, it is this identification of Malay with Muslim by Malays themselves— stressed earlier—which influenced the perceptions of Werndly and Va-

---

15. It may be noted that the Muslim natives of the Southern Philippines are still often referred to as "Moros."

lentijn of the "Malays"; and, particularly in the case of Valentijn,
which produced a somewhat ambivalent mixture of respect and hostility toward them.

In these eighteenth-century writings, we do not find the assumptions of inherent racial superiority and contempt for the "lazy native"
which accompanied nineteenth-century colonialist expansion, and of
which Clive Day's notions in *The Policy and the Administration of the
Dutch in Java* (1904) may be cited as a typical example. The Industrial
Revolution in Europe led to the systematic exploitation of colonies for
raw materials, involving the establishment of large-scale commercial
undertakings such as plantations, which depended upon native labor
for their development. This led the Europeans to view the association
with the colonized peoples as a master-servant relationship. While the
land-starved peasant of overpopulated Java was a ready source of
labor, in other areas such as the Malay peninsula, the local people saw
little advantage in working for such concerns. This gave rise to the
notion of the "lazy native."

In the early eighteenth century, however, the relationship between
the Europeans and the inhabitants of the archipelago was structured
around trade, and the prowess of the Malays in this area merits the
respect of both writers. Werndly's appreciation of the Malays as
traders is particularly strong, perhaps because his first direct impression of "Malays" was seemingly gained in 1718 at Padang (p. 256),
the people of which are still renowned for their business acumen.

Earlier, we observed that the writings of Werndly and Valentijn
were still very much a part of the European commonplace tradition.
Both writers reveal a relative lack of the skepticism and critical attitude stemming from an awareness of inconsistency which arose during
the nineteenth century as a result of the knowledge explosion and
technological revolution of the age of Romanticism. In the eighteenth
century, the *loci communes* of tradition were there for the use of one
and all, and the Romanticists' professed unswerving insistence on
originality was yet to come. In such an intellectual environment, it was
accepted practice to glean material, often verbatim, from the writings
of others, with or without acknowledgment, and such material might
be taken over and accepted without comment or any attempt to establish its accuracy. We have seen an example of this in Valentijn, who
quotes verbatim from Tavernier without acknowledgment or comment. Werndly, too, in spite of a scarcely veiled dislike of Valentijn,
gleans much material from the latter, and while it is true that he cites

Valentijn as one of the sources for his *Boekzaal,* comparison of the latter with Valentijn's comments (see Sweeney and Tiwon, 1986) reveals that he copied material verbatim from Valentijn without any indication that he was quoting. Valentijn's confusion between the *Hikayat Hang Tuah* and the *Sulalātu 's-Salāṭīn* is also reproduced by Werndly without comment.

It is hardly surprising, therefore, that the views of Werndly and Valentijn on Malay beliefs and scholarship should also reveal this relative lack of skepticism, compared with European writings of the nineteenth and twentieth centuries. The Bible, especially for these two clergymen, was still the ultimate source of knowledge, and in this sense they were much closer intellectually to Muslim scholars of their time for whom, too, a holy book, the Qur'an, constituted the font of all science. Thus, for example, it might at first seem strange that Valentijn finds it necessary to take seriously enough the claim of the Achinese and Minangs that they are descended from Alexander the Great to have to conclude that if this be true they must be bastards, "for their colour and skin are too different" (I:58). Yet when we read Valentijn's contention that Noah made the first ship, and that all other vessels must be descended from it no matter how much the heathens may swear that this is not so (I:5), we realize that even the most outlandish Malay beliefs (by modern standards) will not immediately appear ludicrous to a man of Valentijn's time and background. And while the scholarship of Werndly appears to us relatively more "scientific," his scholarly opinions are also firmly anchored in the teaching of the Bible, so that, for example, he takes it for granted that Hebrew is the original language of mankind (p. xlix).

In general, it can be said that the views of Werndly and Valentijn on the Malays reveal little of the condescension which Malays later came to expect in the writings of Europeans concerning Malay culture, and which, in this age of liberalism and guilt over the colonial past, has often tended to be transmuted into exaggerated praise, which yet still bears a patronizing flavor. This expectation is reflected in the need felt by Ismail Hussein (1966:48) to emphasize that, in making such positive remarks about the Malays, Valentijn had no reason to be merely attempting to "satisfy the Malays or put their minds at rest, for who would be able to read his writing in Dutch?" Valentijn and Werndly did not live in an age of tolerance and liberalism. While we note a relative lack of condescension, we also detect a certain hostility, which is clearly directed at the Malays as Muslims. This, of course, accords with what has been said concerning the two writers' perceptions of Malay culture as being an integral part of the Islamic tradition. They were not concerned with one relatively small ethnic group, but with a supra-national tradition, which they felt was a formidable rival throughout the East. Indeed, for over a thousand years, up to as late as the siege of Vienna by the Turks in 1683—only forty-odd years before Valentijn wrote—Christian Europe had feared Muslim domination. It is worthy of note that the hostility of Werndly and Valentijn toward Islam is expressed in conventional terms; it is a formulaic or schematic hostility rather than one based upon personal experience. Thus, for example, Valentijn inserts the phrase "however dull they may otherwise be" (III:26) when speaking of Muslim "priests," and whenever Werndly refers to Muhammad, he finds it necessary to add in epithetic fashion "the false prophet." In this respect, we are reminded of Skinner's remarks concerning the conventional insults leveled by both Makassarese and Dutch in the Mengkasar war, where "the 'dogmatic' nature of the author's insulting epithets is typical of individuals holding (whether from conviction or mere conformity) 'totalitarian' views on Good and Evil" (1963:11). And this tendency, of course, is characteristic of the still-formulary nature of discourse in residually oral societies, as has been convincingly argued by Ong (1967:83–85).

We may now attempt to assess the observations of Werndly and Valentijn in the specific area of Malay literature.[16] It is immediately obvious that they have no interest in the exotic "native woodnotes wild" so typical of the age of Romanticism. For both Werndly and Valentijn, the primary aim of studying Malay literature written by Malays—as they repeatedly stress—was to acquire a good Malay style, and it is for this reason that a preference is expressed for works which are free from large numbers of foreign words and phrases. The common complaint of nineteenth- and twentieth-century Malaici that traditional Malay literature is overly repetitious and conventional in style is conspicuously absent from the observations of Werndly and Valentijn. Indeed, Werndly's criticism of two of the works in his *Boekzaal* is that the style was too terse! This is not, in fact, surprising in light of what was noted earlier concerning the repetitive style of both

---

16. Where no references are supplied for quotations in the following paragraphs, the source is the translated passages in Sweeney and Tiwon, 1986.

Werndly and Valentijn, for copiousness and decorum were still the marks of good composition in the early eighteenth century.

Also characteristic of its time is Valentijn's remark linking his evaluation of the literature with his estimation of the language as an effective instrument of rhetoric: The language "is in itself uncommonly sweet, mellifluous and charming, and a powerful medium in which to express oneself. Various works, written in this language and cited by us above, and a great number of fine songs in which many things of yore are preserved, give clear evidence of this" (vol. V, 1:310–11).

The complaint that Malay literature was not "original" but a mixture of foreign influences would have seemed strange to Werndly and Valentijn. For them this "book Malay" was a learned language of Muslim scholarship; indeed Valentijn includes his list of Malay works and observations upon them in his chapter on "the Religion of the Moors." It was taken for granted that the literature of a learned language should draw together material from a wide variety of sources; indeed it is this feature which made it worthy of study! It was clearly no matter for surprise to Werndly and Valentijn that versions of books in their lists were also found in other languages, not merely of the Muslim tradition but also in European languages, as evidenced from their remarks on the *Hikayat Kalilah dan Dimnah,* found, *inter alia,* in Latin, Greek, and Dutch.

A number of works merit the praise of Valentijn and Werndly for their content. They were not concerned with "literary value" in the modern sense; indeed, mere tales appear to have been of little interest to them, being dismissed as "fictitious accounts," and "trivial matters" without further comment. The works that found favor with them were all "useful" as sources of knowledge. Thus, for example, in Werndly's estimation, the subject matter of *Sulalātu 's-Salāṭīn (Sejarah Melayu)* is of the "highest value" as a historical source. The "excellence" of the *Mir'ātu 'l-Mu'min* lies in its usefulness for "gaining knowledge of Mohammedan theology." The *Tāju 's-Salāṭīn* contains "very many moral stories and lessons" according to Werndly, while Valentijn considers it "a noble book," and "the best Malay book that I know." It is understandable that the *Tāju 's-Salāṭīn* should have appealed to Europeans still entrenched in the classical tradition steeped in rhetoric: in its wide assortment of potted wisdom it bears an unmistakable resemblance to European *copie books* or commonplace collections. It owes not a little, moreover, to the ideas of Aristotle and Plato. It is significant that Valentijn perceives its role as similar to the *Cyropaedia* of Xenophon, in which the latter presented his ideas on training and education. When we compare the views of Werndly and Valentijn on the *Tāju 's-Salātīn* with those of later writers such as Winstedt (1958:114–16), for whom the work was "poorly written," was of "small literary worth," and was "atrocious" in its language, we realize that such evaluations tell us more about the changing literary tastes in Europe than about any intrinsic quality of the Malay works themselves.

It cannot be denied that Werndly and Valentijn had but a sketchy knowledge of certain areas of Malay literature. For example, as already noted, Valentijn, followed by Werndly, confuses the *Hikayat Hang Tuah* with the *Sulalātu 's-Salātīn*. In other places, too, Valentijn tends to say more than he can justify. Teeuw (1966:438–39) has drawn attention to a notable instance of this in Valentijn's remark on Hamzah Fansuri, "a man renowned among the Malays for his wonderful Sjaiers and Poems, makes us familiar with his native town when in his grandiloquent verses he raises as from the ashes its ancient lustre and past splendour and recreates the past days of its glory" (vol. IV, 1:66). A similar passage is cited by Doorenbos (1933:1). Yet while such praise tells us little about Hamzah's *syair,* it does reveal Valentijn's positive expectations of Malay literature, and these, of course, were formed by his experience of those areas of the literature with which he had indeed acquired some familiarity.

Werndly, too, has not been considered by modern scholars to be very informative about Malay poetry. As Teeuw (1966:439) has noted, the "poems" listed in the *Boekzaal* may not be poems at all, and Werndly's listing them as such may well be based upon a misreading of Valentijn. Furthermore, Werndly bases his remarks on Malay poetry upon examples in the *Tāju 's-Salātīn,* which are largely translated from or modeled upon Persian and Arabic poetry. Yet it is incorrect to say that he was entirely unfamiliar with the *syair:* the *nazam* he quotes (pp.224–25) from the *Tāju 's-Salātīn* is indeed in *syair* form (Sweeney, 1971:66–67),[17] and his remarks on this poem are most informative in revealing the standards by which he judged Malay literature, for in this passage he provides the yardstick of Dutch

17. This is the poem commencing with the line: *Bahwa bagi raja sekalian* (Roorda, 1827:117).

poetry. He considers that of all the poems he has quoted, this one is the most similar to Dutch poetry, and further remarks that "were I to compare this poem with the Dutch poems of former centuries, it would surpass these; and for this reason the Malay poems are not to be despised, although they are not put together with such precision as our present day [poetry]" (p. 226).

The generally positive evaluations of these eighteenth-century Europeans contrast quite sharply with those of the nineteenth-century Romanticists. Yet the works of traditional Malay literature which evoked these very different opinions were still the same works. The radical change of taste had taken place in Europe. While an awareness of this shift alerts us to the dangers of accepting the views of the Romanticists as absolutes, it is not our purpose to somehow "rehabilitate" traditional Malay literature by suggesting that the eighteenth-century scholars were more "correct" in their assessment, and that it should replace the more negative views. On the contrary, if we were concerned with personal predilections, we would no doubt find the taste of the nineteenth century closer to our own. But again, I would emphasize that our aim is not evaluating; it is understanding. In light of the considerations examined in this chapter, it is clear that many of the assumptions and attitudes of the pre-Romanticist period were closer to those of a radically oral manuscript culture than were those of more recent scholars, and help us to gain some understanding of the workings of that manuscript culture.

For us literates, a study of oral tradition cannot but be an exercise in writing. We must begin with the assumptions of the literate and move laboriously toward an understanding of orality through the barriers of our literacy. And an examination of our literate starting point requires a consideration of the shifts in the patterns of European literacy during the periods in which our predecessors studied traditional Malay society.

CHAPTER 3

Displacement and Development

Before we attempt to examine the relationship between orality and literacy in Malay society, a word of caution is perhaps necessary. While an awareness of the developments in the technology of communication in Western society is essential for an understanding of the assumptions and attitudes of our print-interiorized predecessors and ourselves concerning Malay language and literature, we should avoid allowing the model which made possible this awareness to determine our perceptions of orality and the consequences of literacy in Malay society. Otherwise, what was a relational model in the context of Western society will produce a reductionist thesis when applied to the Malay situation. "Orality" and "literacy" are not independent entities subject to immutable laws; they can only be observed in the context of specific societies, and studied in relation to the social structure of the society in question.

Several points emerge from this. First, any attempt to explain cultural change even in one society—not to speak of human society in general—purely in terms of the development of literacy is doomed to failure, for the interrelationships with other social forces are so complex it is usually impossible to distinguish clearly between cause and effect. Widespread literacy may be seen as an enabling factor; it is, for example, a prerequisite for the development of large-scale urbanized societies: but then other forces must be at work to promote the development of that literacy. Concentrating only upon the mechanics of literacy and excluding consideration of those forces may well lead us to unjustified generalizations. An example of this is the argument that emphasizes "the technological restrictions imposed by non-phonetic systems of writing, where the sheer difficulties of learning the skill mean that it can be available only to a limited number of people"[1] and then as proof for this contention points to a society with a low level of literacy possessing such a system without taking into account such factors as social and economic motivation and opportunity.

Similarly, an attempt to assess the "implications" or "consequences" of literacy without fully taking cognizance of the cultural peculiarities and diversities of human societies will lead the scholar to equate the concept of "fully literate" with his own standards of literacy, which, in the case of most Anglo-American writers on the subject, will be those of liberal-democratic bourgeois society, and to assume that the potentialities lie only in this direction. Then, the perception that the Soviet Union is still residually oral, for example, will lead to the conclusion that with the further interiorization of print, the Soviets will unwittingly be transformed into liberal democrats.[2] Another example of how generalizations can obscure cultural particularities is the assumption made by Lord (1976:131) that "writing as a new medium will mean that the former singer will have a different audience, one that can read," and that the "new reading public" will demand change. We have seen that such a view is not at all borne out by the Malay facts.

Of course, the tendency to perceive the Western development of literacy as a universal pattern is encouraged by the fact that Western expansion has transplanted Western notions of literacy and Western technology of communication, from printing machine to computer, into most parts of the Third World, so that in the Malay-speaking areas, for example, we observe a pattern of development in the past hundred-odd years which appears to parallel what evolved over many

---

1. Goody, 1968:19. His example was China, which is in fact far more literate than he suggests. And in Malaysia (at least before independence), the higher level of literacy among Chinese (in Chinese) than Malays in Malay may be explained by the fact that the urban-based, business-oriented Chinese had more uses for literacy than did the predominantly rural Malays. Given the same level of motivation and opportunity, of course, it is likely that acquiring literacy in Chinese is more demanding than in Malay. See further, Sweeney (1980:5, 10–11).

2. This was the conclusion of some students of mine (Americans), who, having read Ong's (1967:257) comments to the effect that Russia is emerging from a strongly residual oral culture, compared them with Goody's (1968:55) view, which associates democracy with widespread literacy.

centuries in the West. I am not arguing that such perceived similarities are merely an illusion. I do believe, nevertheless, that the ease with which scholars are able to agree on the universality of patterns of literacy may sometimes stem from the cultural assumptions they themselves hold in common, leading them to see the unfamiliar in terms of the same familiar schemata. I am not, however, advocating extreme relativism. It seems irrefutable that certain applications of the technology of the word tend to have certain predictable consequences; but it would be unwise indeed to assume that such tendencies will be realized everywhere in the same ways. We may take as an analogy the use of the wheel, which in most places tends to increase mobility; in Tibet, however, with its mountainous terrain, the wheel was adopted as an instrument of prayer, although perhaps it enabled prayer to be performed more rapidly than before.

Thus, while an appreciation of the system of communicating, storing, and retrieving knowledge in one society may well provide insights into the workings of the system obtaining in other societies, I believe we must follow the Durkheimian practice of studying one society at a time or at least in this case one language area at a time. Any generalizing must then be based upon the comparison of entire systems. Otherwise, the tendency is to universalize one's findings from this study of a single system. I have noted elsewhere, for example (1980:35), that some of Lord's (1960) conclusions, while no doubt valid for the Yugoslavian society he studied, are not entirely applicable to traditional Malay composition. Nevertheless, the thoroughness of Lord's Yugoslavian research provides us with a solid basis for comparison. However, when a scholar does not anchor himself in the study of a particular system, there is a danger that he will be led to cull "facts" from the four corners of the globe in order to support a preconception, even though the phenomena observed have no intrinsic content in themselves and derive meaning only from the system which produces them. Here, I am not merely rebuilding straw men from the past, for such global culling is still not uncommon. In Ruth Finnegan's *Oral Poetry* (1977), for example, her Malay "facts" are twice removed from their context: the outdated perceptions of Wilkinson are a major source of her information, and Wilkinson's remarks are themselves used out of context to support her own position.[3]

3. For example, an unidentified "local 'folk version' " of the *Ramayana* is presented as an example of oral poetry (p. 165). In view of her source (Wilkinson, 1924), this must be Maxwell (1886), which—apart from some runs unrelated to the *Ramayana*—is prose.

In light of these considerations, it should be emphasized that my concern here is not to generalize upon questions of orality and literacy merely using the Malay case as an example. Rather it is my aim to gain a clearer understanding of the complexities of Malay discourse. Thus, in observing that Malay society is still strongly orally oriented, I am not attempting to argue that all the features of that society's discourse can be explained away purely in terms of the "nature" of orality. It is not my intention, furthermore, to reduce the complexities involved to a simple dichotomy between orality and literacy. While it cannot be denied that even a minimal amount of literacy has a very considerable effect upon thought processes, it must be emphasized that "literacy" is not some undifferentiated condition. In the Malay world the situation is particularly complex: distributed among five modern nations (Indonesia, Malaysia, Brunei, Singapore, and Thailand), in anthropological terms the Malay-speaking areas consist of a myriad of distinct societies, for some of which Malay is a mother tongue and for others a learned language. In spite of the establishment of mass education and the introduction of the modern panoply of print and elec-

---

Or, in view of Finnegan's notion that repetition "is one of the main criteria by which we tend to distinguish poetry from prose, in both familiar and unfamiliar cultural traditions" (p. 131), is all traditional Malay prose to be classed as poetry? The reference to Wilkinson's comments on *hikayat* singing being in a "transition stage" (p. 26) does not take into account his notion that the presentation represented a "compromise" between earlier works intended to be read visually and "recited" oral material. With regard to the "metaphorical unity" of the *pantun* (p. 114), the example Finnegan gives is a Romanticist poem inspired by the *pantun,* and the unity she perceives is in the former. She twice (pp. 108, 123) emphasizes that the "structure" of the *pantun* is "particularly complex and demanding," it "makes great demands of understanding and unravelling from its audience and might seem an obviously *written* form. . . . The puzzle is largely resolved when one discovers that the *pantun* is sung very slowly," for this gives an opportunity for the "lengthy and selfconscious reflection said to be typical of the appreciation of written literature." Again (p. 108), the example is an English *re-creation* of a *pantun.* These examples are, of course, written forms. One must ask by what standards is the Malay *pantun* complex? Of whom is it demanding? Obviously it makes great demands upon the Westerner unfamiliar with the idiom and with the formulas and patterns which provide the prefabricated materials for the orally composed *pantun.* It need not be sung slowly; many tunes have a fast tempo. Indeed the *pantun* is a good example of the Parry-Lordian formulaic composition which gives Finnegan so many problems, caused to some extent, it would seem, by misunderstanding (see, e.g., p. 71: the italicizing and misinterpretation of "any" in "*any* group of words"). Other problems concern "the fairly common genre of self-praises" (p. 117), of which "Malay poems" are a prime example, but no evidence is offered. Also, the generalization that "syllable counting is a common basis for metrical forms" "in the east" (p. 93) is ill advised. References and explanation of the Malay magician's receiving and delivering poems in spiritualistic seances (p. 208) would be welcome. Also on the traveling Malay storyteller (p. 157), an old chestnut (ultimately from Maxwell, 1886), which, I suspect, is to some extent a European projection of perceptions concerning the medieval troubadour.

tronic media, it should not be thought that the Malay world has
simply undergone a transformation into the Western idea of modern
literate societies. The new media of communication were not merely
superimposed upon the old: Western print technology did not suddenly replace the old radically oral manuscript culture, which then
died without trace leaving the new print-based culture to function
according to some universal pattern. Rather, the new technology was,
to no small extent, assimilated by the old, and indeed, appeared initially to strengthen it.

A concrete example of the way the new technology seemed to give
new life to the old was the proliferation of "manuscripts" made possible toward the end of the nineteenth century by the introduction of the
lithographic process. In numerous other, often more intangible, ways,
old habits persisted, though usually in modified form, so that many of
the formulary features associated with oral composition—or at least
with composition for aural rather than visual consumption—are still
detectable in the written composition of modern print-based Malay
society. Yet the new medium, while seeming initially to strengthen the
old, is gradually undermining it.[4] The possibilities offered by Western
models of print format and punctuation have been exploited, making
the lithographic "manuscript" largely obsolete. It is clear, furthermore, that Malay written composition (and as a result literate speech)
is rapidly becoming less formulaic.

A case in point is the cultivation of proverbs and "sayings." Over
the past twenty-five-odd years I have observed a relative decline in the
use of such aphorisms in everyday speech on all levels of society. A
survey of Malay writing over the past half century reveals a similar
trend. The publication of numerous collections of such sayings in the
recent past (particularly in the fifties) does not belie this trend; it
rather confirms it, and serves as another example of the undermining
of the old medium by the new: there is a certain irony in the fact that
these sayings, mnemonically patterned for easy retrieval in an oral
society where they function as repositories of knowledge, are made
available as itemized, alphabetically arranged (!) collections by the

4. While this statement was inspired by Ong (1977:82ff), it may appear to contradict Ong's view that "a new medium ... not only does not wipe out the old, but
actually reinforces the older medium or media. However, in so doing it transforms the
old." Obviously, as Ong argues, people still talk after the introduction of writing, and
still write after the introduction of print, but they talk and write in ways impossible
before. However, the old habits are destroyed. Ong himself states (1977:10): "The
world of primary orality was torn to pieces by writing and print."

very medium, print, which has made them obsolescent. Having been removed from the arena of everyday life, they have then been consigned to the fate of a lingering death in the schoolroom, where generations of schoolchildren are subjected to studying them as texts which will have little practical use.

While one of my concerns is with the increasing interiorization of print as manifested in Malay discourse, we should beware of perceiving these developments as a simple progression through time along a clearly marked scale denoting degrees of literacy in Malay. When all the factors have been considered, it may indeed be convenient to think of the development of Malay discourse as a continuum, but we should bear in mind that this need not reflect the individual experience of the users of the language. For many of the inhabitants of the Malay world, the transition was from orality or minimal literacy in Malay, either as a mother tongue or as a learned language, to more advanced literacy in Dutch or English. Here, the individual's ways of thinking are affected not merely by the interiorization of print upon his thought processes, but also by the assimilation of ready-made patterns of Western thought, and of course it is impossible to consider the two processes separately. Such acquired modes of cognition obviously could not be reserved for the individual's discourse in the Western language; naturally enough they had a radical effect upon his speech and writing in Malay, which could (and can) cause considerable difficulty for himself and his audience.[5] A somewhat similar process is experienced nowadays by the speakers of Malay dialects who learn standard Malay, Indonesian, or, indeed, Thai.

The situation in the Malay world is further complicated by the introduction of electronic media, such as radio, television, and telephone. In the West, the impact of these media was upon a society in which print had long had a profound effect upon the thought processes, and although the new secondary orality is reminiscent in some respects of primary orality, it is a much more self-conscious, deliberate, and programmatic orality, firmly based as it is upon the use of

5. For example, the Malaysian poet Muhammad Haji Salleh, after living in the West and being immersed in Western literature, encountered some difficulty when attempting to communicate new ways of thinking to his Malaysian audience during the early seventies, as is evidenced by the confusion created in some circles by his poem *Batu-batu*. The participative nature of modern Malaysian literature (Ismail Hussein, 1976:244) means that a poet's readers are not merely an elite group of literati. (See also Sweeney, 1980:26ff.) The average educated Malay man-in-the-street expects to understand the poetry published in newspapers and magazines, and when he does not, he labels them *sajak kabur* (vague, obscure poems), of which, incidentally, there are not a few.

writing and print (Ong, 1967:301–2). In Malay society, however, the impact of the electronic media was upon a still largely orally oriented culture, so that for the radically oral segments of the populace, particularly in rural areas and among the urban poor, the effect of the new media is to reinforce their oral mental set. Indeed, with tongue only slightly in cheek, one might say that if one were suddenly to replace a performing *Selampit* storyteller in Kelantan with a television set "performing" "The Six Million Dollar Man," the audience might not even blink.

It is hardly surprising, therefore, that a study of literacy in Malay society reveals a remarkable variety in the extent to which writing and print have affected thought processes, and one may find surprising differences in this respect even between two university graduates. A comparison of areas where Malay is a mother tongue and where it is a learned language, as in the greater part of Indonesia, reveals further diversity. While the results of such a synchronic study of discourse in the Malay-speaking world tend to be perceived as a series of gradations on a scale ranging from orality to deeply interiorized literacy, such a perception must take into account the relationship between the orality-literacy polarity and the electronic media.

Of course, an emphasis upon the synchronic must be reconciled with a need to account for change, for an awareness of the developmental perspective is essential for an understanding of the present situation. And, as argued by Goody (1977), such an awareness can help to overcome the "we-they" dichotomy, the idea of the advanced and the primitive, separated by a Great Divide. A study on the synchronic level of the interface between orality and literacy in the present, moreover, may be expected to throw light on aspects of development in the past. For example, a knowledge of the mechanics of oral composition, still observable today, is essential for an understanding of traditional methods of literary production, for although the old palace scribe is now extinct, we are able to discern in his writings many features of schematic composition typical of oral storytelling. We should, however, avoid the temptation of assuming that the continuum perceived on the synchronic level can serve as a model for investigating the historical development of Malay discourse.

Thus, while the study of the professional oral storyteller and his audience, or of the everyday discourse of nonliterate persons, will provide insights into the oral mental set, it will afford us but a hazy notion of what primary oral (or indeed pre-print) Malay society was like. A primary oral society is one untouched by writing or print, where the communication, storage and retrieval of knowledge are exclusively oral operations. In such a society, the storyteller is a central figure, for the verbal storage of cultural information tends in large part to take the form of narrative. The teller is thus no mere entertainer or literary artist; he is scholar, jurist, and custodian of the traditions of his society. Only with the reification of the spoken word made possible by the introduction of writing can the knower separate himself from the known and begin to think "analytically" (Havelock, 1963).

When writing is introduced, it does not merely coexist with the oral tradition, which continues unchanged; it begins to displace various functions of that tradition. This process began in the Malay world at least as early as the seventh century A.D.[6] The chirographically based societies resulting from the introduction of writing remained radically oral manuscript cultures for the next twelve hundred—odd years: the centers of literacy were the courts of rulers, yet even there penmanship was an exclusive art, and only a handful of people would be able to read and write. The ruler himself might well not be included in that group. Correspondence was a task for scribes; writing one's own letters was as demeaning as cooking one's own rice (Sweeney, 1980:14). Yet the importance of writing should not be underestimated, for consumption was largely aural: works were recited in a rhythmical chant, not unlike that still used in some genres of stylized professional storytelling. Thus, as regards the performer's delivery and the audience's reception, a recital of written literature was very similar to a presentation of stylized oral composition created in performance. Paradoxically, it was this radically oral orientation of Malay-speaking societies, in which literacy was not a prerequisite for experiencing the written word,[7] which enabled writing to perform so many functions of transmitting, storing, and retrieving information previously the exclusive domain of the oral specialist. Initially, of course, the teller would hold his own, but the fact that dependence on oral memory was no longer absolute would result in a gradual erosion of (a) the areas of influence

6. This is not to say, of course, that the "Old Malay" of Srivijaya is the direct ancestor of the Malay appearing in the first manuscripts still extant dating from circa 1600.

7. Except, of course, for the reciter.

in which he once reigned supreme, and (b) his standing in those areas which he was allowed to share with the written tradition or those into which writing had made no inroads. We should note, furthermore, that while our perspective as observers from a certain point in this progression allows us to make this distinction, the erosion of his standing in (b) is in actuality part of the process of erosion of the area.

In some of those areas it seems safe to say that writing, initially at least, merely appropriated certain functions of the teller and continued to perform them in the traditional manner, which is to say in a manner still reflecting the workings of an oral tradition as we know them. One example would appear to be genealogies of the ruling class. The genealogy is one of the limited ways in which oral man is able to organize his experience into discrete units. As Goody (1968:32) has argued, the genealogy in a primary oral society requires constant adjustment in order to carry out its function as "a mnemonic of social relationships." This "homeostatic tendency" or "structural amnesia" ensures that memories no longer relevant to present conditions are discarded, or, I would add, transformed, whether in form or function. Over the past two and a half decades, I have observed this tendency in the orally transmitted genealogies of Malay *dalang*s of the shadow-play: although those twenty-five-odd years have in some cases produced several "*dalang* generations," the genealogies of the newest *dalang*s are rarely longer than those I collected in 1962; the most illustrious and most recent names are retained; others are discarded. My point here is that writing appears to have had a far less drastic effect upon this homeostatic tendency in traditional Malay society than might be expected. The transient nature of Malay manuscripts resulting from climatic conditions and the materials used, plus the orally oriented schematic methods of composition (which were indeed reinforced by that transience) continued to allow a large measure of "structural amnesia" usually associated only with oral tradition, and enabled the scribe to adjust his *silsilah*[8] (genealogy) texts to suit existing social conditions. Modern scholars, privy to large collections of manuscripts from various periods and areas, and able to compare many versions of a "work" or several works dealing with a similar topic—not to mention the wealth of external evidence available to

8. A distinction should perhaps be made here between the *silsilah* proper, "containing little beyond the genealogy of the chief" (Newbold, 1839, II:333) or a simple kinglist (see Roolvink, 1967) and the more extensive *silsilah*-based "chronicle," such as the *Sejarah Melayu*. The remarks on displacement appear to be relevant to both types.

us—naturally enough have perceived such changes as inconsistencies and the result of sloppiness, rather than as a method of ensuring the relevance of such works to contemporary needs.

The earliest reasonably detailed references to oral tradition in the Malay peninsula date only from the nineteenth century. Judging from the admittedly sketchy evidence provided by the content of the recorded *penglipur lara* tales and the descriptions of the storyteller's role (e.g., Maxwell, 1886), it would appear that even before the effects of mass education and the wide use of print had been felt, the sphere of interest represented in the written tradition by the state *silsilah* (genealogical chronicle) was no longer even shared by the storyteller. It should be emphasized that I am not equating *silsilah* with *sejarah* ("history"), nor am I concerned with whether written material is more "historical" than oral composition, whether by scholarly standards or by those of Malay tradition. To the Malay *dalang*, for example, the tales of Rama and Sita are as much "history" (*sejarah*) as, say, an account of the reign of Long Yunus of Kelantan, who died at the end of the eighteenth century, and he can muster an impressive array of "evidence" to prove that the events related actually occurred (Sweeney, 1972:257–58; 1983:41). Similarly, the Perlis *Selampit* storyteller presents his tale as part of the history of Kedah. Of course, the fact that most educated Malays would not agree is an indication of the greatly dwindled authority of the teller; but then they would also not attach much authority to the written *Hikayat Merung Mahawangsa* which purports to recount Kedah's past. It is likely that both tales were more widely believed in the nineteenth century. My point, however, is that it was in the written *hikayat* that we find royal genealogies and traditions of the Kedah ruling class, not in the stylized oral performance of the *Selampit*. Havelock (1963:93–94) describes the oral composition of the ancient Greek bard as "the sole vehicle of important and significant communication. It therefore was called upon to memorialise and preserve the social apparatus, the governing mechanism, and the education for leadership and social management. . . ." "It provided a massive repository of useful knowledge, a sort of encyclopedia of ethics, politics, history and technology which the effective citizen was required to learn as the core of his educational equipment" (p. 27). To see large amounts of extraneous material and perceive them as incidental to the epic purpose and a drag on the narrative is to misunderstand that purpose, which was in fact didactic: "the tale is made subservient to the task of accommodating the weight of educational materials which lie within it" (p. 61). This description will certainly not seem relevant to the role of the storyteller today;[9] one might, however, use Havelock's words to describe exactly the function of the *hikayat*, and in particular, the *silsilah*.[10]

The tendency of scholars in the past to see the *silsilah* as a poor attempt to write "history" or as a mishmash of genres merely reveals the assumption that traditional Malay literature possessed the same criteria for differentiating knowledge as the scholar. A *silsilah* contains not only royal genealogies and traditions, and a recounting of past events; it may present such diverse materials as an inventory of elephants (*Hikayat Aceh*), a description of palace building (*Sejarah Melayu*), or lists of customs duties (*Silsilah Raja-raja Berunai*), often told at great length, and all placed in the narrative framework as part of the tale. It is only our expectation that such topics will form the subject matter of separate manuals that leads us to see them as somehow disparate. In traditional Malay society, the *silsilah* was the genre for treating such topics. The narrative is not an end in itself; in the still radically oral manuscript culture, narrative was the chief way to organize knowledge of all types. Thus, in recounting a royal wedding or list of customs duties, for example, the writer does not usually suspend his tale in order to produce a consciously generalized description. He tends rather to tell the tale of a particular raja's wedding or a particular captain's visit.

As in oral tradition, however, the nature of schematic composition encourages the presentation and preservation of the typical. We might say that the use of the schema automatically results in generalization. And, indeed, the writer's awareness that what is true of one raja or captain may apply to others is often revealed in the comment concluding such accounts to the effect that "Such is the custom of rajas . . . " (*Demikianlah adat raja-raja . . .*). This tendency to present such information as a tale is perhaps best seen when an attempt is made to counter it. In the *Adat Raja-raja Melayu*, the request of the Dutch governor of Melaka for a description of Malay custom causes the writer to attempt to write in general terms. For the first few pages he succeeds, as may be seen from his noting of alternative possibilities; for example, ". . . has given birth to a boy or girl," "in a gold or silver

---

9. But see chapter 4.

10. Milner (1982) repeatedly emphasizes the educational function of such *hikayat*, referring particularly to the *Hikayat Pahang* and the *Hikayat Deli*, describing the latter as a "manual."

bowl" (1929:5, 10). Subsequently, however, the account turns into a tale about a particular raja, and recounts the various customs as events in that tale. By reason of the schematic nature of his composition, however, the result does turn out to be generalized. But there are exceptions, which occur when the writer's perceptions/memories of specific events intrude upon his schema;[11] for example, he includes a description of two old women having a *latah* fit at the wedding, which may conceivably have led the Dutch governor, de Bruin, to understand that a royal wedding always includes such a fit! Such idiosyncrasies also occur in oral performance, but the strong tendency to transmit the typical usually results in their eventually being discarded. When they are written down, and particularly when the manuscript is removed from the tradition by being taken to Europe away from the attentions of copyists, such idiosyncrasies may survive.

While I am not suggesting that the *silsilah* was merely a written record of a composition previously oral, it seems likely that it represents to some extent a continuation of a function once performed by the oral teller. In other areas once dominated by oral tradition, writing did not merely appropriate the function of the teller. As the possibilities of writing revealed themselves—often via the adoption of foreign models in which such possibilities had already been realized—some of these areas were radically transformed. Two of those areas were "religion" and "law." These categorizations are, of course, those of traditional literature, represented by the *undang-undang/kanun* and *kitab* literature. Yet while we should beware of assuming that the differentiation of branches of knowledge made by oral tradition corresponded to those of written tradition, which simply displaced them, we should also not assume that oral tradition made no such delineations; that in other words the teller held a monopoly over the preserving of all significant knowledge as seems to be implied in Havelock's reference above to ancient Greece. This will, I trust, become clear in the following chapter. Suffice it to say here that one example of differentiation in Malay oral tradition (based admittedly upon observations in the present) was between the domain of the teller and that of the general purpose *bomoh* (folk practitioner);[12] in short, clearly more than one type of oral specialist existed.

11. Cf. Scholes and Kellogg (1966:40) on the "historical event" intruding upon the *topoi*. See also Worsley (1972:82).

12. This does not by any means imply a simple distinction between "telling" and "magic." An intrinsic part of being a *dalang,* for example, involved spirit mediumship. See further Sweeney, 1972.

It follows from this that a major displacement of various branches of oral specialization—in particular those concerned with what we would now term "magico-religious"—must have resulted from the introduction of literate religion. In particular, the arrival of Islam, which, while revealing a strongly oral—or more accurately, aural— orientation, is par excellence the religion of the Book, could not but have seriously undermined the authority of the oral specialist: the Islamic insistence upon the inviolable nature of the Qur'anic text, fixed in writing, militates against the homeostatic tendency of oral tradition. And even though the Qur'an was in a foreign language understood by few, the task of reciting or memorizing it, albeit un-comprehendingly, depended upon the presence of the fixed text, a concept alien to oral tradition. And while such a concept was not new to the Hinduized Malays, the exclusive and universal nature of a religion such as Islam, based upon a text valid for all peoples and all times, discourages (but by no means prevents) the accommodating of existing beliefs considered to be in conflict with its tenets.

That the association in the mind of the Malay between Islam and writing is a long-standing one and no mere projection from our his-torical perspective is clear from Marsden (1811:289), who tells of an instance of one-upmanship between a Muslim Malay and a pagan in Sumatra. In reply to the Muslim's upbraiding him for his ignorance of religion, the pagan asks him what foundation he has for his beliefs in Allah and Muhammad. "Are you not aware, replied the *Malay*, that it is written in a *Book?*" The pagan (according to Marsden, who pre-sumably heard this from the Malay!) submitted to this argument with "conscious inferiority." It must be emphasized, however, that in speaking of Islam militating against the homeostatic tendencies of oral tradition, I am referring to *literate* Islam. When Islam is separated from writing, it ceases to displace the oral tradition; rather it is assimi-lated by it. For example, Skeat (1953:56) reporting on his visit to Biserat (part of Yala in Malay south Thailand) in 1899, describes a somewhat unorthodox Qur'an class which included, *inter alia,* instruc-tion concerning Moses' role as chief prophet of the Siamese. Skeat then observes, "They had no books, not even a Koran or a slate. Writing being an exceedingly rare accomplishment here, the teaching had to be predominantly oral." Here, we may add, the assimilation is clearly to the nonstylized oral tradition, which, lacking mnemonic patterning, exercises much less control over content than the stylized form. It seems clear, moreover, that the all-pervasive magico-religious practices described by Skeat may be directly related to the low level of Islamic literacy in the area. This example also serves to demonstrate that the displacement of oral tradition in the Malay world did not follow a simple chronological sequence. For example, the fact that Aceh was a center of Islamic scholarship in the sixteenth century should not be taken to mean that this provides us with a date for the displacement of earlier orally controlled practices. And though Patani was known as a center of Islamic Studies in the nineteenth century, it is clear that such displacement varied in proportion to the level of literacy.

The apparent appropriation of "the law" by written tradition provides a noteworthy paradox. On the one hand, only with writing did it become possible to produce a systematic listing of laws such as that found on the Trengganu inscription dating from the fourteenth century. And while the various *undang-undang* texts are rather digests of law than codes, such works could not have taken shape in a primary oral society. On the other hand, there is little evidence that these texts served much more than a ceremonial function. Certainly, according to Wilkinson (1922:3ff), they do not appear to have been regularly used in courts of law. The reason for this, of course, is that the prerequisite for charging someone under section such and such of the *Undang-undang Melaka,* for example, would have been a certain level of literacy. We have noted that the center of literacy was the palace, where a relatively large audience might have access to written works if there were but one literate person, the reciter, available. The administration of justice, however, was not presumably confined to the palace. Yet the use of the *Undang-undang* would have necessitated the presence of a literate at the hearing of every case in court. Thus while the teller may have once been the custodian of at least some aspects of what we would call the law, the absence of such a function in the recorded tales is more likely to be the result of the general eroding of his authority in the centers of power rather than a simple displacement of that function by the *undang-undang* texts.[13]

The European sources from the end of the nineteenth century would seem to indicate that the areas of influence left to (or shared with) the teller by the written tradition were not dramatically larger than today. Yet although the oral specialist's domain of interest was already very limited by the turn of the century, it is clear that he still

13. See the following chapter.

had a much larger clientele than he does at the present, and, most important, that that clientele included the ruling class. For example, the Sultan of Kedah still had an official *penglipur lara* storyteller in 1899 (Skeat, 1953:126). Such royal patronage[14] would obviously lend authority to the words of the storyteller and enhance their normative influence on society.[15]

As writing and later print took over more and more of the functions of storing, retrieving, and transmitting knowledge at the centers of power, the domain of the storyteller became gradually narrower and his role increasingly less important in society as a whole, so that by modern times he had become mainly a soother of cares in the rural areas, concerned chiefly with tales of *Antah-berantah* (Never-never land). Today, he lingers on at the illiterate peripheries of society, revealing but mere vestiges of his former role.

In a previous study of Malay storytelling (1973), I made a distinction between "stylized" and "nonstylized" form. In view of the (then at least) prevailing notion promulgated by scholars such as Winstedt that the "rhapsodist's tales" were told in "shapeless," colloquial language, I had found it necessary to emphasize that, in the absence of writing, Malay storytelling was not limited to the language of everyday conversation, and that just as the language of literature is a stylized form of everyday speech regulated by various conventions, so do we find that oral tradition has developed stylized forms of language and presentation (1973:3). I became particularly aware of this when studying the idiom of the Malay shadow-play, which is one of the more elaborate manifestations of stylized oral form still observable. By the use of various formulary features, such as *wayang* words, epithets, strings of synonyms, runs, the employing of "complicated constructions" created by contorting the morphology and syntax of everyday speech, and various other devices, the *dalang* produces a heightened form of the local dialect, intelligible to the users of that vernacular but clearly set apart from it. It became clear that this phenomenon was by

14. With regard to the last royal patrons of the shadow-play in Kelantan and Kedah, see Sweeney (1972:12, 24).
15. It is clear, moreover, that the magician still had considerable authority in certain areas in the nineteenth century. For example, it is reported (Winstedt and Wilkinson, 1974:172 ff) that Raja Abdullah of Perak held and participated in a *main hantu* (spirit performance) ritual involving possession by spirits, the aim being to destroy the first British resident. The position of the state *pawang*, moreover, was one of considerable authority, the incumbent being a member of the ruling class. With regard to the nominal post of *Bomoh di Raja* (royal magician) in Kelantan and its very literate incumbent, see Sweeney, 1972:17–20.

no means restricted to the *wayang*. Other types of traditional drama, such as the *Mek Mulung* and *Mak Yong,* genres of storytelling such as *Awang Batil* and *Tarik Selampit,* and indeed various nonnarrative forms, as, for example, in the fields of traditional medicine and spirit mediumship, were all found to employ similarly contrived modes of speech. This stylized language is further set off from the vernacular in that it does not employ the intonation of everyday speech: depending upon the genre, it may be presented in the form of song, chant, or strongly rhythmical speech.

Just as penmanship was an exclusive art in Malay manuscript culture, so too in oral tradition, exponents of such manifestations of the stylized form are usually specialists and professionals, and the reverse is certainly the case: professional performances are in stylized form.[16]

Of course, storytelling is by no means a purely professional activity, even for a professional storyteller. Most members of Malay society are able to tell tales, but the language used will normally be that of everyday speech, and the presentation will be amateur. Certain classes of tales, such as numskull and animal tales, are usually told in the nonstylized form. Even when told by a professional storyteller they will be recounted in the language of conversation. He will not tell them ex officio and they do not form part of his marketable stock-in-trade, for, like any other member of society, he is the bearer of amateur oral tradition. And when asked to relate parts of his professional repertoire in a nonformal setting, he will tend to do so in the language of everyday conversation, although his frame of reference will be the stylized mode. Hardly surprisingly, therefore, it is in the nonstylized form that these *penglipur lara* tales were dictated to Malay scribes at the behest of British administrators, and no attempt was made to record or even describe in detail the presentation of a typical professional performance. We find, therefore, that the only examples of stylized oral narrative recorded at the turn of the century were a number of relatively fixed runs, which were uttered even in a nonstylized telling.

In the pre-electronic age it would, of course, have been well-nigh impossible to record a professional performance verbatim: as regards the genres with which I am familiar, the storyteller would have been quite unable to perform in stylized form at dictation speed and still give a typical rendering. A transcriber, moreover, would not have been able to keep up with and record faithfully the language of such a

16. See further Sweeney, 1973.

performance presented at its normal speed. This, however, is somewhat beside the point: it would be anachronistic to imagine that the
problem of the pre-electronic age was merely a technical one. At the
beginning of this century, for Maxwell, Winstedt, and their contemporaries, the only possible frame of reference was, on the one hand,
writing and print, and on the other the everyday language of conversation.[17] In such a milieu, it was no easy task even to become aware of
the existence of such an entity as the stylized oral form, let alone
comprehend its significance.[18] The spoken word was seen as an unwritten, indeed defective, form of writing. In taking down an oral tale,
therefore, the logical procedure was to have it tidied up and put into
an acceptable form. It may perhaps seem strange that although scholars had certainly heard the stylized form (e.g., Maxwell, 1886), they
did not consider it worthy of further investigation or even recognize it
for what it was. The reason is that they equated it with the language
of the book. This is particularly well illustrated by a number of European reports which clearly confuse the stylized performance of orally
composed tales with the chanted recitation of manuscripts. Newbold
(1839, II:327), for example, speaking of the fondness of the Malays
for hearing recited the *Hikayat Hang Tuah,* proceeds to describe what
appears to have been a *penglipur lara* performance, where the teller
may be heard "relating portions from memory of these popular romances." Indeed, the confusion persists to this day, as may be seen in
Milner (1982:4, 39).[19] The fact that the presentation and consumption
of both written and oral composition appeared so similar apparently
led some European observers who saw a teller without a text to assume that he had learned it off by heart.

A highly literate culture tends to assume that the natural way of
communicating or recording the significant and important is via the

17. Predictably, Snouck Hurgronje constitutes something of an exception. Already
in 1900, he had an article entitled "Islam und Phonograph," though his focus was not
upon oral tradition but rather upon how the phonograph would be judged by Islamic
law. Of course, at the turn of the century, electronics had yet had almost no effect on
the psyche.

18. We note, however, that by 1927 (and particularly by 1940), Voorhoeve had
made some observations in this respect. See the following chapter.

19. For example (p. 38): "Rulers also had their own storytellers, *Penglipor Lara,*[57]
who read aloud Malay tales to the populace,[58]" the first footnote reference being to
Skeat's mention of the Kedah storyteller, the second to *hikayat* reciting in Sumatra as
described by Anderson (1826). On page 4, a useful reference to the reciting of *hikayat* in
East Sumatra is provided (Gibson, 1855). But in the next paragraph we are told that
"these storytellers" were often wandering minstrels of the type described by Maxwell,
who were oral tellers.

medium of written style, and discourse will veer between the poles of casual, everyday conversation and formal literary style, depending on the context. The illiterate in such a society is denied this possibility and is rightly seen as a deprived individual. In an oral society, however, if discourse were limited to the relatively ephemeral language of everyday conversation, that society would not survive. It should be noted that the possibility of memorizing verbatim a long, fixed text arises only with the possession of writing, without which such a text could not be produced.[20] In order to make possible the preservation and retrieval of knowledge, therefore, oral societies developed modes of discourse which appear to us as highly stylized when compared with the language of everyday speech. The use of strong rhythms, mnemonic patterning, abundant use of parallelism, and other formulary devices makes it possible to encapsulate far larger chunks of knowledge for storage and recall than is possible in the vernacular. This "poetised speech," as Havelock (1963) calls it in his study of Homeric Greece, was the only instrument available for preserving and transmitting cultural information, and formed an "enclave" within the vernacular of an oral culture, providing it with its cultural memory. This "oral enclave of contrived speech . . . constituted a body of general education conserved and transmitted between the generations" (1971:41), and was, in addition, the idiom in which were framed short-term directives, messages, and legal decisions (1963:106ff).

In seeking to establish the relationship between this contrived, poetized speech and the vernacular, Havelock contends that in any culture, apart from the ephemeral converse of daily transaction, there is also an area of preserved, significant communication, which in a literate culture is the language of the book. While everyday speech may be seen as fundamental, and the language of literature derived from it, "the idiom and content of . . . the preserved word set the formal limits within which the ephemeral word can be expressed," for it contains "the maximum sophistication" of which a given epoch or culture is capable, and establishes the thought forms of that culture. Similarly, in an oral culture it is in the area of preserved, significant communication, framed in contrived, poetized speech that the maximum degree of sophistication is found, the state of mind revealed therein being the general state of mind (1963:135). Putting cart before horse, which is

20. The level of "fixity" observable in Malay oral transmission may be illustrated by the form of the *wayang* prologue (Sweeney, 1972:348–52).

the only way for us literates to gain an insight into the oral mentality, we may say that the function of the oral stylized form may be equated with that of literature as a frame of reference for the vernacular.

In a society newly acquainted with writing, the notion of the written word as a more "correct," "tidied-up" version of the vernacular, or the assumption that all subjects of daily conversation may equally well be written about, would be strange indeed. When writing begins to displace an oral tradition, the first effects are upon the stylized enclave of significant, preserved communication. One of the most widely perceived advantages of writing is its capacity to preserve the spoken word, thereby relieving the mind of the burden of memorization, and it was in the area of contrived speech that this burden was greatest. Initially, moreover, it would have seemed pointless to preserve in writing that material which had not been considered worth preserving in the pre-writing era, that is, speech not processed for storage in the stylized form. Thus, in the context of the Malay-speaking world, when we speak of the displacement of the oral tradition by writing and the dwindling role of the oral specialist, it becomes clear that we are particularly concerned with the shrinkage, transformation, or depreciation in importance of the enclave of contrived speech which was his domain.

It should be emphasized at this point that the erosion of this enclave is not necessarily an indication of a radical change in the general state of mind of a society. Thus, in the Malay-speaking world, while the role of the oral specialist became gradually more peripheral, the oral thought processes reflected in his principles of composition survived to varying degrees in written composition, much of which reveals the signs of schematic structure typical of oral composition, such as strongly distinctive motifemic patterning on the level of plot, character typing, themes, parataxis, repetition, copiousness, parallelisms, formulas, and formulaic expressions (Sweeney, 1980).

It might be wondered why the composer in writing, apparently relieved of the burden of memorization and the need for rapid-fire composition before a live audience, would nevertheless continue to rely upon the use of so many formulary features. The main answer, of course, lies in the nature of the writer's audience: the use of such schemata would still be essential for effective communication with a nonliterate, listening audience. A further consideration is that the new freedom from memorization was but a relative one: in a manuscript culture, "visual retrieval"[21] is still very rudimentary. The traditional

21. This term is taken from Ong, 1977:162.

Malay manuscript with its pages solidly packed with writing, unbroken by chapter headings or paragraphing and little or no space between words—not to mention the absence of indexing—was not designed to facilitate rapid retrieval of information. This made it imperative for the writer to continue to memorize much of his inventory of composing materials in relatively large chunks; and to ensure retention, such materials had to be typical, that is, schematic.

A third factor was the degree of ambiguity possible in the *Jawi* spelling of traditional composition, which was modeled upon that of Arabic (cf., e.g., Shellabear, 1901). The fact that Malay had more vowels than Classical Arabic and lacked the complex morphology which simplified somewhat the reading of Arabic meant that the deciphering of many Malay words was highly problematic. In the seventeenth century, open vowels in final syllables were frequently not represented in Malay orthography, so that, for example, l-a-l might indicate either *lalu* (then) or *lali* (ankle); l-a-g might represent *laga* (clash), *lagi* (more), or *lagu* (tune). After the seventeenth century, it became the regular practice to include such final vowels, but vowels in closed syllables were still omitted in the orthography, so that the spelling t-m-b-ng might represent any one of the words *tambang, tambung, tembang, témbang, tembung, tembong, timbang, tombong, tumbang, tumbung*. The word intended by a writer could therefore be ascertained only when in its context, and for this it was essential that the context was familiar, indeed predictable, to the audience. When even a phrase consisting of two of the words cited above (e.g., *timbang lagu* and *tumbang lagi*, etc.) could be orthographically identical, it was necessary to rely heavily upon formulaic constructions. There is thus a clear correlation between the degree of difficulty in deciphering the spelling and the formulaic nature of the composition. In speaking of "pre-alphabetic" scripts, Havelock (1982:71) contends that "the range of ambiguity in decipherment stands in inverse ratio to the range of possible coverage supplied by the content. If you want your reader to recognize what you intend to say, then you cannot say anything and everything you might want to."

This, however, needs to be qualified in the Malay context, at least. The notion that written composition must remain formulaic because the orthography is ambiguous would ignore the possibility that the script may be adjusted. It is equally valid to argue that it is the formulaic nature of the composition which allows the spelling to be ambiguous. This is certainly borne out in the case of Malay. It seems clear that the gradual shifting away from the formulaic is reflected in the spelling changes over the past four hundred–odd years from the so-called pre-Classical Malay to that of modern times. A prime example is the writing of the nineteenth-century Munsyi Abdullah. His radical departure from the schematic composition of traditional Malay literature is also reflected in his spelling:[22] we find that he regularly employs vowels in closed syllables (e.g., as in hamp*i*r, hid*u*ng, bang*u*n); a much lower level of formulary usage made it necessary to ensure that words were easily decipherable to a greater degree from their form and not merely from their context. There was, however, a limit beyond which *Jawi* could not keep pace with the development of modern Malay.[23] This became particularly clear to me when I assigned some Malay students the task of romanizing *syair* texts such as *Syair Ceretera Bijaksana,* published circa 1923, which is an adaptation of a "John Sinclair" detective story.[24] The students found much of this *syair* impossible to read. Not only were most of the (European) names undecipherable; they were not set in the familiar *syair* formulas, which, as we see below, could be changed or replaced almost at will by the reciter.

From our historical perspective, it is easy to perceive a variety of possibilities open to the composer newly acquainted with writing.[25] When, however, we attempt to see the possibilities of writing from the viewpoint of the Malay scribe in a still radically oral manuscript culture, it becomes difficult to imagine what incentive he would have had not to use the schemata of tradition. What other method could he have used to take their place? The tendency among some scholars to use their knowledge of the growth of the individual in a literate culture in order to speculate and generalize on the development of literacy in a *society* has tended to cloud perception on this point. Thus, for example, Lord (1976:134) contends that "when a tradition or an individual goes from oral to written, he, or it, goes from an adult, mature style of one kind to a faltering and embryonic style of another sort." The illiterate who learns to read and write in a society already

22. See, for example, the reproduction of the lithographed *Hikayat Abdullah* (Djambatan & Gunung Agung, Djakarta, n.d.).
23. The use of Arabic vocalization was a little too laborious, and would still not have enabled a distinction between "e" and "o," "i" and "u." Though improvements could have been made to rectify this and also to denote "e" pepet (schwa), the fact that *Rumi* (romanized) had been introduced by the colonial authorities and was readily available led to a general shift toward *Rumi*. (See, e.g., *Memoranda '50,* 1962.)
24. See further Roff, 1974a:463.
25. See further Sweeney, 1980:36–38, upon which the following two pages are based.

possessing a long-established literary tradition and a reading public merely has to acquaint himself with existing methods and assimilate the readily available patterns of literate discourse. And in the case of the pre-school child of literate parents, the speech patterns he absorbs from infancy are those of literate individuals, even though he himself is still preliterate. For a *society* newly introduced to writing, however, the only written models available will be those of the culture from which the writing system is acquired. An aspiring writer who wished to make use of those foreign models would not merely require a mastery of the language and literature of the "donor" culture but also, if communication were to be effective, he would have to be capable of translating the foreign patterns into the terms of the "literary grammar" of the local audience, that is, a listening audience, familiar only with an oral tradition. I am not questioning the extent of foreign influences that have made themselves felt throughout the history of Malay literature; however, in the context of *how* a composer worked, it seems inconceivable that a writer who aspired to compose in the new medium for a traditional (i.e., listening) audience stories of the type to which it was accustomed would abandon the tried and trusted methods of oral composition for the unfamiliar methods of an alien culture.

By no means all works written in Malay were composed schematically in accordance with these patterns, however. The most obvious exceptions are those materials translated from foreign languages, and works in Malay by writers of foreign origin, such as Nuruddin ar-Raniri, or Malay writers steeped in a foreign tradition, such as Hamzah Fansuri. In this respect, it is well to remember the international character of Islam and the role of Malay as the major Muslim language of Southeast Asia. Thus, when in centers of Muslim scholarship such as seventeenth-century Aceh scholars used the Malay language for expounding questions of theology and philosophy for the members of their coteries, the resulting literature might well be labeled "Muslim" rather than "Malay," in the sense that it might equally well have been written in Arabic or Persian.

In all these cases, however, if there were to be effective communication with a listening Malay audience, such works would have to be geared to the mental set of that audience. Indeed, it is this requirement that accounts for the fact that so many Malay works originating from foreign sources are adaptations rather than direct translations. In other words, they have been "reassembled" using the traditional "literary grammar" of the Malays. It was the same need which led Hamzah Fansuri to employ the *syair* form, which was structurally very similar to the orally composed *pantun,* but which served as a vehicle for him to introduce his new ideas to the Malays in a familiar form.

The situation of the writer of traditional Malay literature as he composed his tale was not at all unlike that of the storyteller. The main difference is that the latter composes in performance for his audience, whereas for the writer, creation and presentation constitute two separate processes. Yet this is only partly true. The writer does, in a sense, create in performance: he performs for his postulated audience. It is clear, moreover, that the traditional Malay writer composed with a maximum of auditory imaginings—indeed it is likely that he actually intoned the words—for that listening audience.[26] Unlike the oral teller, however, the scribe wrote down the words, thus producing a fixed text.

Of course, there is no audience feedback to affect the writer's composition. Yet one cannot generalize on the influence of such feedback in oral tradition. While a shadow-play audience can sometimes radically alter the course of a performance by its reactions, in other genres, such as the *Tarik Selampit,* I have found that the audience feedback has much less effect upon the teller's presentation. It may be argued that the writer has time to spend pondering in search of *le mot juste.* But let us remember that the Malay writer was not seeking to be original or unique. Why spend time pondering when he had a ready-made system of composition which would provide him with the right word every time? The idea of a writer laboring over draft after draft would have been an alien one indeed; and paper was too valuable a commodity for such a practice to be encouraged. Lord's words (1976:128) concerning the supposed benefits of dictation for the oral teller might well be applied to the "possibilities" of writing for the Malay scribe: "It is vastly important that we do not make the unthinking mistake of believing that the process of dictation frees the singer to manipulate words in accordance with an entirely new system of poetics. Clearly he has time to plan his line in advance, but this is more of a hindrance than a help to a singer who is accustomed to rapid-fire association and composition."

This reference to dictation is perhaps relevant in another respect. Even when the Malay palace written tradition was long established

---

26. Day (1978:442) suggests that in Javanese, composition or even copying may have involved such private, oral performance.

with its own style and idiom, and was thus not merely attempting to transcribe the oral stylized form, it seems that in many cases texts were dictated to scribes. This, incidentally, would help to explain the role of the aristocratic "writers" such as Raja Culan of Perak (*Misa Melayu*) and Raja Ali Haji of Riau, for the actual task of writing was one of relatively low prestige. What the process of dictating involved is not entirely clear. Kern's (1956:15–16) observations on a manuscript of the *Silsilah Kutai* imply that at least part of the final word choice was the work of the dictator. On the other hand, the *penglipur lara* and farcical tales adapted into writing under British sponsorship were dictated in everyday language by nonliterate tellers. The task of composing the tales in *hikayat* language was performed by scribes in the palace tradition.[27] It is conceivable that the *Hikayat Pelanduk Jenaka*, a written version of mousedeer tales produced in precolonial times was composed in similar fashion. It seems likely, therefore, that the degree to which the scribe actually recomposed or merely copied down the words of a dictator may have depended to some extent upon the standard of literacy possessed by that dictator.[28]

The strong oral orientation of the scribe may perhaps be illuminated somewhat by examining the methods traditionally used to recite from manuscripts. Some indication of this was provided for me by an old lady in Kelantan who sang part of the *Syair Siti Zubaidah* from a lithographed *Jawi* text. She had not previously learned this *syair* (or another version of it) by heart. Her reading often did not coincide

27. For example, Maxwell (1886:88, 115) mentions that tales were "taken down verbatim . . . by native writers," and "reduced to writing for me." Raja Haji Yahya, who is said to have put *Malim Deman* into "grammatical prose" (Winstedt, 1957a:flyleaf), may have himself been more of a patron or supervisor than the actual scribe: in *Awang Sulung* (Winstedt, 1957b:flyleaf), he is said to have given assistance in putting it into literary shape. Whether (a) taking down verbatim and (b) putting into literary shape constituted two separate processes is unclear but seems doubtful. Maxwell does not mention two processes, but his text is clearly in written style which could not be that of the illiterate teller. Winstedt (1957b) seems to be claiming to have taken down *Awang Sulung* himself, which is highly doubtful, especially in view of Kern's (1956:16) observation that the romanization of *Seri Rama* to which Winstedt puts his name is clearly not his own work. Several other transcriptions and romanizations by Winstedt are obviously the work of Malay scribes (in part or in toto) and it appears that Winstedt saw his role more as patron and supervisor in such undertakings, in which sense he was still operating in the palace tradition.

28. This is not to suggest, however, that those aristocratic authors who might be presumed to be literate, such as Raja Ali Haji, would always work by dictation. Skinner (1978:467) argues convincingly that such authors may have been more patrons than authors, and, giving the example of Raja Ali, suggests that while he may well have written or dictated material, much of his work may have involved more supervising and checking the activities of his secretarial staff.

with this particular text and it was clear that she had a large stock of alternative phrases (mainly of the length of half lines) with which she replaced phrases in the text, particularly where the text was corrupt. For example, phrases such as *berdalang hati* (a misprint for *berwalang hati*) and *kuripa dijunjung* (for *kurnia dijunjung*) caused her no problem; she simply replaced them with *berdebar hati* and *budi dijunjung* respectively. Even when the text was clear she often chose to replace the wording with a phrase of her own; for example, *yang leta* became *yang nyata; mengeluarkan dia tempat yang cela* became *mengeluarkan kekanda di dalam penjara*. These kinds of changes are of the type often encountered between a manuscript and a copy of it. From this it seems likely that the hypothesis advanced by Macknight (1981) concerning Bugis chronicles that "the transmission of text from one manuscript to another—from an 'original' to a 'copy'—is oral rather than visual" is also applicable to the copying of Malay *hikayat*. I would suggest, furthermore, that an awareness of such methods of copying may throw some light upon the process of composition proper, for it provides additional support for my previous contention that the Malay scribe had a ready stock of prefabricated materials on the level of specific word choice.

In view of these considerations, it might seem surprising that the idiom of the traditional Malay scribe should be so different from that of the stylized form of the oral storyteller—at least, judging from what survives of that form today. Of course, as I have argued previously (1980), not all traditional Malay literature is uniformly schematic in structure, and while the writer is bound to establish schematic common ground with his audience, he might well adjust his schemata in order to wrestle with the specific. But even in the case of the most schematically composed literary "romances," the idiom is very different from that of the oral *penglipur lara*. The explanation lies in the fact that the oldest extant Malay manuscripts are already the product of perhaps a thousand years of development, during which time the language of writing grew into a distinct dialect. In the case of the oral enclave of contrived speech in the Malay world, it would appear that the stylized form was closely tied to the local vernacular. And while the chief exponent of the stylized form was the oral specialist, the oral enclave was not, as we shall see, his exclusive domain. With regard to writing, however, the means of production were entirely in the hands of specialists, and this naturally encouraged the development of various conventions, in keeping with the exclusive nature of the art. Writing itself was of foreign provenance and was exposed to foreign influences to a far greater extent than was the sphere of the oral specialist. It was in the estuarine palaces that those foreign influences first made themselves felt. As writing began to displace the sphere of the oral specialist, the palaces increasingly became the domain of the scribe, and the oral specialist was gradually eased away from the centers of power where influences from abroad were strongest. Written language, therefore, developed into a literary enclave of contrived speech clearly distinct not merely from the vernacular, but also from the stylized oral enclave of significant and preserved speech which it gradually displaced.

Based upon what may still be observed, it would seem that the oral stylized form tends to be closely tied to the dialect of the area in which it is used. It is clear, however, that the use of a written dialect could transcend the confines of the area of a single spoken dialect. Various factors encouraged the growth of a certain uniformity of idiom: the reification of the word divorced from its speaker made possible by writing afforded the scribe direct access to a variety of sources from a much wider area of the Malay world than were available to the oral specialist. Thus, in the Straits of Malacca area, for example, manuscripts circulated widely among the various "states":[29] a glance at the catalogues of manuscript collections reveals that manuscripts of the same tales were acquired over a wide area. Even texts specifically concerned with the affairs of one state, such as *silsilah* texts, were known far beyond the confines of that state, and there was much mutual borrowing of material. Such a practice would not have smacked of plagiarism in a milieu where the building blocks of composition were the commonly held schemata of tradition. With writing, it became possible to incorporate and manage larger chunks of discourse in (relatively) fixed form than when dependence upon memory was absolute, even when the underlying principle of composition was basically similar.[30]

It would seem, moreover, that the awareness of a wider audience beyond the confines of his own *negeri* was sometimes exploited by the

29. And, indeed, further afield. For example, the *Syair Perang Mengkasar* (Skinner, 1963) reveals influence of Hamzah Fansuri's poetry, written in Aceh fifty years previously.

30. For example, the preface of the *Bustānu 's-Salātīn* was appropriated by later versions of the *Sulalātu 's-Salāṭīn* (Winstedt, 1938:35). Material in the *Hikayat Raja-raja Pasai* is also found in the SS (Winstedt, 1958:127; Sweeney, 1967). The preface of SS has been appropriated by the *Hikayat Merung Mahawangsa* (Winstedt, 1958:133; Siti Hawa, 1970:1–2).

writer of a *silsilah* text. Thus, for example, while the primary audiences postulated by the writers of the *Sulalātu 's-Salāṭīn* (*Sejarah Melayu*) and the *Bustānu 's-Salāṭīn* were in Johor and Aceh respectively, there is evidence that both writers gave some thought to the effect their works would have upon audiences in their rival state.[31]

Wide circulation of manuscripts does not, of course, imply mass distribution. Manuscripts were precious commodities circulated among the literate few. The scribes were key figures in an exclusive network, and this must clearly have encouraged the sense of belonging to a highly select coterie. Judging from what little evidence is available, moreover, scribes were not always natives of the states in which they enjoyed their patronage.[32]

Factors such as these tended to promote a certain uniformity of idiom in the written medium. This uniformity was of course observed by scholars such as Winstedt. However, subject as they were to the expectations of a mass-literate print culture, scholars created a norm of "correctness" entirely unrealistic for the manuscript culture of the Malay world, and this insistence on print standards of uniformity tended to obscure the fact that there were numerous varieties of written Malay, some being more closely tied than others to the local dialect. My point is, however, that the written dialects tended to transcend the boundaries of the local spoken dialect areas more easily than does the oral stylized form.[33]

31. For example, Hooykaas (1947:205) suggests that the Johor *Sulalātu 's-Salāṭīn* (*Sejarah Melayu* or "Malay Annals") was a response to the Achinese *Tāju 's-Salāṭīn* of some years earlier, and points to the similarity of the titles. The fact that Hooykaas did not take into account Winstedt's (1938) contention that the Raffles 18 manuscript of the SS dated from 1535 is fortunate, for Raffles 18 was also entitled *Sulalātu 's-Salāṭīn*, and if written in 1536 could not have been a response to the TS. De Josselin de Jong (1964:241), by accepting the views of both Hooykaas and Winstedt, contradicts himself. However, it has now been generally accepted that Raffles 18 is in fact the 1612 version (Roolvink, 1967; Iskandar, 1967; Sweeney, 1967), and this supports Hooykaas's suggestion. It also seems likely that the *Bustānu 's-Salāṭīn* in its turn was a response to the SS (Iskandar, 1967:40), for it refers directly to the latter work, and appropriated material from it (Winstedt, 1958:132).

32. Amin, author of the *Syair Perang Mengkasar,* was a member of the Malay community and presumably had wide inter-insular contacts. Skinner (1963:41–42) notes that his Malay is very much in the Riau-Johor style and little influenced by Makassarese. Nuruddin ar-Raniri, though more of a scholar in the *kitab* tradition than a scribe, was not a native of Aceh and traveled widely in the Straits of Malacca area (see Voorhoeve, 1951).

33. It may be noted, however, that the shadow-plays of Trengganu and Perak employ an adapted (localized) version of Kelantan/Patani stylized form for the speech of princes and demigods.

Although the practice of writing resulted in the growth of an idiom (or idioms) quite distinct from that of the stylized oral form, the written, no less than the oral, enclave of contrived speech was designed for aural consumption and developed in interaction with a nonliterate audience. While a scribe might well introduce new materials, it was essential that he should adhere to typical patterns conforming with the oral mental set of his postulated audience, and the advantages of literacy were, to no small extent, private to himself. In spite of the different idiom, therefore, we find the same "literary grammar" employed to generate both written and oral Malay composition. It is clear that our predecessors sensed this intuitively, but they were unable to articulate the underlying causes.

Thus, for example, the similarities between the oral folktale (*penglipur lara*) and the "literary romance" have long been noted: Hooykaas (1947:120) observed that the two merged into each other and that it was difficult to distinguish between them. This difficulty, of course, is explained by the fact that the *penglipur lara* tales with which most scholars were familiar were texts that had been transformed into a written idiom from the nonstylized form under British auspices. Yet while the process of adaptation had obscured the differences of idiom between oral stylized and written forms and thus the different patterns employed on the level of word choice, this paradoxically better enabled scholars to perceive the similarities of what was in fact the schematic structure on the level of plot, character type, theme, and so forth. So Winstedt (1923:29), for example, observed that "structurally" the *penglipur lara* tales "have the outline and machinery of all Malay romance," although in almost the same breath he paradoxically describes the former as the "cream of Malay literature," while the literary romance is "tedious and a slavish copy of Indian models." The fact that both the oral and literary forms were created with the methods of schematic composition for a listening audience resolves the apparent contradiction in Winstedt's view: the "slavish" part of the literary romance was clearly the dynamic or motifetic material, rather than the motifemic. The palace, which produced the literary romance, was more exposed to foreign influences than was the milieu of the oral teller, and the author's stock of motifs would tend to be more diverse. I have observed that not all written composition is equally schematic; the writer might well adjust his schemata in order to deal with the specific and present a less collective point of view. Nevertheless, the need to establish common ground with his listening audience ensured that he define his position with reference to the traditional schemata.

It is for these reasons that the development of a written tradition did not cause a radical change in the general state of mind of the Malay-speaking world. It might be supposed that as the oral enclave of contrived speech was gradually displaced by writing, the kinds of thought processes underlying that stylized oral form would no longer find mutual reinforcement in all areas of communication on all levels of society, and that the nonliterate segment of the populace for whom this oral enclave was their cultural frame of reference would find themselves increasingly isolated from the intellectual mainstream of society. In fact, however, as we have seen, while writing displaced the oral stylized form, it did not displace the thought processes which produced the latter, for these were still the thought processes of the writer's audience, so that regardless of the private advantages of literacy for the writer, his starting point had to be the oral mental set. Thus, while the medium of preserving the significant and important had changed, this cultural store was still fully accessible to the nonliterate. With the advent of mass education and visual consumption of writing, however, the individual unable to read was denied access to the written enclave of significant and preserved speech, and the nature of his oral thought processes, furthermore, consigned him to an increasingly isolated and deprived segment of society. Here, the only area of preserved communication which embodies his state of mind is the now similarly peripheral domain of the oral specialist. The isolation of the illiterate has been alleviated to some small extent by the growth of the electronic media; yet even here, his access to information is restricted. The orality of these media is a "print-based" orality; the message is usually pre-composed in writing, and only the presentation is oral. It may be argued that much of literate Malay discourse still reveals a strong oral orientation, so that many of the thought patterns are still familiar to the illiterate mental set, and this is true of programs such as drama, the offerings of disc jockeys, and many commercials. But more serious informative material such as news broadcasts and commentary are presented in language which is often too analytical and uses too many subordinating constructions for the paratactical oral mind to grasp, particularly in the area of reports translated from the offerings of foreign press agencies.

So far, I have tended to emphasize the distinctions between the language of significant, preserved communication and the casual converse of daily speech, or what I have termed the "stylized" and "non-stylized" forms. At this point it is necessary to clarify the relationship between the two and explain my contention that both forms may be said to reveal the same thought processes at work. In the case of storytelling this is fairly clear: the stylized form is mainly distinguished by its highly rhythmical presentation and its much more distinctive patterning on the level of word choice, the two factors being of course closely related and interdependent. Apart from this, however, both forms employ the same types of patterning on the level of plot,[34] character typing, themes, et cetera, and insofar as the principle of composition in both is schematic, it would be wrong to assume that the nonstylized form is not at all programmed for retrieval merely because it is relatively less distinctively patterned on one level—that of word choice.

Of course, the principle of schematic composition is not restricted to storytelling, be it stylized or nonstylized. As we shall see in chapter 5, the orally oriented individual perceives and discusses the topics of the daily round in a highly schematic fashion, by which I mean he apprehends experience in much larger chunks than does a highly literate individual. Other features shared in common by the stylized and nonstylized discourse of oral persons are repetitiousness, copiousness, and the use of an adding or juxtaposing style rather than a subordinating one. Indeed the relationship between the stylized and nonstylized forms may best be appreciated by considering the stylized form as the result of taking the features of everyday conversation and exaggerating them.

While it is true that the chief exponent of the oral stylized form is the oral specialist, be he storyteller or folk practitioner, etc., this should not be taken to mean that he had sole proprietary rights to the oral enclave of contrived speech: the *pantun,* for example, was the property of one and all. The *pantun* was no romantic extravagance; it was an essential means of communication, indeed the only means of expressing certain emotions. That these emotions were conventional and framed formulaically did not mean that they were any the less genuinely felt. Indeed, in most societies people tend to think and feel in terms of such time-tested distillations of experience. It is only our Romanticist heritage which causes us to insist that what are in fact

34. For plot patterns in numskull tales, see Sweeney, 1976. Many types of tales of course are presented in both stylized and nonstylized form, and share the same patterns except on the level of word choice.

fairly predictable human emotions are somehow unique and should be clothed in unique language.

A similarly widespread form of stylized speech was the *nyanyian*[35] *kanak-kanak* (children's songs, i.e., in fact, songs *for* children). It might be wondered how some of these songs could have had a normative function when the words are often well-nigh meaningless gibberish. In fact, a major function of these songs was to instill into the individual's mind from infancy the rhythms and mnemonic devices of tradition and to condition the mind to certain patterns of expectation and fulfillment. For example:

Cing cing pering	Ching ching pering
Kapal sudah laju	Ship now moving fast
Turun hantu putih	White ghost comes down
Belayar pukul satu	Sails at one o'clock
Peram peram pisang	Banana ripens ripens
Pisang masak layu	Ripe banana wilts
Menyelam dalam dulang	Dive into a tray
Disambar bapak yu	Pounced on by Daddy Shark
Pokok bunga melur	A jasmine tree
Tanam tepi batas	Planted at the edge of the dike
Itikku bertelur	My duck lays an egg
Ayamkau menetas	Your chicken hatches one
Ayun lambut-lambut	Swaying along supply
Sampai kubang babi	Arrive at pig's wallow
Takut Keling janggut	Frightened of bearded Indian
Lari tak ingat lagi	Run, forgetting oneself

While forms such as these are clearly set off from the language of everyday conversation, the distinction is not always so clear. I am not referring merely to the fact that the speech of orally oriented individuals appears to be highly schematic and repetitive to a print-literate person, or that the vernacular employs—as in other cultures—large numbers of conventionalized utterances of greeting, parting, and the like. My point is rather that the vernacular constantly draws upon the enclave of preserved speech, and in an oral culture this cannot be done by paraphrasing a written source, which may always be checked to confirm accuracy. The wisdom of an oral culture is encapsulated in mnemonic patterns which must constantly be repeated if they are to

35. Note that the term *nyanyi* appears to have been the earlier term to denote the quatrain now known as *pantun*. See chapter 9.

survive. Paraphrasing them would swiftly result in the loss of the pattern and thereby the wisdom. It is for this reason that the discourse of an oral culture is heavily dependent upon the use of relatively fixed utterances in stylized form, such as proverbs and other "sayings." While these are delivered in the intonation of everyday speech, their use of parallelism, assonance, alliteration, et cetera, ensures that the form produces its own, often distinctive rhythm.

Such utterances are not merely used to underline a point; they *are* the point. The individual *thinks* in these formulas. In a print culture, proverbs may sometimes still be used, and indeed perform a part of their old function: on the one hand, they carry with them the weight of tradition, and on the other, the fact that they sound right seemingly adds validity to the thought they express. For example, the acoustic equilibrium of *Lain dulang lain isinya, lain orang lain hatinya* ("Different trays have different contents; different people have different hearts") persuades us that the ideas expressed are indeed to be equated and fit well together. The difference, however, is that in a print culture, the proverb is used to illustrate or support a point made separately. For example, in a recent newspaper article, Sri Delima, the Malay writer and columnist, highly literate in both Malay and English, presented her argument concerning "pride," and then by way of underlining her point, added: "The oral tradition goes: *Kalau hidung tinggi semua orang benci*" ("If the nose is held high, everyone will hate [you]").

Similarly, in the formal speeches of educated individuals, one often hears a *pantun* used to reinforce and enhance a point. For example, at a farewell party, the guest of honor will, after expressing his gratitude, often end with a "gratitude" *pantun,* which is likely to be prefaced by a remark such as, *Sebagaimana kata pantun tradisional* (As the *traditional pantun* goes . . .). By way of contrast, in the actual traditional, that is, oral, context, the *pantun* itself is the message. For example, one may still occasionally hear old ladies negotiating wedding preparations in *pantun,* and traditionally, the medium of courtship was often the *pantun.*

Of course, what survives of the stylized oral form in modern discourse will tell us little about the interaction between the stylized and nonstylized in the past. Just as the study of the oral specialist today can give but a hazy picture of his central role in former times, so too an examination of the discourse of the modern illiterate will provide only limited insight into the everyday speech of pre-literate or even pre-print Malay society. Today, the illiterate has been relegated to the ranks of the dispossessed, and he is wholly dependent upon the literate for the preservation, communication, and retrieval of knowledge required for the functioning of society. Though his thought processes are still formulaic, he need no longer preserve the orally produced sayings of tradition by constant repetition. He realizes that the weight of authority lies not in his folk wisdom but in the printed and electronically processed word, and this awareness is clearly reflected in his speech: he hears the ideas and concepts of literate, analytical thought, but not being privy to the thought processes which produced them, he takes them over and uses them as formulas. As the ideas of the literate change, so, too, will his stock of formulas. He has thus become much more of a receiver than a producer of formulas.

This tendency of the illiterate, and indeed of the residually oral, to think in formulas is intuitively understood by the governments of Malaysia and Indonesia, and exploited to their own ends. This is done by deliberately creating formulas, in the form of slogans, mottoes, and catchphrases for adoption by the masses. It might be said that the slogan has become the new proverb. Like the proverb it is constantly repeated, but now only for its effect upon the recipient, that it may become part of the stock of formulas which determine his attitudes. Like the proverb, moreover, the slogan is often mnemonically patterned, again only to ensure that it sticks in the mind of the listener, thus no longer to ensure its survival. Examples of such neo-proverbs in Malaysia are *Pemuda harapan bangsa, pemudi tiang negara* ("Young men are the hope of the nation; young women are the pillar of the state"); *Bahasa jiwa bangsa* ("Language is the spirit of the nation"). We may note that the Malaysian national motto is also mnemonically patterned: *Bersekutu bertambah mutu* ("Unity enhances quality"). A somewhat more aggressive example from Indonesia produced during the Japanese occupation and reactivated for the Confrontation with Malaysia (1963–65) was: *Amerika kita setrika, Inggeris kita linggis* ("America we shall iron flat; England we shall fix with a crowbar"). The hundreds of signs now posted around Jakarta and other cities are more concerned with arousing civic consciousness. For example: *Anda dan hukum bagaikan ikan dan air* ("You and the law are like a fish and water"); *Mati akibat ngebut mati yang sia-sia* ("Death from speeding is death in vain"); *Kebersihan pangkal kesehatan* ("Cleanliness is the basis of health"). The force of such sayings lies in the fact that they are succinct, acoustically balanced, and relatively concrete. Their impact is aural. The tendency of one immersed in print culture is to think in abstractions and compose for visual consumption. When this tendency is not resisted, the resulting neo-proverb may communicate little to the orally oriented. For example, *Mengolahragakan masyarakat, memasyarakatkan olahraga,* while something of a tongue twister, is at least acoustically balanced. The thought pattern underlying it, however, is much too abstract for a slogan. The translation in comparable English might be "Sportizing society, societizing sport." The person who can immediately grasp the concept is likely to resent having it presented to him in such a form. The corollary of this is the slogan which, though it remains on the level of the relatively concrete, fails to make any aural impact: an exhortation posted in Blok M, Jakarta, appeared to announce that "Development will not succeed" (*Pembangunan tidak akan berhasil*). The initial impact of this slogan failed to impress upon the reader that there was a vital qualification to the effect that development will not succeed unless we cooperate shoulder to shoulder, and so forth, but this made it far too long to achieve the desired effect.

Apart from the mnemonically patterned neo-proverb, much use is made of the catchphrase, which, being short, sticks easily in the mind without the help of mnemonics, provided it is constantly repeated. Examples of such phrases in Malaysia are *sains dan teknoloji* (science and technology), *pembangunan negara* (nation building), *buku hijau* (green book—to encourage home gardening) and *revolusi mental* (mental revolution).

I should emphasize that the use of these "new proverbs" and neo-traditional sayings is not a cynical or sinister attempt at mind control, but stems rather from the oral orientation of those who produce them, or at least from their attunement with their orally oriented audience. This orientation may be illustrated by comparing Malaysian news broadcasts in Malay with those in English. During the sixties and seventies, I was on several occasions asked by English-speaking foreigners to Malaysia why the news in English consisted largely of empty platitudes, particularly when politicians' speeches were quoted. I was accustomed to listen to the news in Malay and had not felt that the politicians' speeches were entirely meaningless; at least they clearly had some effect upon members of my family. Eventually I made a comparison of the English and Malay broadcasts and began to understand how indeed they might elicit very different reactions. For example, an English broadcast which "called on the people to give their undivided loyalty to the nation and work together, for in this way we shall be able to ensure the nation's progress and the strength of Muslim society, and achieve prosperity, happiness, etc." would serve at best as a soporific for the highly literate in English. The same broadcast in Malay, however, is likely to have a very different effect upon its intended audience. This is because the speech consists largely of formulas, each of which is calculated to evoke a certain emotion. Such formulas in the above example are *menyeru rakyat* (call on the people), *taat setia yang tidak berbelah bagi* (undivided loyalty), *kerjasama/gotong royong* (cooperating), *kemajuan negara* (progress of the nation), *keteguhan umat Islam* (strength of Islamic society), *makmur bahagia* (prosperity and happiness).

However, while the use of such formulas is still quite effective upon the orally oriented, it should be noted that their appeal is not to the intellect but to the emotions. It is here that a problem arises: While formulaic propaganda may well succeed where traditional docility, obedience, and conformity are sought, when the aim is to encourage new ways of thinking, a campaign which merely reinforces a tendency to think in formulas is self-defeating. The most revealing example is the "Mental Revolution" campaign in Malaysia of some years ago, which merely added one more formula to the stock, hardly the way to encourage analytical thought.

Clearly, a very different situation obtained in the pre-print era, which was an age of "pre-illiteracy" in the sense that the ability to read and write was the exception rather than the norm among ruler and ruled alike. Thus, while the ruling class certainly depended on literacy, they did not perceive any need to acquire it themselves; writing was a task for scribes, who were at the disposal of the ruler. Obviously, it is not easy to obtain any exact knowledge of everyday discourse in the pre-print era. I have argued that the language of daily conversation is less ephemeral than it might at first seem, for even in that area not drawn from the mnenomically stored stock of significant and preserved speech there is much that is schematically programmed for retrieval. But on the other hand, the homeostatic tendencies of oral discourse ensure that material no longer relevant will be discarded and forgotten. The tape recorder, which now enables us to preserve the sounds of speech—though, one should note, without their context and referents—is a new invention. Previously, the only way to record speech was in writing, and the exclusive nature of the craft ensured that dialogue represented in writing or in spoken narrative committed to writing would be transformed into the written "dialect," a medium far removed from the language of daily conversation, as we note from the changes wrought on the tales collected under the aegis of the British. In such a situation, speech on its most ceremonial and formal level might correspond to or at least approach a written style, but the latter would almost always be uniformly stylized, and thus would offer little insight into the range of possibilities between casual and noncasual modes of speech.[36]

The wide gap between everyday speech and the written representation of speech is still very clearly seen in Malaysian (and, to a lesser extent, in Indonesian) society, and only in recent years has the gap begun to close. Only twenty years ago, characters in Malay films and novels spoke to each other in language which now strikes us as incredibly stilted. Close relations, furthermore, would write to each other in the most formal style.

Only when print is fully interiorized in the psyche does the gap narrow appreciably; it can never fully close, of course, for writing, unlike the spoken word, must always provide context. The process has clearly gone further in Indonesia, where Indonesian[37] is largely a learned language, acquired through the medium of print, and people tend to speak Indonesian more as they write it, or, more accurately, to be less aware of the distinctions between the written and spoken word. The corollary of this is that the individual no longer equates written style exclusively with formal expression, and colloquial speech may be reproduced in writing. Thus, the Indonesian who addresses a friend in a letter with "*Oi, lu gimana?*" ("Oi, how yer doin' mate?") has come a long way from the day, not so long ago, when he would feel bound to commence with sentiments in the vein of *Menghadap majlis sahabatku yang budiman* ("Addressing the presence of my friend possessing wisdom").

It might be thought that the older European books concerned with the Malay language would provide more insight into the nature of Malay discourse. Yet, as we have seen in the previous chapter, scholars such as Werndly felt that the only form of Malay worthy to be

36. There are apparent exceptions, of which the most noticeable is the attempt to reproduce the speech of foreigners. An example of this is the portrayal of Europeans speaking Malay. For instance, in the *Misa Melayu* (p. 84): *Sahaya itu hari membedil . . .* ("That day, I shot . . ."); and in the *Hikayat Marsekalek* (p. 17), Daendels is made to say: *. . . yang gua punya mau di dalam itu pekerjaan* (". . . my wish in that business"). However, the depiction of European speech was usually, in fact, highly conventionalized. The idiom was still that of the *hikayat,* interspersed with features such as inversion of noun or pronoun with *ini/itu.*

37. As distinct from the dialect of Jakarta, the *Bahasa Melayu Betawi.*

written down and used as a model for instruction was, hardly surprisingly for his time, the language of writing, the *Bahasa Jawi*. And even in the nineteenth century, although scholars such as Marsden, Dulaurier, and de Hollander endeavored to classify various types of Malay—in which they were clearly influenced by the distinctions perceived by Werndly—little light is thrown upon the nature of the spoken, as opposed to the written, word. For example, Dulaurier[38] distinguishes *Malay littéraire* from *Malay vulgaire* ("the language of daily life"), but considers the court language as a dialect of the latter although he also views it as a written medium (e.g., the language of treaties), differing from *Malay littéraire* in its use of some words used only at the court. For de Hollander, the "pure" Malay is written Malay, and, as is the case with Dutch, the purity of spoken Malay will depend on the education of the speaker and on the situation (1882:293). Here again, we see the assumption of the print-based society, referred to above, that one speaks, or should speak, as one writes, and this, of course, cannot apply to a radically oral manuscript culture.

It is, however, possible to gain considerable insight from the reports of outsiders—well-versed in Malay and whose standards of comparison are accessible to us—on Malay conversations they have *heard*. In the works of Hugh Clifford, for example, Malays are represented in English translation as speaking in a sententious, almost biblical style, which I found vaguely irritating until I realized that he was attempting to convey his feeling for the formulaic flavor of Malay discourse to his English-speaking readers. In the following passages (1925:64–65) he explains this formulaic style:

> In a discussion among Malays it is ever the man who can *quote* not he who can *argue*, who carries off the palm of debate; and Norris knew that this speech, with its tags of old wise-saws drawn from the proverbial philosophy of the people was well calculated to appeal to his audience.

An example of such a speech is provided by Clifford:

> When men be young they lie in the wombs of their mothers; when they be grown to full estate they lie in the womb of custom; when they are dead they lie in the womb of the earth. Behold, it has ever been my wish to obey the laws and customs of this land of Pelesu. When among the kine, I have striven to low; when among the goats, I have joined in the bleating; when among the fowls, I have crowed with the cocks.

38. "Memoire, Lettre et Rapports à M. le Ministre . . ." quoted in de Hollander (1882:291).

Clifford is said to have spoken flawless Malay.[39] I would suggest that this stemmed not merely from a mastery of pronunciation, vocabulary, syntax, and so on, but from an ability to overcome the tendency to translate his analytical thought processes directly into Malay, and instead think in the formulas of Malay tradition. Naturally enough, for one of Clifford's time, the employing of such formulas could only be thought of in terms of "quoting."

Marsden (1811:198), after acknowledging that a *pantun* of his own composition was dismissed as " '*katta katta saja*'—mere conversation; meaning that it was destitute of the quaint and figurative expressions which adorn their own poetry," observes that "their language, in common speaking, is proverbial and sententious. If a young woman prove with child before marriage, they observe it is '*daulu buah, kadian bunga*'—'the fruit before the flower.' Hearing of a person's death, they say, '*nen matti, matti; nen idup, bekraja: kallo sampi janji'nia, apa buli buat?*'—'Those who are dead, are dead; those who survive must work: if his allotted time was expired, what resource is there?' "

Marsden (1811:283) further remarks that "the Sumatrans in general are good speakers. The gift of oratory seems natural to them," and continues (p. 284):

> In Sumatra you may observe infants, not exceeding the former age [seven years], full dressed, and armed with a *kris,* seated in the circle of the old men of the *dusun* [village], and attending to their debates with a gravity of countenance not surpassed by their grandfathers. Thus initiated, they are qualified to deliver an opinion in public, at a time of life when an English schoolboy could scarcely return an answer to a question beyond the limits of his grammar or syntax, which he has learned by rote. It is not a little unaccountable, that this people, who hold the art of speaking in such high esteem, . . . should yet take so much pains to destroy the organs of speech, in filing down, and otherwise disfiguring their teeth; and likewise adopt the uncouth practice of filling their mouths with betel, whenever they prepare to hold forth. We must conclude, that it is not upon the graces of elocution they value an orator, but his artful and judicious management of the subject matter; together with a copiousness of phrase, a perspicuity of thought, an advantageous arrangement, and a readiness, especially, at unravelling the difficulties and intricacies of their suits.

The contrast we perceive between the two societies (Marsden's and Sumatran) is revealing: on the one hand, we see the print culture, still vestigially oral in that oratory is still a subject of some importance and

39. Personal communication from Dato' Abdullah Mohamed (former State Secretary of Johor), who is able to recount many detailed anecdotes concerning Clifford.

schoolboys still learn by rote; however, they are in a school room, and their instruction by rote is but the preliminary to learning to think analytically. On the other hand, we have a picture of an oral society, where the child is not segregated for the purpose of instruction, but acquires his education by sitting with his elders and absorbing from infancy the patterns and rhythms of the "proverbs" and "*sententia*" which form the stock-in-trade of the "good speaker."

From sources such as these, which are mainly concerned with the level of word choice, we see that in pre-print Malay society, effective thought depended upon the use of the formula at all levels of society. It would also seem that the oral discourse of that time was much less ephemeral than the speech of the modern illiterate. In the pre-print era, the central concerns of society were discussed by ruler and ruled alike in the mnemonically patterned utterances needed for preservation and retrieval in the oral mind. The illiterate today is forced to depend, however indirectly, upon print-based thought, and the neo-proverbs he is given last only as long as the ideas which underlie them are in vogue with the powers that be.

The decline in the use of the traditional formulaic expressions which began after the introduction of mass education has continued throughout the present century. My own impressions, referred to above, may be confirmed by comparing the language presented in various books[40] purporting to teach *colloquial* Malay which have appeared over the years. A revealing example is M. B. Lewis's *Teach Yourself Malay* (1947), excellent for its time but now so outdated that, unlike most of the other *Teach Yourself* language books, it is no longer reprinted. It is not that Lewis's ideas are not valid; rather the level of Malay she wished to impart has changed so much that the language of her book now reechoes the idiom of the past. For example, Lewis places great stress upon the importance of the proverbial expression, for "that is the way they talk. Subordinate clauses are seldom used in conversation" (1947:xv). On a more advanced and literary level, we may cite the work of Lewis's contemporary, Za'ba, who produced the three-volume *Pelita Bahasa Melayu* (1948). Again,

40. It should be noted that until recent years there was no such thing as a "standard" colloquial Malay, and writers of books on "colloquial" Malay were not always aware that the brand they marketed was a regional dialect, as say that of Penang. Furthermore, some of these books teach the bazaar or kitchen Malay reserved for conversation with Europeans, which authors have unwittingly taken to be the language used among Malays. In other cases, the Malay is simply wrong, being merely a mechanical translation of the author's English speech patterns.

a comparison of the Malay style taught by Za'ba with modern usage reveals how much the language has changed. If it be thought that the modernization of the Malay language has been largely a matter of inventing new terms, an examination of Za'ba's works will demonstrate how much of that modernization involves a shift away from the formula, parataxis, and copia toward the abstract, the analytical, and subordination.

If we were asked to put the displacement of the oral tradition in a nutshell, we might reply that the devastating effects of literacy upon formulaic thought are particularly striking in the area of telling time, for "time literacy" is now well-nigh universal, even among the otherwise illiterate. The use of clocks and watches has made almost entirely obsolete the numerous formulaic expressions once used for telling the time of day and to indicate duration. Examples of telling time are: *buntar bayang-bayang* (round shadows, i.e., noon); *toleh tenggala* (changing the plow, i.e., approximately 10:00 A.M.); *matahari ayun-temayun* (the sun hovering, i.e., approximately 4:00 P.M.). Examples of duration formulas are *sepetanak nasi* (the time it takes to cook rice); *seperludah* (the time it takes to spit);[41] *seperpisang* (the time it takes to eat a banana).

41. Also used to indicate distance: as far as one can spit.

CHAPTER 4

The Language of the Oral Specialist and the Effects of Writing

Our consideration of these developments in oral discourse now leads us to ask whether perhaps similar changes have taken place in the language of the professional storyteller, and of the oral specialist in general. So far, we have spoken of the displacement by writing of the oral specialist's areas of influence, to the extent that he has now become a peripheral figure in society, functioning largely as a mere entertainer in the rural areas. We have not, however, considered what effects this may have had upon his language and presentation within the dwindling oral enclave of contrived speech; whether, for example, his language was more mnemonically bound in the past when he played a central role in the efficient functioning of society, for, it might be argued, his stock of cultural information would have had to be preserved in a much more detailed fashion than in later times when he had become a mere entertainer. The question we are asking is, in fact, two-sided: were those areas of the oral enclave whose functions were displaced by writing more rigidly patterned on the level of word choice than those which survived; and in those areas which survived, has the degree of mnemonic and rhythmical patterning been affected by writing, and later by print and the electronic media?

We should first be aware that neither the written sources nor the oral specialist himself will be able to throw much light on these matters. Whereas the classical scholar of ancient Greece possesses a record of the ways of primary orality, paradoxically recorded in writing

(Havelock, 1971:15), it would seem at first sight that the study of that corpus of material known as "Classical Malay" is unlikely to reveal much about the shape of oral materials first committed to writing in the Malay world. And the very fact that traditional Malay literature was schematically composed for a listening audience makes it all the more difficult to detect the presence in literature of stylized oral language transposed directly into writing, especially as adjustments are likely to have been made to suit the written dialect. Thus, the only obviously original oral form found in literature is the *pantun*, which, of course, is likely to have been composed also for and/or in writing.

European sources are equally unenlightening. As we have seen in the previous chapter, there was little awareness of the existence of an oral enclave of contrived speech, and the only examples of stylized oral form recorded in these sources were a number of relatively fixed passages produced by formulaic clustering, such as the runs of the storyteller, and incantations collected from the folk practitioner.

It may seem superfluous at this stage to insist that the storyteller himself will be unable to throw much light upon the nature of his role or the shape of his performance in the distant past. Yet the fact that so many scholars still perceive oral tradition to be some kind of unwritten writing which preserves the words of the past somehow independently of the teller and his audience makes it necessary to emphasize once again that the performance of the oral specialist bears witness only to the time and place of utterance. The homeostatic tendencies of oral tradition ensure that no matter how rigidly patterned an utterance may be, once it loses its relevance for society, it is no longer repeated, and disappears. An example of this tendency on the most basic level is provided by the Kelantan *Tarik Selampit*. In the performance of one old teller, whenever news had to be broadcast to the villagers, a servant of the king would sound a gong (*canang pemanggil*) before making his announcements. In the performance of the teller's pupil, now quite elderly himself, there was no more mention of the gong. Instead, when the servant came to the village, he put up notices and distributed circulars (*sekelar*)! To the educated with some sense of history, this appears as an amusing anachronism. The storyteller himself considered it quite normal. Of course, not all old usages simply disappear. However, the rhetorical function of those which survive may well have undergone radical transformation over time, so that, for example, the use of "archaisms" may come to serve the purpose of emphasizing the distinctive flavor of the storyteller's speech over against the language of everyday conversation.

It should be understood that the language and presentation of the teller are not shaped solely by the need to preserve the significant or respond to the needs of rapid-fire composition. The professional teller is a businessman, and must be able to provide a commodity which his potential customers do not already possess. Every member of Malay society is a bearer of oral tradition, and the great majority are active bearers in varying degrees, but, in the case of narrative, the medium will usually be the language of everyday speech. The professional performer must therefore present his wares in salable form. In this respect, moreover, the storyteller has to produce a mode of speech sufficiently elevated from the language of everyday conversation to be a convincing medium of communication for the gods and princes who feature in his tales.

One possible line of inquiry opens up when we realize that the displacement of the oral enclave by writing in the Malay-speaking world did not proceed at a uniform rate. I am not advocating a cultural evolutionist approach which insists that all areas of the Malay world passed through identical stadia of development. Rather, I take it as self-evident that an examination of the displacement of the oral tradition in the Malay-speaking areas should not confine itself to merely one of those areas, such as the Straits of Malacca, for such an approach can only lead to the normative tendencies of our predecessors. I would suggest that the findings from one dialect area may well provide insight, or at least grounds for educated speculation, into developments in another area, and alert us to the dangers of making overly simplistic generalizations based upon one set of observations.

It is perhaps worthwhile to illustrate this latter point at some length. My comments on the role of the oral specialist in the fields of magic and healing might be taken to mean that writing has played no role in these spheres. Yet, on the contrary, the evidence from other Indonesian societies would seem to indicate that in a number of communities at least, one of the earliest functions of writing was in the field of magic. Indeed, prior to Western influence in the nineteenth century, the Bataks used their script almost exclusively for the purposes of magic and divination.[1] Voorhoeve (1927:12) observes that

---

1. See, e.g., Marsden (1811:383). Writing was also used for letters (Voorhoeve, 1927:9).

"writing for the Bataks is basically an act of magic. The alphabet serves as a means of defence against evil spirits . . . ; instruction in writing constitutes only the necessary preparation to that end in the magic arts." While the Batak lands are not a Malay-speaking area, there is some indication that writing performed a similar function in other parts of Sumatra, particularly in pre-Muslim times. For example, judging from the scanty material available, much of the literature of the Rejang of Southwest Sumatra, which employs a form of Malay and uses a pre-Muslim, Indian-derived script, traditionally appears to have focused upon matters of magic and divination.[2] It appears also that magic was a central concern of Besemah literature, which also uses the *Ka-ga-nga* script.[3] There is little doubt, furthermore, that this is also true of the seventh-century "Old Malay" inscriptions of South Sumatra (Coedes, 1930; de Casparis, 1956).[4]

It is not surprising that writing should be associated with magic power in a society newly introduced to writing or one which remains radically oral, regardless of the function of writing in the donor culture. Writing is highly mysterious to oral man: the power to capture speech in signs is awesome indeed, for the written message appears to be invested with secret meaning, even though the text may have no magic intent. Rockwell (1974:141) notes that Scandinavian rune stones often contained only the dullest of messages, but acquired an aura of magic in later times for those who could not read them, and hundreds of them were "decontaminated" or "defused" by placing them at the entrance of churchyards. The same attitude is also found in the Malay world. For example, according to Paterson (1924:252), the fourteenth-century Trengganu inscription provoked such awe that "the Malays of Kuala Berang were superstitious enough to refuse to handle it." The fact that the stone contained a promulgation of Muslim legal provisions is, of course, irrelevant to those unable to read it. And it seems hardly coincidental that both the seventh-century Karang Brahi inscription from South Sumatra (Coedes, 1930:45) and the Trengganu stone (Paterson, 1924:252) had been placed in front of

2. See Jaspan (1964).
3. Personal communication from my colleague William Collins. "The *karas* (bark-cloth manuscript) in Ke-ge-nge syllabic script was preserved as *pusaka* (heirloom) covering magical arts of omens, portents, divination, gambling."
4. "The imprecations which fill up almost the entire texts of Kotakapur, Karang-brahi and Telaga Batu . . . form together more than half of the epigraphical remains of Çrīvijaya" (de Casparis, 1956:7). Incidentally, the mention of drinking an oath on the Telaga Batu inscription reminds one of the same practice often represented in the Malay shadow-play (termed *minum air sumpah*) when a character enters the service of a king.

mosques, where they were used as flagstones upon which the wor-
shipers washed their feet before entering.[5] This belief in the magical
properties of writing among the illiterate or semiliterate in Malay is
also revealed by the widespread belief in the efficacy of written charms
(*azimat, tangkal*) which are found (among Malays) in Arabic, Thai,
Javanese, and Malay. This reverence for the written word is also
stressed by Voorhoeve (1940:133) and Collins (1979: 262, 277).[6]

In speaking of the displacement of the role of the oral specialist in
the fields of magic and religion, we should be aware that this was
unlikely to have been a simple appropriation of his functions by writing, and that the undermining of his orality is not necessarily to be
equated with the undermining of his role. In a society newly acquainted with writing, for example, the previously oral practitioner
who exploits its magical applications is able to reinforce his position
even though he "undermines" his own orality. An illustration of this
would seem to be Batak society. With regard to the more Indianized
societies of the Malay world, we are largely ignorant of the degree to
which the literate Brahmin, for example, displaced the oral practitioner, but from the evidence of the clearly Indonesian flavor of the
undeciphered curses on the three Srivijayan inscriptions referred to
above (de Casparis, 1956:28, 32) and the situation still obtaining in
Hindu Bali today, together with what we know of the assimilating
tendencies of Hinduism and Buddhism in the Malay world, it seems
likely that the magical practices of the pre-Hindu-Buddhist period
were not merely tolerated but rather reinforced by writing. On the
other hand, with the advent of Islam, such magic practices came to be
frowned upon, at least officially, and replaced at the centers of power
by Muslim writings on astrology and divination (*kitab tib*). The exponent of such practices as spirit mediumship and sorcery was, in many
areas, eased away from those centers of power toward the peripheries
of society, where he was no longer afforded access to the written
tradition. In this sense, we may say that while his functions were
reduced and his role became a less central one, his orality was reinforced or even reinstated. Yet writing is still seen as a powerful force
by oral practitioners, and I have observed that many of them, who are

5. According to Paterson's report, it seems that the question of handling the stone
arose only when the *imam* discovered characters inscribed on it and ordered it removed.
But of course we are concerned with why it was put in front of the mosque to be
trodden on in the first place.

6. See also Newbold's (1839: II, 333) reference to the preserving of genealogies
"with superstitious care, and kept as much as possible from the vulgar eye."

otherwise illiterate, have learned how to trace out in writing certain words, such as "Allah," "Muhammad," which are considered to be particularly useful in the preparation of talismans.

The point of this digression on magic and writing has been to illustrate the complex nature of the process of displacement before returning to our central concern, which is not writing *per se,* but the two-sided question regarding the form of those areas of the oral enclave which were displaced by writing and those which survived. The difference of focus may be appreciated from the example of the Rejang referred to above. While writing in the Rejang area had, until recent times, made but minor inroads into the oral enclave, the Rejang case is of but limited direct relevance to our concern with mnemonic patterning in Malay, for while the Rejang *Ka-ga-nga* literature was in a form of Malay, the oral enclave was in the Rejang language.

The Rejang, however, are but one of the upland peoples of South and West Sumatra whose societies were, until recently, still radically oral, and for at least two of these—the Minangkabau and the Besemah—Malay was their mother tongue. All too often, definitions which insist that the Malays are a coastal or riverine people ignore the fact that they are also a mountain people. It is undeniable that much of what survives in the stylized oral tradition of the coastal areas is not merely shared in common with but is indeed derived from the Minangkabau tradition. This, plus the fact that until relatively modern times little of the oral enclave of contrived speech had been displaced by writing, and that almost all areas of knowledge were still stored, retrieved, and communicated orally on all levels of society, should surely have made the study of Minang oral tradition a prerequisite for the study of Malay discourse in general, and Malay literature and oral composition in particular. It is true that in the past, attention has been drawn to certain aspects of the relationships between Minang and coastal Malay oral tradition, but it seems that little attempt was made to integrate these observations and fully realize the implications of what was being said. Winstedt (1923:37–38) was undoubtedly correct in his view that the bulk of the *penglipur lara* tales collected in Malaya under the auspices of the British "came into the Peninsula by way of Menangkabau." Indeed, in discussing the "metrical passages" of these tales, he drew attention to close similarities of meter and language with passages of the Minang *kaba Cendur Mata* and with the "sayings in which is embodied . . . the constitution" of Negeri Sembilan, whose inhabitants are descended from Minangkabau immigrants and speak a Minang dialect. Yet Winstedt understood these metrical passages to be merely poetic islands in a sea of prose (Sweeney, 1973:27). He was unaware that the *penglipur lara* delivered his whole tale in these short stretches of utterance, and that these passages differed from the body of the text only in that they were relatively more fixed in form, being "runs" of clustered formulas. Thus, while Winstedt made an educated speculation based on "the analogy of other ancient literatures" and the "rude ballad" form of the published *Cendur Mata* that this "rugged metrical form" was "the vehicle of all Malay rhapsodist literature," he wrongly believed that the form survived only in "stock purple patches" of the *penglipur lara*. And again, while he perceived the similarities with the incantations of medicine men and *adat* sayings, he felt that the latter survived only in "a few legal sayings" (1923:8).

Hooykaas (1947:14), moreover, remarked that "the old legal situation of the small Malay communities may perhaps still be found in its purest form among the Minangkabaus in Sumatra, or in Negeri Sembilan in Malaya, whence a number of them made their way in the nineteenth century." Hooykaas does not, however, elaborate on this observation, for the remainder of his remarks are largely adapted from Wilkinson (1922, 1925) and, following Wilkinson, all his examples of "legal maxims" are taken from Negeri Sembilan, not from Minangkabau. In this respect, it is surprising to note that even some Indonesian scholars such as Alisjahbana (1948), himself a Sumatran, when writing on traditional Indonesian poetry drew the bulk of their examples of *kata adat* from British studies of Negeri Sembilan, and not directly from Minangkabau.

Clearly, scholars of Malay literature sorely needed more information on the Malay oral and literary traditions of Sumatra. In 1940, Voorhoeve, one of the few Dutch scholars of Malay possessing extensive first-hand knowledge of several languages and literatures of Sumatra, provided scholarly support for Winstedt's speculation referred to above. He observes that throughout the South Sumatran area, tales such as the Middle Malay *andai-andai* and the Lampung *tetimbai* (also in Malay but with a strong admixture of Javanese words) reveal a strong measure of uniformity of language and style. He further notes that "the form is broadly the same as that of the Minangkabau *kaba:* rhymeless lines of mainly nine to ten syllables, with a strong rhythm and frequent use of parallelism. . . . I am inclined to accept that this is the real Malay story form, and that the prose of the classical Malay literature, with its endless *maka, sekali peristewa,* . . . etc., is a product of the schoolish translators from Persian and Indian languages. Or better, that it was they who elevated this natural awkwardness, which one also finds, for example, in the Batak tales, to the level of literature, with an easy-going neglect of that form deeply rooted in Malay language consciousness, the *kaba* form, which is closely connected with *sja'ir* and pantun" (1940:133).

It is clear that Voorhoeve (1927:15) had perceived in Batak oral composition a distinction between what I have termed stylized and nonstylized form.[7] Subsequently he was able to expand this observation to cover a much wider area: "Over practically the whole of Sumatra there exists this distinction between the simple folktale and a more literary form: in Atjeh *haba* and *hikajat*, in Mandailing *obar-kobaran* and *toeri-toerian*, in Minangkabau, *tjurito* and *kaba*" (1940:133). Included in the "more literary form" are the *tetimbai* and the *andai-andai* mentioned above. While these South Sumatran "epic songs" are "almost exclusively transmitted orally" (1978:92, also 1940:133), a few examples exist in traditional manuscript form (i.e., not merely written down for foreigners). Similarly, the Middle Malay *juarian* (question and answer between man and woman), similar in form to the *andai-andai*, are transmitted both orally and in written form (1940:134ff).

I was at first surprised that Voorhoeve had seen fit to include both oral and written versions in the category I would have termed "oral stylized form," which, in my experience, differed considerably from traditional Malay literary style. Yet Voorhoeve was clearly following local custom, and from his description there did not appear to be a noteworthy difference of form or style between written and stylized oral materials. The Minangkabau case reveals a similar lack of differentiation between oral and written materials in much of the traditional narrative. Thus, literary versions of the *kaba* differ little in form from the oral versions, and both are included in the genre *kaba*. Van Ronkel (1909:474), for example, remarks that the *kaba* manuscripts are "mainly in poetic form, overflowing with peculiar expressions."

It would seem from the evidence of South and West Sumatran writings that the literary style is much closer to oral composition, and represents an earlier[8] stage of literary development than that found in

---

7. That is, he notes that the *obar-kobaran* is a simple form told in everyday language, while the *turi-turian* is a "literary and musical work of art." Although he uses the term "literary," he is clearly referring to oral composition.

8. This does not, of course, imply that they were chronologically anterior to "Classical" Malay.

"Classical" Malay literature. I do not accept Voorhoeve's negative assessment of that "Classical" Malay style, which I consider to be the inevitable result of the development of a written dialect in the hands of an elite anxious to emphasize the exclusive nature of its craft. However, one cannot but concur with Voorhoeve that the "rhymeless line" of the Sumatran tales is the basic Malay story form. Indeed these short, parallelistic stretches of utterance are the basic units not merely of narrative, but also of the *kata adat,* incantations, and indeed of the *pantun,* and ultimately, after literary refinement, of the *syair* form. Whereas scholars in the past have seen this "rhythmical verse" as "the Malay's first essay in poetry" (Winstedt, 1958:145), it should be noted that the motive was not "poetic" in the modern sense. This method of processing speech was a highly pragmatic way of storing knowledge orally.

I feel therefore that any investigation of the development of "Classical" Malay—or indeed literacy in Malay—must focus upon these basic units. Indeed, even in certain extant texts of traditional (i.e., classical)[9] Malay there are indications of the influence of these units of speech. Examples of such texts are the *Hikayat Raja-raja Pasai* and the *Silsilah Kutai,* in both of which we encounter instances of the short, mnemonically patterned stretches of utterance so typical of oral style. For instance, in the *Hikayat Raja-raja Pasai,* there is the oft-repeated passage[10] (with expected variation):

> Ayohai Dara Zulaikha Tingkap
> Bergelar Tun Derma Dikara
> Tiadakah kau dengar genderang di Tukas
> Palunya tabuh-tabuhan
> Hari nin dinihari, bulanya terang
> Semalam musuh dari mana kutahu datangnya?
> Berapa kutahu banyaknya?
> Siapa kutahu pertuhanya?

> Oh Dara Zulaikha Tingkap
> Entitled Tun Derma Dikara
> Hear you not, the wardrum at Tukas?
> Beating a rally
> It is not yet dawn, the moon is bright
> By night an enemy from where I wonder?
> How many of them I wonder?
> Who is their chief I wonder?

9. As distinct from the written versions of Sumatran oral forms. It seems we cannot escape from this term!

10. This passage (Hill, 1960:78) has been corrected by reference to the manuscript (MS67, Royal Asiatic Society).

Other passages of the same type are:

> Duduk ia di balai panjang
> Penuh sebalai panjang
> duduk ia di jambar panjang
> penuh dengan sejambar panjang . . .
> (P. 77; also three times on p. 76)

> Sat they in the long hall
> Packed was the long hall
> Sat they in the long shelter
> Packed was the long shelter

and:

> Jika hamba mahu derhaka
> Jika Pasai sePasainya
> Jika Siam seSiamnya
> Jika Cina seCinanya
> Jika Jawa seJawanya
> Jika Keling seKelingnya
> Tiada dapat melawan aku
> (P. 87; cf. also p. 86)

> If I wish to commit treason
> If it's Pasai the whole of Pasai
> If it's Siam the whole of Siam
> If it's China the whole of China
> If it's Java the whole of Java
> If it's Kalinga the whole of Kalinga
> Will not prevail against me

And another passage of such clustered formulas is:

> Jika ia memakai cara Jawa serupa Jawa dan
> jika ia memakai cara Cina serupa Cina [etc.]
> (P. 85; cf. also p. 75)

> If he wore Javanese style he looked Javanese,
> If he wore Chinese style he looked Chinese [etc.]

The *Silsilah Kutai* is even more illuminating. Kern (1956:16), in some extremely perceptive comments, notes the occurrence of a considerable number of "short rhythmical passages" of "stereotyped descriptions," which alternate with the prose parts of the work but are not distinguished from them by the format. He observes that this parallelistic mode of expression is known in Kutai by the technical term *"taki,"* a peculiarity of which is that some of the words used therein do not belong to everyday speech; this results from the use of archaisms, foreign words unknown to the vernacular, and common words which, however, are given "what may be said to be an arbitrary sense." It may be noted that this is strongly reminiscent of the idiom of the stylized oral form of the Malay *dalang* and storyteller (Sweeney, 1972, 1973).

One of the many examples of these *taki* (Mees, 1935:165; Kern, 1956:17) relates the traditional words of a prince's representative at a marriage proposal ceremony:

> Dititahkan oleh Dewa Aji
> disuruh oleh Dewa Ratu
> hendak mengandung, hendak mengapang[11]
> hendak berteduh di kayu agung
> hendak berlindung di kayu besar
> hendak berlindung kehujanan
> hendak bernaung kepanasan
> (jikanya seperti orang pandai)
> hendak menggantikan pisau di tangan
> hendak menggantikan pahat di jari
> (sekarang ini orang tiada tahu)
> akan penjerat tangga rentas
> akan penjerat jamban hanyut
> minta jala, jala benang
> minta jala, jala sutera,
> minta jala lalu boleh
> minta rengge, lalu dapat.

> Decreed by Dewa Aji
> Ordered by Dewa Ratu
> seeks to carry, seeks to embrace
> seeks refuge in a great tree
> seeks shelter in a big tree
> seeks shelter from rain
> seeks shade from heat
> If in manner of artisan
> seeks to change knife in hand
> seeks to change chisel in fingers
> nowadays people know not
> of the tying of broken ladders
> of the tying of drifting bath-houses
> asks for net, net of thread
> asks for net, net of silk
> asks for net and acquires it
> asks for dragnet and obtains it.

11. This line is unclear. Kern notes that the reading *menggepang* ("embrace") was suggested to him (1956:94).

Kern notes that these passages are distinguished from the prose parts of the work not merely by their rhythm but also by the use of parallelism, and observes that this is "typical of the rhythmical parts of the Malay so-called *penglipur lara* tales and of the Minangkabau *kaba* and the Middle Malay *andai-andai* in their entirety" (1956:18). He observes, furthermore, that the same form is found in the Kutai tales, called *pekenan*.[12]

Kern knew the *penglipur lara* tales only from the versions written down for the British, and we now know that these tales are also rhythmical in their entirety (Sweeney, 1973). It is important to note, however, that our knowledge of the (British-sponsored but Malay-executed) process of writing them down, which involved preserving the form only of the oft-repeated runs of clustered formulas and turning the rest into prose, can perhaps throw light upon the presence of the rhythmical passages in the *Silsilah Kutai* and the *Hikayat Raja-raja Pasai*—for these, too, as is clear from the fact that they are regularly repeated, are clearly runs. It is likely that the tales were originally told in their entirety in these short stretches of utterance. With writing, however, the original rhythm would begin to break down, the only parts able to preserve their form somewhat longer being the relatively fixed runs. Yet while I have argued that some degree of mnemonic patterning was still needed in aurally consumed writing, the strong patterning of the orally composed tales, found especially in these runs, was no longer functional. In a particularly illuminating comment, Kern remarks:

> How the rhythm of such fixed expressions can be corrupted may be seen in the development of the strophe:
>
> | bedil demi perumpung tunu | Guns (sounding) like reeds |
> | egung-gendang demi ka- | popping |
> | cang diaru | Gongs and drums (sound- |
> | | ing) like beans being |
> | | stirfried, |
>
> where the compound *(e)gung-gendang* can be conceived as one word. [Then] we find:
>
> egung-gendang demi kacang diaru
> suara bedil demi perumpung tunu
>
> Here the addition of *suara* (sound) somewhat spoils the metre. . . . But this expression still does not completely conform with the *hikayat* style, which

---

12. Lines are of four, sometimes three, words (Kern, 1956:18).

turns it into: *Maka orang pun membunyikan bedil seperti perumpung tunu,
egung-gendang seperti kacang diaru* or *Maka berbunyilah egung-gendang
demi kacang diaru, tembak bedil demi perumpung tunu.*[13] Just one little
step further, one single conjunction more, and there is nothing left of the
original rhythm. (1956:20–21)

Clearly, we are observing here what should be an entirely expected
feature: the transition from an oral to a written style. Kern, however,
did not see these developments in such terms. For him, as for so many
other European scholars, this was no development, but "rather a retro-
gression." Yet if we apply the logic of this view to Europe, we would
still be communicating significant knowledge in "rough rugged" verses
akin to those of *Beowulf*.

When we reexamine the written versions of the *kaba*, we see little
evidence of this transition from an oral to a written style. This is not
to say, of course, that the Minangs did not possess a more "developed" written style. On the contrary, the existence of a number of
Muslim *hikayat* written in a variety of "Classical" Malay is an indication of this.[14] My point is, however, that matters of the most central
concern to Minang society as a whole continued to be preserved,
retrieved, and communicated orally in spite of the presence of writing.
And the written form of the *kaba* is strong evidence of the oral orientation of the society: writing did not succeed in displacing the *kaba* or
in replacing it with some foreign-derived literary form; neither did it
gradually transform it into something else. The form of the written
kaba reveals that the scribes were not merely concerned with recording the content of the tale, which could then be "elevated" to new
heights of literary splendor; on the contrary, they preserved also the
traditional oral style, an indication that this style was sufficiently
meaningful and prestigious to be preserved in writing. Unlike the fate
of the oral *cerita*, which became *hikayat* in "classical" Malay, the oral
genre *kaba* remained a *kaba* even when written.

The strongly oral orientation of traditional Minang society is only
fully realized when we allow ourselves to look at Minang discourse as
a whole. It is my belief that in the past, Western scholars have been
hindered from doing this by their natural tendency to view Minang
discourse in terms of their own categorization of knowledge, so that

13. That is, "People discharged their guns like . . ." and "The gongs sounded
like . . . , the firing of the guns was like. . . ."
14. See also the description of royal letters and warrants (Marsden, 1811:337ff).
Reference may also be made to the pre-Muslim Pagarruyung inscription of 1356.

Minang tradition came to be carved up and studied in terms of "the law," "literature," and "history," without sufficient consideration of the Minangs' own principles of classification. The scholar of literature, for example, tended to see "*adat*" as somehow not literature, and left its study to the jurists; and, again, the work of those jurists, in particular the magisterial work by Willinck (1909), appears to have received little attention from literary scholars. Or again, when scholars attempted to study both "law" and "literature," the subjects were usually kept rigidly apart, as, for example, in Wilkinson's *Papers on Malay Subjects,* where "Malay Proverbs" and "Malay Law" constitute two separate papers. It seems that Hooykaas (1947), who based his chapter "Spreekwoord en Rechtsspreuk" on these two papers of Wilkinson, felt the arbitrary nature of the distinction, for he includes material from both in the same chapter, and indeed notes examples of "proverbs" and "*adat* sayings" which are identical. And of course they are: *pepatah* is the term used for both of what Europeans have seen as distinct categories. Nevertheless, Hooykaas (1947:13–14) feels that he must keep them apart and employs an equally arbitrary distinction to the effect that *adat* sayings have "compelling force," whereas the proverbs are merely the subject of conversation, and that as *adat* sayings, these "what are themselves in no sense profound proverbs have here acquired a limited, special significance."

Although Wilkinson provides an extremely perceptive description of what constitutes *adat* ("right procedure," "right action in the matters of everyday life as well as obedience to the laws of the land") and observes that *adat* is not coextensive with "law," his belief in some Platonic form of "the law" leads him nevertheless to equate the Minang idea of *adat* with "law," and to assume that the Minangs make the same distinctions as he does between "law" and "history," so that he finds it necessary to rationalize the presence of "history" in *adat* with the words, "old sayings, even when historical in character, are generally considered by Malays to be included in *adat*, 'law,' for although they are not really law, they serve to explain or elucidate the law" (1922:9–14). The same assumption of the existence of "the law" is seen in Willinck (1909:50), who, while noting that law is transmitted among the Minang in "aphoristic sayings," feels that "the aphorisms in question . . . were, however, always more allusions to the existing law and could not be considered as laws proper." In fact, as we now understand, such *kata adat* or *pepatah/petua* were not illustrations of a point; they were the point.

An appreciation of the way the Minang classification of knowledge differed from that of the West may be gained—paradoxically, in that our focus is upon the orality of Minang society—from texts, such as the written versions of *tambo,* for, on the one hand, these reveal what materials were considered appropriate for inclusion under one rubric and, on the other, the fact that Western reactions to these texts are available enables us to highlight further such differences. Thus, for example, the Western scholar who studies the *tambo* with the preconception that Minang categories are the same as his own will likely assume that the Minang is confused and lacks the gumption to distinguish "history" from "law." Willinck, for example, has the notion that the *tambo* "have always tried to pass as history books rather than as sources of legal knowledge," although "they are mainly nothing but collections of fairy tales." They also "lose themselves . . . in moralizing precepts," and "now and then under all that worthless material there lies buried here and there a vague allusion to one or another rule of positive law" (Willinck, 1909:55). Willinck concludes (1909:55) that "at best, these *tambo* have some worth for the literary scholar"(!). This rigid imposition of Western categories has hindered us from understanding Minang tradition on its own terms, and indeed, has taught Indonesian/Malay scholars to view their own cultures from a Western perspective.

Thus, the temptation to see the *kaba* merely as "literary art" will tend to obscure the fact that it functions as the purveyor of what in a print culture would be differentiated into many branches of knowledge, each of which would merit a distinct genre. Had Willinck understood the tendency of oral tradition to preserve knowledge in narrative form, he would have realized that much of the "legal" knowledge he was seeking was preserved in the *kaba.* The observations of Taufik Abdullah (1970) are particularly illuminating in this respect: a *kaba* deals with "the ideal conduct of life in accordance with adat." The *Kaba Cindua Mato* is "a standard reference work for Minangkabau adat theoreticians and guardians," and "a considerable number of adat sayings" are based on it. It "relates the tradition of Minangkabau royalty," and provides "the ideal model for the Minangkabau monarchy," demonstrating "the ideal political and social structure of Minangkabau in operation." Taufik also draws attention to "the people's belief in the characters as historical figures," the descriptions of the "geography of the Minangkabau World and its neighbors," and of "community settlement patterns" (1970:3–4, 13). These observations will surely bring to mind Havelock's remarks on the social encyclopedia of oral tradition quoted in the previous chapter.

While Taufik Abdullah's discussion is mainly based upon printed editions of the *Kaba Cindua Mato,* this should not be taken as an indication of the demise of the *kaba* as an oral form; his approach rather reflects the proclivities of the scholar to study a "text." From the study of Phillips (1981) which, surprisingly, is the first detailed study of the *kaba* as an oral performance, it is clear that the *kaba* as an oral form is still a very central concern of the Minang community, and, indeed, forms a basic part of the education of the young (Phillips, 1981: e.g., p. 2).

In spite of the strong oral orientation of traditional communication in Minang society, expressed in the various verbal manifestations of *adat* such as *pepatah, kaba, tambo, pidato,* and so forth, it should not be forgotten that this is also an age of mass education in Indonesia. Even at the beginning of the twentieth century Willinck (1909:44ff) found that the Minang people considered the *adat* age (*masa adat*) to be past. Although a number of Dutch jurists wished to see "ample space allotted to a *living and growing adat law,* which should not be ousted by Western law, nor locked up in codification" (de Kat Angelino, 1930: II, 184), it is clear from Willinck (1909:47) that, after the establishment of the Dutch administration, the areas of authority left to the *adat* were those of "family and property law," and even here we see that the *adat* had been chopped up to suit Dutch categories of "law." Those areas of *adat* perceived by the Dutch to fall into the categories of constitutional and criminal law were replaced by Dutch law. The Minangs, therefore, referred to the Dutch period as the *masa rodi* (the age of [Dutch] authority).

Again, according to Willinck (1909:51–52): with the advent of the *masa rodi,* cases were no longer settled "among the marketgoers in a council chamber open on all sides," and henceforth, members of the public were absolutely forbidden to involve themselves in the proceedings. The result was that the Minang gradually lost his ancient love for and interest in the law, so that by 1909 only a few people still understood the *adat* and comprehended the old *petua.* This provided a stark contrast with what Willinck had heard of the *masa adat,* when the Minang "sucked in, as it were, the knowledge of his law with the mother's milk." "The various *petua,* said to have been the common property of well-nigh every Minangkabauer during the *masa adat,* are today much less understood by the average man. Then, people would

take the greatest pride in knowing many *petua,* and the greatest pleasure in applying them in every conversation and at every debate. He
who knew the most would be known as the most learned and smartest
man in his *negri.*" The *tukang pidato* were "the pillars . . . of the
literary art in the Minangkabau world," and it was they who made it
their business to dispense *petua* on every possible occasion. *Orang tua*
(elders, old people), furthermore, were regarded as the keepers of the
store of *petua,* and thus played a predominant role in the legal tradition. But in past times, the common man, too, had a great liking for
discovering the secrets of his *adat,* and "one might almost say that
every Minangkabauer of the *masa adat* was a natural jurist."

It is clear that by Willinck's time the oral tradition had been significantly displaced by the Dutch presence. The implementation of Dutch
justice, moreover, did not merely result in the appropriation of areas
of oral tradition, such as those displaced by Dutch criminal law: according to Willinck (1909:52–53), it also led to the appearance of
many *undang-undang* writings in the Minang dialect. It is clear, therefore, that a study of the interaction between oral and written Minang
traditions cannot afford to focus exclusively upon discourse in the
Minang dialect, or to treat the Dutch presence merely as an alien
intrusion which can safely be ignored. While both oral and written
composition in the Minang dialect reveal a strong oral orientation,
only when this composition is examined in the context of discourse as
a whole in Minang society may a balanced perspective be obtained;
only then does one become aware of the large areas of oral tradition
which were displaced by Dutch, and later Indonesian, print culture.

It seems clear from Willinck's account that during the *masa adat,*
those areas of discourse perceived by Willinck to concern "the law"
were still firmly within the oral enclave of contrived speech. Yet while
the oral specialist was the chief exponent and custodian of the *kata
adat,* he did not by any means possess sole proprietary rights to them.
This, of course, accords with what we have observed above concerning pre-print Malay speech in general. While stylized oral *narrative*
constituted a body of general education, particular skills were needed
to produce it, and its composition therefore tended to be the exclusive
domain of the specialist; the layman would, of course, be familiar with
the patterns and themes of such narrative, but his role was rather that
of recipient than of producer. The wisdom of oral society was consequently also encapsulated in *adat* sayings. This area of the oral enclave
of contrived speech with its short, relatively fixed, self-contained units

was so designed that it could easily be drawn upon by the vernacular for use in dialogue. Equating *adat* with "the law" merely because European law displaced part of the *adat* produces an extremely limited, indeed distorted, perception of the scope of *adat*. The *kata adat* were, in fact, the repository of all knowledge that depended for its validity and force upon a specific word choice. Obviously, if such sayings were to possess any authority and have the weight of public opinion behind them, it was necessary that they should be known and accepted by all members of a community, and this was possible only if the sayings were in relatively fixed form.

Of course, "relatively fixed" in an oral tradition is a far cry from the frozen text or rigidly standardized expression made possible by writing. Thus, in the *kata adat,* similar sentiments could be expressed in slightly different ways. For example, the duties of an individual toward his sister's offspring, and vice versa, may be compared:[15]

Ko malu mambangkitkan	Kurus dipagapuk
Ko haus mamberi aye	Senting diparimbah
Ko litak mamberi nasi	Sakit dicarikan obat
Ko lului manyalami	Lului disalami
Ko hilang mancari	Hilang dicari
Ko sakit mengobati	Mati ditanam
Ko mati manam	

(Willinck, 1909:408, 413)

The *adat* sayings were by no means fossilized and could vary over space and time. An example of how a saying adapts to existing circumstances is provided by Taufik Abdullah (1966:12; 1970:12): The aphorism *Adat bersendi alur, sarak bersendi dalil*[16] in the course of time became *Adat bersendi sarak, sarak bersendi adat;* this again developed into *Adat bersendi sarak, sarak bersendi Kitabullah*. Here we see the essentially conservative nature of the *adat* saying. The change may be effected only within the framework of the known and accepted traditional schema. Incidentally, it should not be forgotten that our awareness of such change is made possible only by the existence of written documentation, whether this originates in the local written

15. "If shy, give them encouragement; if thirsty, give them water; if weak, give them rice; if fallen in, dive after them; if lost, search for them; if ill, give them medicine; if dead, bury them." The second passage is similar, only "if thin, to be fattened" and "if short, to be lengthened" requiring translation.

16. "*Adat* is based on propriety, religious law is based on (correct) interpretation (of the scripture)." *Kitabullah:* the Qur'an.

tradition or in the reports of foreign observers. In the absence of such documentation, an oral society would tend to obliterate the memory of these adjustments.

Where no such adjustment has been necessitated by changing social circumstances, the *adat* sayings may exhibit remarkable stability over time and space, as may be revealed by comparing those of Minangkabau and Negeri Sembilan. For example, the saying *Salah makan mamuntahkan, salah tarik mangembalikan* (Willinck, 1909:696) differs little from *Salah makan dimuntahkan, salah tarik dikembalikan*[17] (Wilkinson, 1922:32). This degree of variation may occur in the same community, as we have seen from the example above.

The *adat* saying provides clear evidence that oral man is capable of preserving a large volume of knowledge in relatively fixed form. The principle of organization, however, is very different from that of a printed text, which has a beginning, an ending, and a fixed sequence. In the case of nonnarrative materials, this sequence may be determined by some abstract principle of classification or by alphabetical indexing. The corpus of *adat* sayings in oral tradition could have no such fixed sequence. Like language, it has no beginning or ending; the "index" is the human situation. The sequence in which the sayings are presented will be in response to the needs of the immediate situation, or more accurately, to the schemata which determine the perception of a "situation." Within the scope of this response, a number of sayings may cluster to form a passage of relatively fixed sequence, although considerable variation is still possible in that sequence, which again may be illustrated by the above example from Willinck.

A comparison of the *kata adat* with oral narrative as presented in the *kaba* reveals that only in the runs of the narrative is there a comparable degree of fixity on the level of word choice; indeed, many of the utterances occurring in runs are, in fact, *kata adat*. The language of the main body of the narrative varies from performance to performance (Phillips, 1981). It would therefore be unwise to assume on the basis of studies of the discourse of ancient cultures preserved in writing that in an oral culture, (*a*) narrative[18] is the only way to preserve the significant, or that (*b*) it is in narrative that the maximum possibilities of verbatim memorization in an oral culture are necessar-

17. "Wrongly eat, cast it up; wrongly take, return it."
18. Of course, most *kata adat* are themselves narrative units, but they do not form part of a larger *narrative* structure.

ily realized. In a culture such as that of ancient Greece, which developed from an oral to a written style without the benefit of foreign models obtained from a culture in which the problems faced by a primary oral culture were already solved, the obvious material for transcription in writing would be narrative, for the principle of organization had long been established in oral tradition, narrative being one of the earliest ways in which man organized experience. It would not, however, have been possible to produce a collection of sayings and aphorisms at such a stage of development, for, as I have argued above, no framework or system of indexing existed in oral tradition which might have been adapted by writing to classify such material. The aphorism was, of course, used in oral narrative. However, the structuring of narrative was based upon human experience, and the only model available for employing the aphorism in that narrative was that provided by the human situation. It was thus in this context that aphorisms were first recorded in writing. It may be speculated, however, that their occurrence in the written versions of ancient Greek oral epic is merely the tip of an aphoristic iceberg.

This is certainly the case in Minang society. The fact that many areas of Minang discourse still reveal a strong oral orientation, even though the *masa adat* is long gone, enables us to appreciate the vast amount of mnemonically fixed knowledge preserved in the *kata adat*. A perusal of the *kaba*, be it in oral form or enshrined in writing, gives little indication of the extent of this mnemonically preserved knowledge. It is only the availability of foreign methods of classification, originating from print-based culture, which has allowed the production of collections of *kata adat;* and, as I have already observed, it is, ironically, the potentialities of print which sound the death knell of the *kata adat*. Without these collections, and without access to the living tradition, one would tend to reach conclusions similar to those of Havelock concerning ancient Greece (1963:93) that "epic" was the only way of preserving the significant.

However, the relative lack of verbatim memorization in the *kaba* should not be seen as an indication that narrative is any the less an efficient preserver of knowledge than the *kata adat*. On the contrary, such fixed language was unnecessary in stylized narrative. The *kata adat*, which consisted of independent units or self-contained clusters of units, depended not merely for their force but also for their continued existence on a fairly fixed choice of words, for the unit or cluster did not form part of a larger formal, that is, verbalized, structure. In the case of narrative, however, the stretches of utterance are organized on several schematic levels (e.g., plot, character typing, themes, etc.) into a coherent whole. Thus, on the level of word choice, the formulaic or substituting mode of composition produces an adequate degree of stability to ensure the preservation of what is significant, although when a relatively fixed passage is needed to achieve a certain effect, that is, when a specific choice of words in a certain order has to be preserved, this may indeed be realized, as in runs.

We need not speculate on whether the form of the *kaba* was even more stable during the *masa adat*. The orally produced *kaba* is still a central concern of Minang society, and is regarded as an important vehicle for communicating knowledge. It is sufficient for our purposes to know that the form in which the *kaba* is produced today provides enough stability to enable it to perform the function of preserving and disseminating the significant. If it were now possible to compare this form with that of the composition of storytellers who have been displaced to the peripheries of society, we might well gain some insight into that process of displacement and its effects on the stability of a tale. Of course, if such a comparison were to have any validity at all, the genres compared would have to be closely related. A comparison with an entirely different genre such as the *wayang kulit*, for example, would be, as we shall see, of but minimal value. Such a related form would seem to be the *penglipur lara* tales of tellers such as Mir Hasan and Pawang Ana, which, as noted above, are generally accepted by scholars to be of Minangkabau origin. While the stylized form of these tales was not recorded, one may still find tales of this type performed in Pahang.[19] Evidence for the view that these tales—or better, the mode of composing them— are of Minangkabau origin is provided by (*a*) the tellers themselves (for example, Esah bte. Mat Akil, who performed *Raja Donan,* stated that she learned the tale from her Minangkabau grandfather); (*b*) formulas which carry with them the assumption that the Minang universe is the basis for all comparisons (for example, in Jidin's renderings of *Bongsu Pinang Peribut* and *Raja Muda,* it is said of a princess that, in the whole of Minangkabau and Sumatra, there was none to compare with her: *Selilit Pulau Perca, sealam Tanah Minangkabau, ta'ada tolok bandingnya*); and, most important, (*c*) the

19. For a description of these genres, see Sweeney, 1973.

structuring of the stretches of utterance. One of the best examples to demonstrate this is Esah's rendering of *Raja Donan,* for the form is still close enough to that of the *kaba* to make a comparison worthwhile. An examination of the most typical stretches of utterance in Esah's performances reveals their identity of structure with the *kaba* form. By "typical stretches," I mean those units of speech which, whether used separately or clustered in runs, are relatively fixed in wording and are the basic formulas of composition. These units are of almost uniform length, containing mainly nine syllables. For example:

> *Cindai jantan melilit pinggang; keris cabut di dalam sarung.*
> Silk sash enfolds the waist; *keris* is unsheathed from scabbard.

They are also characterized by the abundant use of parallelism, and each stretch of utterance corresponds to one phrase of the melody. These units are thus identical in form to those of the *kaba,* and indeed to those of the South Sumatran tales examined by Voorhoeve (1940, 1971) and Collins (1979), referred to above.

When, however, we examine those parts of the tales which are not fixed in wording, that is, the main body of the narrative, we see that the structuring of Pahang tales such as that performed by Esah is much looser on the level of word choice than that of the *kaba* form. This fact may be demonstrated by the use of three criteria: length of utterance, use of parallelism, and reliance upon formulaic substitution.

In the *kaba,* the stretches of utterance of the whole performance are of almost uniform length (i.e., nine syllables), whereas those of the Pahang performance are regular only in the runs; in the body of the narrative, the "lines" are much more irregular in length.

There is a much higher incidence of the use of parallelism in the *kaba* than in the Pahang performance. As this may seem to contradict the findings of Braginsky (1975) and Phillips (1981), it is necessary at this point to define my use of "parallelism" in this context. In the widest sense, two or more stretches of utterance are parallelistic when they are felt to be balanced against one another rhythmically, even though they are only approximately similar in length. By such a criterion, all the "lines" of both *kaba* and *penglipur lara* tales are in parallelisms. Here, however, I am using "parallelism" in a narrower sense. For two or more such stretches of utterance to be considered a parallelism, they must, in addition to having rhythmical balance, also possess a similar grammatical structure involving some degree of word repetition—be it only a repeated preposition, postposition, affix, or particle—in corresponding parts of the stretches of utterance. It is possible, moreover, for only half lines to enter into parallelisms as, for example, in:

Sembah ng ampun beribu ng ampun, *Harap di ng ampun* duli tuanku.[20]

Phillips (1981:114–16), however, includes both structural and semantic repetition under the general heading of parallelism. Braginsky (1975), on the other hand, uses parallelism to mean syntactic parallelism, but apparently this may or may not feature lexical repetition. It is this latter understanding of parallelism which is most relevant in the present discussion, for it is also used by Phillips (1981a) in his comparison of Braginsky's remarks on *penglipur lara* tales with his own findings on the *Sijobang kaba* form; this comparison leads him to the conclusion that there is a lower percentage of parallelisms in *Sijobang* than in the *penglipur lara* tales, and that "it might seem reasonable to suggest a correlation between *Sijobang's* lower percentage of parallelisms and its higher rate of syllabic regularity, compared with *cerita penglipur lara* verses (on the lines of Braginsky's correlation between the declining incidence of anaphora and the rising degree of syllabic regularity in *bahasa berirama*)" (1981a:5).

In comparing the findings of Braginsky concerning these passages with the *Sijobang*,[21] Phillips is undoubtedly correct in concluding that the former contain more parallelisms. This would no doubt be the outcome even if we were to use my definition of parallelism rather than Braginsky's, which appears to be particularly concerned with anaphora. However, there are two other factors to be considered. Braginsky, who was apparently unaware of my 1973 study of Malay storytelling, bases his findings only upon the *runs* of the *penglipur lara* tales. Hardly surprisingly, such runs reveal a high degree of mnemonic patterning, for only thus could they continue to exist orally in relatively fixed form. In contrasting the frequency of parallelism in *penglipur lara* tales with that in the *kaba* form, if we compare only the runs of the former with the entire narrative of a *kaba* performance, we shall obviously find that these runs contain more parallelisms than does the *kaba* as a whole. When we compare a complete rendering of, say, Esah's *Raja Donan* with the *Sijobang* performance, however, we find

20. And, we may note, the two halves of the first line also parallel each other.
21. Which was the task he set himself. The following should not, therefore, be construed as a criticism of Phillips, to whom, furthermore, I am most grateful for explaining to me parts of Braginsky's Russian text.

a *far* higher incidence of parallelism in the *kaba* form. Indeed, in a personal communication, Phillips informs me that "there is a great deal of syntactical parallelism all through *Sijobang*," and that in this respect the runs of *Sijobang* are "perhaps not so strikingly different from the main body of the story as with *penglipur lara*."

Secondly, Braginsky's comments on *syllabic* regularity in the *penglipur lara* are again based upon his study of the runs in the versions published by the British, which were all dictated. Phillips draws attention to the lower degree of syllabic regularity in passages of *Sijobang* which are spoken rather than sung (1981:106). I believe this to be true also of the *penglipur lara* tales: when sung or chanted, the runs tend to be more regular than when recited or dictated. I feel, therefore, that using Braginsky's figures for a comparison with sung renderings of *kaba* will give misleading results.

While Braginsky's contention that the high incidence of lexical repetition in incantations has a direct correspondence to a lack of syllabic regularity[22] may well be valid, I believe that a consideration of the mechanics and constraints of *oral* composition would have afforded an opportunity to ascertain the significance of his statistics.

An examination of the sung or chanted *penglipur lara* tale reveals that the runs are more regular syllabically *and* contain far more parallelisms than the body of the narrative. The body of a *kaba* rendering, moreover, is syllabically more regular *and* reveals a higher incidence of parallelism than the body of the *penglipur lara* tale. I do not see, therefore, why syllabic regularity and frequent use of parallelism should be regarded as tending to be mutually exclusive. On the contrary, I would argue that both are powerful tools for producing the mnemonic patterning so necessary for the survival of knowledge in an oral tradition in cases where a high degree of specific word choice must be preserved. That these two tools may work together in stylized Malay narrative is demonstrated by the fact that a higher incidence of both syllabic regularity and parallelism is found in runs than in the body of the performance. That these are the parts of the tales programmed for preservation on the level of word choice is proved by the

22. It is perhaps relevant to note that incantations in Kelantanese are often quite irregular in length, for most of the units consist of names and epithets, some of which are much longer than others. Such incantations are not rigid in form; they are recomposed to some extent each time they are uttered. The same *dalang* who produces incantations of irregular length will, however, compose *pantun* of much more even length. We should not assume, therefore, that the incantation is now a fossil, no longer produced, which has developed into a shorter, more regular form. Both coexist.

fact that they can be repeated and they do indeed survive in relatively fixed form. Furthermore, the fact that the *kaba* reveals in general more syllabic regularity and a higher incidence of parallelism than the *penglipur lara* form is an indication that the *kaba* is better equipped to preserve the significant on the level of language.

It may perhaps be wondered why I have placed so much emphasis upon the use of parallelism when, in fact, this feature occurs in only a minority of lines. The answer is that while parallelism by definition can occur only in consecutive lines, the principle generating it (by my definition above) is exactly the same as that underlying the production of formulaic substitutions of the "Parry-Lordian" type, whereby formulaic lines and half lines are those which "follow the basic patterns of rhythm and syntax and have at least one word in the same position in the line in common with other lines or half lines" (Lord, 1976:47). It is these productive patterns which clearly form the basis of *kaba* composition. As Phillips notes (1981:110), they "constitute the grammar of the special, limited language of *Sijobang*." Thus, while variety of expression is encouraged in *kaba* composition (Phillips, 1981:116), the structures or patterns which generate the language of the *kaba* form are relatively fixed and limited in number. This feature, combined with the uniformity in length of the stretches of utterance give to the *kaba* a stability on the level of language which is clearly lacking in the Pahang performances. While the runs of the latter still reveal in relatively crystallized form the results of formulaic substitution within a symmetrical framework, in the body of the performance, formulaic patterns, while still present, are much less precisely used, and do not keep the stretches of utterance within the confines of a regular length; indeed, not infrequently, the length and form of an utterance may approach that of nonstylized, everyday speech, from which it is distinguished only by its sung presentation. An example of this may be seen in the second line of

Dipasang dian tanglung pelita,
Bangkit nga lah Raja Diu pergi ke kolam bersiram dua suami isteri.[23]
(Sweeney, 1973:34)

The relatively much lower degree of mnemonic patterning in the performances of Pahang tellers such as Esah than in *kaba* composition

---

23. "Candles, lanterns and lamps were lighted. Raja Diu arose, went to the bath tank and bathed together with his wife."

is a further indication that the *kaba* remains a much more efficient vehicle for the preservation of significant and important knowledge on the level of word choice. I believe that this may be directly related to the relative degree of importance accorded to these modes of stylized composition in their respective societies. On the other hand, in Minangkabau, as we have seen above, the orally produced *kaba* is still central to the concerns of society as a whole, for it constitutes a body of general education, and indeed embodies the general state of mind. Obviously, society will endeavor to ensure that such knowledge is preserved in as stable a form as possible. It is not enough, however, to explain this stability merely in terms of some ill-defined notion of public awareness of importance; we must rather attempt to appreciate the mechanics involved. In saying that the *kaba* embodies the general state of mind, we are implying that the thought processes which produce the *kaba* form are not restricted to use in the *kaba*. In more specific terms, we may say that the methods of presenting and preserving the knowledge contained therein are reinforced on other levels of communication: the short stretch of mnemonically patterned utterance used in the *kaba* is also the basic unit of the *kata adat, pidato, tambo,* and so on.

This presents a striking contrast with the situation of the Pahang teller, who is an almost forgotten figure in Pahang society; even in his own rural milieu his tales are no longer a central concern, and performances are few and far between. The thought processes revealed in his composition no longer embody the general state of mind, for the methods he employs receive little reinforcement from other modes of stylized oral communication, most of which have already long been displaced by writing.[24] Indeed, he may not even have heard another teller's performance in decades. There is thus no longer an effective system of checks and balances on the production of stylized stretches of utterance, and this tends to undermine gradually the stability of these units of composition.

Further evidence of how the weakening of the system of checks and balances results in the undermining of the stability of a tale, and of the stylized oral form in general, is provided by the Malay shadow-play. In a previous study of the genre (1972), I observed that the stability of the *Rama* repertoire of the *Wayang Siam* seemed to

---

24. The only form still tolerably alive which uses the basic unit of utterance is the *pantun*. The proverb is very much on the decline.

vary in direct proportion to the degree of popularity it enjoyed, and illustrated this by comparing the situation in Kelantan, on the one hand, with that in Perak, Kedah, Trengganu, and Patani on the other. In Kelantan, in contrast with other areas, certain factors seemed to exercise some control over the content of the basic repertoire: a large number of *dalang*s knew, and at times performed, the story; and a large part of at least the older section of the populace was well acquainted with it. A *dalang* who made radical changes in a well-known episode not compatible with existing levels of expectation laid himself open to criticism from the audience. Further, although a *dalang* might receive an idiosyncratic version from his teacher, he was unlikely to restrict his accumulation of repertoire to the one source and was[25] able to refresh his version from other sources. Where there are few *dalang*s who know the story and where it is now little known in the society, the perpetuation of idiosyncrasy is far more likely (Sweeney, 1972:261).

When these findings are considered in the context of Walter Anderson's (1923:397ff) so-called "law of self-correction," it becomes clear that the effectiveness—indeed validity—of this "law" varies in direct proportion to the frequency of performance of a tale. By now, it is perhaps superfluous to reiterate that in oral tradition, knowledge is preserved only by constant repetition. The less frequently a tale is performed, the less stable it becomes, and the more likely it is that large parts of the knowledge preserved therein will be forgotten.

It should be emphasized at this point that I am not equating popularity or frequency of performance of the *Rama* tale with that of the genre, nor attempting to explain the waning importance attached to the *tale* as a symptom or result of a gradual decline of the *genre*. On the contrary, in Patani the *wayang* still enjoys considerable popularity, even though the basic *Rama* tale is less frequently performed and less stable in form than in Kelantan.

However, while these remarks may throw some light upon the mechanics of the weakening of the system of checks and balances as manifested in the dwindling sources of reinforcement and correction, they do not explain why the basic *Rama* tale has become increasingly less important in the estimation of both performers and audiences of the *wayang*. It might perhaps be argued that my study of the *wayang* (1972),

---

25. In 1968, I was still able to use the present tense. Since then, most of the old *dalang*s I knew have died, and far fewer people today know the basic *Rama* tale.

being largely a synchronic one, is not capable of detecting change. I would reply, however, that (a) my study indicates that the *Rama* tale in Patani, Kedah, Trengganu, and Perak was once much more frequently performed; (b) comparative work concerning differences between the generations reveals that even in Kelantan the basic repertoire of younger *dalang*s is far less complete than that of older *dalang*s; (c) older *dalang*s' knowledge of the tale in Patani matches in length and complexity only that of younger *dalang*s in Kelantan; and (d) although I speculated in 1970 (Sweeney, 1972:77) that younger *dalang*s might fill out their knowledge of the tale in the course of their careers, I have not found that this has occurred in the intervening years. I believe, therefore, that I am justified in speaking of a general decline in the knowledge of the basic *Rama* tale in the Malay shadow-play.

I would argue that the adverse fortunes of the *Rama* tale are to be explained in terms of the changing role of the *wayang*, from being a purveyor of knowledge and preserver of the significant (which of course had to be entertaining in order to be effective) to becoming merely a vehicle of entertainment.[26] In more general terms, these changes provide us with an example of the erosion of certain functions of the oral enclave of contrived speech.

I am aware that the *wayang* is no longer a central concern of Kelantanese society as a whole. Indeed, in a broader context, when measured against the importance of writing, print, film, and radio, the oral enclave of preserved speech was already in 1962 (when I began my study of oral composition) clearly peripheral as a preserver of knowledge. Yet in certain areas of the rural milieu in which the *dalang* operated, considerable importance was still attached to the knowledge he purveyed. In Kelantan, for the older *dalang*, at least, the *Rama* tale represented a vehicle of general education, a purveyor of knowledge, a record of history, and a source of power. This was revealed not merely in what the *dalang* said in conversation, but in the nature of his postulated audience. And one may be sure that the creation of that postulated audience was determined by the *dalang*'s knowledge of the attitudes and expectations of the flesh-and-blood audience who attended his performance. This is not to deny that the denizens of the invisible world such as the *jembalang* or spirits of the puppets played an important role in the *dalang*'s postulated audience, as is revealed in

---

26. And it may be noted that the differentiation between entertainment and what is not entertainment (didactic, magico-religious, etc.) is a relatively new development.

the use of various *bilangan* (runs) which were often identical in form
to invocations and were perceived to possess a certain ritual value, or
in the various ritual practices performed within and without the
drama.[27] However, this part of the postulated audience, too, is determined to a large extent by the current beliefs of the audience of flesh
and blood. When society no longer attaches importance to such beliefs, the invisible audience becomes much less prominent in the
dalang's estimation, especially as his appeal to such beings loses its
calculated rhetorical effect upon his actual audience. The changing
function of the *wayang*, from being a purveyor and preserver of
knowledge and a source of power to becoming a vehicle of mere
entertainment, is thus again reflected in the erosion of the ritual importance of the *wayang*, for it is clear that the decline in knowledge of
the *Rama* tale has been accompanied by a corresponding decline of
ritual knowledge and practices.

It is perhaps noticeable that in relating my comments concerning
the *kaba* and Pahang performances to my findings on the *wayang*, I
did not attempt a comparison on the same level of composition: in my
consideration of the *kaba* form, I was particularly concerned with
stability on the level of specific word choice, whereas my discussion of
the *Rama* tale and the *wayang* was more general in its purview, although certainly concerned with the level of plot. My justification of
this method of operating is twofold: on the one hand, it is my contention that the principles underlying the system of checks and balances
that control the stability of a performance are not merely applicable to
only one level of schematic composition; on the other hand, a simple
comparison of the degree of fixity on the level of word choice between
the Pahang tales and the *wayang* that failed to take into account other
levels of composition would produce extremely misleading results. I
have argued that in an oral tradition important knowledge is processed for survival, to the extent that the degree of stability of stylized
oral material may be an indicator of the importance accorded it by
society. A comparison of the language used in the *wayang* with that of
the Pahang tales might seem to indicate the presence in the latter of a
higher degree of mnemonic patterning than in the *wayang*. Certainly,
stretches of utterance are more regular in length; indeed, it would
seem that *wayang* speech was never divided into short, regular units

27. See further Sweeney (1972). An example of a ritual exigency within the drama is
portrayal of the death of Rawana, when a yellow canopy must be installed and various
spirits invoked to ensure that the performers and audiences are unharmed.

delineated by the patterns of melody or chant. And yet I would argue that, whether as purveyor and preserver of knowledge, or even merely as a vehicle of pure entertainment, the *wayang* is accorded much more importance, is held in much higher esteem, and is far more popular in its own milieu than is the case with the performance of the Pahang teller in his milieu. The apparent contradiction is resolved only when we examine other levels of schematic composition. Then we see that the relative lack of mnemonic rigidity on the level of word choice in the *wayang* is amply compensated for by the very high degree of stability on the level of character typing: here the performer is no longer reliant merely upon verbal memory; character is encapsulated in the iconography of the puppets, the various traits which constitute a type being encoded in the appearance of each puppet.[28]

Whether or not *wayang* speech was once relatively more fixed in form is impossible to demonstrate. It is demonstrable, however, that where there was a perceived need to preserve a specific word choice, this was readily accomplished, as is clear from the form of the *bilangan* (runs) and invocations of the older *dalang*s I studied. Here, the use of parallelism and other mnemonic devices enabled the *dalang* to preserve long passages in relatively fixed form.[29] In this area, too, however, I have observed a general decline in the use of these fixed passages over the past two decades, and this accords with my comments above concerning the depreciation of the ritual aspects of the *wayang*.

While the recent history of the Malay *wayang* provides us with a good example of how the oral enclave of contrived speech is eroded and its function displaced, this process is not necessarily to be taken as a sign that the genre itself is being displaced at the same rate. On the one hand, it is true, the spread of mass education, the stream of information provided by the modern media, and the ease with which information may be preserved by those media have led to an awareness that much of the knowledge preserved in the *wayang* is no longer suited to the modern age, and that the oral methods of preserving that knowledge are obsolete and inefficient by modern (i.e., print-culture)

28. Incidentally, in Java, although characters are more recognizable as individuals, the encoding of traits is so important that genetic origins may be overridden by the need to portray characteristics, so that, for example, Vibhisana is portrayed as a refined type even though he is the brother of the *raksasa* (ogre) Dasamuka (Ravana). In the Malay *wayang*, Vibhisana (Mah Babu Sanam) is depicted as a *raksasa*.

29. The longest *bilangan* I collected were those of the (in 1968) eighty-five-year-old Amat Ismail (died 1969) and the fifty-five-year-old Karim (died 1971) whose *bilangan* for Seri Rama varied between 250 and 300 words in length. See also Sweeney, 1972 (chapter 5).

standards. A good illustration of this growing awareness was provided
by reactions to the news in 1969 that the Americans had landed on the
moon. Awang Lah (died 1974), the greatest *dalang* of his time, for
whom the *wayang* was the source of all important knowledge and
power, proclaimed that the news could not be true, for, "in the *wayang* it says there are seven layers of sky.[30] They could not have got
through those." Two of Awang Lah's pupils, discussing his views
afterward, felt that what he had said "might have been true once, but
now times have changed."

On the other hand, the genre survives. It is clear that for the
younger generation of *dalang*s, the *wayang* is increasingly a vehicle for
entertainment rather than a source of general education. In this context of the *wayang* as an entertainment business, our earlier comments
(inspired by Ong) regarding the ways in which a new medium apparently reinforces the old initially but eventually changes it or even
destroys it are applicable: it is indisputable that the new media of
communication, including print, film, tape recorders, and now television have had a very significant effect upon the presentation of the
wayang, and indeed many of the devices used by these media have
been consciously appropriated by the *dalang.* For example, the insistence of the Kelantan state government on a three-hour limit for performances, based of course upon what is considered a reasonable
length for a performance by Western media standards, has forced the
dalang to present his wares in a much more concise format than was
formerly the case. Again, his model for accomplishing this is the format of the film and television drama. This is in fact now expected by
his audience, who have become familiar with the instant entertainment
provided by the electronic media. Indeed, even the methods of organizing a performance are now based upon what obtains in the cinema:
whereas the *wayang* was once performed mainly for rites of passage,
the vast majority of performances today are organized as a business
enterprise, involving the sale of tickets. The modern *dalang* does not
operate by half measures: standard equipment nowadays includes a
loudspeaker, amplifier, and throat microphone, which enable him to
assume a much more intimate ethos than formerly, the model again
being the electronic media. Some *dalang*s make extensive use of the
tape recorder to provide music, usually from the sound track of Hin-

---

30. *Tujuh Petala Langit* (Sanskrit: *sabta petala*). It would be irrelevant to say that
this is not originally from the *wayang;* he learned it from the *wayang.*

dustani films, before the performance commences, or even to record the performances of other *dalang*s who are thought to have something worth appropriating. There are even *dalang*s who feel that colored footlights add just the right touch!

The new media, moreover, play a significant role in the development of repertoire. Many *dalang*s, especially in Patani, adapt the plots of Hindustani films to the *wayang*. Increasingly, *dalang*s make use of material they have read in published sources. Literacy also enables *dalang*s to make summaries of their repertoire in writing; for example, many of the tales of Hamzah, the star pupil of Awang Lah and a leading *dalang* today, are recorded in a notebook in summary form. There is even a tendency for the new generation of *dalang*s to note down in writing other materials, such as *bilangan* and invocations, although, as mentioned above, much less attention is devoted to these than was once the case.

As was seen in the relationship between magic and writing, here again the *dalang* is attempting to ensure the survival of his livelihood, the *wayang,* even though this entails undermining the orality of his craft.

CHAPTER 5

Schematic Language in Everyday Speech

In the introduction to this study, I have drawn attention to the arbitrary nature of any attempt to carve out an area known as "folklore" from the discourse of the Malay-speaking world. The creation of such a distinction leads to the notion that the society we are studying itself perceives its own tradition in terms of a twofold division into "literary art," on the one hand, and everyday conversation on the other. The distinction I have made between stylized and nonstylized form should certainly not be construed as providing support for such a notion. The motivation to produce the highly patterned language of the stylized form was not the self-conscious concern with aesthetics of the modern literary artist. Rather, as we have seen, such mnemonic patterning was the only way to preserve the significant when the level of specific word choice was important. The use of these formulary features was thus by no means the exclusive domain of the oral specialist; effective thought depended upon the use of the formula at all levels of society and in all areas of discourse. Yet while the stylized form is distinguished by its much stronger patterning on the level of word choice, this does not imply that the nonstylized form is therefore entirely ephemeral. An examination of stylized and nonstylized storytelling reveals that both forms employ the same principle of schematic composition on the levels of plot, character typing, and so on, and it would be wrong to assume that the nonstylized form is not programmed for retrieval merely because it is less distinctively patterned on one level—that of word choice.

What then of the language of everyday speech? Granted that the vernacular draws heavily upon the formulas of the oral enclave of contrived speech in the form of *kata adat,* et cetera, there still remains the bulk of the casual round of daily converse which is in nonstylized form. In storytelling, be it in stylized or nonstylized form, what may be said is determined by the schemata available to the teller and expected by his audience. Of course, the question of intentionality is all-important, and a given schema may be adjusted when it is perceived for whatever reason to be inadequate to the composer's purpose. He cannot but begin with his given schemata, however; it is these which determine his perceptions of the world to be represented in his storytelling. Not everything which may be narrated in the nonstylized form can also be told in the stylized form, and vice versa. The mental set of the teller is shaped by his medium and style, by the composition of his audience and his standing with that audience. Thus, for example, a major area of nonstylized storytelling is devoted to the numskull tale, featuring a peasant as protagonist. The mental set of the teller in stylized form, however, would tend, in the traditional context, to screen out the possibility of presenting such a peasant character as the hero of his performance. The stock of schematic building blocks available determines a very predictable hero type: the schematic pull, if unadjusted, will produce a young, handsome, unmarried prince as hero.

To the highly literate individual unfamiliar with the still-strong oral orientation of much of the Malay world, it might seem that it is this schematic structuring of storytelling, be it stylized or nonstylized, which sets off storytelling from the language of everyday conversation. The composition of a tale, where given schemata determine the teller's initial perception and shaping of his material, would seem to be a highly artificial process, contrasting strongly with the seemingly "natural" language of the daily round, where one is dealing with "reality" unhindered by such barriers to a clear perception of things as they are.

In fact, such a distinction would be highly arbitrary. On the one hand, as I have argued in the introduction, the difference between the schematic composition of an oral society and the modern "literary" composition of a print culture is one of degree, not of kind. On the other hand, a set of given schemata is a prerequisite not merely for the writer or teller, but for anyone who would speak, for only thus may he perceive order where otherwise there would be meaningless chaos. To adapt Gombrich's (1969) observations on visual perception in pictorial art, we may say that man does not so much talk about what he sees; he rather sees what he can talk about. If this were all that could be said on the matter, there would be little point in saying it, for what is true of all speech will hardly afford us any specific insight into Malay conversation. My point is, however, that in the still orally oriented areas of Malay society, the schematic "chunks," not merely of storytelling but also of everyday conversation, are much bigger than those of a print-interiorized culture. We have already seen that on the level of word choice, Malay conversation traditionally made wide use of the mnemonic patterning and strong rhythms of stylized or contrived speech. I would now argue that on other levels, too, which may be compared with those of plot, theme, character type, and so on, of the storyteller, orally oriented conversation is much more schematic in structure than the speech of highly literate individuals, with the result that what is said in a certain context may often be highly predictable.

The foreign scholar who spends perhaps a maximum of two years in "the field" does not easily become aware of this, however. For him the language is still refreshingly new; many turns of expression seem quaint; there is a constant element of surprise. And, not infrequently, although he resides in the community he is studying and learns to speak its language, he may exist in a different dimension, for he is unaware that the choices available in the language he is learning do not coincide with those of his own culture; and until he becomes aware of the possibilities, he may feel that he has learned to express himself on any subject, without realizing that in expressing what he considers are normal human sentiments he may be failing completely to adjust to and meet the level of expectation of his audience essential for effective communication. An example on the most basic level is that of the Western anthropologist in Malaysia whose wife had committed a *faux pas*. He felt that he should put matters right by explaining to his audience of relative strangers that he and his wife loved each other very much,[1] but that she was feeling a bit miserable. The reverse is also true; in attempting to understand, the researcher will tend to naturalize what he hears in terms of his own view of the world. Of course, if this were all that were to be said on the matter, we would

---

1. This was the first time his listeners had heard such a public profession of marital harmony, which, moreover, seemed quite irrelevant as part of an apology.

merely shrug it off as a problem of cross-cultural communication. However, the scholar who studies an oral or orally oriented society faces the complex problem of bridging the gap between his own highly literate, "schemata-fragmenting," analytical thought processes and the schematic, paratactic patterns of the people he is studying, who, unaccustomed to reifying speech, cannot detach themselves from what they know but rather identify with it.

The situation is very different for the literate foreigner who learns to speak standard Indonesian,[2] which is a learned language of writing and the print-based medium of communication of a modern state.[3] With certain mental adjustments, it is true, he is able to express himself and be understood on most subjects of his own choosing by a relatively large section of the populace. The question of what proportion of Indonesian thought processes is based on Western influence and how much is the natural consequence of the development of mass literacy is irrelevant here, and cannot be answered anyway, for Indonesian literacy did not develop in a vacuum. The problem for the scholar who wishes to assimilate to a radically oral or orally oriented society, however, is that he must learn a very different way of looking at the world: he must acquire the thought patterns of the oral mind; he must deny himself the opportunity of being able to discuss many things; it must become natural for him not to think in abstract or analytical terms. The scholar usually has neither the time nor the inclination to assimilate in this way; indeed, paradoxically, his constant need to analyze militates against his being able to learn to think nonanalytically. On the other hand, the individual without scholarly pretensions who elects for whatever reason to be accepted as a member of such a society and endeavors to assimilate to it does not automatically acquire the ability of interpreting his experiences for the world of scholarship. My own experience in such a situation is that one tends to develop two personae, which are to a large extent sealed off from each other. Indeed, only when fate decreed that I should attend university after four years on the margins of literacy in Kelanta-

---

2. And increasingly so, *Bahasa Malaysia,* which is a learned dialect.

3. Indeed, modern, mainstream (i.e., Jakarta) Indonesian society is very much a newspaper culture. One must be a regular reader of the paper merely to keep abreast of the new words constantly appearing in print. Many of these are acronyms, which are particularly characteristic of a print culture. These acronyms are formed by arranging the first *letters* of words in a group, or selected syllables from those words (or a combination of both initials and syllables), into a new word. Such a combination is *gali* (*golongan anak liar*; lit.: "group of wild children," i.e., "delinquents"). So numerous are these acronyms it has been found necessary to produce dictionaries merely of acronyms.

nese society did I become aware of this dual persona, and conscious of the fact that I could switch from one to the other depending upon my audience. Only much later, however, did I attempt to confront the one with the other.

That this is not merely a problem of reconciling the norms of two mutually alien cultures is attested to by the fact that Malaysian Malays and Indonesians from orally oriented backgrounds who are trained to think in the analytical modes of highly literate, visually consuming print-based culture experience a similar problem, though in reverse. However, the fact that many Malays succeed in deeply interiorizing the thought patterns of print culture only after studying in the West again precludes our distinguishing between what in these new modes of thinking and expression is peculiar to Western culture and what is the natural outcome of becoming more highly literate. What can be said, nevertheless, is that those Malays receiving higher education overseas who complain of "cultural schizophrenia" are usually from strongly orally oriented backgrounds. That the use of the vague catchall "cultural difference" is inadequate to explain what is experienced by such an individual on the level of verbal communication is demonstrated by the fact that he does not have difficulty expressing himself to and being understood by an audience of highly literate persons in his own language and society. It is usually when he returns to his oral roots and attempts to fit in and still "be himself" that he becomes particularly aware of being schizophrenic. I would argue that this is felt more by the individual who receives his higher education abroad than, say, in Kuala Lumpur,[4] due to the fact that he is cut off from his oral roots for a much longer period of time. Also, his being trained to think analytically in a foreign language militates against his being able to lapse into the oral patterns of his own language. Even in the case of students who have not been abroad, it is noticeable that those individuals who received their secondary education via the English language medium tend to possess a higher degree of ability to think analytically, argue systematically, and express themselves on an abstract level in *Malay* than students from the Malay stream.

Of course, merely by studying a language which possesses a long-established tradition of print literacy one does not automatically acquire the ability to exploit the possibilities of the learned language and

4. In Indonesia, however, those who travel to Jakarta from the "outer islands" experience something similar.

express oneself on a similar level in one's own language. On the one hand, the student who remains in a strongly oral milieu will tend to speak a noticeably formulaic type of the learned language. Often, the speech patterns are entirely Malay, as in this example, heard in Malaysia: *Q. Anybody inside? A. Body!* Indeed, even the words are often a mixture of Malay and English, producing *"rojak"* (a mixed salad). The use of this "Malaylish" is considered to identify one as a member of the English-educated elite and is felt to be a way of improving one's English! For example: *Kita mau practise kita punya Englishlah* ("We want to practice our English"). Other examples: *Half past eight 'dah, ada news 'kan?* ("It's half past eight; there's news on, isn't there?"); *She want to cut the cake sendiri; dia nak cut sendiri* ("She wants to cut the cake herself; she wants to cut it herself"); *Maybe hujan, better take payunglah* ("It may rain; better take an umbrella").

On the other hand, the mere acquisition of a high degree of print literacy in a foreign language is no guarantee of effective communication of the thought processes made possible by that literacy. The determining factor is the audience: the inability of the audience to think in abstractions or argue in syllogisms, for example, will pose a formidable barrier to the communication of certain ideas. It is not merely that the ideas, objects, or events discussed may be unfamiliar; rather it is the way of thinking about them that is alien. It is thus that the individual returning to Malaya in past decades when Malay print literacy was still in its infancy would find the "literacy gap" too wide to be bridged over a wide range of topics. The disorientation such individuals experienced on returning home was, I suspect, responsible for leading them to the mistaken conclusion that they had "forgotten how to speak Malay." This kind of notion, still occasionally encountered when I first lived in Malay society, earned for such individuals the scornful tag of *"Mat Salleh celup"* ("a dyed Brit").[5]

The question of dialect must also be considered briefly. Obviously, many of the differences in modes of expression stem from the use of various dialects, and are not to be explained away in terms of orality and literacy. On the other hand, the tendency to shrug off all such differences as the result of mere variety of dialect will grossly oversimplify matters and surely hinder us from learning more of the development of literacy in Malay society. Thus, for example, to say that

5. Sometimes this tag was richly deserved, as in cases where such a person might claim to have forgotten how to eat with his hands.

Kelantanese and Perak Malay differ from standard Malay (Malaysian) because they are "dialects" is merely to state the obvious, and reflects the normative attitude of the literate speaker of "standard" speech, which is itself a dialect. Such an observation acquires significance for our present purposes only when it is realized that a considerable number of those differences result from the fact that standard Malay is a learned dialect, which depends for its existence upon writing and print. As I shall argue, many of the features which I identify as revealing an oral orientation tend to be shared in common by the unwritten dialects but are much less apparent in the standard dialect. This helps to explain why, for example, a Kelantanese peasant may be unable to make head or tail of the national news broadcast from Kuala Lumpur, but will have little difficulty communicating with the speaker of another (nonwritten) dialect.

Of course, when we think in terms of speakers rather than of dialects, we see that there exists no simple correspondence between oral/unwritten dialect and literate/standard dialect. Every speaker of standard Malay also possesses a "mother dialect." His level of education and also the nature of his audience will determine the extent of oral orientation in his speech when speaking either dialect. Thus, a literate native of Kuala Lumpur who knows no Kelantanese may be able to make himself easily understood by the peasant who had such difficulty with the analytical language and subordinating constructions employed by the news reader.

The aim of this digression has been to demonstrate why the schematic nature of conversation in the more orally oriented sectors of Malay society has not been immediately obvious to observers, be they Malays or foreigners. As my use of "orally oriented" is intended to emphasize, we are not dealing with a simple dichotomy of oral and literate, but with a whole range of tendencies. Thus, for example, the notion of a clear correspondence between rural/urban and oral/literate ignores the fact that the speech of large sectors of the urban population reveals a strong oral orientation. Similarly, there is no simple correspondence between oral/literate tendencies and the medium employed: not everything that appears in print reflects interiorization of print-based thought; much that is published in Malaysian newspapers, particularly, reveals a strongly oral tendency.

Furthermore, while the Malay who studies abroad is enabled to detach himself from his own milieu and view his language from a new perspective, it seems that the tendency has been, naturally enough, to assume that differences observed in modes of expression all result from the fact that two languages are involved, and thus the possibility that certain of these differences might be explained in terms of varying degrees of interiorization of print in the psyche has not been considered.

If we bear these factors in mind, I believe it is possible to distinguish some of the tendencies in the everyday speech of Malays which may be regarded as typifying either an oral or a literate orientation without giving the impression that there exists "a great divide" between the two. The first indication of oral orientation to be discussed is the use of relatively large schematic chunks.

An examination of the way in which people recount events experienced by themselves and by others reveals that existing "plot patterns" tend to determine the shaping of the account. It might be argued that such a pattern merely reflects "reality," that is, that events might, in fact, really have occurred in that pattern. And indeed, in the case of a sequence of human actions which does conform to a set pattern, we might seem to find ourselves in a chicken-and-egg situation. A good example for our present purpose, therefore, is the account people give of their encounters with ghosts, for here we may assume that events did not occur as told, and we are thus afforded the opportunity of observing how a certain level of expectation may determine if not always the initial perception of an incident, then at least the eventual retelling of it.

A widespread encounter-with-ghost experience concerns the man riding home on his bicycle along a route that will take him past a graveyard. He sees a remarkably beautiful woman at the side of the road and she asks for a lift on the back of his bike. As they approach the graveyard, she gives vent to horrible shrieks of laughter and flies up into a tree. He realizes she is a *pontianak* (in Java, *kuntilanak*), and rushes home terrified. I have heard this incident related on a number of occasions in Johor and Selangor, usually by people who claim to be well acquainted with the individual involved. The incident is also well known in Indonesia.[6]

In Pontian, Johor, in 1960, I was afforded the opportunity of observing how the experience may acquire its familiar shape in the re-

6. For instance, it is said that various individuals have had such an experience near the cemetery in Blok P. Kebayoran Baru, Jakarta, where it so happens, prostitutes are frequently to be seen. The *pontianak* tale will remind folklorists of the American "vanishing hitchhiker."

telling. A man returned home one night on his bicycle looking slightly shaken, and informed his family and a few neighbors that as he passed the graveyard, he had heard a loud cackling sound. Within a short time, in the retelling by others, the incident had acquired its usual form. Initial speculation rapidly led to conviction that the man had met a *pontianak,* and the beautiful woman was made to appear, not out of nowhere, but from the mental pattern, the level of expectation of the hearers. Months later, I heard the typical *pontianak* experience told by a friend of the protagonist in his presence, and was intrigued to note that the protagonist clearly accepted that this was indeed the true version of the incident. While the individual involved may himself perceive such an incident immediately in terms of the pattern, I believe that the experience usually acquires its typical shape in the retelling, whether by himself or by others. The first recounting of any incident or experience often takes the form of a question-and-answer dialogue rather than pure narrative. Initially, the teller may well be inarticulate; his remarks may appear confused. However, certain elements in his remarks will act as cues both to his hearers and himself. Cues in the above account would be: riding home on a bicycle; graveyard; sudden noises; and perhaps even the presence of a woman. These are typical motifs filling the slots of the characteristic pattern. One finds that the questions of the hearers tend to nudge the speaker's account into this typical shape.

A further illustration of how the "plot pattern" shapes the incident is provided by the *mulut masin* pattern. *Mulut masin* (lit. salty-mouthed) is applied to persons whose words are so powerful that whenever they express a hope or a fear that something may befall, it will surely come to pass. The typical pattern features two parties and consists of: (*a*) some slight, real or imagined, of the possessor of the *mulut masin* by the second party; (*b*) a hope or fear expressed by the former; (*c*) separation of the two; (*d*) the realization of the hope or fear to the detriment of the second party.

A specific manifestation of this pattern is the following: In 1962, an individual was about to drive a jeep from Lemal to Tok Uban (both in Pasir Mas, Kelantan). A party of about eight people, including a prominent *haji* from the *madrasah* (religious school) in Lemal, asked for a lift. Explaining that the jeep springs (being weak) were likely to snap, the driver[7] avoided taking the party. The *haji* expressed the hope

7. Who, incidentally, had neither license nor insurance.

that the driver would be careful near Cical Tinggi, as the bumpy road might cause the springs to snap. The driver set off, and as he approached Cical Tinggi, for no apparent reason the springs broke, and he had to walk home.

This is the account which was told to me approximately ten days after the incident occurred. The account was of particular interest to me as I was the driver, and I knew that my springs had not broken; indeed, nothing at all untoward had occurred on the journey home. However, elements (*a*), (*b*), and (*c*) were more or less as I recalled them. The combination of slight, *mulut masin,* and fear expressed were the cues for those present to perceive the incident in terms of the familiar schema, which, to be complete of course, demanded the introduction of the mishap. Such was the strength of the schematic pull that even though I assured the teller of the account that no mishap had occurred and I could prove it—people in Cical Tinggi had seen me drive by—I found that my version of things was apparently much less convincing than the account molded by the existing pattern.

This specific realization of the pattern is of some interest in that it is not the most common one: I have observed that usually the main cue is an actual mishap. The pattern is then completed by tracing the cause of the mishap and producing motifs to fill the slight and hope/fear slots.[8] I am not suggesting that mishaps are always attributed to the slighting of the possessor of *mulut masin.* There are indeed a number of alternatives. These alternatives nevertheless do tend to contain the common denominator of interdiction and violation of interdiction, of which the *mulut masin* motif may be seen as one of the variants.

These two cases are illuminating in that there is a clear discrepancy between what actually happened (or at least my perception of what happened) and the recounting of the incidents, and this enables us to observe the power of the schematic pull. In the recounting of most everyday activities and experiences, however, such discrepancy is much less obvious; the account seems to accord much more with "the facts," which makes it far more difficult to perceive a schema at work. It would be necessary to observe a large number of happenings, incidents, or experiences of various types, and in each case compare what actually happened (or one's own perception of it) with how others recounted it, in order to see whether set patterns emerged.

8. This often constitutes a major part of the diagnosis by a *bomoh* (folk practitioner) when he attempts to trace the cause of illness or mishap.

It is, of course, much simpler when we are able to begin with a pattern and observe whether and how it affects the perception and recounting of happenings. We do, in fact, have this opportunity. The patterns I am referring to are the plot schemata of tales in oral (and indeed written) tradition. I have observed that these schemata may determine how an incident is perceived, or at least recounted. To illustrate this we may take the example of the numskull tale. In a previous study (1976), I discerned a number of typical patterns in this kind of tale, many of which feature the character Pak Pandir. A considerable number of these tales reveal the pattern of order, separation, misinterpretation of order with possible dire result, return, revelation, reproach. My reason for drawing attention to this is that on a number of occasions when listening to people recount some instance of stupid behavior they have witnessed, I have noticed that their account followed the same pattern. While this case may seem to be somewhat different from the preceding in that all the events actually "happened," it must be emphasized that the same process is still at work. The incident is perceived in terms of familiar schemata. The given pattern enables the observer to make selections which accord with that pattern. As before, in perceiving the incident and/or in recounting it, the teller or his listeners recognize cues which guide him or them into a certain pattern. Furthermore, while speaker and audience are unlikely to be conscious that the shape of the incident as related is determined by a given pattern, they may well become aware of the similarities between their end product and a tale or tales which typify the pattern employed. Thus, for example, I have heard people comment, "Oh, that is just like a Pak Pandir tale."

The account produced by succumbing to the schematic pull of a pattern may appear to coincide with what "actually happened" in another sense: the given pattern may determine not merely how people perceive or recount an event they have witnessed; in matters concerning human activity, the patterns may also be prescriptive, and may determine the course of the activity itself. While this observation may seem to be a commonplace, I would contend that, considered in the context of Malay discourse, it may throw some light on why so many of the descriptions in Malay literature and oral composition have been considered "stereotyped" and "clichéd." I would contend that the use of highly schematic descriptions is not always designed merely to answer the exigencies of oral or written composition for a listening audience by providing conveniently large, prefabricated chunks of easily memorized stylized language. This may be seen from the fact that a description of similar activity in everyday language is almost as schematic. I believe that in many cases of organized human activity, the description also reflects the schematic nature of the activity itself. This may be illustrated by considering the theme of "arranging and holding a wedding." When one hears the events encompassed by this theme recounted by a number of different people, especially in rural areas, one is impressed by the complexity and uniformity of the accounts. For example, a fairly typical description of a wedding in Melaka contained thirty-three distinct stages,[9] commencing with the *merisik* (sounding out the girl's parents) and ending with the *meruntuh balai* (dismantling the wedding "pavilion"). Merely to observe that descriptions of weddings are uniform because they reflect the uniform structure of actual weddings would be fatuous. It would be surprising if they did not. In contending that the patterning of the account reflects that of the activity itself, my point is that the distinctive patterning of the accounts extends down even to the level of specific word choice used in reproducing the speech of the actors featured in those accounts. Furthermore, the formulas used are the formulas which shape the conversation of people actually involved in wedding activities, and those conversations, even when apparently informal, are in fact highly patterned. An example of such a conversation is the *merisik*. Traditionally, this involves an informal visit to the prospective bride's parents by an elderly or middle-aged female representative of the man's family. It commences with the usual greetings and polite preliminary small talk of any visit, which themselves tend to follow fairly set patterns. A typical example[10] would be:

VISITOR: *Assalamu'alaikum! Oi tuan rumah!* (Peace be upon you! Oi, householder!)—Spoken from in front of the house.

HOUSEHOLDER: *Wa 'alaikumussalam! Oh! Cik———! Jemputlah naik!* (And peace upon you! Oh! Mrs. ———! Please come up)—Uttered in tones of surprised delight.

9. Recorded by Abdullah Abdul Majid of Melaka: *Merisik, menghantar tanda, naik belanja separuh, jemput makan, mengumpul waris, meletak kerja, menegak balai, membuat pelamin, membuat rempah bawang, hantaran belanja separuh, hantaran persalinan, persalinan serba satu/dua, balasan hantaran persalinan, melangkah bendul, bayaran mas kahwin, helah lelaki luncur, helah perempuan ganda, berinai kecil, berinai besar, nikah gantung, majlis pernikahan, mandi berhias, nasi adap-adapan, bunga telur, duduk bersanding, jemput besan, makan besan, menanti sembah, datang bertandang, hari bertandang, orang baru, hari mandi-mandi, meruntuh balai.*

10. The following is based upon an account recorded by Mohamed Jan Abdul Ghani of Melaka.

VISITOR: *Tak mengacau* (or *mengganggu*) *pulak 'ni?* (I won't be in
                the way?)—Spoken on entering.
HOUSEHOLDER: *Mengacau apa pulak! Duduklah!* (How could you be in
                the way! Sit down.)—The suggestion that the visitor could
                be in the way must be refuted with a show of indignation.
                One would never say "Well, actually I am rather busy."

The visitor may then inquire after the other members of the household.
The host will offer betel (*Jemputlah sirih*), and remark—if appropriate—that her guest has not visited her for some time (*Lama Cik— tak
ke mari ya*). The guest will say something to the effect that "Everyone
has affairs to attend to" (*Masing-masing dengan hal*).

The serious talk may then commence. The visitor will remark that
an important wish/matter has brought her here (*Datang ini ada hajat
besar,* or *Inipun ada hal besar maka datang*). The following exchange
will involve various allusions to flowers (the girl) and bees (the boy).
Traditionally this might include the trading of *pantun*. The visitor may
say that she hears there is a flower blossoming in this house. If it has
no owner, one would wish to pluck it (*Katanya di rumah ini ada
bunga yang sedang kembang. Kalau belum ada tuannya ingin pula
hati 'tu nak menyuntingnya*). The host is likely to pretend to misunderstand, and her reply will refer to the flowers in the garden. The
visitor will refer to the flower in the house. She may then use another
allusion. For example, "If one has a bird, one should find a cage for it;
it will appear radiant only when hung under the eaves" (*Kalau ada
burung 'tu elok dicarikan sangkarnya, barulah berseri kalau disang-
kutkan di tepi cucuran atap*). The host must then oppose the idea that
the house flower is pretty or fragrant. "It is a jungle flower. What bee
would want its honey?" The visitor must quickly dismiss such a view.
"What bee would not desire the honey of this flower? There is indeed
a bee which has such a wish. Let us make a long story short (*pendek-
kan kata, simpulkan pendapat*); let us match the flower with the
bee. . . ." The host must maintain the ethos of humility with sentiments such as "The palm of my hand is small; I therefore hold out a
tray" (*Kecil tapak tangan, nyiru saya tadahkan*), implying that a large
vessel is needed to accommodate this great good fortune—even though
she may have already decided to reject the suit. The host will then
observe that she must consult with "her (the girl's) father" and "the
owner of herself (the girl)." The visitor is likely to receive this with
aphoristic agreement to the effect that "It is all right to squabble in the
beginning; let us not have sour faces later on. That which is lucid may

be made even clearer. That which is knotted we shall unravel; that which is intricate we shall solve. Let us not find ourselves in a situation where the house has been completed but the chisel can still be heard" (*Biar kita berkelahi dulu, jangan bermasam-masam muka kemudian. Lagi terang lagi bersuluh. Yang tersimpul kita uraikan; yang kusut kita selesaikan. Besok, jangan rumah sudah pahat berbunyi*). The host's request for two or three weeks to deliberate is agreed to, and the visitor pretends to take her leave, perhaps asking at the same time how are the young people of the house, this latter being an allusion to the "intended." The host will, of course, insist that she wait for some refreshment. This will be prepared and served by the prospective bride (if she is at home), the intention being to demonstrate her wifely qualifications to the visitor. The refreshment will be praised by the visitor and complimentary allusions made to their preparer. These compliments will be scorned by the host, her mother. The visit will then conclude with more aphorisms.

The scholars who have criticized the clichés and stereotypes of traditional Malay literature would, one might imagine, reach the conclusion that such accounts are equally as hackneyed after hearing (or more likely reading the transcriptions of) but two or three of them. And yet the mental set which produces such a patterned account is also the mental set which organizes and participates in actual weddings "on the ground." In other words, the activity is no less schematic than the description of it. Indeed, such a schematic description of a wedding recounted for members of one's own community would normally tend to be *prescriptive*, for it is here that the typical is emphasized. It is this, of course, which must be taken into account by the modern reader of such apparently tortuous descriptions in *hikayat*, and underlines the need to consider intentionality. In a *hikayat*, as in a prescriptive oral description, what is given should be typical. One would surely expect a manual on how to organize a wedding to be typical, and one would not think of it as clichéd. The *hikayat* encompassed this function. It seems particularly clichéd to us because it presents such prescriptive material as part of a tale. It may be argued, furthermore, that it is in the nature of ceremony that it should have a fixed form, and a traditional wedding in the West is also a distinctively patterned activity. Again, the difference is not one of kind but of degree; but that degree is quite a considerable one. Not merely the wedding ceremony, but also the matchmaking, preparation, and aftermath are all highly structured. Thus, if, for example, the legendary meeting between Western suitor and prospective father-in-law were to approach the schematic level of Malay matchmaking, one would have to imagine a situation where the father did not merely inquire, "Are your intentions strictly honorable, young man? And what are your prospects?" but put his questions in poetic form and perhaps even chanted them.

I should stress here that I am not at all implying that whenever a Malay describes a wedding he is going to trundle out a long schematic account such as that referred to. As always, intention must be considered. Prescription demands the typical and the patterned. When a Malay returns from a wedding and describes what happened, he naturally takes for granted his audience's familiarity with the typical—although his account will be defined by reference to it—and is likely to pay most attention to the atypical.

We have seen how the task of preserving knowledge in an oral culture necessitates the conservation of wholes. This is achieved in traditional Malay society by employing schematic composition, which militates against the fragmentation of preshaped chunks of knowledge. This use of distinctive patterning is not, however, confined to verbal performance. Many other activities are similarly patterned, and, I would argue, for the same reason: to ensure that the knowledge of that activity is not fragmented and lost. In this respect it is important to note that in traditional Malay society, this distinctive patterning is not merely a feature of *rites de passage* such as weddings, but of everyday activities and technical processes, so that many more activities take on the aspect of ceremony than in the West. I should emphasize that I am not attempting to reduce ritual to a mere device for preserving the knowledge of various activities. Nevertheless, ceremonializing an activity clearly does provide it with a distinctive and memorable shape.

I am not suggesting that there is no need for conservation of wholes in Western society. In the case of technical processes, for example, there is often considered to be but one correct way of doing something, and in a fixed sequence of steps. The difference, however, is that a print society has much more of a choice: whether to conserve or whether to fragment and refine. And the conservation of wholes can be guaranteed by the use of manuals. The oral person must ensure that each stage of a process is clearly delineated and easily retained, for he has no manual to refresh his memory. It often seems to a Western observer, therefore, that many aspects of technical processes in traditional Malay society are not an intrinsic part of the process and might well be dispensed with. In the building of a house, for example, many tasks may appear to be performed in a very roundabout fashion, and every step of the process is accentuated by ceremonial acts.[11] Regardless of the ostensible explanations of such apparently extraneous activity, and acknowledging that such activity may have various functions, I would argue that these activities are an important factor in the preservation of the technical knowledge of traditional Malay society.

I have observed that the descriptions of certain activities reflect the schematic nature of the activities themselves. The activity and the prescription for it reinforce each other and ensure the survival of both. Some qualification is necessary here regarding technical processes. A description in everyday language of house building, for example, would not provide a detailed technical explanation of the process. Such processes are learned by demonstration and imitation,[12] and any verbal explanation will tend to accompany the activity itself. Furthermore, the process often produces a concrete, nonverbal core formula, so that in house building, for example, the basic schema is a house.[13]

In cases where there is no such tangible schema, technical details may be cast in formulaic language. I have observed this particularly in lists of items such as ingredients for rituals, where the use of mnemonic devices facilitates memorization of the various items. For example, in a list of herbs to be used in the *Berjamu* (feast for spirits) ritual of the Malay shadow-play, one hears:

> *c*emara di *c*ita, *j*itung *yang* *r*ampak, *j*erai *yang* *r*indang . . . [The *ch*erished *ch*emara, the *j*itung *which is* leafy, the *j*erai *which is* *l*ush]

where the items to be remembered are the herbs *cemara, jitung,* and *jerai.*

A word of caution is necessary here: I have found that the items in such lists may function as slot designators rather than as indicators of a specific item. With reference to the items in the list above, for example, it is not uncommon for a *dalang* to substitute another herb for one stipulated in the list. A more striking example is a list of offerings for spirits in the same ritual. This includes: *Dadar bertih, tepung kendung, bedak boreh, minyak celak, bunga canga, limau langir, sirih pinang* (omelets and parched rice, various sweetmeats, powder and cosmetic

---

11. See, for example, Yakof, 1975.
12. See, for example, Sweeney, 1972:44ff, 1973:2ff.
13. Compare Havelock, 1971:38.

saffron with oil, oil and kohl, various flowers, limes and other traditional materials for cleaning the body, betel and areca). When one
examines the items which fill these slots, one finds that an assortment
of lipstick, hairspray, rouge, plastic combs, and pomade has taken the
place of the traditional cosmetics mnemonically preserved in the run.

Incidentally, I would draw attention to the many and varied formulaic lists of items included in descriptions of weddings in *hikayat,* and
especially in *silsilah* texts. On the basis of the evidence from the oral
tradition, I suggest that many of the items are also slot indicators, and
it would be unwise to take all the items in such lists at face value. I
would also suggest that awareness of this tendency should alert us to
the danger of accepting uncritically in the context of traditional Malay
literature the view that information in fiction produced as a background (to the action) which makes specific events seem plausible
"must be recognizable as factual by the contemporary reader" (Rockwell, 1974:117). Many of the formulas of the *hikayat* serve as background to the action, but it would be unwise to accept them at face
value. What is factual is that such formulas were a common device in
traditional Malay verbal performance.

Although both rites of passage and technical processes were highly
schematic and ceremonialized in Malay society, with the advent of
mass literacy it was the technical processes which changed more rapidly. The relief from the burden of memorization opened the way to
streamlining the process to the basics needed for maximum efficiency,
and the economic incentive to do this was obvious. And while the
more literate members of society might perceive the advantages of
streamlining activities such as weddings, the organizers of such affairs
tend to be elderly ladies, the most conservative members of the community, for whom adherence to the *adat* and the accruing of prestige
therefrom may well outweigh the advantages of not incurring the
heavy debts associated with such occasions.

A common enough criticism of Malay literature both traditional
and modern is that the characters tend to be two-dimensional cardboard figures which do not speak or act like real people. Of course,
our expectation of even the most "realistic" of novels is not, in fact,
that they provide us with reality, but that the characters will perform
in accordance with the conventions of realism. The creation of this
illusion of reality is not the natural tendency of all men; it is rather a
highly artificial process requiring rigorous selection and careful crafting, and an audience whose mental set has been geared to understand

the convention. In fact, attempts to present unmediated reality, such as the program advocated by Sartre,[14] actually violate the convention of realism. I have drawn attention to the wide disparity between the language of everyday speech and that of written style. In this context, the faithful reproduction in writing of the actual speech of living people becomes not merely boring, but often unintelligible, as I have demonstrated to Malay students by transcribing verbatim conversations and narratives recorded in the language of everyday speech. For those who may think I am flogging a dead horse, it should be noted that the outworn notion of "realism" as somehow an absolute ideal, a universal criterion of good literature, is still espoused by many Western scholars of Malay literature, and has been bequeathed to the Malays themselves.

I am not suggesting that there is anything wrong with using the convention of realism in literature. I am arguing first that realism may not necessarily be germane to a writer's purpose: on the one hand, he may be able to achieve his desired effect only by violating the convention of realism. On the other hand, in a society where writer and audience are still attuned to the stylized oral tradition, the introduction of "realism" will itself constitute a violation of existing conventions. I am arguing secondly that while the modern Malay author may indeed be attempting quite self-consciously to produce "realistic" writing, his ideas of what constitutes "realism" may not accord at all with those of the Western scholar, who consequently still complains of cardboard characters. A not infrequent result of this is that Malay writers and critics pay lip service to the principles expounded by the Western scholars, and level the same criticisms at other Malay writers. Yet in such critics' own literary productions, the characters are often just as stereotyped by Western standards as those of the writers they criticize. The principles have not been internalized or reinterpreted; there is still a tension between what the critic says and what he knows; a term such as "cardboard characters" becomes just one more of the formulas to be used when one is involved in "literary criticism."

Let us now examine the implications of some of these points. In earlier studies, I have drawn attention to character typing in traditional Malay oral performance (1972, 1980), and traditional Malay literature (1980), and I have argued that this is an intrinsic feature of schematic

14. Booth (1961:52) draws attention to the "absolute durational realism" of a British film which followed Sartre's principles by portraying eighty-eight minutes of action in eighty-eight minutes. The film was less than successful.

composition in Malay oral tradition. In order to preserve, retrieve, and even communicate knowledge in an oral society, that knowledge must be cast in a distinctive mold and must be typical. One might conceivably argue that what initially gets preserved becomes typical, but be that as it may, that "typical" becomes the basic schema for the continued preservation of information thereafter. In such a situation, the number of character types which can be handled effectively is necessarily limited by these constraints. In the Malay *wayang,* for example, where the visual immediacy of the puppets is an aid to verbal memorization, one finds about nine basic types.

The advent of writing may relieve the burden of memorization, making it possible for the writer to fragment his schematic chunks without fear of thereby losing the knowledge contained therein. He is thus able to observe human nature more closely and adjust and refine his character schemata. His audience may then be led to perceive their fellow humans with these refined schemata, producing increasingly complex perception of human types both in literature and in everyday life.[15] I am not arguing for a black-and-white distinction between orality and literacy: the oral composer may well juggle with and refine his character types to some extent.[16] My point is, however, that in the transmission of the "mold" used to cast those types, it is the typical which will tend to be preserved, for if the embellishments are not worked into the pattern, they will be lost. My use of the term "embellishment" indicates a further difference: the constraints of medium and audience discussed above discourage the oral composer from violating and fragmenting his schematic core.

The realization of these possibilities is certainly not guaranteed by the advent of writing. We have seen that aurally consumed Malay manuscript literature retained many of the features of oral composition, and the structure of the typical literary "soother-of-cares" tale was no less schematic than its stylized oral equivalent, with *dramatis personae* from a number of clearly defined types, whose appearance and behavior conform to prescribed patterns.

---

15. Thus, rather than seeing one's wife as a Siti Dewi—as did the late *dalang* Awang Lah—one may begin to perceive her character according to the model of, say, Maria or Tuti of *Layar Terkembang* (Alisjahbana, 1937) or even Tini of *Belenggu* (Armijn Pane, 1940). The popular television drama exerts a counter-effect. I have known not a few Malay women sojourning in the United States who have learned to perceive life through the soap opera.

16. See, e.g., Sweeney, 1972:291ff.

Western scholars usually disapproved of these "stock characters," but there was nothing to be done about it, for "Classical" Malay literature was supposedly dead. They pinned their hopes on the "new" literature, which was, they felt, to no small extent their baby. Indeed Hooykaas (1961:53) clearly sees it in these terms: He considers modern Indonesian literature to be the child of a Malay mother and a European father, the mother being the language and the father the European literary spirit. The compartmentalization of approach discussed in chapter 1 tended to obscure the continuity between the old and the new. And so, when the cardboard characters continued to appear, something was felt to be wrong, for the Malays were now supposed to be writing novels, not *hikayat*. There were new character types, to be sure, but they were still types. Scholars were somewhat nonplussed; surely it was now high time for Malay writers to draw upon the rich variety of character in everyday life. This, I believe, illustrates the dangers of studying literature in a vacuum. For the scholars, the problem seemed to be a literary one, a problem of technique. They obviously took it for granted that on the level of everyday experience, the Malay's perception of the complexities of human character accorded entirely with their own. A more intimate familiarity with Malay society would perhaps have convinced them that character typing is not some artificial device peculiar to literature. On the contrary, modes of perception which produce such character types in oral performance and literature are the same modes which determine how members of society perceive one another as fitting into a limited number of types.[17]

The wide disparity between the perceptions of the highly literate and those of the still radically oral segments of the Malaysian populace may be illustrated by the very different attitudes expressed towards Malaysian television drama. A good example is the *"Drama Minggu"* (Weekly Drama), about which critics have frequently been extremely scathing, labeling it hackneyed and clichéd, and bemoaning the usual cardboard or wooden characters.[18] Yet they grudgingly have to acknowledge that it is one of the most popular programs on Malay-

17. It is perhaps superfluous to add at this point that the perception of type as type is possible only from our viewpoint. "Type" is no objective category; it is only the fact that our literary schemata are much more fragmented that causes us to perceive the larger chunks of oral or orally oriented composition as formulaic.

18. See, for example, *The Star,* August 31, 1980.

sian television among the Malay community. And when one investigates the reason for this among those who never miss the program—many of whom will walk half a mile to the home of someone who owns a television set—one finds a high level of consensus that the characters portrayed are remarkably true to life. It appears that the somewhat stilted language and exaggerated acting[19] of such dramas are discounted by the audience as a normal feature of the stylized presentation expected in dramatic performances. The contrast between these types from everyday life and the prince or demigod type of the *hikayat* is sufficiently great to convince the audience that the characters of "*Drama Minggu*" are just like real people.

It is now often said—as here in the words of Goody (1968:61–62)—that a "major emphasis of literate culture" is "the stress upon the individual" and that "on the whole there is less individualization of personal experience in oral cultures." A problem, of course, is that "individualism" is a very subjective term; for example, many Europeans who visit the United States, supposedly the bastion of individualism, are dumbfounded by the uniformity, conventionality, and predictability of American life; and even more so when they read the announcement of a leading San Francisco department store that it is holding a seminar on individualism to "teach you how to become a very unique individual." It seems that a true individualist must conform to a very narrow set of rules! Apparently he is just one more character type. It would be unwise indeed to assume that this "individualism" is an indication of extreme literacy, or that a striking contrast would result from a comparison with a less individualistic, more orally oriented society.

A more fruitful approach is suggested by Havelock's documentation of the separation of the knower from the known in ancient Greece: the task of Homeric man "was not to form individual and unique convictions but to retain tenaciously a precious hoard of exemplars." It could not occur to him "that he has a personality apart from the pattern of his acts." The poetic tradition must be accepted uncritically or else it fails to survive in living memory. "Its acceptance and retention are made psychologically possible by a mechanism of self-surrender to the poetic performance, and of self-identification with the situations and the stories related in the performance." Only when the

19. As when a character, wearing shoes in the house (which is generally taboo in the house of a Malaysian Malay) gazes out of the window, chin propped on hand, and speaks to other characters present with his back to them. Thus was portrayed "contemplation."

"I" can stand apart from the tradition and examine it can there be a self-conscious separation of the knower from the known (Havelock, 1963:198–99). This development is possible only with the advent of writing, which allows the separation of speaker from the remembered word, and relieves some of the burden of memorization, releasing psychic energy which may be used to examine and reexamine what can now be seen as an object (Havelock, 1963:208).

The Malay-speaking world is not, of course, one of primary orality, nor has it been for over a thousand years. Writers of *kitab* literature, moreover, are clearly no strangers to the doctrine of the autonomous psyche. This is evident not merely from the emphasis placed upon the self by Muslim scholars at the very least from the time of Hamzah Fansuri and Nuruddin ar-Raniri, but also from the ability of these scholars to isolate and examine abstract concepts. I shall return to this in the following chapter. My point here is that it is precisely these features which distinguished the writings of the small coterie of Muslim scholars from the great bulk of Malay manuscript literature, which was intended for a nonliterate audience. The introduction of mass print literacy into the Malay world began barely a hundred years ago, and sizable sections of the population remain radically oral in orientation. Even among the more literate members of society, old habits die hard, especially as many of their interlocutors are far less literate than themselves.

Only when the knower is separated from the known can "the self" itself become an object of the knower. It is understandable, therefore, that many members of Malay society are little given to self-analysis: the individual is so much a part of his situation that he is unable to extricate the center of that situation—himself—for the purpose of introspective examination of that self. This might seem to be belied by the Malay usage *tahu diri* (knowing oneself). In the traditional context, however, this does not carry the connotation of knowing oneself as the result of analyzing one's soul and examining one's conscience. It refers rather to knowing one's place in society. It implies that an individual understands, and acts in accordance with, the patterns of behavior appropriate to his station in life. The reactions of the Russian peasants interviewed by the Soviet scholar Luria (1976) to questions about their own qualities are exactly the kind of response one might hear from Malay peasants in a similar context. This reaction is perhaps best typified in the response, "What can I say about my own heart?" The more old-fashioned Malay would not merely be in complete accord with this sentiment; he might even find it difficult to tell a questioner his own name.[20]

Ong (1982:55), commenting on Luria's findings, speaks of the "touching and humane directness" of Luria's informant quoted above. And foreigners have often concluded that the Malay's reluctance to discuss his own qualities is an indication of some innate sense of modesty. Yet the Malay would not see such a response as particularly direct, humane, or modest; rather it would be merely stating the obvious. Judgment of one's character must be based upon one's speech and actions. These are observed much more clearly by others, who are therefore much better qualified to judge one than is oneself. "Knowing oneself" in such a context does not depend upon an internal sense of rectitude derived from the conviction of the individual conscience. It resides rather in apprehending from the reactions of others to one's behavior that one is behaving correctly. Good name is all-important, and good name depends on judgment from outside, a judgment which is based entirely on externals. Appearances are everything. And it goes without saying that this is as true of knowing others as knowing oneself. The ability to analyze oneself is a prerequisite for analyzing the "self" of others. When I know internally that I am right in spite of appearances and the opinions of others, I am much more able to consider the possibility that appearances may lie when I am judging the conduct of others.

In a society which sets such store by appearances as a basis for judgment, the misinterpretation of appearances may well have more far-reaching effects and be more difficult to disprove than in a modern industrialized print-based culture where there is more concern with the internals, with the workings of individual psyches. It is for this reason that *fitnah* (slander), which tends to involve a deliberate misinterpretation of appearances or creation of false appearances, is so feared. Indeed, it is well known that General Nasution of Indonesia announced in 1966 that "*Fitnah lebih jahat dari pembunuhan*" ("slander is worse than murder"). *Fitnah* is a common motif in traditional Malay literature. The Western reader may feel that these accounts of slander are quite unconvincing: the motives of the maligned character seem to be so obviously pure, yet the attempt at slander succeeds so

20. Traditionally, Malays would even "shew much disinclination to tell their own names or the names of their parents, and if thus interrogated, look confused, desiring one of their companions or bystanders to perform this service for them" (Newbold, 1839, II:176). And I have observed this reluctance even today in Patani.

readily[21] and the postulated audience does not appear to be expected to feel any distaste for the characters (usually including the ruler) who believed the slander. The explanation, of course, resides in the fact that when externals form the basis for judgment, appearances are not expected to lie. And when something is actually seen to happen, purity of motive is of little consequence. The breaker of taboos, for example, must suffer, regardless of the reason for the transgression.

The importance of appearances may be illustrated by two examples from my own experience. In 1962, I was working on an irrigation project in Tok Uban, then a very undeveloped area twelve miles from Pasir Mas in Kelantan. Working with me was a Malay clerk about my own age (early twenties) who became a close friend and confidant. One night, en route for home, he came to a ditch rendered almost impassable by the monsoon rains. He encountered a village girl coming in the opposite direction. He assisted her over the ditch and spoke to her briefly. This incident was observed by two local youths and was soon blown up into a major scandal. It was said that the two had been "in close proximity" (*berkhalwat*) and had been caught in the act (*tangkap basah*—lit. "caught wet"). Threats of violence were made against my friend, whom I advised to return to his village near Kota Baru, the state capital, until things quietened down. The outcome of all this was that he married the girl and all was well. My friend was understandably distressed by the affair, but did not feel he had been treated unjustly. He knew that his motives were "sincere" (*ikhlas*), but he felt what really mattered was that they had indeed been seen together.

Often, the only way to counter appearances is with other, more convincing appearances. I, too, was once involved in a similar situation to that just described. In 1960, in Keluang, Johor, I was planning to enter into partnership with an elderly coffee shop proprietor, the father of five children (two girls, three boys), and there were hopes that I would marry his eldest daughter. He slept in the shop, and I shared a small rented shack with the children, including my "intended." Shortly after we moved in, a neighbor called in, told us he was the *pegawai maksiat* ("sin officer"), and informed us that we were committing "close proximity" (*khalwat*). The closest proximity I had enjoyed was, in fact, to clasp hands (*berjabat salam*) with the girl

21. I am not thinking primarily of the stable, schematic *hikayat*, where the plot pattern demands that *fitnah*, like other forms of deception, should always succeed for the tale to develop. Rather, I would refer to works such as the *Hikayat Hang Tuah* and the *Sejarah Melayu*. See also my *Reputations Live On* (1980a).

through the regulation layer of cloth.[22] My solution was to march up to the *imam*'s house wearing a *songkok* (a black velvet cap)—for in those days, the wearing of a *songkok* was one of the hallmarks of the good Muslim. My argument centered on the fact that I could be seen to be a good Muslim; the *imam* himself had observed me attending Friday prayers. It helped, moreover, that my accuser had misrepresented himself: he turned out to be the sin officer's driver. I also argued for my innocence and sincerity of motive, and explained that my being unemployed forced me to share accommodation with my friend's children. It was clear, however, that the *imam* was more convinced by my appearance of sincerity than by my arguments for it.

In an oral society, the great bulk of knowledge is *common* knowledge. Specialized knowledge, too, must be common to the group of specialists in order to survive. Indeed, private knowledge may well be viewed as dangerous, as in the case of the magician; and it is dangerous precisely because it is secret—the content of such knowledge often consists merely of meaningless syllables. This private knowledge, moreover, is not the result of private thought; it is received (as a whole) from a teacher. And while there is of course private thought in an oral society, it will not survive unless articulated in a memorable form. The preservation of knowledge necessitates the conservation of wholes, and a vital aspect of this is the regulation of behavior and speech, which thus tend to follow very distinctive patterns. Indeed, in a milieu where the conviction of the individual conscience has little social significance, the individual's sense of identity depends upon his conforming with the patterns appropriate to his status, age, and roles in society. The nonconformist is seen as a threat to the solidarity of the group, and personal idiosyncrasy is not encouraged (Sweeney, 1980:25ff). It might thus be said that the traditional (i.e., orally oriented) Malay tended to see other members of his society in terms of stereotypes, and took it for granted that he himself should conform to one or more of those types. It is perhaps needless to add that he would not be able to articulate matters in these terms. We should remember incidentally that both "stereotype" and "cliché" are metaphors from print technology.

Knowing one's fellow men, therefore, may be compared to recognizing a character of the Malay *wayang;* we may not be able to recognize the individual character, but the iconography, speech, and move-

---

22. One should not touch the skin of a woman who is not *muhrim* (too closely related to marry).

ments will always enable us to place him in a clearly defined type, which encompasses a relatively narrow range of appearance and behavior. The highly literate individual, be he Malaysian, Indonesian, or Westerner, might well find this somewhat suffocating. One hears Europeans observe that it must be difficult being a Malay, "with all those forms to observe," and many a Malay, after studying overseas, voices his anxiety about not being able to fit in when he returns to his village. The orally oriented Malay, of course, feels none of this. On the contrary, knowing the types and observing the forms enable him to know his fellow men and himself, and afford him a strong sense of security and of belonging. A stranger from one's own society is never really a stranger, and a first meeting with someone is a much less unpredictable experience than, say, for an urban Westerner. One begins with far more assumed common ground, and one may usually predict quite accurately the course of the conversation.

An easily recognizable traditional type in Malay society was that of the *haji/lebai,* who might be identified by his white skullcap and might also sport a small beard. In one of the most popular numskull tales of *Pak Pandir,* these are the two features by which Pak Pandir was supposed to recognize the pious individuals he was to invite to a feast (see Sweeney, 1976:33–34). The *haji/lebai* type would also wear a sarong rather than trousers. A particularly convincing sign of piety would be a bruise on the forehead, the result of constant contact with the floor in prayer. In the mosque at Friday prayers, one would expect to find this type at the front of the congregation. His conversation would tend to center on topics concerned with the hereafter.

This may seem similar to the stereotyping found so offensive by the modern Western liberal. In Malay society, however, this kind of stereotype served and to no small extent still serves as a model. He who wishes to become a pious individual, for example, will emulate the prescribed pattern. And conforming with the stereotype enables recognition of oneself and others as belonging to a specific type.

When I first began to live in Malay society, I found this constant insistence on conforming to externals very difficult to accept, and especially so in the matter of wearing one's religion on one's head. I was regularly enjoined to wear a *songkok.* I clearly still entertained the Western notion that religion should be a private matter of personal conviction. It troubled me, therefore, when pious friends in Johor Baru insisted that we should go to the front of the congregation at Friday prayers. I observed that it seemed hardly very humble to push one's way to the front. They replied that we would obtain more *pahala* ("grace") at the front; "that is where the *orang alim* [the learned and pious] are, and one can be seen." The modern Westerner may find this apparent display of piety highly distasteful. The Malay who insists on such forms would argue that he is showing off his "Islamness," not himself. The accent is more upon solidarity with the group than upon self. In an orally oriented society, constant attention to the patterns is needed to preserve those patterns and ensure the continued stability of society.

When we apprehend the importance of externals in establishing a sense of identity in traditional Malay society, it becomes much easier to understand, and indeed sympathize with, the hostility of many Malays in the late nineteenth and early twentieth centuries toward the idea of wearing Western-style trousers (particularly without a protective sarong) and of allowing one's children to learn English.[23] In such a milieu, the adoption of Western dress and speech would indeed alter one's identity in the eyes of one's fellow members of society.

There has been a slow but sure erosion of the *haji/lebai* type in recent decades. This is not to say there are fewer *haji*s; on the contrary, more people have been making the pilgrimage than ever before. Rather, the type serves as a model for fewer people, and is associated by many in the more urbanized and literate sector of the populace with being behind the times.

This erosion of certain types may be explained to some extent by the growth of literacy, which made possible a higher level of self-awareness and consciousness of personal worth. In the sphere of religion, the new awareness was particularly noticeable in the increasingly analytical and critical attitudes of the *kaum muda* (modernists). On the level of first-hand experience, I was particularly struck by the stark contrast between the traditional *haji* type and individuals such as Yusof Zaki, a Kelantanese writer and publisher, whom I first met in 1961. For him, religion was a matter of one's own heart. The sense of personal identity resulting from self-criticism and self-analysis made it unnecessary for him to maintain a "type" identity.[24] Yet the influence of the type was still apparent from his need to react against it and avoid being typecast by others.

23. See, for example, the *Hikayat Abdullah* (1953:149ff), which roundly denounces such attitudes.
24. Though learned in religious scholarship, and a *haji*, he affected neither the title nor the dress of the type, preferring slacks and a sport shirt.

This change may be viewed in the context of the process of schema and correction: it should be emphasized that unless an individual is privy to the thought processes which produced the correction, the result of that adjustment will constitute for him merely a new schema. Thus, with regard to character typing in Malay society, the appearance and behavior of those individuals whose personal conviction causes them to react against typecasting may, for those who have not experienced a similar change in their way of thinking, become the template for merely one new type; in the present example, the traditional *haji* type is replaced by the modern, trendy *alim* type, where the emphasis is still upon appearances; the sentiments of the Yusof Zakis are echoed, but they have become formulas.

It is clear that while urbanization, increased division of labor and specialization, and other aspects of "nation building" have resulted in more variety of lifestyle, the need for "typecasting," though gradually weakening, is still strong, as evidenced by the appearance of new stereotypes, which usually turn out to be new manifestations of older types. For example, two easily recognizable types in the early seventies were those of "the important official" and "the important official's wife." The male of the species might be recognized by his bush (or safari) jacket and his expensive car. When I began living in Kuala Lumpur in 1970, I became aware that the range of acceptable brands was fairly limited; the typical cars for this type were Volvo and Mercedes. Riding on buses was not for this type. I was informed by my dean in 1970 that my intention of going to Kelantan by bus was not a good idea: "A university lecturer should not be seen on a bus." A newly qualified magistrate in Kelantan who could not afford the desired Volvo reacted with distaste to my suggestion that he might buy a secondhand Toyota like mine, and he emphasized that one could not neglect appearances, for "one must guard one's status" (*jaga taraf*). This type spoke the idiom of "*rojak*," a mixture of Malay and English, and one might predict that casual conversation would revolve in fairly set patterns around matters such as superscale salaries, success on the stock market, golfing performance, and what the P.M. said. The type attached great importance to titles, which were to be seen and heard. The *Tan Sri Datuk Dr. Haji*[25] type of today would quickly be recog-

25. *Tan Sri:* a Federal Malaysian "knighthood." *Datuk:* a state "knighthood." The honorary doctorate is very popular and is always included in the list of titles. The world champion in title length may well be Brunei, where a single official's titles may contain nineteen words. See, e.g., *JMBRAS* 1981: 3, 71.

nized by the Sri Indera Bangsawan Diraja of two hundred years ago, wearing the appropriate style of clothing, using the appointed mode of speech, riding on a particular type of palanquin, and shaded by a certain type of parasol.

When externals are so vital for establishing identity, even a slight misrepresentation of appearances can have a seriously destabilizing effect on society. Traditional Malay society was thus regulated by a strict protocol in matters of apparel, speech, and behavior. The wrong choice of verb when addressing royalty, or the wearing of the wrong color jacket, might cost an individual his head. Today, while impersonation for obviously nefarious purposes is still, hardly surprisingly, a risky matter, type—when status is involved—is regulated much more by money. Thus, the office boy may well affect the dress of his superiors— nowadays usually a safari jacket—but the iconography is flawed when he is seen riding off on a bicycle or a Honda 50cc.

I should emphasize that I have not been attempting to produce a blanket description of important officials. Rather, I am describing a type, which determines the behavior of many individuals, who establish their identity by conforming to that stereotype. If it be wondered why the power of the type should persist among a group that received a Western education, it should be pointed out that colonial education did less than might have been expected to break down the traditional, schematic modes of thought of orally oriented Malay society. Information tended to be apprehended in large chunks; the colonial administration did little to combat this tendency, for the emphasis was upon training rather than education. It was also safer to provide a colonized people with collections of facts rather than to teach them the analytical and critical modes of thinking which produced those facts. Collections of facts thus acquired by rote become mere formulas to the recipient. It was fine for colonized people to echo platitudes about the Western democracies, equal rights, and love of freedom, for example. But if they were to fragment such formulas and examine their implications for themselves, the formulas would soon acquire a hollow ring.

Westernization for many Malays was thus a formulaic kind of Westernization. New dynamic material might be adopted, but it tended to be placed in the old slots. The slots themselves changed much more slowly. One is reminded of the character types in the Malay *wayang*, where a type such as a refined prince or *patih* (officer) may be given modern embellishments but the type is still clearly recognizable.[26]

So far, we have discussed type as a model for behavior and appearance. There are, of course, many negative stereotypes, particularly of people outside one's community, such as Chinese, Indians, Arabs, and Malays of other states. Trengganese, for example, are considered "mean" by Kelantanese, and are expected to inform one that "*Rumah saya jauuuuh*" (My house is ever so far away! I.e., too distant to be visited). These stereotypes, most commonly revealed in the popular ethnic slur, have little effect on their targets; the latter are often unaware of being stereotyped.

Unfavorable stereotypes of members of one's own community may well tend to function as negative models. For example, a woman who becomes a stepmother may well wish to avoid being seen as conforming to the pattern expected of this type. One might imagine that criminals would prefer not to advertise themselves as the criminal type. In fact, however, the stereotype of the villain—well-known from the *bangsawan, wayang,* and popular drama, with exaggerated posturing and nasty laugh—does appear to serve as a model for many violent criminals. A parallel in the West would be a burglar who did in fact affect the striped jersey and black mask of the burglar in the old comic strips. The rhetorical thrust of such behavior is to intimidate one's victims by meeting their expectations of villainy. The reliance on appearances is clearly seen in the recent drive in Indonesia—by undisclosed elements—to rid the country of "recidivists" by ambushing and shooting them. To go by reports of newspapers such as *Pos Kota,* all those found shot had tattoos! The constant formulaic association of "recidivist" and "tattoo" (*residivis bertato*) in the press led many nonrecidivists with tattoos to burn off this new mark of the criminal.

26. See, for example, Sweeney, 1972:56, 1972a:25ff. An interesting example of formulaic Westernization is seen in the embellishments and changes in the "young-man-about-town-in-the-evening" type: in the sixties, the long-sleeved shirt rolled up to mid-forearm, tight pants, plentiful pomade, and *rokok sigaret* (i.e., modern cigarettes in a packet as opposed to palm leaf cigarettes) gave way, to a large extent, to long hair, "hippy" attire (and sometimes *ganja*). The Western flower child traveling through Asia in search of inner truth often appears to have imagined that he had met up with like-minded brothers in philosophy, only to find (if he was perceptive) that the "hippiness" was usually only on the surface, a mere appearance. But that appearance, hardly surprisingly, caused considerable alarm in Malay society; and in some cases this was well justified: the drugs used frequently led to tragic results.

We have seen how a type may gradually acquire negative connotations in the case of the *haji* type. This happens particularly when those conforming to a type become aware that the type was imposed upon them by those more powerful. Peasants, for example, might awaken to the fact that self-effacement and extreme deference to one's superiors, and the philosophy of life that "this world is not for us Malays; we'll get our reward in the next," did not benefit them one jot, and that the social stability ensured by adherence to such patterns was to the advantage only of those in power. This was of course realized by the colonial powers, who even attempted to strengthen the image of the "good peasant."[27] Ironically, the stereotype was undermined, particularly in Indonesia, by ideas of democracy and socialism which managed to filter through from those same Western cultures. As in the case of the modern *alim,* however, the reaction created new formulas: Soewarsih Djojopoespito in her *Buiten het Gareel* (1940), for example, provides a picture of the schematic socialist.

For many women in the West, the patterns of behavior associated with being a "good middle-class housewife" have come to be seen as a negative stereotype, imposed by chauvinistic males. Often, the sympathy Western feminists feel for their apparently submissive Malay sisters is misguided. The Malay wife of the non–ruling class is traditionally a working wife. The Kelantanese woman wholesaling rice with numerous male workers at her beck and call, and perhaps married several times, could hardly be seen as a mere drudge. A glance at the universities in both Indonesia and Malaysia, moreover, reveals far more women in positions of authority than, say, in the United States. In contrast to this, however, there is a type which may be labeled "leisured wife of important official" (or "W.I.O"). The great increase in numbers and visibility of this type over the past three decades in Malaysia would appear to reveal a trend which runs counter to developments in the West. One finds confirmation of this even on the level of details such as styles indicating gender. Whereas many English-speaking Western women now insist on being "Ms." rather than "Miss" or "Mrs.," the opposite trend is apparent in Malaysia: both single and married women were traditionally styled *Cik.* Now, however, the new middle class has opted to follow the old Western practice of distinguishing between single women and married women, who are now styled *Puan.*

27. See Sweeney, 1980:6; and further, Roff, 1974:139.

The leisured W.I.O. is not a new type. However, the growth of a moneyed, urban Malay middle class over the past three decades has enabled many more individuals than before to aspire to be identified with this type. The old slot, furthermore, has been filled with a large measure of formulaic Westernization, involving the acquisition of material goods and the affectation of the external manifestations of Western behavior patterns (the latter having been acquired to no small extent from observation of the lifestyle of colonial officials). It is expected that the *nouveaux venus* will advertise their new status in order to convince the world of its legitimacy. In a society where appearances are so vital, this leads to a considerable amount of conspicuous consumption. As with the "important official" type, however, the range of choice is fairly limited, and patterns of behavior and speech are distinctive and predictable. Gatherings of this type take place in showplace sitting rooms, rather over-amply stocked with expensive and highly visible furnishings; mementos of foreign travel alias shopping trips, such as model Eiffel Towers; and paintings, which usually include the regulation picture of *kampung* house, padi field, and flame-of-the-forest tree, mass-painted in Jakarta.[28] Activities in this venue include coffee mornings and Tupperware and Avon parties. Conversation, carried on in "I-you *rojak*," is highly predictable.

Again, it must be emphasized that this is not a generalized description of officials' wives. It is a stereotype which exists in the mind and serves as a model for many. There are few, perhaps, who would view this type as an object for pity. I would contend, however, that she who conforms to this type is indeed a victim: of a limited, formulaic education, and of the still-widely held notions that a woman who does not have to work is indeed lucky and that her leisured existence is conspicuous evidence of her husband's prosperity. It is clear that increasing numbers of women who have received higher education and are learning to fragment the formulas are unable to endure the lifestyle of the "leisured W.I.O." type.

I have spoken of the typing of people within and without the community. Only in the former case does the type serve as a model. A somewhat more complex situation arises when a person perceived to pertain to an extraneous type is accepted into the community. The example with which I am most familiar is that of the European who

---

28. Such paintings are themselves composed in a highly schematic fashion, being the work of several individuals, each of whom is responsible for a part of each painting: one man paints all the houses, one all the padi fields, one all the trees, etc.

"becomes a Malay" (*masuk Melayu*), that is, a Muslim, and lives in Malay society. In the late fifties, I became aware of the then-current Malay stereotype of "the Englishman." This, again, was not a blanket description of all Englishmen, producing a grotesque caricature; rather it consisted of a number of expected or suspected tendencies, which included the possibility of being "*sombong*" (proud), getting drunk, being too free with others' wives (as evidenced by ballroom dancing), acting fairly, being *kasar* (unrefined)—he might, for example, put his feet on the table, and show anger; it also included being a good and faithful husband (from a woman's perspective) or a victim of "queen control"[29] (from the male viewpoint).

The Malay did not, of course, expect all Europeans to possess these qualities in equal measure. Not all Englishmen were *sombong*, for example; but the expectation is revealed in the warm reaction of the Malay toward the European who showed a little geniality, and was thus adjudged "not *sombong*." And it is not uncommon for a European considered insufferable by his countrymen to gain a great reputation among Malays for being "*baik*" ("nice") merely by affecting a little formulaic geniality.

The European who "becomes a Malay" will naturally be expected to conform to a new set of rules. Traditionally, he was no longer said to be a European. In 1960, I was walking in Segamat with a friend from a nearby village, when an acquaintance of his passed by and inquired about his European friend. My friend's subsequent comment to me was "*Dia tak pandai tengok orang*" ("He doesn't know how to look at people"; i.e., he cannot recognize various types of people). The implication seemed to be that if one can be told by one's appearance, then I should have been recognized as a "Malay" by my appearance.

This does not mean, however, that a European in this situation escapes from the European stereotype. On the contrary, it now becomes a model for him—a negative model where unfavorable qualities are concerned. As with "not *sombong*," it is still necessary to observe that he does not drink. Or if he is seen having a drink, the reaction is, "Well, what do you expect?" On the plus side, an occasional visit to the mosque may well earn him an undeserved reputation for piety. He may imagine that the passage of time will break down the stereotype as people come to know him as an individual. He may find, however,

---

29. These two English words have been combined to produce this Malay phrase implying domination by one's wife.

particularly if his social interaction is with orally oriented people, that even those closest to him still tend to see him more as a type, so that after many years of marriage, for example, a marital disagreement may cause his wife to complain, "But Europeans are good to their wives!"

Earlier in this chapter, I observed that literacy, by relieving some of the burden of memorization and separating the speaker from his words and reifying them, may lead to the articulation of a more refined and complex perception of human nature, both in literature and in everyday life. This might seem to accord with Goody's (1968:62) view that one of the factors causing "greater individualization of personal experience in literate societies" is "the immense variety of choice offered by the whole corpus of recorded literature," and (1968:69): this "individualization . . . had to do with the capacity to extend one's experience through time and space by what one reads, thus providing an intellectual history that is different, often radically so, for each individual in the society." This may be true to some extent of modern Western societies, though it should be noted that one's choices, interpretations, and experiences are constrained and shaped by the conditioning of one's time and place. Certainly, by comparison with the audience of the oral storyteller or reciter, the reader is offered more freedom of choice if only because he can decide when he wants to read, but this does not necessarily translate into variety, for Goody's assumption that "the whole corpus of recorded literature" will offer "immense variety of choice" is not universally valid, as is evidenced by the Malay case. On the one hand, in pre-print Malay society, the advantages of literacy were largely private to the scribe, and the relationship between author and audience produced a corpus of literature containing many features of schematic oral performance, one of which was the prevalence of character typing. On the other hand, the mere acquisition of print literacy does not necessarily result in a sudden increase in variety of choice; and more specifically in the present context, it need not precipitate a fragmentation of stereotype and a richer appreciation of the individual. On the contrary, standardization and proliferation of text made possible by print may reinforce the stereotypes by codifying them.

Controlled experiments are not possible in studying the growth of print literacy, for it is always part and parcel of much wider change, and the economic incentives which promote mass literacy also lead to greater specialization and its corollary, increased division of labor. Concentrating only on literacy leads to reductionism, as may be illustrated by comparing the situation in Indonesia with that in Malaysia. On the level of literature, it has often been commented that Indonesian literature has progressed further than that of Malaysia, and in particular, that the characters portrayed are more realistic and reveal more psychological depth. The explanation is usually held to lie in the fact that Indonesian is more "developed" and better able to deal with abstractions. This might be attributed to the fact that as a print language, Indonesian has been used more widely by more people over a longer period of time. Furthermore, for most Indonesians, Indonesian is a learned language acquired through the medium of print; the patterns learned are those of a written language. Yet while the growth of mass literacy is undoubtedly a vital factor in the breaking down of stereotypes, it is by no means the only factor. This may be illustrated by comparing the effects of urbanization in, say, Kuala Lumpur and Jakarta. The relative homogeneity of the Malay community in Malaysia still allows the newcomer to Kuala Lumpur to operate with his existing set of stereotypes. A different experience has long awaited the new arrival in Jakarta: he finds that the types which served him well enough in Minang, Bali, or Aceh, are of little use to him. He learns to beware of assuming too much from appearances; appearances are no longer absolute. The "fellow Malay" sitting next to him in a train may turn out to be a *haji*, a Jesuit priest, or an organizer of Protestant schools. The fragmentation of traditional stereotypes has long been taking place in Indonesia, and the attitudes and assumptions of Jakarta have, to a large extent, become the national norm. Indeed the obsolescence of traditional stereotypes is implied in the national motto, *Bhinekka Tunggal Ika* ("Unity in Diversity"). Of course, new Indonesian stereotypes have arisen, but appearances are no longer considered absolute. One may say that there is more awareness of type as type.

The dependence of Malaysian Malays on typecasting became apparent to me in 1960, when I twice observed the "misreading" of Indonesians by Malaysian (then Malayan) Malays. On both occasions, it was taken for granted that the Indonesians were Muslims: one of the Indonesians found himself in a discussion which assumed that he, too, would feel uncomfortable eating food prepared in pots which had previously been used to cook pork. Eventually he revealed that he was a Christian Batak! The reaction was, "How can that be? He's clearly a Malay." The other incident involved a Javanese Catholic narrowly escaping arrest during Ramadhan for eating in public.

We have observed that literacy makes possible the fragmentation of character type in particular, and schemata in general. We should beware, however, of assuming that mass literacy will necessarily mean the end of formulaic thinking. It is undeniable that literacy, by relieving the burden of memorization and allowing the speaker to detach himself from his speech, makes possible more contemplative and analytical modes of thought and a sharper awareness of inconsistency. One's givens may be reorganized and readjusted without danger of losing them. Yet the number of people in any society who are privy to the thought processes involved in the reaction against and correction of the existing schemata is relatively small. The growth of mass-literate print culture does not imply an increasingly high level of analytical thought throughout society. For the mass of the populace, the fragmentation of existing schemata provides a proliferation of yet more schemata. Literacy thus offers a greater number and variety of schemata than in an oral society, which must be more conservative of wholes and preserve its schemata in larger chunks.

Again, it would be unwise to assume that all members of a literate print culture take equal advantage of the variety of schemata available. The success of such schematic compositions as the novels of Barbara Cartland indicates that a handful of stereotypes is sufficient to satisfy the literary appetites of millions. Pronouncements on individualism should also be treated with caution. It would be rash indeed to assume that the profundities uttered by those nouveau Californians engaged in raising their consciousness and otherwise relating to and knowing themselves are in fact the product of deep analytical thought and therefore indicate a high level of literacy. All too often such pronouncements are merely formulas echoed by empty and unthinking minds.

Apprehension of experience in terms of a limited number of stereotypes is further encouraged in the United States by commercial television, both in its advertising and programming. The lowest common denominator of taste to which it aspires in order to prosper must include the 20 percent of the adult population functionally illiterate. The result is that the variety of schemata is strictly limited. The glossy finishing, plastic packaging, and technical gimmickry do not conceal the highly schematic structure on every level of composition.[30]

30. One of my students, Jesse Nierenberg, spent a month watching the rerun of "The Six Million Dollar Man" every night. His subsequent paper demonstrated that each episode had basically the same plot. At the age of ten, my daughter demonstrated her grasp of the schemata of one such American television series, even though her mother tongue was not English. Toward the end of an episode, her brother was about to change the channel, when she restrained him, saying that she wished to hear "the last joke."

It is important to bear these considerations in mind when referring to "Western print literacy," for Western scholars of Third World societies often have a very idealized notion of "literacy" in their own society, based upon the standards (real or imagined) of their academic coterie. It is this rarified notion of literacy which becomes the scholar's yardstick in assessing levels of literacy in the Third World society he is studying. What is more, the generalizations made about that society are often based upon a very narrow range of findings, usually obtained in a particularly orally oriented area of the society. In speaking of the greater development of Western literacy compared with, say, that of Malaysia, therefore, we are considering first the extent to which the potentialities of writing have been exploited in the two societies, and second the proportion of the populace able to share in the thought processes involved in the realization of those potentialities.

CHAPTER 6

Write As You Speak: Audiences and Abstractions

A favorite exhortation of English teachers in Britain was (and no doubt still is): "Write as you speak!" The assumption was that the speech of the common man is simple and to the point, and it was felt that writing should reproduce that common speech. This notion originated in the Romanticist reaction against the verbosity of the neo-classical tradition. In fact, the language advocated by the Romanticists was a highly literate mode, made possible only by writing, and shorn of the stylized oral features so typical of the neo-classical tradition.

Considering this maxim in a Malay context is a useful way to introduce one of the concerns of the present chapter—the oral orientation of written Malay—and enables us to demonstrate the futility of insisting that one should write as one speaks in a still orally oriented society. What the Romanticists were actually advocating was: write as you should be speaking, and the way you should be speaking is with the literate patterns of a print society. The application of this maxim to Malay is undertaken in C. C. Brown's *A Guide to English-Malay Translation* (1956): one should write in the language of the *Sejarah Melayu*, which Brown mistakenly believes to be the "true" spoken Malay. The language of the *Sejarah Melayu* is, in fact, very much a written idiom. In one sense, of course, traditional written Malay is similar to the oral enclave of contrived speech: it is a schematically composed, highly stylized mode of speech produced for aural consumption. Unlike the speech advocated by the Romanticists, therefore, it was not shorn of its stylized oral features; it was also very distant from the supposedly simple conversational speech of the common man. The mode of writing advocated by Brown, moreover, was not merely a written dialect quite distinct from spoken Malay; it was the written dialect of pre-print, manuscript Malay culture, and, as we shall see, had his efforts met with success, the continued use of that dialect could only have hindered intellectual development and restricted abstract thought.

On the other hand, if the Malays had attempted to write as they really spoke, the results would have been strange indeed, whether they chose the nonstylized form of everyday conversation or the more elaborate style of *wayang* and professional storytelling. It is clear that the British did not really expect the Malays to write in the language of everyday speech: one need refer only to their practice of having the "shapeless colloquial" language of nonstylized storytelling put into "grammatical prose" by palace scribes. And this was of course wise; the speech of a literate person in a print society may resemble his written style quite closely, because the patterns he uses are literate ones, developed by writing. Especially if raised in a literate milieu, he will have interiorized those patterns from infancy. The speech of oral persons is not so based upon the written dialect, and when recorded and transcribed may be quite incomprehensible. For example, my students in Penang were asked to read one another's transcriptions of the tales they had recorded and had great difficulty in understanding them. An attempt to write in the language of stylized oral narrative would also produce results very different from those envisaged by Brown. It would certainly not be "simple" or "precise." Reliance upon the schema, the use of repetition, and general copiousness—so necessary for communication with a listening audience *in an oral milieu*—produce a style which appears hackneyed and verbose when consumed visually.[1]

Compared with a transcription of stylized oral performance, the language of the *Sejarah Melayu* appears as a model of conciseness; and even the most schematically composed of *hikayat,* such as *Indera Bangsawan,* seem quite terse on the level of word choice. The copiousness of the oral teller is tempered by writing: the scribe still needs to ensure effective communication between reciter and audience, but neither scribe nor reciter is any longer in the rapid-fire situation of the professional teller. However, insofar as the principles of schematic composition were used by teller and scribe alike, one might say that

1. See chapters 7 and 8 for examples.

the scribe still wrote as the oral specialist spoke, or rather chanted. The *Sejarah Melayu*, which attempts to overcome the purely schematic and wrestle with the specific, represents a moving away from the oral tradition; nevertheless, by the standards of print culture, it was still strongly orally oriented. Were the twentieth-century Malay to espouse the language of the *Sejarah Melayu*, he would, in effect, be moving in a counter direction to that taken by the scribe of the *Sejarah Melayu* himself.

Of course, all this might seem to be merely academic were it not for the fact that the pull of oral habits is still formidable in Malaysian and Indonesian society. The battle of the more intellectual poets and writers over the past sixty years to avoid clichés, to fragment stereotypes, and generally confront the schematic has been a fight against oral tradition. Their language is not merely more literary, but more literate than that of the mass of the population. The modern writer may employ the convention of "realism" to create the illusion of "real" speech, but he does not aim to write as most people speak, or as he himself must speak much of the time if he is to be understood. A survey of popular culture, be it writing, film, drama, or song, reveals the still-strong oral orientation of society. If one pauses to examine the lyrics of modern pop music, one finds a form still very close to that of the *pantun* and *syair*. As if to emphasize this to me, as I was writing the notes on which this is based, my neighbor's radio was blaring out formulary sentiments to the effect that

Marilah kita bernyanyi	Let us sing
Irama cinta nan murni,	Rhythm of pure love
Tiada duka nestapa,	There is no sadness
Penawar hati yang rindu.	Soother of a longing heart.

Even in the realm of modern poetry, until quite recently, it was the custom to "declaim" poems in a highly stylized, rhythmical manner, involving a gradually rising tone and a sudden drop at the end of the line. Judging from the efforts of my students in Johor in 1960, and those of my son some years later, much the same rhythm tended to be used for any *sajak*.[2] The purple patch, moreover, is still favored even by highly educated persons. At a university literary club award ceremony in 1980, for example, the vice chancellor opined that "*Bahtera*

---

2. In a personal communication, Ismail Hussein suggested the possibility that the style of declamation originates from the *Bangsawan* (Malay opera). Incidentally, an early description of the "Sumatran Opera" is found in Gibson, 1855:170.

sastra belayar dengan megahnya di lautan semudra" ("The barque of literature sails proudly through the briny deep").

In the following, I shall attempt to examine in more detail this oral orientation, focusing particularly upon the writing of persons from oral backgrounds. To the child of highly literate parents who acquires their speech patterns before attending school, learning to write might seem merely to involve transposing those patterns into orthographic signs. In a milieu where the gap between the spoken and the written is much wider, learning to write entails acquiring a new dialect, which is the problem faced by Malaysian Malay children. And for most children in Indonesia it involves learning a new language. However, the study of vocabulary, grammar, and spelling is but one part of becoming literate. No less important is learning how to supply context and create an audience in the absence of actual listeners.

The loss of context and the need to supply it are perhaps best observed when speech is removed from the human situation in which the words were uttered, and is recorded verbatim in writing. As will be shown, this constituted an important part of the problem faced by my students who found the transcriptions of narrations by illiterate story-tellers largely incomprehensible. Of course, the need to supply context is not limited to transferring something into writing. When relating an incident orally to a person who did not witness it, one must assess how much one's immediate audience does or does not know. This we take so much for granted that we become aware of it only on encountering an extreme example of apparent ineptitude. This may be observed when a person from a small face-to-face community, who, being illiterate, has only first-hand experience of interacting with his fellowmen, is suddenly required to function outside his community. For example, a youth from a remote village in Kedah accompanied his uncle to Penang and then got lost. He approached several complete strangers and asked them, "*Mana Pak Cik?*" (Where's Uncle?). A second example occurs in Clifford (1899:165), where a woman from an isolated district seeks Clifford's help: "It never occurred to her that her words might need explanation or preface of any kind, in order that they might be rendered intelligible." In both cases, the protagonists took for granted that everyone knew who they were; they had never before been in a situation where they had had to explain themselves. An example of the obverse, again illustrating an inability to assess audience, is provided in Emily Innes (1885, II:13–14): when Innes revealed her unfamiliarity with Malay custom, a Malay "volunteered, with an air as if he hardly expected us to believe him, such pieces of information as that in the Malay country many plants grew from seeds, which were put into the ground, and after a time became young plants." He also explained that ducks swim better than chickens thanks to webbed feet.

Fortunately, such examples are not typical.[3] One might perhaps wonder, therefore, why a person who has learned to write a little may have considerable difficulty communicating a piece of news effectively. This may be illustrated by the example of the letters written by a relative in Kelantan. Usually, her letters tended to be mainly formula, always with the stock opening: *Kakanda telah menerima surat adinda dan pahamlah segala isi kandungannya. Kakanda di sini dalam keadaan sehat walafiat dan harap lebih-lebih lagi bagi pehak adinda.* ("I [elder sister] have received your [younger sister's] letter and understand all its contents. Elder sister, here, is in a condition of health and well-being and hopes for even more of the same for younger sister.") There would follow a few statements on purchases, visitors, and things she was sending, concluded with a formulaic closure. On one occasion, however, she announced the death of a cousin with the bald statement: "So-and-so is dead; he died of poisoning." This was frustrating to say the least, for so many questions were left unanswered. None of the hows, whys, wheres, or whens had been provided. This is a typical case, and the explanation lies in the fact that, though narrative is the primal way of relating experience, it does not presuppose monologue but rather dialogue. Narrative in the everyday language of an oral milieu requires an immediate audience, indeed an interlocutor. The initial relating of an incident will tend to take the form of conversation; often, it is related entirely in response to questions from listeners. Then, the bald statement "So-and-so is dead" is a good attention-getter. The audience will play a major role in the shaping of the narrative from then on. Even if a narrator were able to anticipate all the details of interest to her listeners, she would not expect to deliver a monologue to a passive audience.

The writer of a letter must do exactly that. She must attempt to imagine the mood of her reader and anticipate his reactions to her

---

3. At the other end of the scale we have the Minang, whose tradition of *merantau* took him out of the environs of his own society to travel in foreign parts. There he would learn that the modes of speech suitable for converse in his own village were no longer adequate; he would learn to adjust to a variety of audiences. This may well have contributed to the famed *lidah petah* (skill with words) of the Minang.

words. As far as she is concerned, furthermore, that reader is merely a decoder of signs; he does not see her expressions and gestures, nor hear her intonation. Everything to be communicated must be verbalized and then channeled into those signs. Of course, the orally oriented person is unlikely to be conscious of this as a problem; it occurs to her to write only what is available to her in this medium, and traditionally, this involved relying upon the numerous formulary features which governed Malay letter-writing. The postulating of one's audience, for example, was provided for by clear-cut schemata. When reading letters between friends and relatives who one knew to be on the most intimate of terms, one might wonder at the remarkably impersonal tone and sameness of voice until one realizes that the audiences are prefabricated. The formulas used carry with them a certain voice which picks up a particular audience, such as "mother," "sister," or "lover." In the last chapter, we spoke of "typecasting." In conversation, the need to adjust to personal idiosyncrasies produces a certain modification of the type. In letters, the audience postulated by the formulas is pure stereotype.

Letters might well consist entirely of formula. Letters between rajas might often appear to have nothing to communicate: almost the whole letter could well be *puji-pujian* (compliments), a major part of which would be the listing of titles and epithets of sender and recipient. Marsden (1811:337ff) who provides a translation of such *puji-pujian,* was clearly exasperated by the extravagance of these "preambles." It would seem, however, that often the main point of a letter was the *puji-pujian* itself, for it is here that the writer confirms or attempts to establish his relationship and standing with the addressee. A letter may be completely formulaic, moreover, when the writer needs to express only the most generalized sentiments. Love letters, particularly those from anonymous admirers, tended to rely entirely upon formula. A letter I read in 1961 consisted only of protestations that the sender *"Makan tak lalu, tidur tak lena, mandi tak basah," "Hendak mencapai gunung tangan tak sampai," "Bantal berendam air mata"* ("Eating I have no appetite, sleeping I am not rested, bathing I do not get wet," "I would grasp mountains but my hands do not reach," "My pillow is soaked with tears"). It concluded with a formula acquired from a P. Ramlee[4] film: *"Perasaan yang bergelora ini sudah lama terpendam dalam kalbu saya"* ("These tempestuous feelings have long been locked away in my heart").

---

4. The romantic hero of dozens of Malay films.

One of my first impressions of Malay society in the late fifties was that large numbers of young people corresponded with pen pals, contact with whom was made through the pages of magazines such as *Fesyen,* which published their particulars, including "likes," consisting usually of "reading magazines, listening to the radio, corresponding." At that time, dating was still uncommon, and writing to pen pals provided a way of communicating with members of the opposite sex. I was often allowed to read such letters received by friends, and was struck by the remarkable uniformity of the content; the writers depended so much upon formulas that their personal quirks could rarely be detected. The ethos was pure "pen pal type."

In such correspondence, a modest stock of schematic chunks enables even a relatively unschooled person to produce a letter which is reasonably consistent in style. However, when the writer finds it necessary to go beyond the generalized sentiment and deal with the specific, a major disjunction of voice may occur. Interesting examples of this may be seen in the nineteenth-century Kelantanese letters published by Skinner (1965). The splendid ethos assumed at the outset, produced by picking up the voice carried by the *puji-pujian* formulas, seems to us to fall flat when the writer has to deal with particularities. It is also here, where the writer has to transform the colloquial into the medium of writing, that the problem of supplying context and anticipating one's audience becomes acute. Of course, the writer himself may not be aware of any problem; it becomes apparent, however, in the frustration experienced by his readers, as in the account of the relative who died of poisoning.

An opportunity to observe the difficulties faced by an orally oriented person who is forced to verbalize everything he wishes to communicate (even when provided with an interlocutor) is provided by modern technology. It does not, perhaps, occur to the Westerner accustomed to talking on the phone from infancy that a phone conversation differs considerably from a face-to-face conversation, and he may find it strange to observe old Malay ladies absolutely terrified of answering the phone. Gestures, facial expressions, and body language become meaningless, and it requires considerable adjustment for an adult oral person formed in his ways to adapt himself to this. For example, he must learn that he can no longer point out directions. I recall a new office boy at the National University of Malaysia giving directions to someone over the phone concerning the whereabouts of the post office by jabbing his hand vigorously in the direction of the post office and repeating heatedly, "*Sana, sana!*" ("Over there, over there!").

Not only does narrative presuppose dialogue in the sense I have discussed above; the speaker's narrative itself may tend to take the form of dialogue when he describes the interaction between the persons involved in his account. Comparison of the conversations and narrations of Malays at various levels of education reveals that the nonliterate use far more direct than indirect speech when reporting the words of others. Literates may employ direct quotations when it is felt necessary to achieve a certain dramatic effect, or to reproduce a specific tone of voice or an utterance thought particularly worthy of note. Usually, however—and especially when the audience is also literate— reported speech predominates. The use of reported speech requires a certain distancing from the actual words heard, and a measure of subordination and analysis. This is not to say that the oral person uses no reported speech: often the shift from direct to indirect involves merely the substitution of one pronoun; as for example, *Dia kata,* *"Aku tak mahu 'gi ke sana"* (He said, "I don't want to go there") becomes *Dia kata dia tak mahu 'gi ke sana* (He said he doesn't/didn't want to go there). And the traditional preference for omitting personal pronouns wherever possible may mean that the need to make such a distinction does not arise, as for example, *Dia kata tak mahu 'gi ke sana* (He said, don't/didn't/doesn't want to go there).

It is significant that, even when the use of indirect speech does not involve the speaker in what he might see as unnecessary complexity, he still tends to opt for direct speech. Indeed, it is not unusual for a speaker who reports an utterance then to repeat it in direct speech, as for example, *Dia kata dia tak mahu 'gi ke sana.* *"Malas eh," dia kata,* *"Buat apa aku 'nak 'gi ke sana? Tak mahu eh," dia kata.* ("Can't be bothered," he said. "What do I want to go there for? I don't want to," he said.) For the oral memory, it is important to preserve the dramatic flavor of the event related. The oral person recreates scene after scene, adding event to event, and each event involves actors and action. Speech is a part of that action; the narrator is able to retain the speech by keeping it as action, and reproducing actual utterance. People do not talk to each other in reported speech.

This partiality for the use of direct speech is well illustrated by the tendency of many persons who hear utterances related in reported speech to "redramatize" it. For example, I informed an in-law that "so-and-so feels it isn't necessary to rent a marquee (actually a parachute) for the wedding because it would cost too much." Later, I overheard the in-law telling her mother, "So-and-so said, 'Why rent a tent?' he said. 'We don't need it. It would cost a lot and we can't afford it,' he said." Similarly, one may hear a newspaper or radio report dramatized in the retelling. For example, I recall hearing a person who could read a little relaying news about the 1979 confrontation between the United States and Iran in terms of Carter and Khomeini having a heated dispute: " 'Well,' says Carter, 'you have to hand back those hostages,' he says. 'Why should I? What are you going to do about it?' says Khomeini."

The tendency to turn any account into drama is, hardly surprisingly, particularly strong among *dalang*s. Indeed, even when a *dalang* relates a tale in everyday speech, after he warms up he often omits indications of speaker (e.g., X said, Y replied) and presents the tale as drama (Sweeney, 1972:49ff). As I was known to have collected large numbers of tales, I was often asked by *dalang*s to provide them with materials they could use in performance. These I would summarize, using much reported speech. When I requested a third person to ask the *dalang* to tell him the tale (before the *dalang* had performed it), in the resulting account almost all the reported speech would be transformed into direct speech. It is this tendency which constitutes a major reason for the difficulty a *dalang* faces when attempting to summarize a tale. I met only two *dalang*s who were appreciably more able to compress their material; both of them were literate. It is worthy of note, however, that the written summaries of tales made by both of these *dalang*s for their own use were far more copious than is the norm in modern Malaysian and Indonesian printed materials; both summaries included a very considerable amount of direct speech (which, furthermore, was not intended to be preserved verbatim).

The strong tendency to put actual utterances into mouths is clearly revealed in all types of traditional Malay narrative, and this contrasts strongly with the far more frequent use of reported speech in modern writing. True, one finds large amounts of dialogue in novels, but, as pointed out above, its use is the result of a conscious choice to employ it as a dramatic/literary/stylistic device. We would not expect all the interaction between characters in a history book to be presented as live utterance in the manner of the argument between Carter and Khomeini, as was the usual approach in traditional narrative. In traditional Malay writing, moreover, a character's thoughts and intentions are also usually presented as direct speech. The use of the phrase *fikir dalam hati* ("thought in the heart") is not an indication of an attempt to probe into the psychology of the character. It is rather a device which enables the character to continue talking even when he is alone, and the content of his thought is as externalized as when he is addressing another character. Similarly, the device allows the character to reveal intentions which must be concealed from other characters, somewhat in the manner of an aside, although a character never addresses the writer's audience directly. Even when speech is reported in traditional Malay narrative, the strong pull to present actual utterance is revealed in the way sentences not infrequently revert to direct speech. For example,

> Surat Kyai Demang ada pulak mengatakan mintak tolong seboleh-bolehnya kepada konsil dan kemandur . . . karena hamba tiada tahan hati hamba diperbuatnya oleh Holanda. [Kyai Demang's letter also stated that he asked for help if at all possible from the council and the commander . . . because I cannot stand being so treated by the Dutch.]
>
> (*Hikayat Nakhoda Muda*, p. 149)

The greatly increased use of reported speech in modern Malay/ Indonesian is to be seen as one aspect of the general development away from the orally oriented paratactic style of traditional Malay literature toward a much more subordinating and analytical mode of written composition. The much more frequent use of *bahwa* to introduce and subordinate reported speech is a useful indicator of this shift. In traditional Malay, *bahwa* served mainly as a sentence heading, a function which survives today for the most part only in legal usage as an equivalent of "whereas." As a device for subordinating reported speech in Malay manuscript literature, however, its use was relatively infrequent, but commoner in *kitab* literature than in the palace tradition.[5]

At the beginning of this chapter, I implied that the task of postulating an audience is not confined to the writer. It would be quite incorrect to assume that because the speaker or teller has a "real" audience he has no need to postulate one. For that matter, the writer, too, has a real audience. Anyone, anywhere can theoretically be the real audience of anything written, but this has no bearing on the audience postulated in the text. We may say that the writer, unlike the speaker, does not face his intended audience; in reply it might be said that he is able to visualize his audience in the mind's eye. It can be argued that the writer's

---

5. In the *Sejarah Melayu* (Winstedt, 1938:180), we read: . . . *mengatakan bahwa Raja Legur hendak menyerang Pahang* (". . . saying that R. L. intends to attack Pahang"). On the use of *bahwa*, see Winstedt (1927:161), van Ronkel (1899:52ff), Drewes (1950:104ff).

intended audience may not be the audience actually postulated in his writing; in other words, the audience implied in the text, discernible only from a close reading, may not be that intended by the writer.[6] In fact, however, the speaker's being in the physical presence of his potential listeners does not give him an immediate advantage over the writer. Such a notion results from the assumption that the presence of a listener produces some psychic reaction resulting in immediate spiritual communion with that listener. On the contrary, the speaker must assess his listener and select the voice he feels most appropriate. The presence of that flesh-and-blood listener may help in his choosing and refining that voice. That he is still postulating an audience becomes particularly clear when he miscalculates, as, for example, when his listener feels he is being talked down to. The reliance on stereotype in oral Malay society enables a speaker to bracket his listener with relative ease and allows for a certain economy of voice. The need to postulate an audience becomes even clearer when a speaker addresses a group consisting of a variety of types, as is often the case in storytelling or public speaking. The storyteller does not cater to the individual whims and quirks—as though these could be miraculously understood—of each of his listeners. He assumes the ethos of storyteller. That ethos requires a certain voice, and that voice postulates a certain audience with which he hopes his listeners will be able to identify. Even when he can choose his audience, only his own estimation tells him that this is indeed his intended audience, and should this assessment be accurate, it is still possible that the audience postulated in his performance does not accord with that intended. The notion that because a performance is live it is somehow more "natural" is meaningless. The voice to be used is learned. The tale is presented in terms of tales already told and/or heard. Of course, a performance is no one-way street: the speaker assumes the ethos of teller; those present must assume the role he assigns them—that of storyteller's audience. The teller's opening words—the initial contract—inform the audience of what they may expect, and in particular indicate the voice to which they must attune themselves.

Although both writer and teller postulate their audiences, the major difference is that the reaction of the teller's audience may have an immediate effect upon the course of a performance. They may reject

6. For example, an academic may write a tract intended for, say, politicians or bankers which turns out to be much more in tune with an audience of academics.

the terms of the initial contract: when everyone decides to watch television or go to bed, grandmother may decide not to continue with her tale. They may feel that the teller is not keeping to the terms of the contract. The sentence "People used to be tickled by the strange habits of Charlie-Sharp-Arse" (*Awang Si Punggung Tajam*), as an initial contract, leads to expectations of being amused. When the audience realizes that the teller intends to lecture them on morals, or that he has become completely confused, their reaction may result in a modicum of audience repostulation on the part of the teller.

In view of the importance attached to social cohesion in traditional Malay society, which is also reflected in its literature and oral performance and again seen in the fact that traditional written and oral composition was communally consumed, it is not surprising that a limited choice of voice was available to scribe and teller, which resulted in a relative uniformity of audiences postulated. Reliance upon traditional schemata was essential for the presentation and understanding of a tale. The nature of audience conditions and the composition of that audience—it might include all age groups—made it imperative that the performer did not depart from the patterns which the audience had come to expect. An audience did not expect to be surprised; there was no convention of violating convention. The performer did not have to labor to achieve common ground with his audience, for it was already assumed. In oral performance, therefore, the initial contract offers no surprises. Indeed, it is standard practice for many professional storytellers and *dalang*s to employ the same contract for every tale they present. For example, Awang Lah, the most famous Malay *dalang* of modern times, would always commence with a relatively fixed (i.e., by oral standards) passage to the effect that:

> So ends the telling, so ends the tale of those in the land of Selurah Tanah Jawa, breaking open the *wayang* tale, the account, the story in the (operating) box of Membarum Dewa. Who is it possesses to utter the *wayang* tale? The children and grandchildren of Sirat Chekrawati have broken open the *wayang* tale, the yarn, the story in the box of Membarum Dewa.[7]

7. This translation endeavors to reproduce the "distortions" of this stylized mode of speech (see Sweeney, 1972:63ff). The Malay is: *Maka hilang royat hilang cerita orang dalam negeri Selurah Tanah Jawa, memecah cerita wayang hikayat jitra di bangsal Membarum Dewa. Siapa yang punya berucap cerita wayang? Anak cucu Sirat Cekrawati telah memecah cerita wayang bari jitra di bangsal Membarum Dewa.* The variability of this formula may be seen from Sweeney, 1972:353 & 384.

Other examples of such openings as used by professional storytellers, including both *tabik* and *konon* formulas, may be consulted in Sweeney (1973:25). Indeed, one may take the initial contract so much for granted that one may well miss the beginning of a performance without fear of any surprises. Similarly, with the Malay *hikayat* of the "soother-of-cares" type, the loss of the first page of a manuscript—a not-infrequent occurrence—would cause little confusion to audience or reciter. In such schematically composed tales, the terms of the contract would be taken for granted, and that contract is reinforced throughout the text or performance.

While audience reaction *may* affect the course of a performance, it would be quite incorrect to assume that this is always so. In stylized oral performance, the teller who chants or sings his tale may appear to pay little attention to his live audience. Ismail Hasan of Perlis, for example, performs with his face buried in a cloud of incense, and claims to be in a state of trance. The (usually blind) *Selampit* of Kelantan, similarly, seems little aware of the presence of listeners when he sings or chants. In the few places where he uses dialogue closer to everyday speech, he may permit himself a small smile if his hearers find something amusing. I have six renderings of the *Cerita Raja Budak* by Mat Nor of Bacok, recorded over a period of ten years under varying audience conditions;[8] comparative work indicates that audience response or lack of it has only a minimal effect on the performance.

Such chanted and sung tales might almost be said to have a "built-in" postulated audience, and the course of a performance may be affected by the composition, status, and reactions of those actually present as little as the recital of a written "soother-of-cares" *hikayat* or the singing of a written *syair*. In contrast, the *dalang* of the Malay shadow-play is much more responsive to his audience. Not only is he likely to assess his audience before commencing; he will monitor their reactions during the performance and adjust his presentation accordingly (see further Sweeney, 1972:288 ff). Loud approval of battle or comedy scenes may spur him on to greater efforts and usually causes him to extend them. When most of the audience starts talking, he may find a change of direction is needed. In the *wayang*, moreover, reactions may be framed in most specific terms. A person who feels he did

8. As my presence as a part of the audience would have been a constant, I contrived to have performances given where I and/or tape recorder were conspicuously absent.

not contract to listen to the *dalang* singing all night may remark, "*Ah, nyanyi pula*" ("Gawd, he's singing again"). A feature of the *wayang* which permits this is the screen interposed between performer and audience. The critic would be somewhat more restrained if he suddenly observed the *dalang* glaring at him!

It is this interaction and the ability of the *dalang* to respond which enables the *wayang* to keep up with the times in a way the performer of the chanted or sung tales apparently cannot. Ismail Hasan, the *Selampit* performer of Perlis, is apparently aware of a problem. His solution, however, has not been to alter his chanting style; his tales, mnemonically patterned for survival, have crystallized into a fairly set form which is apparently not to be tampered with.[9] Rather he intersperses his chant with comic routines in everyday speech, which sometimes take over the whole performance. The sudden shifts in voice may have a somewhat startling effect: in the chanting, the voice is distant and impersonal. Indeed, Ismail stresses that he is merely relaying the words, which are channeled through him from beyond.[10] With the sudden switch to everyday speech, an entirely different person seems to materialize before us. And the audience must immediately assume the new role assigned it: we are to keep our distance no longer, but to become the amused and responsive intimates of the speaker.

The chant, song, or rhythmical speech of a stylized performance ensures a certain distance between teller and audience. In a non-stylized, amateur performance, however, the language employed is that of everyday speech, and although the story is set off from the stream of the daily round and the speaker assumes the ethos of storyteller, that ethos, the voice it requires, and the audience it creates will be directly determined by his standing with those present on the plane of the daily round. In other words, his everyday relationship with his listeners will be clear from the interaction between them during the storytelling. Thus, if he briefly takes off the mask of teller in order, say, to press coffee on his guests, ask for a cigarette, or quieten a grandchild, the change of role may hardly be noticed by the audience. Sometimes, the voices may be so similar that the audience may initially

9. Although in fun he will sometimes use his rhyming speech to talk about mundane matters in the course of conversation.
10. See Sweeney, 1973:12ff. It may be noted that a likely model for the introduction of these comic routines is the role of the clowns in the *wayang, Mak Yong,* etc. In *Selampit,* however, these routines are not an integrated part of the chant performance. The contrast between the speech styles, moreover, is not apparently calculated to elicit a specific effect from the listeners.

take the utterances to be part of the tale, as is evident from students' comments on tales they collected. In contrast, the professional story-teller who drops his mask may create quite a jarring effect. For example, when a *Main Puteri* (spirit mediumship) performer suddenly broke off his chant to ask for a glass of water, and when a *dalang* interrupted his narrative to demand that someone turn down a loud radio, there was a very clear break, which some members of the audiences found amusing. In nonstylized storytelling, to the contrary, the exact point at which a person assumes or relinquishes the role of teller may not always be apparent. This important fact is often obscured by the use of the tape recorder: when "record" is pressed, the conversationalist falls silent; a clearing of the throat is heard, and an entirely new voice then intones a formula such as "*Pada suatu hari*," or "*Adapun . . .*". Students of mine who rightly avoided creating such a sudden shift[11] often found considerable difficulty in deciding where to begin and end their transcriptions in order to extricate "the story" from the teller's stream of speech.

The explanation for this is twofold. On the one hand, the speaker may ease himself gradually into the role of storyteller. This is particularly the case when he attempts to make the voice employed convincingly his own; when he merely echoes a voice he has heard, the transition may be more abrupt. On the other hand, a distinction between the initial contract of the performance and the external social contract is often unclear. In literature or stylized oral performance, the external contract—buying the book or ticket, inviting the teller or reciter—is clearly delineated from the initial contract of the "text." In nonstylized storytelling, however, the exchange, say, between grandmother and grandchildren which leads to her telling a tale may itself contain the beginning of the tale which includes the initial contract. It may even contain the main point of the tale. For example, "Yes, the elephant is the strongest of all the animals in the jungle, but he is not the king." "Who is the king of all the animals, Grandma?" "That's Mr. Mouse-deer. He's very small, but he's very wily. He was able to make all the other animals his subjects." "How, Grandma? Tell us about it. . . ."

Although the interaction between teller and listeners in the non-stylized form reveals their relationship in everyday life, this does not mean that a person may tell the same story with equal ease to any

11. They were encouraged to record the whole session or at least wait until the teller had begun to ignore the presence of the recorder.

group of persons with whom he or she has intercourse in the daily round: acquiring the facility to assume the ethoi appropriate for interacting with the various types of his society does not automatically provide him or her with the ethos required to tell tales to all those types. This enables us to demonstrate further that the voice needed to postulate a particular audience is learned from stories previously heard and told. The fact that some tales are told only to certain groups ensures that the voices available to tell those tales are strictly limited. The researcher may be puzzled sometimes when he is told that a person is a good storyteller and yet finds that this is not borne out in the performance. Not infrequently, when Malay students of mine seeking tales of a certain type encountered a person reputed to know a lot of them, they would find the person quite articulate until the question of telling a tale arose, whereupon the potential teller would grin nervously and fall silent. The students' conclusion that the person did not really know the tale was often not correct. The problem was that he or she had never told the tale (or heard it being told) to adults. The only voice she could use would produce a postulated audience of children, and she was too aware of the discrepancy between what she could postulate and her listeners of flesh and blood.

A somewhat bizarre solution to the problem was found by my son's second cousin, a nineteen-year-old rural Kelantanese with little formal education, who was staying with us. One evening, some older guests, also Kelantanese, came to visit, and the talk turned to my interest in Pak Pandir tales. They heard that the cousin knew some of these and pressed him to tell them one. After many protests, he agreed, on condition that he could face the wall while telling it. He explained later that he had been imagining himself telling the tale to his small brothers and sisters. Of course, he appeared to be talking down to his actual listeners: "Well, you know what a *pipit* bird looks like, don't you?"; "A billy goat has a beard, you know." But his listeners, having coerced him, had to accept his conditions and assume the role he had assigned them.

It appears that the difficulty of telling a tale encountered when the audience one is able to postulate does not accord with one's assessment and perception of one's actual listeners is a problem faced particularly by oral people. I have observed from experiments that literate, reasonably well-read persons are able to deal much more easily with the problem. The literate does not depend for his choice of voice upon memory of tales heard or told personally in specific human situations. He is acquainted with a variety of voices from his reading. Furthermore, from his experience of writing, he is familiar with the idea of recounting a tale or event without the presence of actual listeners. When requested to relate such a tale or event by individuals to whom it is not normally told, therefore, he chooses a suitable voice and postulates an audience exactly as he would in writing. He knows, moreover, that there is a tacit understanding between the (literate) listener and himself about what is happening. I have found the presence of a tape recorder useful in demonstrating the difference of approach adopted by oral and literate individuals in such a situation. I am referring not to its function as a recorder of speech but to the effect of its presence as *audience* upon the speaker. The fact that both types may be nervous about being recorded and about subsequently hearing their own voices is largely irrelevant in this instance. The point is that the literate person in this situation tends to "write" the tale in speech. He intends his account to be a self-sufficient whole; he postulates his audience as he would in writing, and the presence of listeners may become but a minor distraction. It is also noticeable that he will tend to provide the kind of context which would not be necessary were he having a normal conversation or telling a tale without the tape recorder. For example, a statement such as "Puteri Hijau lived on that hill over there" with a casual wave of the hand or directional pursing of the lips, might become "Puteri Hijau lived on Bukit Naga, to the south of this village, Kampung Jawa." In contrast, the oral person does not readily appreciate the idea of his everyday speech being lifted out of its immediate context, or of speaking for an absent audience unfamiliar with the surroundings to which he is referring. He aims his tale much more at his actual listeners. This, of course, contributes to the relative unintelligibility of much of the speech of the oral teller when it is transcribed into writing, referred to above. In contrast, the transcribed speech of literate tellers performing for literate individuals and/or the tape recorder[12] is usually much clearer for the reader. My remarks should not, however, be construed to imply that oral tradition is unable to produce an account which does not depend for its intelligibility upon the immediate human situation. Our present concern has been the recounting of tales in the nonstylized language of everyday speech; in stylized composition, which must be presented to a variety of audiences, the presentation tends to be much more verbally[13]

12. See chapter 8.
13. In the *wayang*, of course, there is the visual aspect of the puppets.

self-sufficient: a prerequisite for providing a tale with a "built-in" postulated audience is the ability to detach oneself from a specific situation.

That the literate's ability to postulate a variety of audiences derives from his reading experience may also be illustrated in negative fashion: when he is required to recount a tale for the telling of which no voice is available from his reading, he, too, has problems. Thus, for example, a Kuala Lumpur student asked a literate friend of his, a Kelantanese, to tell him some tales in Kelantan dialect. The Kelantanese was naturally unable to pick up a voice from literature and postulate a reading audience, so he attempted to imagine himself telling the tale to Kelantanese friends. He, too, would have been well-advised to face the wall, for the presence of his friend and the tape recorder constantly distracted him, resulting in a telling which veered strangely between the adding patterns of oral speech and the subordinating patterns and abstractions of literate speech. For example, he found it impossible to maintain the style of

> "Kalau sekala kawan pekong tak rajin tak betul." Bila kena sebutir batu atas kepalanya, pengemis tua 'tu pun lari. Lari, dia 'gi 'nusup congok alik tong sampah. . . . Kena pula atas 'pala pengemis tua itu. "Aduh," katanya, kohor-kohor kuat.

> "Usually, when yours truly lobs one, he don't miss." When he caught a rock on his head, the old beggar ran off. Ran off he did. Ran off and hid behind a garbage bin. Then he caught another one on 'is 'ead, the old beggar did. "Ouch!" he says, louder and louder.

He would, therefore, constantly revert to a literary style such as

> Si pengemis itu pun, bila mendengar sahaja perintah isterinya itu, dia pun teruslah pergi ke perigi itu lalu meminta ataupun memohon kepada ikan itu supaya direstui ataupun dimakbur[14] ikan permintaannya itu. . . . Pada kali ini si nelayan itu menempuh berbagai-bagai kesulitan untuk sampai. . . .

> As for the beggar, no sooner had he heard his wife's command than he immediately went to the well and asked or requested the fish that his request should be granted or fulfilled by the fish. . . . On this occasion, the fisherman experienced many difficulties in arriving. . . .

The problem for the oral person of postulating an audience which is quite disparate from his perception of his actual listeners may be clearly observed when he is required to produce definitions or descrip-

---

14. *Makbur* is a hypercorrect form of *makbul*. In Kelantanese there is no way of knowing from the spoken dialect whether the written form requires "l" or "r" in this context. Ironically, it is here in the literary style that oral orientation is apparent.

tions of common objects. A. R. Luria (1976:86–87) has drawn attention to the apparent inability of illiterates to define even the most concrete things, such as "a tree," and Ong (1982:53–54), commenting on Luria's work, relates this to the "situational, operational" mode of thinking of the oral mind. It is my belief that before accepting the evidence of this inability at face value, we must consider more carefully the questions of audience and intentionality. The oral person's audience is an immediate one. In communicating information, he makes certain assumptions about that audience. The reaction of the Malay to a question when he believes his questioner already knows the answer is revealed in the old saw: "*Sudah gaharu cendana pula*" ("It was sandal wood and now it is eagle wood"), alluding (with assonance and rhyme) to "*Sudah tahu bertanya pula*" ("Already knows the answer but still asks"). A genuine request for information would be seen to merit some effort to explain. For example, a fisherman asked by a visitor from town to describe a certain type of fish trap would quite possibly be able to describe it in exquisite detail. True, he still considers it in an operational context: his model for describing it may well be the process of constructing it; he is unlikely, furthermore, to see any point in confining himself to a description of appearance and omitting an account of the use to which it is put. If he had a specimen to hand, moreover, it would be far more logical to show it than to describe it. But a tree? Such a question would be likely to raise doubts about the questioner's sincerity or indeed sanity.

The ability afforded by a relatively high level of literacy to postulate a variety of audiences in the absence of, or regardless of one's assessment of, actual listeners is a major enabling factor in formulating definitions, where one need no longer be attempting to fulfill a genuine need for information. Rather, one learns the convention of describing things that "everyone knows," which necessitates postulating an audience which has a strong partiality for the logical and succinct, but is quite unfamiliar with the term defined. Malay students, even at university level, often have difficulty in creating such an audience, as may be seen from examples such as "*Cerita lucu ialah satu kumpulan cerita lucu yang merupakan unsur-unsur lucu yang membolehkan orang ketawa ketika mendengarkan cerita-cerita itu.*" ("Comical tales are a group of comical tales which constitute comical elements which enable people to laugh when hearing those tales.") Here we notice how the assumption that everyone knows the meaning of *cerita* and *lucu* ("tale" and "comical") leads to their inclusion in the definition of the terms.

However, merely acquiring the ability to describe something "everyone knows" still does not guarantee success in producing a "definition." We experience life through time, and perceive it as a sequence of events. It is natural, therefore, that the basic way of recounting that experience should be narrative, and this cannot but include the description of things, activities, and institutions. The strength of this tendency is best seen when we are required to curb it. This, of course, happens in school when we are taught to define terms and write "analytically." In producing definitions, we have to overcome the "something-is-when" approach. In describing qualities, institutions, activities, events, and so forth, our perception of them as happenings through time leads to the production of narrative, as in the following translated examples from Malay university students: "A wedding is when two people get married," "Justice is when we act fairly to other people."

However, to satisfy the requirements of a modern education, we must learn to extract "concepts" from their operational situation and freeze them. It is only writing that enables us to remove such items from their context, attempt to assign a fixed meaning to them, and thus formally conceptualize and categorize them at a higher level of abstraction. Of course, the problem of overcoming the "something-is-when" tendency is not peculiar to Malays; it was my experience in Britain that teachers would attempt to eradicate the habit at elementary school level, and a successful candidate in the eleven-plus exam would have conquered it. That so many Malay students have made it to university with the tendency intact is indicative of a still-strong oral orientation.

The persistence of this tendency is hardly surprising: it is only since the introduction of mass, that is, print, literacy involving the widespread visual consumption of writing that the need has been felt in the Malay-speaking world for large-scale formal conceptualizing. Scholars have long commented upon the paucity of "abstract" terms in Malay. For example, C. C. Brown (1956:18) sees this as one of the hallmarks of what he calls "true Malay" in contrast with "modern Malay" or Indonesian (p. 4), which he scornfully dismisses as mere translation; for him, a sentence of Indonesian is "in fact an English sentence with Malay words substituted for English ones" (p. 7). Apparently, Dutch did not count! For Brown, "the average Malay has been hitherto (and long may he continue to be) a *country* man: and true Malay . . . is an ideal country man's tongue" (p. 10). Apparently feeling himself entirely justified in dictating to Malays how they should use their own language—he was, after all, colonial Malay language examiner of Malays in Malaya—he insisted that the style of "true Malay" was that of the *hikayat*. As is clear from his model translations, Brown demanded that the Malay country man continue to employ what was in fact the paratactic style of oral/aural tradition, and denied him the possibility of producing abstractions. And, putting aside Brown's failure to distinguish between spoken and written modes, we may note that his assertions concerning the terseness of traditional Malay style are rather belied by the fact that his Malay passages are over a third longer than the English originals (even though those originals are set in a Malay context).

Teeuw (1955), writing a year earlier, provides a more acceptable view of the situation. Although his remarks are not framed in terms of the development of a print-based culture from that of a radically oral manuscript society, Teeuw is clearly aware of the inevitability and indeed necessity of the changes which produced modern Indonesian. He notes how much longer and more complex sentences are in Indonesian than in "classical" Malay. And even more germane to our immediate concerns are his observations regarding the enormous increase in the frequency of derived substantives of the *ke-an* and *pe-an* types in Indonesian, "words which as a rule stand for what we would call abstract concepts" (1955:12), and which "are hardly found at all in a classical piece of historical prose." While not denying that the awareness of the need for so many abstract terms was prompted by external forces, Teeuw rightly contends that in producing those terms, Indonesian was able to exploit the existing possibilities of the language in a process of "autoproductivity." Teeuw wisely avoids stating categorically that Malay traditionally had no abstract terms. On the one hand, as Ong (1982:49) points out, even "so 'concrete' a term as 'tree' does not refer simply to a singular 'concrete' tree but is an abstraction, drawn out of, away from individual, sensible actuality." And it is clear that there is no simple concrete/abstract dichotomy in traditional Malay composition, be it written or oral. On the contrary, there are many levels of abstraction, and the would-be dichotomizer will realize this when faced with concepts such as *adat* ("custom"), *iman* ("faith"). On the other hand, *Bahasa Jawi,* the Malay of Muslim scholarship, was certainly not devoid of the more abstract terms, as an examination of *kitab* literature quickly reveals. Indeed, I would contend that it was the efforts of the writers of *kitab* literature to convert

Malay into a suitable medium for Muslim philosophy and theology that earned for much of that literature the condemnation of scholars such as Winstedt, who, for example, judged the *Tāju 's-Salāṭīn* to be written in "atrocious" Malay (1958:114). For him, as for Brown, "true Malay" was the aurally consumed *hikayat* created for a nonliterate audience. And even though the British scholars judged the (originally) oral *penglipur lara* tale to be the cream of Malay literature, that judgment was based upon their reading of the adaptations of these tales into *hikayat* form.

Rather than merely asserting that there are few or no abstract terms in traditional Malay, therefore, I consider it worthwhile to examine some of the different options available to the composer of traditional Malay manuscript literature and to the writer of modern Indonesian and Malaysian print literature. With the exception of some *kitab* writing, almost all traditional Malay literature is in narrative form. Havelock (1963:151–52) has argued that in an oral culture, "the entire nervous system . . . is geared to the task of memorization." The various motor reflexes activated were "closely linked with the physical pleasures." "The audience found enjoyment and relaxation as they were themselves partly hypnotized by their response to a series of rhythmic patterns, verbal, vocal, instrumental and physical." Havelock might have written these words about the effects of a performance of the Malay shadow-play. In a previous study (1972:35–36), I wrote that "the attitude of the religious conservatives is still very much against the *wayang,* and the reason often given for this is the mesmerizing effect that the *wayang* and its music are alleged to have on many individuals." "The opponents of the *wayang* . . . speak in disturbed tones of those persons who, 'on hearing the first strains of the orchestra are unable to control themselves further but rush down from their houses to the place of the performance, and sit, almost mesmerized, until the end of the show.' " Indeed, a specific term, *angin,* is used to describe this susceptibility to be moved greatly by the rhythm of speech and orchestra; it implies a capability of identifying completely with the performance,[15] and this may cause the experiencing of intense

15. This effect appears to have also extended to the recitation of written composition, and underlines again the similarity of presentation and consumption between traditional Malay oral and written materials. Gibson (1855:174), describing the reciter of a manuscript and his audience, tells us that the former "rocked his body, he waved his hand; and men and women, youths and coolies, slid off their mats, and drawing near, with swaying heads, and moving hands, kept pace with limb and sympathetic look to the songs of their land, the sagas of Sumatra." One might suppose that Gibson had read Havelock! I am indebted to Milner (1982) for unearthing Gibson.

emotion, which, if not controlled, may result in trance (1972:42). Other genres of Malay oral composition have been the target of Muslim criticism for the same reason. An example is the Kedah-Perlis *Selampit's* performance of *Malim Deman*. This might seem difficult to fathom if we consider only the content of such tales, which appear to be quite innocuous by Muslim norms. My own experience of such reactions in Kelantan and Patani particularly, indicates that it is the effect of the performance which is held to be unacceptable.

That the antipathy of Muslim orthodoxy for stylized oral composition should so resemble Plato's hostility toward the poets is no coincidence: the burgeoning of Islamic scholarship during the European Dark Ages owed much to the legacy of Greek civilization. Greek philosophy was widely translated, studied, and developed. The Platonic insistence on separating the knower from the known, and the recognition of the known as object, reveals itself in the emphasis placed by Muslim scholars upon the power of reason and rationalism. Islam insists that *nafsu* (the passions) should be subservient to *akal* (reason). For the Muslim scholar, a performance which demands that its audience should surrender themselves to its spell smacks too much of *nafsu*. Only by detaching oneself from the performance—an option made possible by literacy—can the *akal* gain ascendancy.[16]

During oral composition in performance, no such possibility for detachment and contemplation in silence of an idea exists either for teller or for audience. As Havelock (1963:167; 1971:48–49) points out, the fact that a performance is itself a series of rhythmically coordinated actions, of praxis, inclines the teller to choose words which lend themselves to a parallel enactment and which can be acted out in the imagination. "This means that the preferred form of statement for memorization will be one which describes 'action.' But acts can be performed only by 'actors'; that is, by living agents who are 'doing things.' This can only mean that the preferred format for verbal storage in an oral culture will be the narrative of persons in action, and the syntax of the narrative will predominate." While actors and actions are easy to visualize—and visualizing is important for effective

16. One might wonder, therefore, why such practices as *wirid* and *tahlil*, which weave a formidable rhythmic spell, should exist in Islam. I would argue that Islamic scholars faced a similar situation to that of Plato. Both were confronting oral tradition. Paradoxically, the fact that Islam should find it necessary to oppose so strongly such surrender to a performance is an indication that such tendencies were still a potent force. The obvious solution was to harness them and channel them into an acceptable form. If there was to be surrender to a rhythm, it should be to one that proclaims that there is no God but God; for surrender to the one God is the basic tenet of Islam.

enactment in the imagination—causes, principles, categories and relationships are not.

These remarks are applicable not merely to Malay oral composition, but also to schematically composed traditional palace literature. We notice, for example, that in the *hikayat,* qualities are always tied to an actor. We hear of a raja who is just, of a country which is prosperous. But we do not encounter a focus upon justice *per se* or prosperity *per se.* An actor is always needed to portray the quality. I am not suggesting that such actors only appear in specific tales, or that it is not possible to present generalized wisdom. As in proverbs, the account of the actors and their actions and qualities need not be tied to a specific human situation or temporal context. For example,

> Raja bernobat dalam alamnya,
> Penghulu bernobat dalam sukunya
> Buapa bernobat dalam anakbuahnya
> Orang banyak bernobat dalam terataknya
> Ayam itik bernobat dalam kandangnya
>
> The raja rules[17] in his world
> The chief rules in his province
> The elders rule among their followers
> The commoners rule in their dwellings
> The fowl rule in their coops

is good for all places and all times. But the form is still narrative, and the actors and actions are still easily visualized. It is only when those qualities or actions can be isolated as entities in themselves that they can become the focus of contemplation and the subject of statements. This, of course, involves the nominalizing of what in Malay may be termed "verbals": verbs and adjectives.[18] In oral tradition, these words are understood from their many manifestations when applied to various actors. Plato, however, sought to isolate the one from the many: the nature of the quality *per se,* and the definition of the quality would take the form of the timeless present. The concern is no longer with what is done or with what aspects may be assumed, but with what *is, always.* (See Havelock, 1963:256ff.)

It might, perhaps, be imagined that Malay, being a tenseless language, could not conceive of the idea of a timeless present. Such a view would be parochial indeed, for the assumption would be that Malay developed in a cultural vacuum, and to accept such a notion

17. Literally: "sounds the royal drum of sovereignty."
18. In this I follow the classification of Asmah Haji Omar (1968).

would be to deny Malay the possibility of absorbing Greek or Muslim philosophy. Malay was the language of Muslim scholarship in Southeast Asia, and Malay scholars were no strangers to the ideas of Plato.[19] Malay Muslim scholarship was well aware of the quality *per se* and the concept of the timeless present. For example, *Wujūd itulah 'ainu 'l-ḥaqq* ("It is Being which is the substance of the Reality") in the *Kitāb al-Ḥaraka*, ascribed to Syamsuddin al-Samaṭra'i (van Nieuwenhuijze, 1945:313); or a negative: *Ḥaq Subḥānahu wa Ta'āla bukan 'irādh* ("The Almighty Truth is not possessed of surface") in *Tāju 'l-Salāṭīn* (Roorda van Eysinga, 1827:30); *Adapun perkara syari'at sendirinya pertama . . .* ("The matter of the law *per se* is firstly. . . .") in the *Sharābu 'l-'Āshiqīn* of Hamzah Fansuri (Doorenbos, 1933:180; al-Attas, 1970:302). Naturally enough, the majority of terms used for abstract concepts in such writing are Arabic. It is particularly worthy of note, therefore, that in Malay *kitab* literature, many words which in traditional palace writings functioned as verbals tied firmly to actors are isolated from such a narration and nominalized. Examples of words thus reified as concepts and subjected to scrutiny are: *berahi* which becomes *yang berahi itu*, as an equivalent of *al-'ishqu*, "passion"; *mati*, which becomes *yang mati itu*, as an equivalent of *al-mautu*, "death" (in the *Sharābu 'l-'Āshiqīn* of Hamzah Fansuri; Doorenbos, 1933:201–2). Also: *. . . bahwa yang tiada itulah dahulu daripada yang ada* (". . . that that which is not is anterior to that which is") in the *Tāju 'l-Salāṭīn* (Roorda van Eysinga, 1827:18). Particularly in the writings of Hamzah Fansuri, we observe how words such as *panas* and *dingin*, usually functioning as verbals[20] are turned into

---

19. Apart from this, however, it would be quite erroneous to assume that the absence of tense in Malay means that the Malay is somehow less aware of the "pastness" or "presentness" of events related, unless of course one insists on taking one's perceptions of what happens in English as absolutes. I am not thinking merely of modern Indonesian or Malaysian; the speech of oral persons speaking their regional dialects reveals acute awareness of what is present and what is past. As stressed above, context is all-important in the speech of oral persons. The scholar who hoists a sentence out of the stream of orality and attempts to analyze it without a knowledge of the human situation in which it was uttered and of the assumptions shared by speaker and listener may well conclude that the sentence is "ambiguous." Or when he takes the nuances possible in English as the norm, the choices offered in Malay may seem very limited. If he learns to think in Malay, however, he becomes aware of the nature of ambiguity in Malay terms. This, of course, is impossible when a language is perceived as a collection of "linguist's sentences," delivered as monologue. Ambiguity becomes apparent from the response of the listener.

20. This is not to say, of course, that words such as *panas* never functioned as nominals. In *Hikayat Seri Rama* (Ikram, 1980:161), for example, we read: *. . . maka panas pun terlalu sangat* ("the heat was too great").

concepts: *Seperti panas lengkap pada sekalian alam . . . Selang panas lagi demikian* ("Just as heat is distributed over the whole world . . ."; "Considering that the nature of heat is thus . . ."); *Satukan hangat dan dingin* ("Unite heat and cold. . . .")(in Doorenbos, 1933:189–90, 59).

The process of abstracting the *per se* from its many contexts is uncommon in traditional court literature intended for communal, aural consumption. And although C. C. Brown (1956:18) does not examine the implications of his findings, he notes that in Malay there are "very few abstract nouns: and I doubt if there is a single instance in the whole of the *Sejarah Melayu* of an abstract noun [by which he appears to be referring mainly to those produced by the use of the *ke-an, pe-an* affixes, which may nominalize verbals] being used as the subject of a verb. In Malay the practice is to state what is done, felt, etc., rather than to describe the result of an action or a state of feeling." The similarity of these remarks to Havelock's findings quoted above is worthy of note. It is only with the advent of print, mass education, and visual consumption of writing that the nominalizing of such verbals to form abstract concepts began to occur on a large scale.

Of course, the isolation of the *per se* in abstract concepts did not result merely in the production of timeless equations. The concepts themselves could also become actors. This is already a common practice in *kitab* literature; for example, *budi hendak menjadi raja, berahi hendak menjadi fakir; . . . Kata budi: "Jangan dilawan"* ("Rationality will become a king, the passions will become a pauper"; ". . . Says Rationality, 'Do not fight.' ") in Doorenbos (1933:201). Now there were two options: as before, one might still focus upon the king or the country, and describe them as being just or prosperous. But one could also consider the quality *per se,* and observe how it was manifested in various ways, to what degree and in specific contexts. Thus, one might speak of the *keadilan* (justice) of this or that raja, the degree of *kemakmuran* (prosperity) of this or that country.

The additional option offered by the use of such abstractions made possible by literacy may be illustrated by the ways in which a person may be said to have a short memory. The oral person might say, *Dia cepat lupa; Dia selalu tak ingat; Dia pelupa* ("He quickly forgets"; "He often does not remember"; "He is a forgetter" [i.e., forgetful]) where the focus is upon the person as actor and his action (or lack thereof). The advent of literacy does not kill off such expressions, but it offers the possibility of isolating the concept of memory and then commenting on its particular manifestation in an individual: *Daya*

ingatnya terbatas ("His memory is limited"). I am not suggesting that
an illiterate will not use this; once it becomes common parlance, he is
quite able to employ it (although he will still feel more comfortable
with the actor-event pattern). I am saying that literacy is necessary to
produce the usage.

Such is the pull of narrative on the human mind that no sooner has
the *per se* been extracted and reified as the one from the many than it
may itself be recruited as an actor and sent on narrative service. The
obvious initial model for this is human characters, and concepts become simple personifications as in the example of *berahi* and *budi*
above. Personification, moreover, is an effective way of introducing
the abstract to the oral mental set. The development in the use of the
abstract in narrative resulting from the growth of mass print literacy is
well illustrated by the prose of Iwan Simatupang. For example, in the
sentence *"Keratasapuan biru di langit malam yang masih muda, me-
nyiramkan kesejukan maaf ke dalam dadanya"* ("The evenly brushed
quality of the blue in the night sky, which was still young, poured the
coolness of forgiveness into his breast") (Simatupang, 1982:62–63),
the author takes the compound word *sapu-rata*—("sweep"/"brush"
and "even"/"level"), which carries the connotation of "sweep clean,"
"cover completely," inverts it to form a trope, turns it into an abstraction, and then makes it the actor in his sentence, the object of which
involves the use of two more abstractions. This comes as no surprise,
of course, to the reader of Iwan Simatupang's other works, of which
the best known is the novel *Merahnya Merah:* "The Redness of Red."

CHAPTER 7

The Adding Mode in Stylized Composition

NARRATIVE SEQUENCE

While Havelock's contention that oral storage of cultural information must take narrative form is convincing, his arguments concerning the activation of the motor reflexes by the rhythmic patterns of the performance are, in the Malay context at least, valid for the stylized form only. The strong pull of narrative is equally evident in the non-stylized form. And although stylized and nonstylized composition reveal considerable difference of idiom—particularly on the level of specific word choice—both employ similar basic principles of composition. Indeed, many of the devices of the stylized form are in fact exaggerations of features of everyday speech. It is necessary to add, therefore, that the choice of the narrative mode for "epic" is surely first and foremost due to the fact that narrative is the "primal way" (Ong, 1977:244) man has to organize experience, and thus knowledge. He perceives himself experiencing events in a certain sequence through time.[1] When he relates his experience, it is in that sequence. And when a speaker contracts with his audience to assume the narrative mode, the

1. Which is not to say that a traditional Malay would articulate it in these terms. However, for our present purposes it is unnecessary to examine the implications of the "revolution of time" (*peridaran zaman*), or to consider the conceptualizing of an abstract "time" in Malay. While oral Malay tradition did not isolate a concept of "time" *per se,* the role of Malay as a learned language of scholarship should not be forgotten. Abstract "time" was familiar to Muslim scholars, and was derived from the same source as the Western concept of time. Here, however, I am merely stating that the Malay sees an episode in life as consisting of events following one another.

listeners will take it for granted that events of the narrative are represented as following one another in the sequence they are related. Without wishing to propound universal rules, I believe this to be true of
both Malay, the language about which I am writing, and English,
which I am using to write about it.[2]

2. It might perhaps be thought that this could safely be assumed. That such a view
cannot be regarded as self-evident is apparent from the fairly recent discussions in
American linguistic circles concerning "iconic motivation." Haiman (1980:533) observes that the most widespread of such motivations "is the iconicity of sequence,
whereby events are described in the order of their occurrence." He draws attention,
however, to Alton Becker's claim—made in an oral presentation—that, in Haiman's
words, "even this kind of motivation is foreign to a number of South-East Asian languages, among them Burmese and Old Javanese. Specifically, he claims that a native
speaker of Burmese will understand that a apparent from series of instructions are [sic] to be followed
in the order given only if sequence is marked by extra grammatical signs: the unmarked
interpretation is one of SIMULTANEITY." Becker (1979a:218) uses the term "narrative
presupposition" to refer to iconicity of sequence. By "narrative presupposition," he
means "the presupposition in English (and other, but not all, languages) that in two
succeeding clauses with past tense verbs, unless otherwise marked, the events referred to
happened in the same order as the clauses. . . . In many languages (e.g., Old Javanese,
Burmese) this presupposition does not hold and narrative order is a marked strategy."
Obviously, a language without tense cannot have "tense iconicity." "Narrative presupposition," by virtue of the wording of Becker's definition, must be restricted to languages with tense, for only these can have "past tense verbs." Does this then imply that
in languages without tense, sequential relations are not assumed unless they are specifically marked? A problem one encounters in responding to Professor Becker's views is
that, for the most part, they were presented orally. Haiman (1980), Errington (1979a &
b) and Zurbuchen (1976), for example, all refer to oral presentations or personal
communications. Professor Becker himself has published little on these matters. Thus,
his definition quoted above was consigned by him to a footnote, and his comments on
sequence in Malay are restricted to a few brief statements to the effect that, "Temporal
order is neither regularly marked nor presupposed, either between sentences or between
clauses, though it may be inherent in some scripts . . ." and "Temporal sequence in
Classical Malay is usually marked by a combination of the two terms *sa-telah* . . . and
sudah" (1979:249–50). These comments are not clear to me. They are open to, and
have been subjected to, a variety of interpretations. Initially, the use of "presupposed,"
read in the context of Becker's remarks on Burmese, seemed to imply that unless
sequential relations are specifically marked, they are not assumed, and the use of such
phrases as *setelah* and *sudah* is necessary to indicate that one incident is represented as
following another. In other words, in the absence of temporal markers, a Malay will not
assume that the order of events related is that of their supposed occurrence. In a
personal communication, however, Professor Becker stresses that this was not his intention at all. Rather, his aim was to argue that the centrality of tense in establishing
textual coherence in Indo-European languages should not be projected onto languages
which do not possess tense, for there is a tendency for scholars to read into Malay texts
the temporal relations of English. However, as my initial interpretation of his remarks
was similar to that of Errington's (1979a & b), who accepts this interpretation as a
given, I consider it worthwhile to point out that in Malay narrative, both oral and
written, in a series of sequentially unmarked utterances relating events, it will be assumed by a Malay—unless there is some indication to the contrary—that the events are
portrayed as occurring according to the sequence in which they are related. My aim in
the present chapter and the next is to examine adding and subordinating style in Malay
composition rather than to demonstrate the existence of iconicity of sequence. Nevertheless, I believe that the data presented will show that the Malay does not have to use

Even a list of events, such as a recounting of one's activities of the day, will tend to follow the sequence of the events as they were experienced; for example, an illiterate Kelantanese, asked to describe what he had done one morning, responded, "*Ah jadi, hamba bangun, 'gi mandi telaga, pakai baju, er 'pas 'tu makan sikit. Pas—er, 'gi kerja sawah*" ("Ah well. I got up, went to bathe at the well, put on my clothes, er and then I had something to eat. Then, . . . er, I went to work in the ricefield"). In a list of activities, the possibility exists, however, of giving precedence to certain of those activities, even though this may throw them out of sequence. The rhetorical effect desired might, for example, incline one to mention first that one prayed or worked before speaking of one's visit to the cockfight, though in fact one went to the latter first. In preparing a program of activities or list of items such as a shopping list, the oral person will imagine a sequence of events. For example, a former (illiterate) servant of my wife's family in Jakarta would narrate to herself the process of cooking the dinner, which necessitated enumerating the various ingredients needed, before setting off for the market. And although the literate has the additional option of writing a shopping list, he shares with her the process of trying to remember where he bought a particular item, or where he lost something, by narrating the events of the trip according to the sequence in which they occurred. And, as observed in the previous chapter, the description of an object may be modeled upon the process of making it, and the recounting of that process will follow the sequence of the steps in that process.

---

temporal/sequential markers in order to indicate that events occurred according to the sequence in which they are related. On the contrary, Malay speech—particularly that of oral individuals—employs *far fewer* such sequential markers than does modern English. Incidentally, one might ask why English makes so much use of the "and-then-and-then" device. Indeed, the simple juxtaposing of events in modern English is not at all the usual style of narrative. The staccato delivery of, say, "He came in, sat down, removed his hat, looked at me in a funny manner" (or in a Cockney dramatic present: "He comes in, sits dahn, takes 'is 'at 'orf, looks at me all funny like") strives for a certain dramatic effect. If sustained for more than a few sentences, however, it sounds bizarre; not so in traditional Malay narrative, oral or written, where simple juxtaposing may continue for much longer stretches. Furthermore, an examination of narrative sequence must surely take into account the use of an adding or subordinating style. With the former, events related tend to follow the order in which they are supposed to have happened more closely than when subordinating devices are used, for the latter allow the order to be violated, as in "He went after he had written the letter." Even when traditional Malay narrative employs subordination, we still note a tendency for sequential constructions to follow that order. For example, the *setelah* clause precedes what happens next. (Of course *sebelum* is an exception.)

A stretch of narrative is always highly selective. An attempt to
relate *everything* that occurred over a stretch of only five minutes in
but one locale would require volumes. The selection is determined by
bringing to bear the existing "plot" patterns, which necessitates the
filling of certain motifemic slots. It should be noted, however, that it is
a convention—and an effective rhetorical device—of Malay storytelling to refer to this selectivity and to pay lip service to the fiction
that a full account would (and that the teller could) include much
more detail in the order of occurrence. For example, *"Dia pun, Daud
pun keliklah, sampai ke rumah. Kita pintas tanjung, tak kira becak-
becak 'tu, kita pintas tanjung sampai ke rumah"* ("So he, so Daud
went back, arrived home. We'll take a short cut here, not bother about
the trishaw and so on, we'll take a short cut [and have him] arrive
home"). This device is most frequently used when a journey is mentioned. Comparison with other tellings of the tale by the same or other
persons usually reveals that nothing of relevance to the tale has, in
fact, been omitted. It is conceivable that this method of treating
journeys in the nonstylized form is influenced by the way such transitions are represented in stylized telling. In the *wayang*, for example,
characters are depicted as traveling by passing them across the screen
several times with orchestral accompaniment. And in the *Tarik Selampit*, a journey usually requires a song (although the words provide
little information).[3] The fact that this feature is absent in nonstylized
telling may create the feeling of there being a gap. In the stylized form,
such transitions may be omitted, but the teller will then feel it necessary to point out that he is abridging the course of events, and specific
formulas exist for this purpose. For example, *Kita pintas tanjung, kita
ambil rantau* ("We cut over the cape, we pass the curve of the river").
Similarly, in nonstylized telling the speaker may tell us that a character
got dressed, "but we needn't go into that; we'll just say he got himself
ready," and we may wonder what there is to abridge in such minor
detail until we realize that in stylized telling, considerable time may be
devoted to the account of a character's donning his attire prior to
momentous action, and relatively fixed runs are used on such occasions. Sometimes, however, reference to abridgment is made con-

---

3. He does not match words against melody: when he sings, the words immediately
become trite, and are often no more than nonsense syllables. The basic narration is
much more monotonous; this is necessary for effective communication. A richly melodic
rendering of a tale would distract the listener from the words and relegate them to a
position of secondary importance. (See further Sweeney, 1980:22.) A similar situation is
found in Italian opera.

sciously to create the impression that the speaker is selecting the most important details from the chain of events. For example, "*Hor, dia masak 'ga-'tu 'ga-'ni; ah tak payah duk royat hak masak 'tu. Kita kira dia hidang nasi*" ("Well, she cooked something or other; ah, there's no need to tell about the cooking; we'll say she served the rice"). The point to be made from these references to abridgment is that they reveal the underlying assumption that events are strung out in time and are to be told according to the sequence in which they occurred, for otherwise, the notion of the shortcut would make no sense. This is also seen from the reactions of the audience and the response of the teller: one may hear questions, particularly from children, referring to actions which have no relevance to the progression of the tale, but which are recognized from the patterns of daily life as being associated with an activity mentioned in the tale. For example, a child may ask, "But didn't she pound the rice first?" The speaker is likely to respond, "Oh yes, but I passed over that."

A further indication of the storyteller's awareness of the necessity to narrate events in the sequence they are supposed to have happened is provided by the Malay *wayang*. When a *dalang* is about to relate or perform a complex tale such as the basic part of his repertoire, the *Cerita Mahraja 'Wana,* he takes time to sort out the various threads of the tale and ensure that he tells them in sequence. He may refer to this process as "*isi*" (literally "to fill," i.e., "to load himself") (Sweeney, 1972:78–79). During the course of the performance, he will begin one move, take it to a certain point, and then suspend it while he picks up the other threads and develops them to the same point. A formula such as *Hilang royat dulu X, timbul tersebut Y* ("The account/telling of X disappears/recedes, the mention of Y appears/arises") is used to this end. The cutoff points may vary from performance to performance, and structurally similar episodes (such as battles against three enemies) may vary in sequence, but the *dalang*'s avowed aim is to relate the events— which are for him *sejarah*, "history"—in the order of occurrence. And this is very clear from his reaction when he inadvertently omits an episode and has to include it at a later point, or when he realizes that he has told something out of sequence: he will endeavor to rectify the situation by providing explanation or weaving in the omitted material in the manner of a "flashback." Furthermore, although the sequence of episodes may vary from *dalang* to *dalang* (see Sweeney, 1972:87), each *dalang* will aver that he is relating events in the sequence of occurrence.

Occasionally, a storyteller may omit an episode or incident which appears vital for an understanding of the tale. The Western scholar who concentrates only on "the text" may look in vain for the logic of the tale, and may be forced to conclude that it "lacks coherence," or that the Malay has no understanding of cause and effect, or that perhaps the Malay does not take for granted that events are related in the sequence according to which they are supposed to have occurred. The scholar's speculations along these lines might seem confirmed if he were able to observe that the audience of such a telling may perceive nothing amiss. For example, a tale collected in Melaka featured a protagonist born with a buffalo's head. Later on in the narration, a princess is courted by a handsome young prince; the protagonist appears to have disappeared, and no reason has been given. The explanation, of course, lies in the fact that, even though the listeners had not heard this particular tale, they were familiar with this plot pattern: when the hero of a tale is born with a grotesque appearance and the tale is clearly not intended to be farcical, the audience will expect that his appearance is but a *sarung,* or "envelope," and that when he gains access to the princess's chamber, he will emerge from that envelope. The audience took this for granted and had not even noticed the omission.

THE ADDING MODE

Of particular importance in the study of narrative progression and of the effects of widespread literacy on traditional Malay written composition is an examination of the methods used to link narrative elements. Comparison of the following two passages with the extracts from traditional composition presented later in this chapter provides us with an opportunity to observe the difference between a subordinating and an adding style.

1. In Alisjahbana's *Layar Terkembang* (1937:41), Tuti comments on the religious practices of modern educated man:

> Tidak peduli ia tiada tahu, apa jang disebut dan diutjapkannja, tapi dalam perbuatan jang tiada diketahuinja, jang oleh karena itu baginja mengandung rahsia itu, diredakannja perasaan takutnja akan rahsia mati jang njata kelihatan kepadanja mengantjamnja.

> He does not care that he has no knowledge of what he utters and recites, but in those deeds of which he has no understanding, which, because of that, contain for him a mystery, he assuages his fear of the mystery of death, which he clearly perceives to be threatening him.

2. Lest it be thought that such complexity was the monopoly of writers using "High" Malay, it should be stressed that popular literature (the so-called *sastra liar*—"wild literature") of the early twentieth century, much of which was written in "Low" Malay, was also capable of achieving a relatively high level of complexity. The fact that "Low" Malay is now regarded as a substandard dialect does not mean that its users were but semiliterate. On the contrary, it had developed into quite a sophisticated literary medium. In Kwee Tek Hoay's *Boenga Roos Dari Tjikembang* (1930:98), for example, an old lady describes an apparition:

> Pada bebrapa tetamoe itoe Oewa tjerita dengen soenggoe-soenggoe bahoea jang orang banjak hormatken *boekannja* satoe gambar, hanja satoe orang prampoean moeda jang tjantik, jang ia liat teges ada berdiri di hadepan itoe gambar, dengen dilipoetin oleh tjahaja terang jang bergoemilang.

> In great earnestness, Oewa told several guests that what the people were paying respects to was *not* a picture, but rather a beautiful young woman, who she clearly saw was standing in front of that picture, bathed in a brilliant glow of light.

We note that each of these passages consists of but one sentence. The ideas contained in them do not merely follow one another. They have been grouped in fairly complex relationships, made possible by the use of subordination, which also includes embedding of some clauses in others. It is writing which *allows* one to "analyze" the content of one's statements in this way before they are externalized, particularly when the constraints of composing for aural consumption have been removed. Once acquired, this ability is used not merely in writing: such literate patterns become part of one's thought processes and are employed in everyday speech. The oral person, on the other hand, tends to use much more of an adding style; idea follows idea, event follows event, with little attempt to subordinate one to another. One may well argue that it is in the nature of narrative, be it oral or written, that event should follow event. Notice, however, how modern "literate style"—both in English and in Malay—discourages the simple linking of sentence to sentence with an adverb and/or conjunction. When being taught to "write as you speak" in an English elementary school, one was discouraged from using the "and-then and-then" style when writing and speaking, and indeed was encouraged to disguise the fact that one perceived the events related as following one another in this way by employing more subordinating constructions.

Evidence of a strong oral orientation is revealed furthermore when a person does not merely use an adding style when writing narrative, but lapses into that narrative adding style even when he is attempting to write analytically or descriptively.

Bijleveld (1943) draws attention to the widespread use of parataxis in the Malay materials he studied, which include written composition, proverbs, *pantun,* and incantations. Indeed, in the penultimate paragraph of his work, he observes—though almost incidentally—that in Malay, the lack of hypotaxis (inherent in the Dutch written language) is linked to the fact that Malay literature is recited. However, his examination of parataxis is limited to its occurrence in the *herhalingsfiguren* (figures of repetition) with which his work is concerned. His explanation for the abundance of these figures in Malay is the Romanticist notion that the primitive has more spontaneity of feeling; the higher the level of civilization the more the feelings are repressed; and it is the person influenced by his feelings who most easily slips into repetition (1943:115). He is thus deflected from a course which might have led him to examine his materials in terms of an oral orientation, and instead applies the accepted distinction of his day: the Lévy-Bruhlian dichotomy between the "primitive" and the "logical-intellectual" or "developed." It is certainly to Bijleveld's credit, however, that many of the features he groups together as "primitive" are those which today we would identify as typical of an oral orientation. Thus, for example, he observes that "the primitive . . . thinks successively, i.e., what first comes to mind is uttered first . . . without first organizing his impressions and enlisting the help of his intellect in putting his thoughts and words in order." On the other hand, "predicative subordination, the linking together of more than one subject or object with one predicate, is not primitive, as it requires the ability to make grammatical abstractions" (1943:11). It is but a short step to the realization that it is writing which is the enabling factor in self-consciously analyzing one's thoughts before they are transformed into sentences.

I have previously (1980:21) drawn attention to Teeuw's observation (1955:12) that sentences in *Bahasa Indonesia* are in general much longer and more complicated than in classical Malay, where parataxis is the rule. In noting that this adding style is typical of oral composition, I referred to Lord's statement (1976:65) that "the poetic grammar of oral epic is and must be based on the formula. It is a grammar of parataxis and of frequently used and useful phrases." It was my contention that the use of the formula and the use of parataxis go hand in hand, that their use is not confined to oral composition, and that their presence in Malay written composition is indicative of an oral orientation. An oral tradition is, to use Ong's phrase, conservative of wholes. On the level of specific word choice, these wholes are the formulas. If these formulas are to survive, they must be linked together rather than subordinated to one another, for subordination would result in their fragmentation and subsequent loss. Of course, our suggesting even the possibility of this in an oral tradition is a projection of the literate mind; for in the absence of writing there is really no alternative to the adding style, so that even when a specific word choice need not be preserved as in much of nonstylized speech, parataxis is still the norm. However, although traditional Malay literature and stylized and nonstylized oral performance all share similar principles of composition—one aspect of which is the use of parataxis—the idioms differ considerably, and this is true of the ways employed to link the narrative units which form a sequence.

STYLIZED ORAL PERFORMANCE

In stylized storytelling, the commonest way of linking the actions in a narrative sequence, whether performed by one or more actors, is simply to juxtapose those actions. For example, a typical passage in the *Tarik Selampit* of Kelantan sounds as follows:[4]

> Tuan Kecil Raja Budak henyal duduk paut sila tarik dulang beremas, buka tengok anak anjing 'ngan anak kucing, capai ambil dulang beremas, lancar seraaang 'kut jendela balik rumah jatuh ke tanah, mampus anak anjing 'ngan anak kucing. Raja Budak pun keluar terbit, "Ya Mahmud pada saya, mu gi ambil Tuan Puteri Selambuk Bunga, wa' terbit padang luas saujana padang, mu gi godam bujur empat puluh lintang empat puluh jalan empat cabang tiga." Lalu Mahmud budak raja berlari masuk dalam istana gi ambil Tuan Puteri. . . .

4. The method of transcription employed in the excerpts from the performances of storytellers in this chapter and the next is basically that used in Sweeney, 1972, 1973. My use of points requires some explanation. Points at the *end* of a word indicate an omission or the cutting-off of an unfinished stretch of utterance. Pauses and hesitation are distinguished by the use of dashes immediately following the preceding word. Points in the *middle* of a word indicate the prolonging of a syllable. In stylized storytelling, this results from the drawing out of the note upon which that syllable is chanted. In the nonstylized form presented in the next chapter, the prolonged syllable is uttered with the intonation of everyday speech. Where the final syllable of a word ends with an open vowel, the vowel is repeated after the points in order to avoid confusion with ellipsis points. Where short excerpts from chanted tales are not printed in lines, a slash (/) is employed to indicate the end of a phrase of the chant. Mere fillers (e.g., *oleh kata*) are placed in parentheses.

Tuan Kecil Raja Budak eased-himself-down[5] to sit, assumed-a-cross-legged-position, pulled the golden tray [toward him], opened [it], saw the puppy and kitten, reached for, took the golden tray, launched it "clang" through the window at the back of the house, it fell to the ground; died the puppy and the kitten. Raja Budak came out-emerged, "Oh Mahmud of mine, you go [and] get Princess Selambuk Bunga, take [her] out to the wide field, the field as-far-as-[the-eye-can-see], you go [and] beat [her] lengthwise forty times breadthwise forty times [at the] four-roads-three-branches." And so then Mahmud the royal servant ran [off and] entered the palace, went [and] got Princess . . .

In a rendering of the tale of *Malim Deman,* recorded in Perlis:

Rasa perut masing-masing rasa belaka, sebenarlah bunting tujuh bulan Tengku...u Si Malam Bongsu...u
Bunting Tengku Malam Bongsu, panggil pula nujum nerus panggil, tujuh orang buka nerus yang ketika, nak tengok atau laki-laki atau perempuaa-aanlah juga...a
Hulubalang pahlawan panggil "Nujum nerus nujum ketika 'engan segera, di balai pesebaaaan agu...ung"
Sampai di balai paseban agung, Tengku Si Malim Dewa pun panggil, "Nujum . . ."

Each of them felt the stomach; all of them felt [it], truly Tengku Si Malam Bongsu was pregnant seven months.
Tengku Malam Bongsu was pregnant; summoned further the astrologers [of] divining, summoned the seven persons to open their divination of auspicious times, wished to see whether male or female also...o
Warriors-captains summoned [them], "Astrologers of divination astrologers of auspicious times, with haste, in the great audience hall."
Arrived at the great audience hall, Tengku Si Malim Dewa summoned, "Astrologers . . ."

Even when one narrative sequence is placed within another, it may not be felt necessary to provide specific linkage; juxtaposition still suffices:

Dia masuk tidur dalam isteri—er, dalam istana isteri tua, bini tua dia, dapat mimpi yang baik rusia molek, wak orang tua lama tiga kali bongkok tiga kali betul masuk menghadap sembah sujud tapak kaki kiri, dia duduk kepala tidur serah keris kecil hulu emas sarung tuasa (tatkala) saruk cincin mata intan bertuah seurat jari manis, diapun kejut jaga leda tidur, bingkas bangun gerak isteri dia tanya khabar, isteri dia kata . . .

He went in to sleep in his wife—er, in the palace of the senior wife, his elder woman; had a dream which was good, of happy intimations; an aged,

5. In the translations of the following excerpts in this chapter, I have attempted to reproduce the repetitions and devices of the originals and achieve a level of intelligibility similar to that experienced by the audiences for which they were intended.

old fellow three times bent three times straight came into the presence, did obeisance, prostrated himself to the sole of the [raja's] left foot; he sat at the head of the bed, handed over a small keris with golden handle silver-gold scabbard; (at the time that) placed a diamond-gemmed ring of good fortune on the ring finger; he was startled-awoke-arose from sleep, sprang up, woke up his wife, asked (her) about it; his wife said...

(Tarik Selampit)

Of course, the juxtaposing of actions does not constrain the teller to relate only events which follow one another. For example, in the following passages, also from the *Tarik Selampit*, contemporaneous actions are portrayed by using the aspect verb *"duk"* (abbr. of *duduk*):

Ah lalu budak dua beradik pun (oleh kata) keluarlah terbit gi duk bergantung di kaki gajah tunggal. Gajah duk makan daun buluh; budak ni duk bergantung dua-dua beradik. Gajah tunggal pun nak tengok budak dua beradik, meranap duduk, angkat belalai, sembah ...

Ah well then the two children brother and sister (as to saying) emerged-came out went hanging onto the feet of the lone elephant. The elephant was eating bamboo leaves; these two children were hanging on, brother and sister. The lone elephant wanted to see the children brother and sister, lowered himself, sat down, lifted his trunk, did obeisance.

Lalu dia pun naik atas sampan kecil lancang beremas, dia pun tiba menuju ke jong kapal. Tuan Puteri Cemara Mas duk nanti dengan air sekendi. Tuan Kecil Raja Budak pun naik atas jong kapal, dia pun (oleh kata) ambil air basuh kaki ga'. Rombak rambut, sapu kaki, pegang tangan, gi 'tak atas kasur tilam permaidani. "Ah ia sungguh duli tuanku ..."

Ah well then he got into the small-boat-golden-barque; he arrived-direction of the junk-ship. Princess Cemara Mas was waiting with a kettle of water. Tuan Kecil Raja Budak got onto the junk-ship; she (as to saying) took the water, washed [his] feet. Undid [her] hair, wiped [his] feet, held [his] hand, went and set [him] down on the quilt-mattress-carpet. "Ah yes, indeed, your majesty ..."

Juxtaposing does not, of course, limit the teller to delivering a series of independent statements, for one statement may become dependent upon another by association. For example: ... *duk tulis seorang gambar; sudah tulis seorang gambar; dia pun lipat-lipat 'buh* ... ("... was drawing a picture; completed drawing the picture; she folded [it and] placed...") indicates completion of the one activity (which may be of relatively long duration) before the execution of the second action. We would translate this using a subordinate clause: "When she had ..." (written Malay: *setelah sudah/sesudah* ...). This usage is also some-

times employed to pick up the thread after a break. For example, in the
Awang Batil of Perlis:

He..i, dia pergi, tepi lopak, dia ng ambil, oh ng ayar, sua tangan, dia ambil
    hirup, dia minum, hilang lapar, a dahaga, ce' ng aya...r
He...i, telah sudah, hilang dahaga, lapar ng ayar, dia capai kayu . . .

He..i, she went, edge of puddle, she got, oh water, reached out her hand,
    she took [and] sucked in, she drank, lost [her] hunger, [and] thirst, sir
    for wate...r
He..i, now she had, lost [her] thirst, [and] hunger for water, she grasped the
    wood . . .

The sections are separated by a long final note, a drumming rally on
his brass bowl, and a *hei*. The *telah sudah* enables him to recapitulate
and serves as an opening formula.

    It should not be supposed, furthermore, that the use of juxtaposing
denies the storyteller the possibility of expressing relations of cause,
effect, reason, condition, and the like. In one sense, of course, merely
being able to follow the plot pattern implies an understanding of
causes and effects; but I am concerned here with explicit mentions of
the ifs, whys, wherefores and becauses. These tend not to constitute a
major element in the purely narrative part of the teller's performance,
which is mainly concerned with presenting a sequence of events, rather
than with providing commentary on or explanation of those events.
However, a wider variety of such relationships between statements is
found in the dialogue between characters, which constitutes a considerable (often the major) part of most performances, for, as already
noted, interaction between characters is usually presented in direct
speech. Of course, much of the characters' speech is itself narrative
when they relate events to one another; similarly, a series of orders,
directions, or intentions will usually follow the pattern of narrative
sequence, as in the commands given to Mahmud in the first example
above. Nevertheless, a considerable part of the dialogue is concerned
with the conditional, with reasons for action, and so on. For example
(from the *Tarik Selampit*): *Tak 'leh apa satu ta' apalah; patik mari
pagi-pagi esok tuanku nak beri gapa-gapa berilah.* We might translate
this: "If I don't get anything, it doesn't matter; I'll be coming early
tomorrow morning. If you want to give me something then, you can."
More literally, "Cannot get anything, doesn't matter; I come early
tomorrow morning, Highness wants to give something, give." Or:
Jangan dibuat ia tak ia begitu budaknya lari. "Don't treat them in

such an unpredictable way or the children will run away." More literally: "Let not be done yes no yes like that the children run." Examples of juxtaposing to provide reasons: *'Dah tuanku tak 'sir, patik nak balik dah.* "As Your Majesty is unwilling, I'm going back." More literally: "Already Majesty does not want, servant intends to return already." Many instances may also be juxtaposed in English: *Mata kelabu 'dah, tak 'leh 'nulis:* "My eyes have become dim; I cannot write."

However, juxtaposing is not the only way to indicate all such relationships. Subordinate constructions are created by the use of certain words, not all of which are found in the written dialect. Thus, for example, in Kelantan, *muga* ("thing") may function with the sense of "due to the fact that" (see Sweeney, 1972:342, 415); for instance: *tak tahu wak, muga saya tak biasa* ("I don't know, for I'm unfamiliar . . ."). Subordinate constructions are also created using words shared in common with the written dialect. Of these, by far the most common is *kalau* ("if"). I am unable to provide the precise rates of frequency for the use of the various "subordinating words" in all genres of stylized Malay storytelling but have established fairly exact figures for a sample of such words in the *Tarik Selampit* and *Wayang Kulit* of Kelantan. The overwhelming majority of these constructions occur in the dialogue rather than in the narrative. A five-hour performance of the *Tarik Selampit* revealed the following figures. The first number indicates how many times a word was used in dialogue, the second, its frequency in narrative: *kalau* (if): 37, 0; *kalau basa* (if it be the case that): 10, 1; *'ka* (abbr. *jika,* "if"): 8, 0; *sebab* (because): 3, 0; *kerana* (because): 13, 1; *muga* (in view of the fact that): 4, 0. In a three-hour performance of the *wayang,* the following figures were obtained: *kalau:* 57, 0; *kalau basa:* 12, 0; *'ka:* 1, 0; *sebab:* 5, 1; *kerana:* 26, 5.[6]

Compared with the instances of "dependence by association" resulting from juxtaposing, the use of subordinating constructions is

6. We may also note the use of *kalau begitu* (15, 2), a phrase which merely carries the connotation of "That being the case," and does not create a condition. I should emphasize that the above is only a sample. Other subordinations involve the use of *pada . . . baik . . .* ("rather than . . . better that . . ."); *jangan ke . . .* ("so far from . . ."); *asal* ("so long as . . ."); and clauses following words such as "know," e.g., *dia tahu kita mari* ("He knows we are coming").

It is perhaps necessary to mention that my apparently interchangeable use of "subordinating" and "subordinate," when applied to "construction," is intended to keep in mind the active and passive aspects of the same entity. "Subordinating" contrasts with "adding" and emphasizes the dynamic quality of the construction.

much less frequent in both the *Tarik Selampit* and the *wayang*. Indeed, many of the occurrences of *kalau* and *kerana* are in parallelisms involving from one to three repetitions of the word in the same stretch of utterance. The greater frequency of subordinating constructions in the *wayang* dialogue (than in the dialogue of the *Tarik Selampit*) is not explained by the fact that the proportion of dialogue is higher than in the *Tarik Selampit* (approximately 80:20 as opposed to 60:40), for the number of words uttered in the *Tarik Selampit* performance used as a basis for these calculations was much greater than that of the *wayang*: approximately 17,000 words (10,000 words of dialogue) as opposed to 8,400 words (6,720 words of dialogue).[7] The explanation lies rather in the fact that the *wayang* is not chanted but delivered in rhythmical speech relatively closer to the intonation of everyday speech. Whereas the mechanics of composing for chant ensure that the result is clearly set off from the idiom of the daily round, in the *wayang,* as I have demonstrated elsewhere (Sweeney, 1972:63 ff) "complicated constructions" are employed, which contribute to the creation of a heightened form of the local dialect. Thus, for example, in what is perhaps the most contorted stretch of the whole performance, Anggada considers the position of one of his father's wives:

> Betul isteri ayah dengan kerana Ajar Cakariwa yang telah menjadikan bonda satu pandan wangi su—yang nama tunggal di atas gunung ada bukit dari hadapan kota dengan kerana abang Raja Hanuman 'gi cabut bukit daripada Ajar Nila Cakariwa yang telah dicarikan pandan wangi pada masa dulu.

The level of clarity this would provide for the *dalang*'s audience may be reproduced in English with:

> [You are] truly father's wife because AC, who created you a fragrant *pandan* (screwpine) er—that's to say one-of-its-kind on a mountain there was a hill from in front of the city because elder brother Hanuman went and pulled up the hill from ANC who had been looked for a fragrant *pandan* in times past.

Clearly the passage is quite "contorted" by the standards of either spoken Kelantanese dialect or literary style. The actual sense is:

> You are truly father's wife because AC created you from a *pandan wangi tunggal* [which was] on a mountain/hill [which was] in front of the city

7. Apart from the shorter length of the performance, there is less speech in the *wayang* because much of the performance consists of action in which speech is not used (see further Sweeney, 1972:56–57).

because Hanuman pulled up the hill for AC, who was looking for a fragrant *pandan* in times past.

The *dalang* can afford to produce such a contorted passage because he
assumes that his audience is familiar with the details, as the episode
referred to had been performed only the previous night. For the audience, understanding the passage merely entailed discounting the com-
plications. What remains are the essential cues for recalling that episode: AC created you from a *pandan;* the *pandan* was found on a
mountain; the mountain was pulled up and brought by Hanuman; it
was placed in front of the city for AC, who was looking for a *pandan.*
In other instances, the subordinating word is prefixed to the main
clause, as in: *Dengan kerana aku mengamuk 'ni, aku tak genap pera-
ngan bapak aku,* where the standard practice (be it Kelantanese or
written style) would place the *dengan kerana* in front of *aku tak . . .*
("I'm running amok because I didn't get enough of a fight in the battle
with my father").

The fact that the *dalang* complicates his constructions does not,
however, fully explain why these "if-why-wherefore" relationships are
somewhat more frequent in the narrative voice of the *wayang* than in
that of the *Tarik Selampit,* and it should be noted that the figures
given above are based on 7,000 words of the latter as opposed to only
1,600 words of the former. The significance of this becomes more
apparent when we see that the instances of dependence by association
to portray these relationships are also more frequent in the *wayang*
than in the *Tarik Selampit.* The explanation again seems to lie in the
fact that the *dalang* speaks—with a strong rhythm it is true—rather
than chants, with the result that his voice tends to be less impersonal;
he is not constrained by the need to fit his words to a phrase of
melody or chant, and is more able to step back from his narrative in
order to comment. A determining factor is the *dalang*'s standing with
the audience. For example, an older, respected *dalang* may occasionally pause to draw out the moral of an episode. An instance of this
may be consulted in Sweeney (1972:292, 368), where the ingratitude
of the mad buffalo is likened to the behavior of some pupils. It is no
coincidence that this passage gives us the highest concentration of
contorted "if-why-wherefore" subordinating constructions in the narrative part of the performance. Incidentally, it may be noted that such
comments tend to be idiosyncratic in the sense that they are not patterned for preservation as a part of the tale—though in themselves
they may well be schematically structured—and are unlikely to survive

in transmission; or, not infrequently, even from one performance to the next. In the context of a whole performance, such comments in the *dalang*'s voice are very few and far between,[8] the more usual tendency being to put them in the mouth of a character. For example, in several performances of the episode concerning Raja Bali and the mad buffalo by the late Awang Lah, a comment was made to the effect that women are clay in the potter's hands. Only in one rendering was it said in the *dalang*'s voice; on other occasions it was put into the mouth of Bali or his wife.

Apart from their use in subordinating constructions, phrases such as *Oleh kerana dengan sebab* and *Sebab mana kerana mana* (respectively, "By reason of and because," and "For what reason for what because") are usually meaningless in their contexts, as in *Oleh kerana dengan sebab sedang tatkala yang bernama maka Mahraja 'Wana pun duk jalan . . .* (By reason of and because while at the time namely well Mahraja 'Wana was walking . . .), where all the words before *maka* (well) function as opener and filler.

Subordinating constructions indicating sequence and other temporal relations are much less frequently used than those concerned with the ifs, whys, and wherefores, and this applies to both dialogue and narrative. In the *Tarik Selampit* and *wayang* performances referred to above, the following words were used as a sample: *bila* ("when"); *sekat* ("limit," "boundary"; may have the sense of "as far as,"[9] "since," e.g., *Sekat dia makan hati lembu 'tu (adapun) lekat perut sengoti* "After eating the cow's liver, she really did become pregnant"); *tengah 'duk* ("in the middle of," "while"); *belang-belang* ("while" = *sambil*); *jaman* ("in times past when . . ."); *masa* ("at the time that . . .").[10] *Tarik Selampit: bila:* 2, 0; *sekat:* 5, 4; *tengah 'duk:* 0, 3; *belang-belang:* 0, 4; *jaman:* 2, 0; *masa:* 2, 1. *Wayang: bila:* 0, 0;

8. The fact that the *dalang* rarely steps in to provide his own opinions during the course of a performance should not be taken as an indication that he does not reflect or speculate. On many occasions, I have sat listening to "off-duty" *dalang*s speculating and opining until dawn! However, in an oral tradition, if such material does not conform to existing patterns, i.e., if it is too original, it will not survive in tradition—within or without performance—unless it is patterned for preservation.

9. It is used not merely of temporal relations but also of spatial ones. In this context, mention should be made of subordinations involving the use of *tempat* ("the place where . . ."); in *Tarik Selampit* it occurred 0, 1, and in the *wayang* performance 2, 2 times. Other frequent relative subordinating constructions are those using *hak* (see Sweeney, 1972:298, 347) and *yang* (both meaning "which") and *hak yang*.

10. A somewhat different treatment of time is expected in the *wayang* in view of the fact that the action is very much in the present: the characters are all there before our eyes, and the *dalang*'s announcements concern the here and now. He tells us that a character has done something, and now he is going to do something else.

sekat: 0, 0; *tengah 'duk:* 0, 1; *belang-belang:* 6, 0; *jaman:* 3, 0; *masa:* 0, 0.

Here again, many of the words that would introduce subordinating constructions of time in written Malay function merely as openers and/or fillers without temporal connotations. Examples are *tatkala, apakala, barangbila* (see Sweeney, 1972:64–65, 338; note also *tatkala* in the dream passage above). *Apakala* as an opener is a favorite of Ismail, the Perlis *Selampit: Apakala dia pun basuh muka siap semua, habis a bela..ka, / Dan setelah itu dia pun bertitah* . . . "(When) he washed his face, all complete, everything finished; And after that he spoke . . ." Sometimes his use of *apakala* appears to result in subordinating constructions, but it is questionable whether they are always consciously produced. For example, the same statement in another performance sounds: *Dan ia pun diambil air sebatil emas, tuan oi basuh, sedang-a kal mu..ka; / Lepas daripada itu apakala siap sudah, ia basuh muka adat istiadat, yang manakan a..da; / Dan pada waktu itu dia pun seri, sedang-a bersabda* . . . ("And he is taken [= takes] a golden bowl of water, sirs oi washes middling-a-kal [his] face; / After that (when) he finishes washing his face with custom and ceremony, whatever-there-be; / And at that time he glow, middling-a speaks"). His intention is clearly not to say, "When ready, he washes . . .";[11] the comma represents a pause, but, as in many such places, it is not a syntactic pause.

Although the actions in a sequence are most commonly linked by simply juxtaposing them, this does not mean that a performance is merely one long listing of actions interspersed with dialogue. As indicated by the reference to opening formulas above, the narrative is broken up into sections. I have previously discussed scene openers and closers (1972:54, 60; 1973:26) and will therefore mention here only that most professional storytellers and all *dalang*s employ one or more formulas which indicate that one section of narrative is being concluded or suspended and another is to begin. For example, *Hilang royat, timbul cerita* (lit., "the account disappears, the story rises"); *kesah*[12] *dulu* X . . . , *timbul tersebut* A . . . ("Ends the tale first of all/for now/of X [doing Y], arises the mention of A [doing B]).

A second type of division is formed by the use of what I have termed "frame phrases" (1973:26). In some of the genres which are

---

11. This is clear from the fact that the common formula is: *Siap sudah basuh muka.*
12. In contrast to traditional literature, in the *wayang* and other east coast oral performances, *kesah* indicates the end of an episode, not the beginning.

musically strophic, that is, where the one passage of music is continually repeated, the beginning and end of the passage are signaled not only on the musical level by a special pattern of notes, but also on the level of utterance, by the use of special phrases, which thus form a "framework" for the narrative. For example, in the *Jubang Linggang* of Kedah: *Oh oh o..h nik o..h...we..i...* at the beginning, and *Timang...nik der, ayo dendang, cik dondang di, di dondang* at the end. In the *Awang Batil,* too, each passage is introduced with *He..i* or *He..i e..i e....i.*

Whether or not the performer employs a frame phrase, there is usually a musical gap between each passage, produced by prolonging the last syllable of the passage and, in some cases, by playing notes on a musical instrument, such as a tambourine or brass bowl. Some performers find it necessary to bridge this gap and pick up the narrative at the beginning of a new passage by repeating the end of the last passage before continuing. We have noted this usage in the *Awang Batil,* which regularly employs the phrase *telah sudah* (followed by repetition) as an opening formula. That this usage is more for the convenience of the performer as a recall and/or stylistic device than simply to achieve effective communication is indicated by the fact that other performers—e.g., Haji Daud, also of Perlis—usually do not employ any such linkage.

In some instances, the word or phrase used to link passages does not precede only events or actions. Ismail of Perlis, for example, regularly employs *dan* ("and") as an opener, regardless of the content, be it description, narrative, or dialogue. Thus, a piece of narrative might sound as follows: "And the king was named . . . / And the queen was . . . / And he said . . . / 'And today prepare food . . . / And today I am going out . . .' " and so on. And although he also employs phrases such as *setelah itu* and *lepas daripada itu,* which clearly seem to refer to the sequence of events, these, too, are sometimes used in the same way as *dan.*

The function of linking-words is not always merely to bridge the gap between passages; they may at the same time be used to emphasize that gap. And in non-strophic genres such as the *Tarik Selampit,* they may be used both to pick up the narrative and to create space. For example, the word *lalu* is often used when a sequence of juxtaposed events is interrupted by a song, or after a verbal interchange between characters. In the latter case it indicates to the audience that the characters' words are concluded, and in general makes it clear that the sequence of actions is to be resumed or that a new sequence is to begin. Similarly, the use of *lalu* creates space[13] between events, as at the start of a new piece of action. This may be emphasized further by enunciating the word slowly and on a rising tone, and preceding it with *ah*. Although *lalu* usually carries the connotation of "then" or "next," when functioning as an opener it need not indicate an advance in the progression of the tale. In the *Tarik Selampit*, for example, *Lalu Tuan Puteri Ratna Paspa sudah (adapun) sembelih ayam / duk berkira nak sembelih serati / lalu serati pun dengar khabar nak sembelih . . .* ("Well now, Princess Ratna Paspa has [filler] slaughtered the chickens / is deliberating on slaughtering the *serati* ducks / And then the *serati* duck hears of the intention to slaughter . . ."). The first *lalu* does not indicate a "then" in the progression of the story. It picks up the narrative after an interruption and recapitulates. After this brief section, the scene shifts to another character in another locale. The use of *lalu* here thus signals the beginning of a new section comparable to what I have termed a "sub scene" in the *wayang;* to put cart before horse, we might compare this use of *lalu* to an indentation for a new paragraph. Other words and phrases which perform a similar function are *Ah ialah* ("Ah yes") in *Tarik Selampit, Maka* in the *wayang,* and *Kalau begitu* ("if that be the case") in both. These words tend to be enunciated in a distinctive manner to make them stand out from their context. For example, both syllables of *maka* may be prolonged.

I am not suggesting that linking-words such as *lalu* are used only as openers in all genres. In a rendering of *Raja Gagak* by Jidin of Pahang, for example, *lalu* is sometimes used to link events related in sequence within a single passage:

> Balik ke seberang laut la nya..ng i..tu
> serta *lalu*lah dia kembali pulang nga nya ke..mba..li
> bawa dua kuntum bunga yang amat harum yang ama..t mele..mpah
> *lalu* dimasuknya ke dalam perut raja ng itu.
>
> Sudah dimasuknya *lalu* disapunya tiga kali dengan sehuju..ng sa..yap
>
> Returned across the sea of it there that
> with that he *then* went back, went home of it went back
> took two flowers highly scented highly pervasive
> *then* placed them in the stomach of that raja
>
> Has placed them *then* he brushes three times with his wing tips.

13. My use of the word "space" no doubt reveals a visual orientation. But we should note that the teller himself may speak of himself "seeing" the tale. Ismail of Perlis stresses that he does not "remember"; rather he relates what he sees in his mind's eye.

While the first *lalu* is more of a filler preceding repetition, the second two carry the connotation of "then," "straight away." Even so, the incidence of *lalu* in this stretch (six times in eleven "lines" of which five are quoted here) is unusually high: in performances of other tales by the same teller its use is relatively uncommon. It would seem that the long lines and prolongation of each line in this particular tale make it necessary to bridge not merely the strophes but also many of the lines with *lalu*. The use of the same word, furthermore, has the rhythmical and mnemonic advantage of producing an anaphoric parallelism. And as we observe below, in an oral milieu, a word once used tends to reproduce itself.

In considering the use of the words used to open passages, I observed that not all words denoting sequence appear to refer to an "and then" in the tale. One example was *lalu* preceding recapitulation in the *Tarik Selampit*. Others are *setelah itu* and *lepas daripada itu* in the Perlis *Selampit:*

> Dan setelah itu semua apakala dia menjadi raja di dalam negeri . . / Dan digelaran ia tuan oi Duli . . . / Dan permaisuri dialah yang bernama . . .

> And after all that, (when) he was the raja in the country of . . . / And he bore the title, oh sirs, of Duli . . . / And his queen was named . . .

Several other examples of *setelah itu* and *lepas daripada itu* which do not precede any progression in the sequence of events are found in Sweeney (1973:36). In all these instances, however, the connotation of "and then" is still present, though it refers not to story time but to telling time: "The next thing I am going to tell you is . . ." This is more easily demonstrated in the study of nonstylized telling and will be discussed further in the following chapter.

TRADITIONAL LITERATURE

In those genres of storytelling which employ a strophic technique, the length of each utterance is geared to the phrase of the melody, or the rhythm of the chant. The fact that both utterance and melody may be stretched or compressed to accommodate each other allows considerable variation in the length of each utterance. There is, nevertheless, a strong sense of balance; each passage is felt to be weighed against the next. This is further reflected in and reinforced by the use of various mnemonic devices such as parallelisms, assonance, and alliteration, which enable the teller to preserve certain specific word choices and also to create new utterances based upon the existing patterns.

The rhythmic monotone employed in the recitation of traditional Malay written composition consisted of a repeated stretch of chant, and in this respect it was not unlike the strophic technique of stylized oral storytelling. The fact that written composition was intended to be chanted implies that the scribe, in the process of writing, would have the rhythm of the chant in his mind rather than the intonation of everyday speech. This is clear from the comment of a reciter of Malay *hikayat* in Lombok, recorded by Judy Ecklund; Ecklund informed me that "the reciters employ only old Jawi works." New books are readily available, but her informants stated that "the language is more modern and is not as well suited for the singing rhythms" (Sweeney, 1980:75). In writing for chant, the scribe regulated the length of sentences and made liberal use of parallelism in order to produce rhythmically balanced utterances. And, in common with the oral teller, he made extensive use of simple juxtaposing in order to relate a sequence of events. For example:

> Maka Maharaja Dasarata pun heran / Maka Maharaja Dasarata pun pergi kepada seorang maharesi Dewata namanya / Maka Maharaja Dasarata pun minta anak pada maharesi itu / Maka maharesi pun memberi empat biji geliga / Maka geliga itu diambil Maharaja Dasarata /
> > *Hikayat Seri Rama* (Shellabear, 1915:54)

> MD was surprised / MD went to a maharisi named Dewata / MD asked the maharisi for a child / The maharisi gave (him) four bezoar stones / The bezoars were taken by MD.

and:

> Maka Laksamana pun berjalanlah tiga hari / Maka Laksamana pun bertemu dengan Seri Rama dan Sita Dewi / Maka Seri Rama pun berjalanlah dengan Laksamana dan Sita Dewi/

> Laksamana traveled for three days / Laksamana met up with Seri Rama and Sita Dewi / Seri Rama traveled with Laksamana and Sita Dewi.
> > *Hikayat Seri Rama* (Shellabear, 1915:76)

Reference may also be made to the examples given in my *Authors and Audiences* (1980:19–20), which were intended to illustrate the frequent use of parallelisms, but also contain numerous instances of juxtaposing.

The commonest construction used to push forward narrative involves the formulaic pattern: (Slot for actor) + *pun* —(Slot for verbal [verb or adjective]) [+ lah], and is particularly effective in reinforcing the sense of balance. However, by no means all juxtaposed actions in sequence use this construction. For example:

> Maka kata Tun Isap, "Orang Kaya, marilah kita amuk orang Haru ini"
> Maka kata Seri Bija Diraja, "Sabar dahulu"
> Maka segala orang Haru pun datang ke tiang agung
> Maka kata Tun Isap, "Orang kaya, marilah kita mengamuk"
> Maka kata Seri Bija Diraja, "Belum ketikanya"
> Maka orang Haru pun dekatlah
> Maka kata Tun Isap, "Orang kaya, marilah kita mengamuk"
> Maka kata Seri Bija Diraja, "Sabar dahulu encik, belum ketikanya"
> Maka Seri Bija Diraja masuk ke dalam kurung
> *Sejarah Melayu* (Situmorang & Teeuw, 1952:192)

> Said TI, "Lord, let us run amok on these Haru people"
> Said SBD, "Be patient"
> The Haru people arrived at the main mast
> Said TI, "Lord, let us run amok"
> Said SBD, "It is not the right moment yet"
> The Haru people closed in
> Said TI, "Lord, let us run amok"
> Said SBD, "Be patient sir; it is not the right moment yet"
> SBD went into the cabin.

Of course, the mere fact that utterances are juxtaposed does not imply that the events related must be supposed to occur in sequence, or indeed that each item in the series must be an event, and this is clear from the form of the verb and the context; description may be included. For example, in *Ada yang menapak, ada yang mengigal, ada yang bertandak, ada yang berserama* (*Sejarah Melayu*, Winstedt, 1938:108) (there were those who ... [performed various types of dance]), the actions are happening simultaneously. And in:

> Maka sampai kepada suatu tanah yang tinggi sedikit / Maka pada tempat itu adalah pula anak sungai / Maka banyak ikan dan binatang perburuan adalah di situ / Maka Menteri Kelahum pun berhentilah ... /
> *Hikayat Merung Mahawangsa* (Siti Hawa, 1970:76)

> [They] arrived at somewhat higher ground / In that place there was also a stream / Many fish and game animals were there / Menteri Kelahum halted ... /,

the narrative is interrupted by description.

Much of traditional Malay literature is schematically composed. On the level of word choice, it is still highly paratactic and formulaic compared with modern Indonesian and Malaysian. However, when compared with stylized oral performance, the incidence of subordinating constructions is much higher, as may be seen from the large number of utterances subordinated by words such as *setelah, apabila, tatkala, karena, sebab, sungguhpun, walaupun,* and *jikalau.* It is particularly in the use of these constructions that we may observe the extent to which the possibilities offered by writing for prior analysis have been exploited. This is not to say that written composition abandoned the oral habit of juxtaposing two utterances in what I termed dependence by association. On the contrary, writing allowed such constructions to become considerably more complex. For example, the use of the pattern *Hendak——tiada——*in oral tradition would tend to produce short, easily remembered utterances such as the proverbial saying:

> *Hendak terbang tiada bersayap, hendak hinggap tiada berkaki*
> (Wishes to fly, no wings; wishes to perch, no legs).

Written composition allowed much longer and more complicated utterances to be produced from such basic patterns. For example,

> *Hendak pun* hamba sekalian persembahkan ke bawah duli Yang di Pertuan *tiada* akan didengarnya; *hendak pun* saya diamkan kalau esok hari atau lusanya sahaya sekalian beroleh malu.
>
> *Hikayat Hang Tuah* (Kassim, 1964:286)

> Were we to inform His Majesty, he would not listen; Were we to keep silent, tomorrow or the next day, we might incur disgrace.

Of course, in oral tradition, the use of such patterns was not limited to proverbial sayings; dependence by association was the normal way of expressing intentions, causes, feelings, and the like. However, the development in writing of subordinating constructions—the models for many of which were of foreign provenance—provided the scribe with a much wider range of choice, so that the balancing of one clause against another to produce a certain nuance became much more of a consciously used stylistic device.

As in stylized oral performance, constructions expressing the conditional, the causal, the concessional, and so forth, occur much more frequently in the dialogue of written composition than in the narrative parts. Of course, the incidence of subordinating constructions is much higher in writing, but, be they subordinating or "associating," the use of such constructions expressing whys and wherefores implies commentary, explanation, and/or conflicting points of view. The writer of traditional Malay literature was still concerned with recounting event after event as he perceived them to have happened; it was not his prerogative to step back from the narrative and offer an interpretation in his own voice. Differing points of view could be put into the mouths of his characters. Of course, considerable variation in this respect may be encountered between different compositions, even of the same genre as, for example, is revealed by a comparison between the *Sejarah Melayu* and the *Misa Melayu,* or indeed, between different parts of the *Sejarah Melayu.* The higher incidence of subordinating constructions of this type in the *Sejarah Melayu,* and in particular the sections concerned with Raja Tengah (*Sejarah Melayu,* Winstedt, 1938:84ff) and the Bendahara Seri Maharaja (*Sejarah Melayu,* Situmorang & Teeuw, 1952:277ff) is indicative of a concern to provide much more commentary and explanation than is the norm in the Malay *hikayat.*[14] For example,

> Setelah Sultan Mahmud menengar sembah Laksamana itu, kabullah pada hatinya, seperti orang mengantuk disorong bantal; karena baginda sedia berdendam2 akan Bendahara Seri Maharaja, sebab anaknya Tun Fatimah itu; seperti kata bidal Arab . . .
>
> *Sejarah Melayu* (p. 285)

> When Sultan Mahmud had heard the words of the Laksamana, they [immediately] met with his approval, as when a sleepy person is handed a pillow, for he already harbored a grudge against the Bendahara SM on account of his child TF. As the saying in Arabic goes . . .

14. Of course, the reverse is not necessarily true; commentary, explanation, etc., do not require the use of subordinating constructions. A clear point of view may be expressed in simple narrative, as for example, in: . . . *maka banyaklah orang yang jahat-jahat dijadikannya juak-juaknya* . . . ("He made many criminal types his followers. . . .") (*Misa Melayu,* 20). Occasionally, a narrator intrudes directly to comment. For example, in the *Sejarah Melayu* (Winstedt, 1938:64): ". . . if all of it were to be told, the listeners would be bored. Therefore, we have shortened it. . . ." One might wonder perhaps how the sporadic appearance of a relatively intimate voice which addresses the "dear listeners and reciters" is compatible with the impersonal ethos of the *Yang empunya cerita* or *Sahibu'l-Hikayat* ("the owner of the tale"). The answer of course is that it was the convention for the writer to represent himself as the mere conveyor of the tale, as though he is sitting there with the audience and mediating between them and the account of the "owner" which he is relaying. And indeed, the notion of holding a copyright would have seemed quite strange to him; after all, composing meant reproducing, using the commonly shared schemata of tradition. Incidentally, an impersonal ethos and highly formulaic style on the level of word choice should not be taken as an indication that the *hikayat* is structurally anonymous. In fact, a high degree of schematic usage on one level of composition may compensate for a lower degree on another level. A case in point is the *Hikayat Hang Tuah.* In a current study, Sylvia Tiwon (1985) demonstrates convincingly that on the level of structure or plot, there is a clear argument and a definite point of view.

Our present concern, however, is more with the question of narrative progression, and it is here that we see a major difference between stylized oral and traditional written composition: in the latter,
subordinating constructions indicating sequence and time are relatively common. Their use enables the writer to emphasize the relationships between actions and to make those relationships more precise than would merely juxtaposing those actions. For example,
... *maka Maharaja Jaya pun matilah. Setelah dilihat Maharaja Jaya
dan Tun Damang mati, maka orang Kampar pun pecahlah. Sejarah
Melayu* (Winstedt, 1938:149) (Maharaja Jaya died. After it was seen
[that] Maharaja Jaya and Tun Damang [were] dead, the Kampar
people broke [ranks]). Rather than merely reeling off three events,
the writer classifies two of them together, shows how they relate to
each other, and ties them to the third. Juxtaposing may, of course,
express a similar nuance. The relationship of the events would be
clear in the everyday speech of oral persons from the intonation: *Ah,
MJ pun matilah. Tengok/Nampak dia mati 'tu, Orang Kampar lari-
lah.* Or: *MJ pun matilah. Mati 'tu, Orang Kampar nampaklah, lari-
lah. 'Tu* (from *itu*) is pronounced on a rising tone, linking "see,"
"die," with "flee" in the first example, and "die" with "see" in the
second. If the passage were to be chanted, however, this intonation
would not be possible, and the emphasis would be less obvious. This,
incidentally, contributes to the impersonal quality of the narrative
voice. And while the patterns of (sung or chanted) stylized oral performance are relatively short and may be recognized by the audience
from their similarity to the patterns of everyday speech despite the
lack of intonation, writing, by relieving the burden of memorization,
allows the use of longer, more involved patterns, subject of course to
the constraints imposed by the nature of the audience.

An example worthy of note for its variety and number of subordinating constructions indicating sequence and time is the following:

Setelah itu maka Maharaja Rawana pun diterbangkannyalah ke udara.
Tatkala diterbangkannya itu maka kata Maharaja Rawana, "Aku hendak
mengalahkan matahari. Sampaikan aku ke langit." Menengar kata demikian maka rata itu pun terbanglah ke udara. Apabila sampai ke hawan
maka panas pun terlalu sangat, tiada lagi terderita oleh Maharaja Rawana.
Maka ia pun menyuruh rata itu segera turun kembali ke negerinya. Maka
sepeninggal Maharaja Rawana pergi menyerang matahari itu, Bergasinga
bertunggu.

Hikayat Seri Rama (Shellabear, 1915:79)

After that, MR was flown by it [the *rata,* his chariot] up into the air. While [he] was being flown, MR said, "I wish to defeat the sun. Take me to the sky." Hearing his words to this effect, the *rata* flew up into the air. When [he] arrived at the clouds, the heat was very strong; [it] could not be borne by MR. He ordered the *rata* to descend back to his land. From the time MR left to go and attack the sun, Bergasinga was on guard.

Here we see the result of prior analysis; actions are classified into pairs, and the relations of the actions in each pair made clear: speaking while flying, flying on hearing, condition (a verbal) of heat on arrival, one character guarding while another is away attacking.

Of course, the complexity possible was limited by the mode of consumption. Thus, it was relatively uncommon for more than one utterance to be subordinated to the same verbal as in:

> Apabila segala anak buah Bendahara pergi berburu kerbau jalang atau rusa, jikalau ia tiada beroleh rusa, maka ia singgah pada (kandang) kerbau Bendahara, maka ditikamnya kerbau itu dua tiga ekor . . .
> *Sejarah Melayu* (Winstedt, 1938:184)

> When the young followers of the Bendahara went hunting wild buffalo or deer, if they didn't obtain any deer, they would call in at the Bendahara's buffalo stable [and] they would stab two or three of the buffaloes . . .

Rather more common was the positioning of subordinate constructions on either side of the main utterance:

> Adapun Tuan Puteri itu selama ia sudah sembuh daripada sakitnya maka iapun beradu bersama-sama dengan ayah bondanya juga, karena ia akan bercerai itu.
> *Hikayat Indera Bangsawan* (p. 63)

> The princess, from the time she had recovered from her sickness, she slept with her father and mother, for they were to be separated.

Subordinating constructions of time and sequence would, moreover, still show a tendency to follow the narrative sequence.[15] Although *apabila* and *tatkala* clauses sometimes violate that order, the *setelah* construction to my knowledge does not: the *setelah* clause precedes the main event. One does not encounter sentences such as *Dia datang setelah semua sudah siap* (He came when all was ready).

Furthermore, the use of various nonsubordinating linking-words, such as *lalu, sambil, seraya,* in written composition made possible the

---

15. With the obvious exception of *Sebelum* . . . ("before . . .").

production of longer sentences than in stylized oral performance; and
the scribe was able to present a sequence of actions within the compass of one utterance, whereas in oral performance we would be more
likely to encounter a sequence of juxtaposed utterances. Here again,
moreover, the use of these linking-words enabled the scribe to pin-
point the relationships between the events in the utterance which in
the oral juxtaposing technique would be accomplished by intonation.
Nevertheless, as with the subordinating constructions, these linking-
words were most commonly used to link only two events within the
one utterance. For example, *lalu* is often employed to emphasize the
beginning of an action and its culmination, as in *Maka segala anak
raja-raja itupun menyambut anugerah baginda itu lalu dijunjungnya di
atas batu kepalanya* ("The princes accepted HM's largesse and placed
it on their heads") (*Hikayat Indera Bangsawan*, 67); *Maka iapun
berteriak2 lalu mati* ("He screamed and died") (*Hikayat Seri Rama*,
80). *Seraya* and *serta* are also used most frequently to form pairs of
actions: *Maka bagindapun tersenyum seraya bertitah* ("HM smiled
and said") (*HIB*, 47); *Maka anak raja-raja itupun heranlah serta berjalan . . .* ("The princes were astonished and set off . . .") (*HIB*, 50).
Not infrequently, however, three or more actions may be presented
in one sentence, and if this includes speech of characters, the result
may be a sentence of considerable length. For example:

> Maka oleh Indera Bangsawan dipegangnya tangan anak raja-raja itu lalu
> dibawanya duduk seorang-seorang pada sebuah kursi di hadapan mahligai
> seraya bercerita kepada segala anak raja-raja itu: "Akan halnya kakanda
> hendak didudukkan oleh baginda dengan tuan puteri, sehingga kakanda
> menantikan adinda juga sekaliannya akan mengerjakan pekerjaan kakanda
> ini."
>
> (*HIB*, 50)

> IB grasped the princes by the hand and led each of them to a chair at the
> front of the pavilion and said to the princes, "About the matter of HM's
> wish to marry me to the princess [it has come] to the point that I am
> waiting for you to organize this business of mine."

In long sentences such as this, whether subordinating constructions
or simple linkages as above (or both) are employed, the style is still
very much an adding style: event is added to event, statement to
statement in short, easily digested stretches. There is very little embedding; one understands each piece as it comes; one does not have to
wait interminably for a final verb, for example, in order to understand
the beginning of the utterance. And of course, a chanted, heard narra-

tive (i.e., one intended for a nonliterate audience) could not be produced otherwise. Thus, we note that the passage quoted above is divided into relatively short, balanced utterances, and the reciter is provided with cues as to where each stretch begins: Words such as *lalu, seraya, akan halnya, sehingga* are clear signals that a new phrase of the chant should begin.

This may be illustrated by excerpts from a performance of the *Hikayat Nabi Yusuf.*[16] Numbers in brackets after a word indicate the number of seconds the last syllable is prolonged.

Setelah kenyanglah ia
Maka diambilnya tongkat itu maka [3] tongkat itu pun kembali
    seperti sediakalanya [6]
Maka Jibril pun naik ke langit [4]
Pada suatu hari pergilah Yusuf bermain-main pada segala saudaranya [10]
Setelah dirasanya dirinya lapar
Maka dihunjamkan tongkatnya ke bumi
Maka tumbuhlah empat cawang daripada segala buah-buahan [3]
Maka makanlah oleh Yusuf, dan segala saudaranya . . .

And:

Adapun ranting zaitun yang kering tatkala diberi Jibril 'alaihi
    's-salam tanam pada Puteri Sarah
Akan alamatnya beranak
Tumbuhlah lalu [2] berdahanlah sepuluh cabangnya [5]
Maka tatkala besarlah anak Ya'kub sepuluh orang itu
Maka [7] diperbuat Ya'kub segala cabang zaitun akan tongkat
    anaknya [9]
Tatkala besarlah Yusuf 'alaihi 's-salam
Maka [4] diambilnya akan [= oleh?] bapanya Ya'kub dari saudaranya
    Asi dengan muslihatnya [15]
Maka marahlah Asi akan Nabi Allah Ya'kub 'alaihi 's-salam
Maka [9] pergilah ia bermain-main pada segala saudaranya [8]
Maka dilihat Yusuf segala saudaranya bertongkat seorang satu
    tongkat pada tangannya
Maka [6] Yusuf pun berkata "Beri apalah akan daku satu tongkat [9]
Seperti tongkat kamu itu"
Maka kata segala saudaranya
"Bahwasanya tongkat kami ini pun diberi oleh bapa kami [15]
Jika engkau berkehendak akan tongkat pintalah olehmu kepada bapa"
Dan setelah didengar oleh Yusuf kata segala saudaranya demikian

16. I am indebted to Professor Judy Ecklund of Tulane for making these recordings available to me. See further Sweeney, 1980:75. Of interest is the fact that an interpreter provides orally an "interlinear" translation into Sasak. The location of the pauses corresponds to what I have heard from old people in Kelantan.

Maka [9] ia pun berlari-lari pergi kepada bapanya Ya'kub dengan
    katanya [5]
"Hei [6] bapaku berilah akan daku suatu tongkat seperti tongkat
    segala saudaraku" [9]
Maka kata Ya'kub, "Nantilah bapa carikan kayu yang baik
Sahaja ku beri jua akan dikau suatu tongkat seperti tongkat
    segala saudaramu itu"
Maka [4] Yusuf pun menangis minta tongkat kepada bapanya [9]
Katanya, "Beri apalah akan daku tongkat sekarang jua
Supaya ku pergi bermain-main dengan segala saudaraku"
Maka [6] Ya'kub pun dukacita hatinya mendengar kata Yusuf [8]
Maka Jibril pun datang pada Ya'kub membawa suatu tongkat [2]
    kayu dari dalam syurga daripada zabarjad yang hijau.

When he was full,
He took the staff and the staff reverted to its usual (shape).
Jibril ascended to the sky,
One day Yusuf went to play with his brothers,
When he felt hungry,
He stabbed his staff into the ground.
There grew four branches of various fruit.
Yusuf ate, and his brothers . . .

As for the twig of olive which was dry when it was given by Jibril
    (peace be upon him) to Princess Sara to plant,
As a sign she would give birth,
It grew and produced ten branches.
When Yaakub's ten children grew big,
Yaakub made the olive branches into staves for his children.
When Yusuf (peace be upon him) grew big,
His father, Yaakub, took him from his brother, Asi, by means of
    a trick.
Asi was angry with the Prophet of God, Yaakub (peace be upon him).
He went and played with his brothers.
Yusuf saw each of his brothers had a staff in his hand.
Yusuf said, "Won't you give me a staff,
Like your staves?"
His brothers said,
"These staves of ours were given us by our father.
If you want a staff, ask father."
And when Yusuf heard these words of his brothers,
He ran to his father, Yaakub, and said,
"Father, give me a staff like the staves of my brothers."
Yaakub said, "Wait until I find a good (piece of) wood,
I shall certainly make you a staff like the staves of your brothers."
Yusuf wept, asking his father for a staff.
He said, "Give me a staff now
So that I can go and play with my brothers."

Yaakub was sad, hearing Yusuf's words.
Jibril came to Yaakub bringing a staff of wood from heaven, made
of green *zabarjad*.

It will be noted that, with the single exception of *tumbuh,* the first
word of every line is a common cue for the beginning of a division of
the narrative; what in translation we would dub a phrase, clause, or
sentence. We may also observe from these two excerpts the importance of *maka* as an opener; even when it follows a subordinated
phrase, it still begins a phrase of the chant. In the one instance where
it occurs in the middle of a phrase of the chant, it is juxtaposed with a
much shorter utterance; even so, it is prolonged for three seconds.

The usage of *maka* constitutes an important difference between
written composition and stylized oral performance. In some genres of
oral performance, such as the *Tarik Selampit* and the *wayang,* as
noted above, *maka* functions as a section opener. In the former, its use
is sporadic (5 times in 17,000 words), *lalu* being the more common
opener. In the *wayang,* it is regularly used to introduce the speech of
the *dalang* after dialogue between characters (69 times in 8,400
words). In traditional written composition, however, *maka* precedes
the great majority of sentences/utterances. Whereas in traditional oral
performance there is no distinction to be made between the tasks of
composition and presentation, in written composition those tasks are
assigned to two individuals (or the same at two different times). The
writer is writing not merely for his listening audience, but also for the
reciter who is to relay his composition to that audience. Apart from
the specific needs of the audience, therefore, the use of *maka* provided
a cue to the reciter to intone the opening notes of his chanted passage.
Maka also reinforced the balance of the rhythm, so that the majority
of utterances became instances of anaphora. And in longer sentences,
where *maka* could not begin each chanted phrase, other words became
conventional openers of subdivisions.

On occasion a scribe might produce a long, relatively involved
stretch of utterance which could not easily be broken up into short
phrases for chanting. This might happen for example when verbal is
piled upon verbal as in **membuat dirinya sakit mengidam hendak makan.** In such instances, the scribe would tend to repeat the sequence in
subsequent utterances, in order to ensure effective communication. For
example, in *Kuda Semirang Seri Panji Pandai Rupa* (Kelantan, 1931:
52), we hear:

... Maka permaisuri pun membuat dirinya sakit mengidam hendak
     makan hati harimau
Maka masyhurlah dalam negeri Kuripan akan permaisuri sakit
     terlalu payah sakit mengidam hendak makan hati macan beranak muda
Berapa2 Sang Nata menyuruhkan segala para menteri para penggawa
     ke dalam hutan menangkap harimau tiada dapat
Dan segala bini para menteri para penggawa pun masuklah ke
     dalam bertunggu sekaliannya
Maka terdengarlah kepada Radin Inu akan permaisuri payah sakit
     mengidam hendak makan hati harimau beranak muda itu
Maka Radin Inu pun berdebar hatinya

The queen affected to be sick craving wishing to eat the liver of a tiger.
It was broadcast in the land of Kuripan that the queen was sick very
     sick indeed craving wishing to eat the liver of a tiger
     [which had] just given birth.
[No matter] how much SN ordered his ministers and officers into
     the jungle to catch a tiger, it was not obtained,
And the wives of the ministers and officers entered the presence
     [and] attended [upon the queen].
It was heard by Radin Inu that the queen was very sick craving
     wishing to eat the liver of a tiger [which had] just given birth.
Radin Inu's heart beat wildly.

By this time even the most inattentive audience would begin to
appreciate what the queen was requesting. And, we may note, the
repetition reinforces the balance.

While the use of subordinating and coordinating devices enabled
the writer to produce sentences far more complex than was possible in
the stylized oral tradition, this did not mean that a writer now
pondered over every sentence. The constructions themselves became
formulas. Thus, a character's reaction to the death of another is commonly expressed with the pattern cited above: *X mati. Setelah dilihat
X mati, maka* ... ("X died. When it was seen that X was dead, ...").
For example, in the *Hikayat Pandawa Lima* (128): ... *mengatakan
Sutomo mati. Setelah dilihat oleh Dangyang Drona anaknya sudah
mati, maka ia pun rebahlah* ... (... saying Sutomo was dead. When it
was seen by DD that his son was dead, he fell down ...).

The constructions also form the patterns for the formulaic production of parallelisms. In the *Hikayat Pandawa Lima* (127), for example,
the same construction occurs five times in rapid succession: ... *MC
mati. Setelah DD melihat akan MC mati, maka* ... *AD lalu mati. Maka
MM setelah ia melihat AD mati, maka ia pun tampil* ... *keduanya lalu*

mati. Setelah MM melihat cucunya mati, maka MM pun tampil . . .
followed by two more *Setelah dilihat* . . . *mati* constructions.

A pattern which regularly repeats itself is the *jika* . . . *maka* construction: for example, in the *Sejarah Melayu* (Raffles 18:76):[17]

> Jika ia ke paseban, di paseban gempar; dan jika ia pergi ke pasar, maka
> segala orang pasar pun gempar; dan jika ia pergi pada kampung orang
> maka segala orang di kampung itu gempar.

> If [but also implies "when"] he went to the audience hall, there would be
> uproar in the audience hall; and if he went to the market, the market
> people would be in uproar; and if he went to a village, the village people
> would be in uproar.

Note also the repeated use of *Dan jikalau* followed by *Dan jangan* in Ken Tambuhan's letter (*Hikayat Andaken Penurat, 50*).

We find the same tendency to produce parallelisms in constructions using the coordinating linkages, such as *lalu* and *seraya*. For example, *Maka lalu diyunusnya*[18] *samsirnya maka lalu ditetaknya* . . . ("He pulled out his sword and he chopped . . .") (*Hikayat Seri Rama,* 80); *Maka Indera Bangsawan pun menyembah lalu duduk* . . . *Maka Indera Bangsawan pun menyembah lalu makan sirih* ("Indera Bangsawan paid obeisance and sat down . . . Indera Bangsawan paid obeisance and ate betel leaf") (*Hikayat Indera Bangsawan,* 46).

Of course, the rhythm of the chant exerts a strong pull toward the production of these formulaic parallelisms, which in their turn reinforce that rhythm. Thus, the possibilities for the development of an analytical style were limited. We have noted that the simple balancing of one utterance against another without linking-words was developed in written composition into a relatively complex stylistic device. Winstedt's words that "finally antithesis becomes a literary artifice" (1927:171) are particularly relevant here.[19] Yet this particular development was not indicative of a shift away from oral habits; rather, writing enabled the scribe to exploit further the possibilities of oral composition. Again we see how new media may initially appear to reinforce the old. And although the greatly increased use of subordinating constructions did represent a trend toward exploiting the choices offered by writing, those constructions were in their turn assimilated to the still strongly

17. Winstedt's romanization (1938:106) omits part of this passage.
18. That is, *diunus, dihunus.*
19. Although in applying this comment to formulaic parallelisms, I am using it in a more specific sense than does Winstedt.

oral habits of written composition. Thus, when a subordinating construction was produced, not only would the constituent parts be balanced against one another in easily presented and understood pieces: the inclination of the scribe who had just produced one such construction was to create another one to balance it, so that the constructions did not merely contain, but themselves became parallelisms.

A common formulaic construction used in advancing a piece of narrative involves recounting an action, following it with *setelah* plus a repetition of that action (using the same word or a synonym), and then relating the next action in the sequence. For example, . . . *lalu mati. Setelah ia mati, hujan pun ribut* . . . (*Hikayat Andaken Penurat*, 55) (". . . and died. After she died, rain came down in a storm . . ."); *Sultan Mahmud Syah pun mangkatlah . . . Setelah sudah baginda hilang itu, maka gemparlah* . . . ("Sultan MS passed away. After HM had passed on, there was an uproar . . .") (*Misa Melayu*, 153). This usage may be termed the "recapitulating *setelah*" as opposed to that which advances the tale in that a new action follows *setelah*: . . . *lalu turun berjalan ke perahu . . . Setelah sampai ke perahu,* . . . ("and set off down to the boat. On arrival at the boat, . . ."). Of course, a new action after *setelah* does not preclude the use of repetition elsewhere; in the last example, *perahu* is repeated; and in the *mati* . . . *Setelah dilihat* . . . pattern cited above, *mati* follows the new action (*lihat*) after *setelah*.

Moreover, the *setelah* construction may function both to recapitulate and to advance the tale. This often occurs when the *setelah* clause follows an action that has been ordered or one that is of relatively long duration. Then, *setelah* (and in the latter case, particularly, often followed by *sudah*) indicates completion of the action, but also serves to recapitulate. For example:

> Maka Seri Rama pun menitahkan Anila Anggada mengampungkan segala ra'yat. Setellah[20] kampunglah ra'yat itu, maka kata Anila Anggada . . .
> (*Hikayat Seri Rama*, 221)

> SR ordered A and A to assemble the people. When the people were assembled, A and A said . . .

and: *Maka baginda pun santaplah . . . Setelah sudah santap nasi, maka lalu . . .* (*Misa Melayu*, 76) ("HM ate. When [he had] finished eating, then . . .").

20. Spelled with *tashdid*.

This usage reminds us of the *telah sudah* construction of Mahmud, the *Awang Batil,* referred to above, and it appears that the function is not dissimilar. It enables the reciter and his audience to recapitulate at the beginning of a new stretch of chant before advancing the tale further. Of course, if its function were merely to bridge the gap, we would wonder why it is not used constantly, and how simple juxtaposition would be possible. It is true that juxtaposed utterances tend to be relatively shorter than those preceding the recapitulating *setelah,* but this is but a partial explanation. The main function of this device in written composition is, I would contend, to create space both in "telling" time and "story" time. I have referred several times to the nature of audience conditions at a stylized oral performance which, apart from the needs of the teller placed in a rapid-fire situation, require that, even though the pace of a performance may be rapid, the content should be unfolded slowly, for not everything is expected to be heard; and this is achieved on the level of utterance (it may also be effected by prolonging the syllables in the chant) by the use of repetition and large amounts of padding, which may consist of mere nonsense phrases. The similarity of audience conditions at a recital of *hikayat* meant that written composition had to be similarly copious in order to achieve effective communication. The scribe was not, however, performing directly for his audience; he also had to consider the reciter whose task was to bring it to life, and to ensure that he found it intelligible enough to recite. On the one hand, this meant that his work had to be entirely self-sufficient as regards the providing of context compared with that of the chanting teller, who composes directly for his listeners, and certainly more so than the performance of the *dalang* (and parts of the *Tarik Selampit*) where the nuances allowed by the intonation of everyday speech may be expressed; in writing a *hikayat,* everything had to be verbalized.

Even more important, however, is the fact that the scribe could not simply intersperse his narrative with nonsense phrases or syntactical distortions, for this would have caused the reciter severe problems in deciphering his text. Rather, he employed what we may term a "codified copiousness." As we have seen from the examples quoted, this involved large amounts of repetition. Yet while the recounting of a series of actions in rapid sequence may appear relatively drawn out and repetitious to a modern *reader,* this would not have been the experience of a traditional listening audience, as may be ascertained from studying the reactions of audiences at a performance of stylized oral composition.[21] The obvious places to afford a *hikayat* audience some respite would be those parts of the narrative which lacked dramatic immediacy. That respite was afforded by constructions such as the recapitulating *setelah,* which itself served to communicate and emphasize that lack of immediacy. The same may be said of many of the linkages such as *Setelah demikian, setelah sudah,* which are commonly used to create space. Actions which were depicted as following one another in rapid sequence were still linked by simple juxtaposing. The result, however, was that juxtaposing increasingly became a stylistic device to express dramatic immediacy.[22]

The equivalent in written composition of the scene openers of oral performance is a number of words which serve as "audible punctuation." In general, these section headings tend to be shorter than the oral scene openers, and consist of words such as *Bermula, al-Kesah, Adapun, Sekali peristiwa,* although they may sometimes be followed by *Maka tersebutlah perkataan* ("Mention is made of . . ."). When a major division of a text was to be indicated, these words would often be written in red ink and/or in thicker letters than the rest of the text. This of course provided a visual cue to the reciter and, when uttered, the words constituted an audible signal to the audience that a new section was about to begin. And as we have seen from the excerpt of chant, visual cues were not limited to section openers; without doubt, *maka* was the most important visual cue of all, but in addition, words which opened subordinate clauses and even dialogue were relatively limited in variety, and were easily recognized as indicators that a new phrase of the chant should commence.

Becker (1979:253–54) considers words such as these in terms of their "heaviness": that "the larger (i.e., larger in scope)" a unit, the heavier will be the "connective," "with heaviness defined purely in terms of the number of words in the first section of the sentence." This observation makes a valid point, but several important factors have not been considered. First, the yardstick given for the "largeness" of a unit is very susceptible to subjective interpretation. In the absence of a for-

21. Members of the audience do not hear or expect to hear every word. Repetition enables them to grasp all the performer is seeking to communicate, and the "plentiful padding" does not bother them at all. Indeed they tend not to "hear" it.

22. In the light of other indications (chapter 4), it may be speculated that the infrequent use of *setelah* constructions in the Beraim Bapa episode of the *Hikayat Raja-raja Pasai*—in spite of the ministrations of a nineteenth-century copyist in Java—points to the oral origins of this text. This should not, of course, be taken to mean that it is therefore older than texts which have more subordinating constructions. The language of the Srivijaya inscriptions apparently used a variety of subordinating devices.

mal criterion there is no way of establishing that what we might see as a major division was actually intended by the writer. Fortunately, there is such a criterion: the use of rubrication and/or thicker letters. From these visual cues it is apparent that the importance or size of a division does not necessarily correlate directly with the number of "connectives" used. Often a major section may be introduced by a single word, such as a huge *Bermula*. This does not imply that Becker's view is invalid. Rather we may say that verbal "heaviness" has been supplemented by a *visual* heaviness. In stylized oral composition there is indeed a tendency to use lengthier openers for the more important divisions of a performance. Here again, however, the actual number of words used may be deceptive: we often find that the syllables of a single word are so prolonged that, in terms of time taken to utter them, they are the lengthiest of openers and serve as cues that a major new section is to commence. And this device is also employed in the chanting of manuscripts. We should be aware, furthermore, that there is a certain hierarchy of these scene openers, from *al-kesah* down to *arakian, kalakian,* and so on. And the importance of openers may be raised by the use of rubrication, as is often found with *syahdan*. But no matter how long a combination one might produce with a *setelah,* a *maka,* or a *demikian,* it would still rank below an *al-kesah* or a *bermula*.

In chapter 3, I observed that a Malay manuscript did not make use of visual space to create divisions, such as indentations for new paragraphs, or gaps to indicate new chapters; nor did it employ the European type of punctuation used in modern, printed *Jawi* texts. A period was occasionally used, as in the *Silsilah Raja-raja Berunai:* V̇; a mere dot would have disappeared in the sea of dots (intended or otherwise) that characterize a page of writing in a *Jawi* manuscript. In speaking of parataxis and subordination in traditional Malay literature, therefore, we should remember that the published romanized texts with their modern European format and punctuation are a far cry from what was seen by either the scribe or the reciter. And confining our study to such texts is to distance ourselves unnecessarily from the text actually produced by the pen of the scribe and used by the reciter. It is all too easy to expect European conventions in such a European-looking text.

Our consideration of a correlation between the time taken to enunciate something and its relative importance prompts us to suggest a wider application: that the prolonging of "telling" time may serve as a device to illustrate the importance of something. Merely to state that important matters take longer to relate might seem simplistically obvious. When, however, we examine some of the interminable accounts of, say, weddings, we may conclude that the length of such passages may not merely be the result of the author's having so much information to convey or to preserve. Often, such accounts appear to be deliberately drawn out by an increased use of repetition and fillers. When this is considered in the context of the performance of such literature, where the listeners are not expected to concentrate at the same level of intensity throughout and where performance time is not limited, one may suggest that it is the length of the telling, the time consumed, that is especially important in emphasizing the momentous nature of an event. For example, in the *Hikayat Seri Rama,* we may wonder why the war between Inderapurinegara and Biruhasyapurwa should be related at such great length, especially as it seems quite peripheral to the main tale. I would argue that by so doing, the writer is able to emphasize the great importance of Rawana's success in bringing peace. Similarly, in the *Hikayat Aceh* (Iskandar, 1959: 100ff), by devoting thirty-five pages (pp. 78–113) of his text to an interminable description of the wedding of Mansur Syah and Princess Raja Indera Bangsa, the scribe underlines the momentous nature of this event. The progeny of this union will be the hero of the *Hikayat,* Iskandar Muda.

That it is often the length of the telling rather than the content of what is told which underlines the relative importance of an event or character would seem to be confirmed by one specific aspect of stylized oral composition. The use of *bilangan* (runs) in the Malay *wayang* provides an example: the importance of a character is indicated by the length of the utterance concerning him. The *bilangan* is often gabbled at high speed, making it impossible for the audience to grasp much of the content.

Of course, this is but one aspect of the "copious" nature of oral and orally oriented composition. In this respect, it is germane to consider further the remarks made earlier concerning "codified copiousness." The facts that the oral stylized form was copious and its use was associated with relatively formal occasions meant that the copious came to be associated with decorum. Thus, in order to be decorous, one's speech, and particularly one's writing, must be wordy. That this is still a widespread tendency in Malay society may be illustrated by a minor incident at the Universiti Sains in Penang in 1980: a colleague, Fatimah Busu, who had been battling valiantly to make her students stop rambling and get to the point, attached a comment to this effect on the grade list she displayed outside her office, and was only slightly amused by the scribble which appeared on the notice the next day saying: "*Awak bukan Melayukah?*" ("Aren't you a Malay?"), intimating that being Malay meant being polite and decorous, that is, verbose.

The transition from an aurally experiencing manuscript culture to the visually consumed medium of print resulted in a significant shrinkage of the traditional copiousness. As I have observed elsewhere (1980:23), I used to feel quite irritated when, on the point of purchasing published versions of works in "classical" Malay, I would discover that they were not copies of manuscripts, but rather "retold" (*diolah kembali, diceritakan kembali*) versions. I would grumble that there was no need for such "retelling," as modern Malays have little difficulty in reading traditional Malay literature. It took me quite some time to realize that the process of retelling involved reducing the degree of copiousness by cutting out repetition and what was, by print standards, redundancy. It is clear that the retellers understood intuitively what I did not: that works intended to be consumed aurally required retailoring for a reading audience.

The transition to print culture began somewhat earlier in what is now Indonesia than in the Malay peninsula (now West Malaysia). A comparison of Indonesian and Malayan written composition in the 1940s reveals that the latter still revealed much more of a need for *copia* than the former. This may be illustrated by comparing Indonesian and Malayan Malay translations of English passages. For example, in the book *English through Pictures* (Richards & Gibson, 1952), first published in 1945, prefaces are provided in forty-one languages. The preface in the original English is 1.3 pages long. The Indonesian translation is 1.6 pages long. The Malay translation is 2.3 pages in length, the longest of all the languages in Latin script. For example, a passage in English reads:

> The load on your memory is kept light. All your attention can be given to seeing how changes in the sentences go along with changes in the meaning. . . . Recordings are available which will speak the sentences to you, with intervals for you to repeat after the speaker.

In Indonesian:[23]

> Kita tidak usah mengingatkan terlampau banyak. Kita dapat memusatkan perhatian kita untuk melihat bagaimana perubahan dalam kalimat sejalan

---

23. The spelling has been adapted into *ejaan yang disempurnakan* (the new Malay/Indonesian spelling) in both cases.

dengan perubahan tentang artinya. . . . Ada juga tersedia piring-piring gramapon, yang mengucapkan kalimat-kalimat itu dengan berhenti-henti, sehingga kita mendapat kesempatan mengucapkannya pula.

In Malayan Malay:

> . . . menjadi ringanlah bebanan itu di atas ingatan kita iaitu tidaklah payah kita senentiasa ingat-ingat apa makna perkataan ini, apa makna perkataan itu melainkan kelapanganlah juga akal kita hendak memperhatikan bagaimana karangan ayat itu berubah-ubah mengikut makna yang dimaksudkan memberi itu. . . . Adalah telah disediakan beberapa buah piring gramapaun yang sudah diperbuat supaya dapat kita menengar bunyi sebutan ayat-ayat itu sebagaimana biasa disebutkan dalam bahasa Inggeris, dan lepas tiap-tiap ayat yang disebutkan itu ada sela bagi kita sendiri pula menyebutkannya menurut bunyi sebutan yang di dalam piring itu.

CHAPTER 8

The Adding Mode: Nonstylized Storytelling

An examination of the linkages used in narrative delivered in everyday speech provides us with a good opportunity to compare oral and literate modes of composition. In a study of over a hundred story-tellings, given by eighty-three[1] persons whose formal education ranged from none at all to completion of high school, a clear difference was observed between the styles of oral and literate tellers. I am not suggesting that once a person acquires a little literacy he crosses a great divide, evidence of which is immediately reflected in his narrative. My repeated use of "oral orientation" is intended to combat such a notion. And in the group of eighty-three people studied, the degrees to which print-literate patterns were interiorized in their thought processes varied considerably. The comparison of "oral" and "literate" tellers does not involve a simple dichotomy, therefore, but rather a contrasting of the poles of a continuum: that is, between the styles of the illiterate and semiliterate (those who have had two years of elementary school at most and read with difficulty) on the one hand, and those who have completed at least three years of high school and read habitually (be this only newspapers), on the other. A literate teller is usually able to vary his style between an oral[2] and literate mode of speech depending upon his audience, but even when narrating to illit-

1. Fifty-one of whom were recorded by my students at Universiti Sains in Penang.
2. That is, in the sense of nonliterate. Both were of course oral in the sense of being spoken.

erates he may find it hard to abandon entirely his literate thought patterns. An illiterate does not have this option: the same oral style[3] is employed whether he be performing for literates or illiterates. One type of experiment which illustrated well the contrast between oral and literate modes of telling involved having a literate hear a story from an illiterate, and then retell it later both to literates and to illiterates,[4] all of whom would be speakers of the same dialect.

THE NONLITERATE

In nonstylized storytelling, we find that oral individuals tend to use an adding style almost exclusively. This is particularly revealed in the extensive use of simple juxtaposition to recount a sequence of events. This does not, however, produce a long, monotonous listing of consecutive actions, as may best be illustrated by quoting a number of excerpts.[5]

A. [Of the hero's catching a white rat which had stolen his watermelons]—
Seberang Perai

'Dah 'tu, dia pi, pi, dia pi, pi, dia cekup tikus yang putih. Puh! Cekup tikus putih, heh. Dia cekup tikus putih pi; tikus putih kata, "Ah, ah, lepaslah aku," dia kata. "Lepas, lepas aku, aku- apa hang mau aku nak bagi." Kata dia, "Aku mau; la aku tak lepas hang." "Hang mau apa?" "Aku mau kain setera puri." "Hang mau kain setera puri; he—hang lepas aku. Balik pi ambil." "Aku tak lepas hang. Kalau hang balik, hang tak mai 'dah. Buah-buah aku nya aku su- suruh hang bubuh mas-mas urai semua. Tak mau bagi jadi buah tembikai 'dah." Bubuh buah- dalam buah tembikai 'tu mas urai. Ambil kain, pi suruh rakyat dia ambil kain setera puri. Mai "Nah" bagi. Bagi, he, dia pun lepaslah.

After that, he went, went, he went, went, he caught a white rat. Puh! Caught a white rat, heh. He caught a white rat, went; the white rat said, "Ah, ah, let me go," he said. "Let, let me go. I—what [ever] you want I will give." Said he, "I want; or I won't let you go." "What do you want?" "I want fine silk." "You want fine silk; all right, you let me go. [I'll] go back [and] get [it]." "I won't let you go. If you go back, you won't come back. These fruit of mine [I] want you to put gold [in] all [of them]. [I] don't want them as watermelons any more." [He] put fruit- in the watermelon,

---

3. Though, of course, this may veer between the casual and noncasual, intimate and respectful, depending upon the situation (see Sweeney, 1972:49, and chapter 6 of the present work).
4. Without the obvious presence of a tape recorder or myself.
5. See note 4 to chapter 7.

gold. [He] got the cloth, went [and] ordered his subjects [to] fetch fine silk. [He] came, "Here" [and] gave [it to him]. Gave it, hm, he was set free.

B. [Of Pak Pandir returning with padi chaff he has bought instead of rice]—Kedah

Pikullah dia pun. Pikul, pikul, sampai nyeberang sungai. Dia tengok ke-rengga 'duk lalu. Kerengga 'duk lalu berderet banyak. Dia kata, "Aku seorang tak kan tak boleh lalu," dia kata. "Ha, kerengga berderet banyak, bergumuh," dia kata. "Aku seorang tak kan tak boleh lalu 'ni." Dia kata, "Aku nak tumpang lalu sikit ikut titi hang 'ni." Dia bercakap dengan kerengga 'tu. Dia kata, "Aku nak lalu." Pergi dia pun, pergi, pergi naik atas ranting bulu . . . h. 'Kan—Bau! belebak jatuh sungai. Tertungging; yang padi tadi habis mengelapung. Padi ringa . . . n. "Tangguk! Depan tangguk," dia kata.

Carried [it] on his shoulder he did. Carried, carried, arrived at the river crossing. He saw red ants passing over. The red ants were passing over in long lines. He said, "I [being only] one person, it cannot be that I cannot pass over," he said. "Ha, the red ants are in long lines, hordes [of them]," he said. "I [being only] one person, it cannot be that I cannot pass over here." He said, "I'd like to join you for a moment in passing over this bridge of yours." He was talking to the ants. He said, "I want to pass over." Went he did, went, went [and] got on the twig of bambo . .o Well [what do you expect] . . Blam! Splat [he] fell into the river. Arse up in the air. The padi just now was all floating. Padi cha . .ff. "Scoop it up! In front there, scoop it up," he said.

C. [Of a person who gives birth to a pig]—Johor

Lama babi 'tu besar siang besar malam. "Eh," kata mak bidan. "Orang beranak manusia, engkau beranak babi." "Apa 'nak buat," kata dia. "Tak-dir Allah," kata dia. Jadi babi 'tu 'dah besar. Kurung bawah rumah. Babi . . . i. 'Dah kurung bawah rumah. Lama-lama. Dia kurung bawah rumah. Besar siang babi 'tu, besar malam. Orang berburu. Berburunya tadi tujuh lapan orang. Terpandanglah babi 'tu tadi. Anak raja babi 'tu. Pergi turun bersiram. Emak dia tak ada. Bapak dia tak ada. Orang pergi kerja.

In time, the pig grew by day, grew by night. "Eh," said the midwife. "[Other] people give birth to children, you give birth to a pig." "What can be done," said she. "God's will," said she. So the pig had grown big. Penned [it] under the house. [A] pig [after all; what do you expect]. [They] had penned [it] under the house. Time went by. They penned it under the house. The pig grew big by day, grew big by night. People were hunting. Hunting just now there were seven or eight people. [They] happened to see the pig just now. The pig princess. [She] went down to bathe. Her mother was not there; her father was not there. [The] people [had] gone to work.

D. [Of a *puteri*[6] performer hiding glutinous rice]—Kelantan

Tuk Minduk 'ni pun pergilah. Bawa pulut tiga gantang 'tu. 'Gi gagau dalam gelap 'tu. Temulah pohon nangka. Pohon nangka 'tu duduk tepi pusu. Duduk tepi pusu. Tapi dia tak tahu. Tak tahu kata pusu. Dia pun rasa pohon nangka 'tu; temu secabang ambil sebungkus, 'tak, selit celah cabang dia. Ambil sa selit celah cabang 'tu. Ambil sa selit. Cukup tiga cabang tiga bungkus. Dia pun marilah. "Sudah dah ke... ?"

Tuk Minduk set off. Took along the three *gantang* of glutinous rice. Went [and] groped in the dark. Found a jackfruit tree. The jackfruit tree sat on the edge of an anthill. Sat on the edge of an anthill. But he didn't know. Didn't know [that's to] say [it was] an anthill. He felt the jackfruit tree. Found a forked branch, took one packet, placed [it] shoved it in the gap [between] the fork. Took [another] shoved [it] in the gap [between] a fork. Took, shoved. Complete, three forks, three packets. He came. "Have you finished ... ?"

E. [Of a lazy character being told to make a fish-trap and catch fish]—Kelantan

"Mak buatlah; biar kita 'gi tahan," buat ke malas dia saat 'ni.[7] Jadi mak dia pun buat. Mak dia buat saat 'ni, 'gilah. 'Gi, 'gi, 'gi [Sungai?—question from listener] Bukan 'gi sungai. 'Gi naik atas pohon durian. 'Gi sangkut di dahan durian. Tahan buah durian. Tahan buah durian, jatuh buah durian dalam 'tu 'tu. Bawa' kelik dianya. Bawa' kelik. "Dum!" rembas atas jemuran. Ga' mak dia kata, "Mu gi tahan di mana Awang?"

"Mother, [you] make [it]; leave me to set it up" [he was able to say, so] lazy this [fellow was] just now. So his mother made [it]. His mother made it just now, [he] went. Went, went, went, (To the river?) [He] didn't go to the river. [He] went [and] climbed a durian tree. Stuck [it] in the branches of the durian. Set [it] up [to catch] durian fruit. Set [it] up [to catch] durian fruit, durian fruit fell into it. Took [them] back [with him] he did. Blam! [He] threw [them] down on the verandah. Well, his mother said, "Where did [you] set [it] up, Awang?"

F. [Of a mother whose child has been wrongly divined by astrologers to be cursed]—Kedah

Dia panggil anak dia, mai 'kut dapur makan nasi. Anak pun makanlah. Mai Tuk raja 'ni, sepak pinggan-pinggan pelanting habis. Marahlah pasal anak celaka 'kan? 'Duk layan dia buat apa? Teriaklah si anak 'ni. 'Dah teriak tadi, dia pun—tahulah kata dia orang—orang benci 'dah. Dia pun

6. *Main puteri:* spirit mediumship used for healing. *Minduk:* the player of the spike fiddle who acts as the medium's control.
7. *Sa'at 'ni:* lit., "this second." Has the connotation of "the one we were talking about just a moment ago."

khabar 'kat mak dia 'kut dia kata, dia nak pi, dia kata. "Nak pi ke mana?" mak dia kata. "Hak 'tu ikut nasib," dia kata. Dia pi, dia pi . . . i jalan, jalan, jumpalah satu tempat itu Merbau Lima [Merbau Lima?—question from listener] Ha, Merbau Lima. [Nama tempat 'tulah?] Ha, nama tempat 'tu. Jadi kayu merbau lima pokok di situ.

She called her child, [told him to] come through the kitchen [and] eat. The child ate. In came the raja, kicked the plates flying all over the place. Angry because the child [was] cursed, [you understand] don't [you]? Paying attention to him for what reason? This child wept. Having cried just now, he— knew [that's to] say people—people hated [him]. He told his mother; he said, he was going to go, he said. "Where are you going to go?" his mother said. "That's up to fate," he said. He went. He went. Walked, walked, came upon a place Merbau Lima (Merbau Lima?) Yes, Merbau Lima. (The name of that place?) Yes, the name of that place. Happens there were five *merbau* trees there.

G. [Of a couple who desired a child]—Kedah

Konon, adalah satu cerita. Mak Miskin dengan Pak Miskin. Ha, lagu 'tu. Depa 'tu sampai 'dah lama kahwin tak dak anak. Hendaklah 'kat anak. Bila 'dah aa—dapat anak, lama tak lama dapatlah anak. Beranak, beranak jadi anak tupai. Jadi anak tupai 'gitu, jadi lama-lama, bela-bela, besar besar, besar besar, koi besar, koi besar, koi besar, lama-lama anak tupai pun lompat sana, lompat sini, lompat sana, lompat sini. Habis pada 'tu, dialah lama-lama, dia 'duk dekat rumah raja. Ha, dia kata 'kat mak dia, "Pilah minang mak anak raja . . . "

It is said, there is a story, Mak Miskin and Pak Miskin. Ah, that's the way it was. They arrived [at the point where they] had been married a long time, they had no child. [They] wanted a child. When [they] had aaa— obtained a child—After some time [lit.: long not long] [they] obtained a child. Gave birth to a child; gave birth to a child, turned out to be a baby squirrel. Turned out to be a baby squirrel like that, well time went by, [they] cared for [it], [it got] big, big, big, big; bigger, bigger, bigger; time went by, the baby squirrel jumped there, jumped here, jumped there, jumped here. After that, he, time went by, he lived near the raja's house. "Ha," he said to his mother, "Mother, go [and] ask for the hand of the princess . . . "

H. [Of a prince who wishes to fly a kite]—Kedah

Anak raja 'tu kah minta ayahanda dia nak pi—padanglah, nak pi main wau. [Mm] Anak raja 'tu, wau maslah, buat wau, pi main wau mas, pilah empat ora . . . ng. Pilah, pi padang nun. Pi, pi, dia lambunglah wau 'tu. [Mm] Raja 'tu, lambung-lambung, wau 'tu putus, 'tu 'tu pi jatuh 'kat situlah, 'kat anak dara muka kuda 'tu. Wau dia 'tu. [Jodoh] Ha, jodoh! 'Tu 'tukah dia ambil, dia ambil bunyi buanglah dia 'tu . . .

The prince, was it,[8] asked his father, he wanted to go—to the field, wanted to go [and] play with a kite. (Hm) The prince, a golden kite, made a kite, went to play with a golden kite, went [in a group of] four people. Went, went to the field over there. Went, went, he launched the kite. (Hm) The prince, launched and launched; the kite broke away, [it] went and fell near there, near the young girl with the horse's face. His kite. (His match) Yes, his match! She took it, did she, she took it and hid it away. . . .

From these excerpts we see that, although the tellers make wide use of simple juxtaposition, the result is not merely a list of actions. For one thing, one of the most frequent actions is speech; a character rarely proceeds very far without opening his mouth, even though he be alone (see, e.g., B), and his words will almost always be dramatized. The stretches of direct speech are usually linked with the phrases *dia kata* or *kata dia* (he/she said; said he/she). These are not employed merely to indicate a new speaker but to punctuate the speech of a single speaker (e.g., B, C). And when, as often happens in dialogue, *dia kata* is used to punctuate the speech of two characters, it may not serve to distinguish between them, as, " 'When are you going?' he said, 'Tomorrow,' he said, 'At nine,' he said." (For an example of this, see A.) *Dia kata* is also used to punctuate indirect speech, which usually differs from direct only in the use of the third person pronoun, as in *Eh, dia kata, dia jalan, dia terbang balik, dia kata* ("Eh, he said, he's going, he's flying back, he said"). (For another example of this, see excerpt F.) On occasion, direct may switch to indirect speech or vice versa, as in *"Anak awak bodoh," dia kata "Tapi kalau mau . . . ada syarat"; Dia mau jembatan mas, dia kata* ("Your son is stupid," he said, "But if he wants . . . there is a condition." He wanted a golden bridge, he said) (Perai). Often, *dia kata* becomes merely a punctuating grunt, reminding one of the performances of Victor Borge. It may be noted also that *kata* is regularly used to refer to questions, answers and orders, where standard practice would employ *tanya, jawab, suruh,* et cetera.[9] Sometimes, all indications of speaker (X said, Y said, etc.) are dispensed with, and the dialogue takes on the form of drama, as in (A).

8. The old lady telling this tale assumed a very nonassertive ethos, to the extent that she appears to ask her listeners to affirm that what she says is so. We may note that the prince-meets-the-princess motif in this excerpt is a common one in Malay tradition. Cf., e.g., *Hikayat Andaken Penurat.*

9. On the other hand, we often find in the *Tarik Selampit* and other stylized telling that *jawab* and *jawab kata* are used simply to mean "say."

In nonstylized telling, the speaker is able to exploit all the possibilities offered by the intonation of everyday speech. Thus, by means of a series of utterances simply juxtaposed, he is able to provide description, commentary, and explanation, while continuing steadily to advance his narrative, and at the same time indicating the relationships between situations and events; whether, for example, they are to be understood as arising and/or happening according to the sequence in which they are recounted.

Even from excerpts as short as the above we are able to appreciate the close interaction possible between teller and listeners in nonstylized storytelling. It is taken for granted that the audience may ask questions and make comments (e.g., excerpts E, F, H), and the teller will, of his own accord, often pause to provide a comment or word of explanation, or question his audience to make sure that they have understood, as in (F). It is indicative of the importance of intonation that the teller's comment may consist of but a single word. It is only the somewhat drawn-out, tapering-off, enunciation of words such as *Babi* (C) and *Padi ringan* (B) which tells us that in this context they are comments carrying the connotation of "What do you expect?" Similarly, it is the intonation of *Orang pergi kerja* (lit.: person/s go work) in (C)—helped again, of course, by the context—which indicates that this is not the recounting of a new action but an explanation of why the mother and father were not there. Again, in (B), the intonation of *Dia bercakap . . . kerengga itu* (lit.: He speaks/spoke with those red ants) indicates that this is not a new action, but an explanation of what PP was doing.

The person unfamiliar with this type of storytelling may wonder how it is that a teller may provide so much explanation and commentary, and yet omit it when it seems most necessary. For example, in excerpt C, a pig is born to humans and grows up. Suddenly mention is made of people hunting; and then the pig is referred to as "the pig princess." The point to be made is that the teller's intended audience would not be at all confused by this. The structure of these tales is highly schematic; the teller takes it for granted that her audience's level of expectation is determined by their familiarity with the schemata which produce the plot patterns. As I have observed in chapter 7, in this particular type of tale where a grotesque character is born to humans, the expectation is that the character will turn out to be, in fact, a prince or princess, and the grotesque appearance is but an envelope which will be taken off later in the tale. Furthermore, if the character is a female, we expect a prince to arrive on the scene and make contact. Thus, in this tale, we take it for granted that "the people hunting" signals the arrival of the hero. Obviously she is really a princess, and the mention of "going down to bathe" plus the absence of the parents leaves no doubt that they are about to meet. The audience's level of expectation is clearly revealed in excerpt H: here, the grotesque character is a girl with the face of a horse. When the prince's kite lands near her abode, a listener comments "*Jodoh*" (match, intended), which carries the connotation that they are destined to marry each other. The listener informed me that she had never heard this tale before, but she knew that the horse head would be only an envelope and that the girl was a princess. Thus, though the motifetic or dynamic material may have been new, her familiarity with the motifemic structure allowed no confusion.

Again, we note that the comment *jodoh*, echoed by the teller, is a single word. Similarly, the use of one word—*cerita* (tale)—enabled a teller from Johor to dissociate herself from the tale she was telling. Sensing that the story might seem somewhat bizarre to her listeners from the city, she paused and said "*cerita*" (i.e., "It's only a story"), trailing the last syllable, and then laughing.

The use of juxtaposition does not imply, moreover, that a tale is a succession of terse, staccato utterances. The content is still unfolded slowly, chiefly by means of liberal repetition. And this allows recapitulation. A teller may also repeat a specific point if she is unconvinced that she has been understood or if a particular emphasis is needed. Often, of course, repetition results from hesitation and false starts. Repetition is also widely used to indicate duration; one is given an idea of how long an action continued by the number of times it is repeated, as in all the above excerpts except (D). Repetition will also be employed when an action is performed more than once, as in (D).

As we have noted in stylized telling, juxtaposing does not confine the teller to presenting a series of independent statements; a statement may become dependent upon another by association, and in nonstylized telling, this is often achieved by repeating an action with a rising intonation, and then following it immediately with the next action or situation. For example, in (E): "Set it up to catch durian fruit. Set it up to catch durian fruit, durian fruit fell into it"; in (F): "Walked. Walked, came upon . . ."; in (G): "Gave birth to a child. Gave birth to a child, turned out to be . . ."; in (B): "Carried. Carried, ..." The repeated action may also be followed by a situation rather than an action, as in: *Sampai ke satu kuala. Sampai kuala 'ni, ada satu pulau* ("Arrived at a rivermouth. Arrived at the rivermouth, there was an island"). This construction may indicate the completion of one action before another begins, and might then be translated "Having . . . ," "when," "after . . . ". The connotation is determined by the context and may sometimes merely have the sense of "and" or "while," as in: *Duduk situlah. Duduk situ ga', buat kerja.* ("[He] stayed there. Stayed there, worked.") Often the repetition is separated from the new statement by words such as *ga'* (in the above example), *'tu* (abbr. of *itu*), *saat 'ni* ("this moment," "just now"), in which case it is the last syllable of such words which is given the rising intonation. On the whole, this construction tends to be used when there is a lack of dramatic immediacy. When used frequently, the result is a somewhat leisurely pace with the content being unfolded very gradually. Frequent use, moreover, tends to indicate that the teller is not exactly overtaxing himself, or on the contrary, that he is proceeding very carefully, recapitulating at every step, to ensure that he achieves the correct sequence. It will be seen that this construction is not unlike the *setelah* construction of traditional literature, where the *setelah* compensates for the loss of everyday intonation. We are also reminded of the *sudah/telah sudah* construction in the stylized oral form: *'Dah makan, dia jalan* (as in the *Awang Batil* of Perlis). This latter usage is also found in nonstylized oral telling, as in (F): . . . *teriak. 'Dah teriak. . . .* But it is less common than repetition juxtaposed with the new statement. Again it is the intonation which determines whether the *sudah* construction is dependent on the following utterance. For example:

> 'Dah habis bakar, dia pun pengsan. Pengsan. Sadar. 'Dah sadar. Dia buat mengucap. Habis mengucap dia pergi ambil air sembahyang. 'Dah habis ambil air sembahyang. Dia pun menyembah laki dia. [Johor].

> When it was completely burnt, she fainted. Fainted. Conscious. She's conscious. She recites the articles of faith.[10] Having finished reciting she goes to take ritual ablutions. Now she's finished taking ritual ablutions. She pays obeisance to her husband.

We see that both *sudah* and *habis* precede independent and dependent constructions. In the former case, the effect is similar to that of the "dramatic present" in English.

---

10. *Dua kalimah syahadah,* to the effect that "There is no God but Allah, and that Muhammad is his prophet"; frequently uttered in times of danger or stress.

The oral individual also makes use of subordinating constructions. And in view of the frequent comments on and explanation of the tale, such constructions are not mainly confined to the dialogue of the characters, as in stylized performance. However, apart from the *kalau* . . . construction, subordination tends to be used much less frequently than simple juxtaposing to express whys, wherefores, becauses, and the like.[11] In the presentations of illiterate tellers, words such as *sebab* tend to be used in short linkages, such as *Sebab 'tulah dia* . . . (That was the reason he . . .), where the word is followed by a nominal. Illiterate tellers made but sparse use of *sebab* clauses such as *Jadi si Buta 'ni 'duk berehatlah kononnya sebab dia 'ni buta* (Perak) ("So Blindy had a rest so it's said, because he was blind"). Worthy of note is: *Cantik tahu! Sebab dia tak mahu, dia kata, buat apa, dia kata, sungguh raja, dia miskin* (Melaka) ("She was beautiful, you know! [That's] the reason he didn't want [her], he said, for what reason, he said, true [he's a] raja [but] he's poor"). This *sebab* construction is in fact an independent "That's the reason" (rather than a "because . . ." or "the reason that . . .") utterance, equivalent to *sebab itu*. Note, too, that rather than use a *sungguhpun* subordination, the teller juxtaposes "true, raja; he, poor." Attention may also be drawn to a usage common in the narrations of oral Kelantanese involving the use of *sabab* (a variant of *sebab*) which carries the connotation "That's why," and is used as a simple linkage: *Sabab dia tak ser* ("That's why [indeed, no wonder] he was unwilling").

An examination was made of twenty-one tellings by illiterates— selected at random from my collected materials—in order to ascertain the frequency of subordinate constructions of this type. Fourteen tellings are from the east coast, seven from the west coast of West Malaysia. The criterion used here for a subordinate construction is an utterance which follows what Asmah (1968) terms "a dependent sentence marker." The utterances included contain a verbal (verb or adjective) or are of the N_1n (or N_1 + Time/Place word) type. Phrases consisting of marker plus single nominal (such as *lepas itu, sebab itu*) are not included. Figures given for the following constructions are: (a) the number of occurrences in 26,500 words for the west coast and in 11,000 words for the east coast; and (b) their frequency ratio to those in the tellings of literates (see listing at end of this chapter).

---

11. Incidentally, I observed that professional storytellers, when recounting a tale in everyday language, tended to use more subordinating constructions than the average for oral individuals.

	West coast		*East coast*	
Sebab ("because")	14	1:2	3	1:3.6
Kerana ("because")	2	1:12	—	—
Dengan kerana ("because")	1	1:10	—	—
Pasal ("because")	11	1:2	—	—
Kalau/Jika/Jikalau ("if")	103	1:0.74	37	1:1.3
Kot-kot (Kedah/Penang; "lest," "in case")	1	1:7	—	—
Muga (Kelantan; "because," "for")	—	—	10	1:1
Walau ("even though")	2	1:4	—	—
Macam mana (Kelantan: *Guana*) ("how")	3	1:3	3	1:1
Macam ("as")	1	1:11	—	—
Awa (Kelantan; "because")	—	—	2	—

With the main exception of *kalau,* which is equally common in the tellings of literates and illiterates, the rate of incidence for these constructions is much lower in those of illiterates. The rate would have been lower still if we had excluded the following usages:

1. Repetition. When several of the tellers used one of these constructions they tended to repeat it immediately. Eight of the fourteen occurrences of *sebab,* for example, were employed by the one teller (from Perak), and four of these were used in the space of fifty words.

2. Several of these constructions did not depend upon a specific main utterance, but rather on the context. For example, half the instances of *sebab, pasal* and *muga* began new sentences and were separated by a long pause from the preceding material to be explained. Most of the occurrences of *muga,* and both of *awa* might be translated as "Well, what do you expect . . ." rather than "because."

It may also be noted that the subordinate constructions of illiterates were much shorter than those of literates. In the sample checked, moreover, no instances were found of two subordinate constructions in the same stretch of utterance resulting in embedding, as in ". . . because, if . . ., he . . ." Incidentally, relative clauses of the *yang/hak* type need not be embedded in a main clause. When they occur in the middle of a sentence, the referent is often picked up after the relative clause (e.g., "The man who . . ., he . . .").

Subordinating constructions of sequence and time are also relatively infrequent in the narrations of oral individuals. For example, in three tales told by an old lady in Melaka, *bila* constructions (i.e., noninterrogative "when . . ."), as in *Bila sampai aja ke sana, ah! Puteri Bongsu 'dah siap, tahu* ("When they had just arrived there, ah! Princess Bongsu was ready, you know.") occurred only twice in approximately nine thousand words. As with *sebab*, *bila* tended to be used most frequently in short linkages such as *Bila 'gitu* ("When like that," i.e., "That being the case"). It is worthy of note, moreover, that a number of attempted subordinations turned out to be what we may term "aborted constructions." An example of this is encountered in (C), where the teller, having said *Bila 'dah a—dapat anak,* finds herself unable to complete the construction, and abandons it. It is also germane to mention that two semiliterate tellers, who were very much aware of the presence of the tape recorder and anxious to attain the heights of formality, employed constantly the "juxtaposing of repeated statements with new statement" construction, but preceded the repetition with *bila,* as, for example: *Anak Raja Rum nak pi menikah. Bila nak pi menikah . . . Anak Raja Rum tadi sudah sehat tubuh badan dia. Bila sehat tubuh badan dia. . . .* (Kedah) ("The son of Raja Rum wished to go and get married. When he wished to go and get married . . . The son of Raja Rum just now, had recovered his bodily health. When he had recovered his bodily health . . .").

The interaction between illiterate speaker and literate listener may often reveal their different speech patterns. This may be illustrated by the following excerpts from a narration by an oral individual in Kedah to a neighbor of hers who was a university student. The student's comments are in square brackets. *Berjalan, berjalan 'tu baru jumpa gergasi. [Jumpa gergasi] Hm* (coughs). *[Bila jumpa dengan gergasi] Bila jumpa dengan gergasi dia kata. . .* ("Walked, walked only then met the ogre. [Met the ogre] Hm (coughs). [When (he) met with the ogre] When he met with the ogre, he said. . ."); *'Dah berjalan sampai Ligur [Bila sampai di Ligur] Sampai-sampai di Ligur 'tu, harap anak raja. . .* ("Had traveled (and) arrived at Ligur. [When they arrived at Ligur?] Arrived-arrived at Ligur, the prince hoped. . ."); *Sampai-sampai malam, suruh makan malam, sampai-sampai siang suruh makan siang* ("Arrived-arrived at night, ordered to eat at night; arrived-arrived in daylight, ordered to eat in daylight"). This is amplified a few sentences later by the student: *Bila sampai pagi makan pagi, bila sampai petang makan petang* ("When arriving in the morning, ate in the morning; when arriving in the afternoon, ate in the afternoon"). This time the teller merely says "Hm." From this we observe the tendency of the student, a native of the same village, to use subordinate constructions with *bila*, while the teller clearly prefers to juxtapose her ideas. The only time she uses *bila* in her narration is as the result of the prompt in the first excerpt. The second time she is prompted, she does not pick up the *bila*. In the third excerpt, we see how the student preserves the balance of the original, but makes it a subordinate construction.

The frequency of use of subordinate constructions of time and sequence may be illustrated by the following figures, based upon the twenty-one tellings cited above:

	West coast (26,500)		East coast (11,000)	
Bila ("when")	16	1:9	3	1:22
Apabila ("when")	1	1:6	—	—
Sampai ("up to," "until")	6	1:5	—	—
Lepas/selepas ("after")	5	1:1.5	1	1:16
Belum/sebelum ("before")	—	—	1	1:8
Masa/semasa ("while")	3	1:10	3	1:3
Sedang molek (Kelantan; "just as")	—	—	2	—
Belang-belang (Kelantan; "while")	—	—	2	1:1

As in stylized telling, the nonstylized narration tends to break up the stream of speech into sections by means of phrases carrying a connotation such as "That being the case" and "After that." Examples of such "section openers" are encountered in (A): "*Dah 'gitu* (lit.: "complete like that," i.e. "well," "then") and (C): *Lama* ("in time"). Other section openers are *habis* ("finish"; i.e. "that being finished"); *lepas 'tu* and *'pas 'tu* ("after that"); *kemudian* ("then"); *bilanya* ("when [that was complete]"); *lama 'tu* ("in time," "after some time"). Other openers are not of the "and then" type, but perform the same function, examples being: *kalau begitu* ("if that be so"; i.e. "that being so"); *tak apalah* (lit.: "it doesn't matter," but carrying the connotation of "O.K.," "well, all right"). The basic purpose of such openers is to indicate that a narrative sequence is complete, and that now we can pause for a moment before continuing. They also indicate that the teller is pausing to assemble the threads of his tale. The frequency of use varies considerably, both from teller to teller and in the narration of a single teller. Some speakers use these phrases hardly at all. Others tend to use them frequently when they encounter problems organizing their narration; once they have warmed up, they may find them much less necessary. For example,

> Dia kata dia nak pi menghadap Tuhan. Lepas 'tu pi tiga orang nun, hm— 'as 'tu pi pula 'tu berjumpa dengan—berjalan berjalan 'tu berjumpa dengan Tuk Haji duk sembahyang. Hm—'as 'tu kata oleh Tuk Haji . . .

> He said he was going to present himself before God. After that he went [there were] three of them, hm—after that [they] went off again [and] met up with—[They] walked. Walked [and] met up with a *haji* praying. Hm— after that, the *haji* said . . .

When this teller from Kedah had organized her narration, she used *'as 'tu* far less frequently.

We find a similar situation in a tale from Perak:

> Belum lagi dapat siapa nak panjat. Lai lai li tampelunglah. Lai lai li tampe- lung. Lama 'tu— Tahu main lai lai li tampelung? Tiga orang duk main pulas-pulas tangan 'tu. Lama 'tu kenalah si— sisiapa 'tu— si Burut. Ah si Burut, lama 'tu yang si Buta 'ngan si Bongkok . . .

> Not yet decided who would climb. [So they played] *lai lai li tampelung.*[12] *Lai lai li tampelung.* After some time—[Do you] know how to play *lai lai li tampelung?* The three of them played twisting their hands [like this]. After some time the one to be "it" was—who was it—si Burut. Ah, si Burut; after some time, si Buta and si Bongkok . . .

Some tellers tend to use such phrases throughout their telling. For instance, a semiliterate teller from Perai would narrate for long stretches punctuating well-nigh every statement with *jadi* ("so," "happens that"). For example:

> Jadi orang bagi tahulah 'kat raja. Jadi raja 'ni ingat dia nak kena bunuhlah. Jadi dia arahlah 'kat—rakyat—Jadi dia kata—Jadi adalah satu Mamak Keling.

> So people told the raja. So this raja thought, he will have to kill [the snake]. So he ordered—his subjects—So he said—So there was a certain Indian Muslim.

The use of *jadi* in modern written composition tends to indicate a direct link with what precedes it, and often carries the connotation of "therefore." While I have translated it as "so" in the above excerpt, there is often no such link, as in the last sentence, and the word

---

12. That is, the "scissors, stone, and paper" game (*Janken pon* in Japanese). It is a way of "tossing up."

becomes merely an audible punctuation device. Similar is the use of *kalau begitu,* which might appear to have a conditional function, but which in storytelling usually serves to indicate that one piece of narrative can be put aside and that something new is to be told.

We may note from the three excerpts above that oral individuals tend to favor the use of one particular phrase at the expense of variety. This is not to say that all oral tellers make exclusive use of but one such word or phrase: For instance, the tellers above also employed other words occasionally; in addition to *lepas 'tu,* the Kedah teller also used *ta' apalah;* apart from *lama 'tu,* in the Perak telling we also encounter a few instances of *lepas 'tu,* and the Perai teller also made use of *habis* and *belakang.* Some tellers may use but one such linkage exclusively, however: a teller from Kelantan, for example, employed only *lalu* throughout the course of one telling. It would appear that once used, such a word or phrase tends to reproduce itself, as has been observed by Bijleveld (1943:1ff), though his focus was considerably different from ours.

I referred earlier to the distinction to be made between "story" time and "telling" time. This distinction is particularly relevant to our present concern: we often encounter "and then" phrases which do not appear to indicate an "and then" in the sequence of the tale being told. The reason for this, of course, is that such phrases do not always refer to the tale but to the telling of it: the "and then" refers to "the next thing I am going to tell you," not "the next thing that happened." When a teller is relating a sequence of actions, telling time and story time will tend to coincide. However, when the sequence of telling does not coincide with the order in which events are supposed to have occurred, or when the "and then" is not followed or preceded by an event, the distinction is clear. This may be illustrated by the following examples: *Kedian hamba nak royat sabit Tuan Puteri Jintan Mas* ("Next, I am going to tell you about Princess Jintan Mas"); *Ha! Pak Pandir 'tu pemalas. Lepas 'tu dia kata . . .* ("Ah, PP was lazy by nature. After that he said . . ."); *Ha, kemudian pada 'tu, negeri raja Islam 'ni, Raja Melayu 'ni, ramai* ("After that, the country of the Muslim raja, the Malay raja, (was) populous"); *Cerita dia betul tak betul dalam sejarah raja saya tak tahulah 'tang 'tu. Kemudian, turun 'kat anak dia . . .* ("[Whether] his account is true or not true in the history of kings I don't know. After that, it befell to his child . . ."); A teller informs us that the prince slept in one palace, his princess in another, and then continues: *Kemudian pada 'tu dia mai satu malam . . .* ("The next thing, one night,

he came . . ."); *Ada satu raja. Kemudian dia, kepala dia botak* ("There
was a raja. The next thing: his head was bald"); *Ada seorang raja. Dia
'ni 'dah tua 'dah. Kemudian raja tua 'ni ada dua orang anak laki-laki*
("There was a raja. He was already old. The next thing: this old raja
had two sons"); A woman is made to choose between her six elder
children and the youngest born: *Jadi mak dia kata, "Sayanglah telur se-
sangkak." 'Pas 'tu, maknanya 'tu, buanglah adik bongsu 'tu* ("So their
mother said, ['One has more] affection for a nest of eggs' [than for
merely one egg]. After that [the next thing to be said is] the meaning of
this is: cast away the youngest sister"); *'Pas 'tu, masa 'tu dia dah bawa
jauh dah kambing . . .* ("The next thing is: at that time, he had taken the
goats far away . . ."). *Lepas 'tu ada satu orang. Nama dia Mat* ("Next,
there was a person. His name was Mat"). The distinction between
telling and tale sequence becomes particularly clear in the narration of a
teller from Melaka: in order to involve her listeners in her tale, she
assigns the roles of various characters in her narration to members of
her audience. Thus, for example, "So the three of you came back (pointing to three members of the audience). You (pointing to one of them)
want to marry the princess, but you (pointing again) refuse." This device is not unique; a teller from Johor employs the same technique.
What is of particular concern to us here, however, is that the Melaka
teller also often pretends to assign the role of telling the tale to a member
of her audience. It is here that we see which "and then"s refer to the
telling and which to the tale; after relating a sequence of actions, she
pauses and says, *Habis engkau kata . . .*("The next thing you say is . . .").

THE LITERATE

In the group of eighty-three tellers studied, fifteen had received a
high school education and were fairly habitual readers, and these constitute the literate pole of the continuum. A comparison of the narratives of these tellers with those of oral individuals reveals some major
differences. These lie not in the tales told, for both oral and literate
tellers presented the same types of tale, and, with the exception of one
person who had obtained her story from a book, all had acquired their
tales orally. The differences are rather to be seen on the level of word
choice rather than, say, of plot. They are particularly noticeable in the
methods employed to link utterances. In short, the style of the literate
is far more hypotactic.
It might be argued that the difference results from the fact that the

literate is speaking standard Malay rather than dialect. But this would be entirely in accord with what I am contending: that the literate teller does have that option. And, of course, being literate presupposes some mastery of standard Malay, which is the written dialect. In fact, however, the literate tellers *were* speaking their own dialects. This was not merely because their listeners were speakers of the same dialects (although this is an important factor): had they been discussing a different topic, such as modern literature, with literates, they might well have spoken standard Malay. Here, however, in narrating "folk tales," the use of dialect was considered more appropriate, especially in those cases where the tale was to be recorded. It is here particularly that we observe how literacy has made it possible for such individuals to create distance between themselves and their oral tradition. Such tales are now seen as "folk tales." They were heard in dialect, and authenticity demands that they should be told in dialect. For the oral person, the possibility of entertaining such considerations does not arise.

Of course, a person's literate thought patterns are not simply suspended when he speaks in dialect. Thus, for example, when two highly literate Kelantanese converse, they do not suddenly revert to oral—i.e., illiterate—speech patterns. Even though they be discussing matters of traditional interest, as, for example, the *wayang,* their literate thought patterns tend to reveal themselves. And when discussing more "modern" topics, their conversation may differ from standard, literary Malay mainly in what the literate Kelantanese might himself call his "twang,"[13] and perhaps in an insistence on using dialect pronouns, aspect verbs, and relative pronouns: the Kelantanese, for example, will signal the fact that he is speaking his dialect with the use of *dema* [*'tu*], the Kedah person with the use of *depa* [*'tu*], instead of *mereka* ("they"/"them"), and both may tend to prefer *'duk* over *tengah/ sedang* ("in the middle of"), *hak* over *yang* ("which"). Thus, although there is a clear distinction between the idiom of an oral person speaking his dialect and that of a literate person speaking the standard dialect, in the speech of a literate speaking his dialect (especially to other literates), that distinction may be much less clear. Then, it is in the differences between his speech and that of the illiterate speaker of the dialect that we may learn a good deal about oral and literate habits. And if the purist opines that the literate is no longer speaking the "true" dialect, the same point is being made: the "true" dialect for the purist is the speech of the illiterate, which would then deny to the

13. Using this English term.

literate person the possibility of expressing in his dialect many of the nuances which have become natural for him.

Thus, although the literate may attempt to tell a tale exactly as he heard it from an oral person, his idiom will still tend to reveal evidence of the workings of a literate mind. This is especially so when his audience is literate, but even when he is relating for the benefit of illiterate listeners, his literate thought patterns may reveal themselves. As we shall see, this need not mean only that he uses literate constructions. In the matter of linkages, for example, he may employ only words peculiar to the dialect; yet in the treatment he affords them, as in striving to create variety where the oral person would be content with repetition, he reveals his literate tendencies.

My point is not that it is impossible for a highly literate person to speak with the patterns of oral speech, but that it requires a certain amount of application to be able to think "illiterate" concerning matters one is accustomed to reading about. Literacy enables us not merely to think about new subjects, but also to think in new ways about familiar subjects, and the literate must accept the fact that he must either abandon the idea of discussing many things in "oral," or attempt to "translate." Usually, the literate contents himself with discussing those familiar things in the old ways when conversing with oral persons; otherwise, problems may arise, as in the case of students who came to accept that "all those old stories" were in fact *sastra lisan* (oral literature): I have overheard students on more than one occasion asking questions such as *"Mak Cik, ada sastra lisan?"* ("Auntie, do you have any oral literature?")

In the following excerpts, we shall observe some typical features of the literate narrations.

A. Dengan sebab 'tu, dia pun timbullah perasaan haloba, tamak. Kemudian, dengan tak lengah lagi, dia kumpul segala rakyat bala tentera dia, langgar negeri 'tu. Kemudian, dalam peperangan 'tu, peperangan 'tu dahsyatlah. Jadi negeri Jayanegara tadi 'ni, dengan sekali dengan raja dia, ha dengan segala rakyat dia, depa berjuanglah dengan hebat oleh kerana mempertahankan tanah air yang depa sayang 'tu; tapi dengan kerana sebab rempuhan musuh 'tu terlampau kuat, terlampau besar, jadi rakyat dengan apa—negeri 'tu a—raja negeri 'tu telah tewas. Habis, sultan tadi 'ni, sultan yang katakan Sultan Arif tadi 'ni . . . [Kedah]

Because of that, there arose in him a feeling of covetousness, of greed. After that, lingering no further, he assembled his subjects and troops, invaded that land. After that, in the battle, the battle was terrible. So the land of Jayanegara just now, together with its raja, er together with all his subjects, they battled fiercely, as [they were] defending the native land that they loved; but because the attack of the enemy was so strong, so big, the subjects and er—the land a—the raja of that land were defeated. Then, the sultan just now, the sultan called Sultan Arif just now . . .

B. Pada suatu hari, waktu petang, saya duduk di atas buaian di halaman rumah saya. 'As 'tu, terkenang bila ternampak burung-burung gagak di atas pokok di hadapan rumah saya; terkenang pula ada satu cerita, beberapa lama dulu berkenaan dengan gagak ini. Ini saya nak ceritalah sikit berkenaan dengan ini.

And:

Kemudian, adalah orang yang pakar-pakar yang- yang ikut sama-sama dengan anak raja 'tu; adalah yang pakar-pakar, orang yang tahu sikit dalam kalangan perubatan. Dia ambil burung 'tu yang tinggal-tinggal sikit 'tu, dia buatlah, dia siasat, dia buat penyelidikan dalam 'ni- badan burung 'tu. [Penang]

One day, in the afternoon, I was sitting on the swing in the yard of my house. After that, some memories came to mind when I happened to see crows on the tree in front of my house; I recalled, furthermore, that there is a story, of quite some time ago, to do with these crows. Now I'm going to tell [you] a little about this.

And:

After that, there was a person who was something of an expert, who was accompanying the prince; there was an expert, a person who knew a little in the sphere of medicine. He took the bird, of which something still remained, he worked [on] it, he examined [it], he did research on er—the bird's body.

C. 'Pas 'tu ditengoknya budak perempuan 'tu mengambik, apanya—bakul makanan dia 'tu. 'Dah 'tu, dimakannya sikit, apanya kuih er—si Azlan 'ni; kemudian diminumnya air pun langsung. 'Dah 'tu ditengoknya budak perempuan 'tu boleh masuk pula dalam satu pintu dekat gua tadi, terus hilang 'aja daripada jalan dia masuk tadi. Tapi sebelum sempat budak perempuan 'tu nak hilang daripada gua 'tu, Azlan cepat-cepat, katanya em—menghergap perempuan 'tu, dipegangnya. Dipegangnya leher perempuan 'tu. Perempuan 'tu menjerit-jeritlah. Kata dia, "Lepaskan aku. . . ." [Perak]

After that he saw the girl take, er what—his basket of food. Following that, she ate a little of er what—Azlan's cakes. Then she had a drink, and drank it right down. Following that, he saw that the girl was able to go through a door by the cave just now, and straight away just vanish from the passage she had entered. But before the girl had time to vanish from the cave, Azlan quickly said em—pounced on the girl [and] held her; he held the girl by the neck. The girl screamed. Said she, "Let me go. . . ."

D. 'Duk tengah berjalan-jalan, satu hari 'tu, anak anjing tadi nampak ada orang-orang tengah bertukang buat kapal di tepi laut. Dia pun 'duk perhatilah orang-orang tadi, sambil-sambil tengok 'kut-'kut ada saki baki makanan yang dibuang. Boleh dia makan. Lama-lama anjing 'ni pun jinak, dan orang-orang bertukang tadi pun suka tengok anjing jinak. Lagi pun dia pandai pula bercakap-cakap. Jadi, hari-harilah dia ulang pi tengok orang-orang bertukang tadi; sampai mak bapa anjing 'tu pun risau, hari-hari hilang, tak ada di rumah. Tapi 'dah dekat petang, dia balik juga. Bila anak anjing tadi bagi tahu di mana dia selalu pi 'duk ulang alik, senanglah hati mak bapa tadi. Satu hari, anak anjing tadi tanya. . . . [Perak]

Walking along one day, the puppy just now saw there were people building a ship at the sea's edge. He watched these people just now, while at the same time looking in case there were any leftovers that had been thrown away. He [would be] able to eat. In time, this dog became tame, and the builders just now were pleased to see the dog was tame. Furthermore, he could talk. So, each day he would go back to see the people building just now; to the extent that the dog's parents became worried; every day disappearing, away from home. But when it was nearly evening, he would come back. When the puppy just now informed [them] where it was he was always going to back and forth, the parents were relieved. One day, the puppy asked. . . .

E. Kemudian, inang pengasuh mai panggil lagi dia; dia kata, "Ha, baik-lah." Dia pun nak pilah, dia kata. Jadi sementara emak dia di rumah 'tu punya menangis, menangis hingga tak sedarkan diri 'dah. Langsunglah dia pun mengambil pisau, tikam diri dia; sebab dia rasa dia tak sanggup nak melihat anak dia 'ni dibunuh oleh suami dia. Dia tak sanggup. Anak 'tu adalah satu-satunya anak yang dia sayang. Kemudian, em—baiklah, anak 'tu pun 'dah siap 'dah semua, sampailah ke rumah. Bila sampai ke rumah, inang pengasuh pun bunuh diri juga, tak sanggup nak tengok . . . [Penang]

After that, the nurses and maids came [and] called her again. She said, "Ah, very well." She was going to go, she said. So, meanwhile, her mother at home was crying like anything; crying until she was no longer conscious [of her actions]. Straight away she took a knife [and] stabbed herself; for she felt she could not bear to see this child of hers being killed by her husband. She could not bear [it]. That child was her one and only child, whom she loved. After that, em—all right, the child was all ready and prepared; [she] arrived at the house. When she arrived at the house, the nurses and maids also killed themselves; [they] could not bear to watch. . . .

F. Bila dengar lagu 'tu, laki bini 'ni pun suka hati. Bila jalan kelik, jumpa saja nyiur gading, dikutip nyiur; kutip, kutip, kutip, hinggalah dua tiga puluh butir. Tapi oleh kerana jalannya sangat jauh, jadi tinggal kelik ke rumah hanya dua belas butir. Dalam lagu 'tu, oleh kerana 'dah boleh dua belas butir nyiur . . .

And:

Dalam pegang 'tu, dia pun royat ke kakak dia semua, "Hei kakak, kakak tak dengarkah sebelum anak hamba 'ni lahir ke alam 'ni, tidakkah kita mendengar bencana alam . . .? Tak kan tak dengar." Jawab puteri lain, "Hamba dengar." [Kelantan]

When [they] heard that [lit.: that tune], this husband and wife were pleased. When [they were on] the road home, [they] found an ivory co- conut tree; [they] gathered up coconuts, gathered, gathered, gathered, up to as many as twenty or thirty of them. But, because their way was very far, therefore, [it was] left [to them] to take home only twelve coconuts. In that matter, because [they] had come by twelve coconuts, . . .

And:

While holding [the child], she told all her sisters, "Oh, sisters, didn't you hear, before this child of mine was born into this world, did we not hear of a disaster . . .? It cannot be that you did not hear." Answered the other princesses, "I heard."

G. Ada satu hari, anak raja—pergi nak memburu. Bila masuk hutan pergi nak memburu 'tu—juga tujuan 'tu kalau boleh dapatlah 'ni—orang-orang jahat 'ni, tapi tujuan yang utama 'tu nak memburulah burung-burungkah, ataupun kijangkah, mana-mana binatang—sudah berjalan, jalan-jalan 'tu, boleh katakan sampai; dua hari, dua malamlah berjalan dalam hutan: ma- suk, berhenti, berehat, 'tu tembak burung-burung. 'Tu lama-lama datang satu tempat di tengah-tengah hutan . . . [Penang]

One day, the prince—went off to hunt. When [they] entered the jungle, going to hunt—also, their intention was, if possible, to catch—these crimi- nals, but their main intention was to hunt birds or mousedeer, etc., various types of animals—after walking, walking and walking, we can say they arrived; two days and two nights they were walking in the jungle: [they] entered, stopped, rested, shot birds. After some time, [they] came to a place in the middle of the jungle.

I referred above to the problems of reading the transcripts of the narrations of oral tellers, and observed that my students found them largely unintelligible when attempting to read them without also lis- tening to the recordings. In contrast, the students found the transcripts of the narrations by the most literate tellers in the group relatively simple to read, for hearing the intonation of the telling was not so crucial to their understanding of the tale. In other words, the more complex sentence structure enabled them to read the correct intona- tion into the texts, whereas the transcribed juxtaposed utterances of the oral teller often gave no clue to the nuances expressed by, or indeed the relationships between, those utterances.

It is the sparse use of simple juxtaposition which particularly distin- guishes the composition of the highly literate from that of the illiterate narrators. The most literate members of the group tended to juxtapose utterances without connecting-words only when a sense of dramatic immediacy was required, as in (C): "pounced," "held," "screamed," "said"; in (E): "took," "stabbed"; in (A): "assembled," "invaded"; or when a simple list of actions is presented, as in (G): "stopped," "rested," "shot," where each action was performed repeatedly. The actions in such a list may be synonyms or near-synonyms, as in (B): "worked," "examined," "did research."

A fair amount of repetition is also found in the narrations of literate tellers. While it performs a similar function, it is used far less frequently than in the narration of illiterate tellers. The literate teller, moreover, often prefers to employ synonyms as in the above example (B), rather than to repeat verbatim. Again, repetition is much less commonly employed to indicate duration (e.g., in excerpt F: "gathered, gathered"). In such cases, it is more usual to employ a phrase such as *beberapa lama* (for quite some time) to indicate duration of an action or event.

The juxtaposing of a repeated statement with the following utterance to create a dependent construction is far less common than in illiterate narration. Similarly, while *sudah* (*'dah*) is used to create dependent constructions, it is less usual for the utterance following *sudah/'dah* to be simple repetition. Thus in (D): *dekat petang,* in (E): *siap,* and in (G): *berjalan,* all following *sudah/'dah* are not repetitions of the preceding utterance.

We observed that one of the commonest actions of the characters in the narrations of illiterate tellers is speech, so that a major element in the pattern of juxtaposing actions consists of the speaking of the characters involved,[14] and the actual words used are usually presented as direct, or at least as very immediate indirect, speech. In this respect, the narrations of the most literate tellers differed considerably, for they contained far less dialogue. On the average, only 14 percent of the telling consisted of dialogue in the presentations of the fifteen most literate narrators, compared with 40 percent in those of illiterate tellers. In the narrations of illiterate tellers, the characters usually explain themselves; in the more literate tellings, it is more frequently the narrator who explains the motives, emotions, and intentions of his characters. Furthermore, while the use of *dia kata* is fairly common, as

14. Usually only two characters speak at one time. See Olrik's "law of two to a scene" in Dundes (1965:135ff) and Sweeney (1979:43–44). When more than two characters appear, there will usually be only two contrasting types. When one finds a group of persons such as the "seven princesses," they will tend to perform a collective role.

in (E), it occurs much less frequently as a punctuation device. There is, furthermore, more differentiation made between "asking," "replying," etc., as in (F).

Worthy of note is the tendency of the literate teller to depict his characters speaking a more literate type of Malay than might be expected in daily conversation, as in (F). For those who favor "realism," and associate it with literacy, this might seem to be a step backwards indeed. But as I argued in chapter 5, realism is a convention. Thus, while it might seem paradoxical that the illiterate portrays the speech of his characters in an apparently more realistic fashion than does the writer, this is not because he is intending to be "realistic": the entire narration is delivered in the same idiom.[15] And the development of written composition does not suddenly produce an awareness of any need to make dialogue sound "real." In traditional Malay literature, for example, the whole composition employs a written style, be it for narrative or for speech; and this practice of course developed from that of stylized oral composition, where both narrative and speech were to be mnemonically programmed for preservation. Until relatively recently, moreover, speech has been highly stylized in modern Indonesian and Malaysian printed literature. There may appear to be a certain irony in the fact that only after decades of print culture does an awareness arise of a need to reproduce casual everyday conversation in writing. In fact, however, there is no irony: the portrayal of everyday conversation in modern literature is a sophisticated literary technique involving the use of the convention of realism, which entails creating an illusion of reality. This is perhaps not always so immediately striking in Indonesian,[16] which, being a learned language, makes more widespread use of written style in conversation, and this is reproduced in the dialogue of literate characters. The working of the technique is best seen when the speech represented is very different from written style. For example, one need only compare the Kelantan dialect as portrayed by Fatimah Busu in her novel *Kepulangan* (1980) with the dialogue of the illiterate storyteller to realize that the former's apparently natural speech is in fact the result of careful crafting and a high degree of selectivity, producing a style shorn of redundancies

15. In professional storytelling such as *Tarik Selampit,* some of the dialogue resembles the idiom of everyday speech. In fact, however, the division is not between narrative and dialogue, but between chant and the intonation of everyday speech. Much of the dialogue is also chanted, in which case it is highly stylized.

16. Of course, this is only relatively so. The speech quoted earlier (chapter 7) from Alisjahbana is far too complex to be used in conversational language.

which, nevertheless, captures the flavor of Kelantanese speech. In the narrations of the most literate tellers examined, however, while not all direct speech is as stylized as in (F), there is no evidence of any attempt to produce a more realistic (or indeed a different) style for portraying the speech of characters.

While juxtaposing is the mainstay of the illiterate teller both in narrating and in presenting dialogue, it has to a large extent been displaced in the narrations of the more highly literate: by far the commonest way of indicating the dependence of one utterance upon another, or the relationship between two independent utterances, is the use of subordinating constructions and of linking-words.

The literate, no less than the illiterate, teller intersperses his narration with comments and explanation, so that in his case, too, the telling is not a recounting merely of event after event. Constructions expressing relations of cause, condition, and the like are thus frequently used in the course of the narration (indeed such constructions are more frequent than in the tellings of illiterates, where there is more dialogue and so more explanation in the speech of the characters), which is not, therefore, an unbroken sequence of constructions concerned with sequence and time. Of course, this is not to say that the use of constructions indicating cause and the like necessarily holds up the advance of events, as may be seen in (F): "because their way was very far. . . ."

Sentences are not merely more complex, but also tend to be considerably longer than in illiterate narrations. Often, more than one subordinate construction may occur in the one utterance. And while "aborted" constructions are not uncommon, they usually arise only when the teller piles subordination upon subordination and forgets to complete them all.

An idea of the frequency of occurrence of subordinate constructions in the tellings of literates may be gained from the following figures, which are based on ten tellings from the west coast (13,800 words) and four from the east coast (3,900 words). Ratios for constructions also found in the tellings of illiterates have been given above. Those constructions and the number of occurrences in the tellings of literates are:

West coast: *Sebab:* 15; *Kerana:* 13; *Dengan kerana:* 5; *Pasal:* 15; *Kalau:* 40; *Kot-kot:* 4; *Walau:* 4; *Macam mana:* 5; *Macam:* 6; *Bila:* 72; *Apabila:* 3; *Sampai:* 16; *Lepas/selepas:* 4; *Belum/sebelum:* 2; *Masa/semasa:* 16.

East coast: *Sebab:* 4; *Kerana:* 2; *Pasal:* 2; *Kalau:* 18; *Muga:* 4; *Bila:* 24; *Sampai:* 7; *Lepas/selepas:* 6; *Belum/sebelum:* 3; *Masa/semasa:* 3; *Belang-belang:* 1.

Constructions which occurred in the literate but not illiterate tellings included:

West coast: *Oleh/dengan sebab* ("because"): 5; *Oleh kerana* ("because"): 1; *Dengan* ("while," "-ing"): 4; *Seumpama/sebagai* ("as"): 3; *Supaya* ("in order that"): 4; *Sedangkan* ("even though"): 2; *Seolah-olah macam* ("almost as though"): 4; *Hingga/sehingga* ("up to," "until," "to the extent that"): 7; *Dalam* ("while," "during"): 6; *Manakala* ("when"): 8; *Setelah* ("after"): 1; *Sambil* ("while," "at the same time that"): 5; *Di samping* ("in addition to the fact that"): 2; *Selagi* ("as long as"): 2; *Sementara* ("while"): 1.

East coast: *Oleh kerana:* 6; *Dengan:* 4; *Supaya:* 2; *Sedangkan:* 1; *Hingga/sehingga:* 9; *Dalam:* 12; *Ketika* ("at the moment that"): 5; *Selagi:* 2.

Apart from subordinating constructions, the literate tellers made constant use of linking-words, as may be seen from the excerpts. Each teller, furthermore, endeavored to vary the words used. A linkage may sometimes be repeated (e.g., *dah 'tu* in excerpt C), but after that, a new word would usually be employed. Often, moreover, linkages precede subordinating constructions, as in (F): *tapi, oleh kerana* . . . Words/phrases such as *jadi* or *kalau begitu* are also used, and often with the same function as in the narrations of illiterate tellers; similarly, "and then" phrases may refer to the telling rather than the tale, but again, in both cases, variety is sought. It may also be noted that the use of *dan* and *tapi* ("and" and "but") is much more frequent in the narrations of literate tellers.

I have several times cited the frequent use of complex subordinating constructions in spoken language as an indication that the patterns of writing have become a part of the thought processes, enabling a much more analytic mode of speech. Significant, too, is the higher incidence of abstractions in the narrations of literate tellers. Less obvious, perhaps, is that the striving (conscious or otherwise) to vary the linking-words at the beginning of utterances reveals a major shift away from oral habits. The tendency to repeat constantly the same opening word or phrase is typical of orality as opposed to literacy. I have mentioned that many of the devices of the stylized oral form arise as exaggerations of features of everyday speech. Thus, the habit of repeating an opening word leads, in the stylized form, to the development of anaphoric parallelism, a vital mnemonic device for preserving knowledge.

The literate can afford to throw away his words; he can always pre-serve them in writing if necessary. And when writing to be read, he may indulge himself in the luxury of employing a varied style, for mnemonic devices are no longer needed. This, of course, also reflects itself in his speech.

A constant in the narrations discussed in this chapter was the pres-ence of at least one literate person (a student or myself) in the audi-ence, and a tape recorder. I have emphasized that the literate person has more options: depending upon the situation, he may choose a more literate or more oral mode. This option is not available to the illiterate individual. Whether or not he performs for a tape recorder and/or literate listener, his basic mode of composition will vary little. In order to establish this, of course, the researcher must ensure that he is not the focus of either the literate or the illiterate teller's narration; this usually means that the researcher cannot set up such a telling, and that when one takes place, he must endeavor merely to overhear it. A problem is that the highly literate person does not normally find him-self in a situation where he is telling traditional tales to illiterates—unless they be children, of course, in which case the possibility exists that he may be consciously shaping his utterances to serve as models of good speech.

A literate person may well be able to relay a traditional tale in oral style if he resists the temptation to think about the tale in new ways; if he battles down his literate tendency to interpret and analyze. A rather extreme instance of what may happen when he does not involved a person who heard a tale and perceived what he considered to be the use of symbolism. When he told the tale to some illiterate persons, he included his interpretation, even including the word "*simbul*," which he then changed to *syarat* ("condition," but here as a variant of "*isya-rat*"; sign), concluding that "*Kita mesti membezakan antara syarat dengan cakap biasa*" ("We have to distinguish between symbols and ordinary speech").

More commonly, the literate is able to place himself in a traditional situation and just tell a story. Even when he is able to assume a completely oral mode of telling, however, he regularly reveals his liter-ate habits by his tendency to seek variety, especially in the choice of words to link his utterances and in his tendency to report speech.

CHAPTER 9

Oral Orientation
in Written Composition

Secondary or indeed tertiary education does not produce some uniform standard of "literacy" in those who complete it. What we were able to term the "literate pole" of a continuum when making a comparison with persons of little or no schooling, now, on closer examination, may be seen to reveal a wide range of tendencies. The group of literates I have had most opportunity to observe were students of Malay literature at the Universiti Kebangsaan Malaysia and the Universiti Sains Malaysia. In 1980, while teaching a course on *sastra lisan* ("oral literature") to fifty students, I was able to pursue my own research project, which involved studying my students' efforts to study oral tradition. It became clear to me that a major problem faced by some of the students was that their own relatively strong oral orientation militated against their being able to distance themselves from that oral tradition. The most salient characteristic of this orientation was manifested in their need to conserve wholes. This revealed itself on every level of their attempts at analysis, from the composition of individual sentences up to the level of structure of their essays. In other words, they were loath to fragment the chunks of knowledge they had acquired.

On the level of sentence composition, preserving the wholeness of the chunk was best assured by the use of the adding style, which is, of course, most amenable to a narrative mode. One found, therefore, that students' attempts to analyze a text often slipped into a summary of the tale. And efforts to discuss characterization tended to produce separate, overlapping narratives. Thus, a character's qualities would be mentioned, followed by "for example, when . . .," which would take us through the events in the plot involving that character. Other characters would then receive the same treatment, which might result in several essentially similar summaries of the plot.

When a student was required to provide commentary, evaluation, interpretation, et cetera—in other words, when he could not easily employ paratactic narrative—he often encountered considerable difficulty expressing himself, for the "and-then" mode is not suited to an analytical approach. Sentences must be brought into confrontation, fragmented, and subordinated to one another. And the subordination of one to another may require the fragmentation of both, involving alteration of both sentence patterns. This necessitates the prior analysis of what is to be said and the construction of the whole sentence before it is written down, at least in its final form. It is this lack of prior analysis which produces the fractured sentences so often found in students' writing. For example, . . . *Bagi orang kampung itu, mereka suka . . .; Bagi Pak Long ia mudah bercerita kepada kita.* ("For the people of that village, they liked . . ."; "For Pak Long, he [found it] easy to tell stories to us.") *Oleh sebab kedatangan Jepun ke Tanah Melayu waktu itu menyebabkan beliau terpaksa berhenti dari sekolah.* ("Because of the coming of the Japanese to Malaya at that time was the reason he was forced to leave school.") *Kepada Pak LP, kerana semasa kecilnya pernah belajar agama kepada Tok Guru HS, belajar cara mendengar ia membaca kitab dan selalu turut mendengar ia membaca kisah IM, jadi apabila . . .* ("To Pak LP, because when he was small he had studied religion with TGHS, learned the method of listening to him read [religious] books and often joined in listening to him read the story of IM, so when . . ."). This sentence continues for several more lines; pattern is piled upon pattern without any realization of the subordinations. The completion of the "so when" does not materialize. If we remove the subordinators such as "to," "so," "because," and "when," we find an adding style which makes complete sense by juxtaposing.

If the problem were merely one of subordinating one sentence pattern to another by adjusting them both until they intermeshed, the result would simply be the production of new patterns which, as we have noted, occurred in traditional Malay *narrative*. The subordinating of one statement to another, however, also demands that the ideas contained in them be consciously weighed against each other in order to determine what relationships may be perceived between them. Problems arise when one can no longer rely upon the conventional relationships of schematically composed narrative. In the oral tradition, of course, two wholes may be made to confront each other: for example, one *kata adat* may be used to counter another, but neither is lost in the process. Now, however, in subordinating one statement to another, the ideas expressed must become interdependent in a much closer relationship than is produced by an adding style.

This tendency to conserve the whole is seen not merely in the difficulty students encounter in reconciling one statement with another; it is revealed on other levels of composition, up to that of structure, or what in narrative would be termed "plot."

We have discussed the possibilities offered by literacy for analytical and critical thought. Yet these possibilities are appreciated only after the fact; that is, by the literate who has acquired the critical faculty. The reverence for the written word felt by the orally oriented is therefore perhaps surprising, until we realize that the reasons for this awe are to be sought in the oral tradition itself: writing is evaluated by the criteria of the oral tradition. I referred earlier to the power ascribed to the word in oral society, and noted how the knowledge of a name gives the possibility of power over its owner, human or spirit. For the oral person, the written word has an even more awesome quality than that of the spoken: writing can literally objectify the word, and the written charm is a prized possession indeed. The aim of a pupil in an oral milieu is to acquire the sum total of his teacher's knowledge and to preserve it intact in his mind. His task is not to confront or argue with his teacher, for such activities are incompatible with the oral transmission of knowledge. In an orally oriented society, writing appears as a super device: now, all the words of one's teacher may be preserved verbatim, and thus even be memorized verbatim! Writing is thus an aid to the oral transmission of knowledge.

This is clearly revealed in the *modus operandi* of some university students: My students would always expect lectures to be delivered at dictation speed. If I attempted to increase gradually my pace, there would be sighs, and eventually pleas to slow down. If I assumed a normal conversational rate of delivery, all the pens would be laid down, and the students would relax; no more notes would be taken until dictation speed was resumed. Essays and examinations were regarded as a test of how faithfully the student had preserved my ideas.

The exam question often functioned as a cue to a certain lecture, and the ever-important activity of question spotting largely consisted of understanding which cue referred to which lecture, and how to tap into that store of knowledge.

Of course, the acknowledged conventions of a university education are not those of the oral tradition. Students are now taught that they must be "critical" and "original." These terms often become mere formulas, however. The student is told to be critical, and he is therefore critical of whomsoever he is expected to be critical (Sweeney, 1980:9). I would regularly offer my students a variety of theories on a specific problem, as, for example, the origin of the folktale, of the *Panji* cycle, or of the *wayang,* and suggest that they evaluate their relative merits. Invariably there were students who would plead with me to tell them the "right" theory. When I offered them an opinion, this would become the "correct" version. In subsequent essays, the "correct" theory would receive endorsement, and the scholars propounding other ideas would be criticized in no uncertain terms. "Being critical" in this milieu often becomes the traditional oral practice of apportioning praise and blame, which will be discussed below.

The need to be original can result in certain tensions: on the one hand, the student has worked hard to acquire as much of his teacher's knowledge as possible. As in the oral tradition, he feels that what his teacher gives him becomes his own. There is a major difference, however. In the oral tradition, one gains authority for one's pronouncements by claiming that they are from one's teacher. For example, Salleh, a performer of the Kedah dance drama, *Mek Mulung,* when narrating his tales to researchers, always interspersed his account with *Guru kata* ("my teacher said"). One's own personal opinions carry much less weight. A *dalang* of the shadow-play will often claim that everything he knows is from his teacher, even though comparative work shows that much of his knowledge derives from other sources (Sweeney, 1972:46ff). If a questioner appears to query a point he makes, he is likely to reply that this was what he was told by his teacher. And a personal opinion is given the authority of tradition if it is ascribed to one's teacher.

The modern student owes just as much to his teacher—perhaps, as we shall see, even more. He, too, is not expected to look for inconsistencies or errors in what he is taught. Yet he is often required to perform what may turn out to be the impossible: to be original. This is especially so if he hopes to publish his essays in literary journals such as *Dewan Bahasa*.[1] Often, the only way out of this dilemma is to assume the ethos of original scholar, regardless of the actual content of his work. We thus see the frequent use of formulas such as *Kalau diperhatikan betul-betul* and *Kalau diteliti* ("If [this] be closely examined" and "If [this] be subjected to scrutiny"), which imply that the writer has spent many long hours analyzing the text. Of course, he is expected to acknowledge his sources; indeed, this is an important part of credentialing himself. But then, the old convention of ascribing everything to one's *guru* will not help the "original" ethos. The student may therefore acknowledge the teacher merely by including a reference to "lecture notes" in his bibliography. Many examples of this practice may be seen in the journal *Dewan Bahasa*. Such references will probably be omitted if the essay is intended for the teacher's eyes alone. On the other hand, the bibliography may become a mere formulary feature, the citations given having little, if any, relevance to what is presented in the body of the article. On several occasions, I have read articles which were almost verbatim transcriptions of lectures I had given. No mention was made of the source, but bibliographies were supplied which had no connection with the subject matter. Examples may be consulted in *Dewan Bahasa* (20/2, 1976:108–12) and *Dewan Sastra* (5/10, 1975:60ff). The writers of such articles are familiar with the term "plagiarism," but, as is true of so many of the terms used in "Malay Studies," it is a culturally Western term, which the student may find impossible to relate to his own actions. He may well be stunned when told that he has wrongly appropriated the material of others. For him, this *modus operandi* is as normal as that of the *dalang* who composes with the schemata of tradition.

My references to formulary features may seem to imply a dependence by students on the use of schemata, and indicate that much of Malay written composition—our present concern being, specifically, literary scholarship and the transmission of literary knowledge—is still very traditional in flavor. On the other hand, the possibility offered by writing of reproducing one's teacher's "performance" *in toto* might seem to indicate that one need rely no longer on schematic composition. Before pursuing further the question of formulaic composition in Malay scholarship, therefore, certain qualifications must be made.

Firstly, I have observed that the pupil in an oral tradition is faced with a large amount of memorization. His task is to acquire and store

---

1. Which became more of a linguistics journal after 1978.

knowledge, not to seek inconsistencies, an activity which may develop only when the burden of memorization is alleviated by writing, leaving energy to be expended elsewhere. It is important, however, not to project our literate conception of memorization onto our perception of oral transmission and imagine the pupil being presented with a rigidly shaped body of information to be acquired verbatim. The prospective *dalang* may acquire his knowledge from a variety of sources. His basic repertoire is usually an amalgam of gleanings from many quarters. This is made possible by the homeostatic tendencies of oral tradition referred to in chapter 3, whereby a *dalang* may discard, synthesize, add, embellish until his repertoire crystallizes into the form which suits him best without his having consciously to analyze or reconcile inconsistencies in a fixed text. It would, of course, be erroneous to suggest that the advent of literacy marks the end of homeostasis. This "structural amnesia" was still evident in traditional Malay literature; even today, in print culture, the ease with which national histories change might seem to attest to the continued survival of this tendency. In a print society, however, multiple copies of a text exist as witnesses to such changes, and revisions are much more the result of conscious deliberation. In this respect, it is worthy of note that immediately following the publication of a new edition of the school textbook on *Pancasila* (the Indonesian state ideology) in 1983, efforts were made to collect all the copies of the previous editions, and they were ceremonially destroyed under the auspices of the minister of education.

The Malaysian university student also acquires his knowledge from a variety of sources. Often, however, he has considerable difficulty reconciling them either in the traditional (i.e., oral) manner, or according to the norms of modern (i.e., Western) scholarship. The pupil of orally transmitted knowledge learns by acquiring a complex of schemata. In the matter of repertoire, for example, the various motifemic patterns become second nature to him. These frameworks of slots come supplied with fillers, of course, but he learns to distinguish the motifemic from the motifetic. He may study under various teachers, but he will find that the basic givens, the motifemic framework, will vary little, if only for the reason that each performer cannot but develop his material in response to, and must meet, the conventional expectations of his (listening) audience. He learns, however, that he can vary much of the dynamic material; that a variety of fillers may fit the same slots.

It might be thought that the orally oriented student who has not yet interiorized the literate thought processes necessary for scientific analysis would simply continue to operate in the traditional manner, and indeed, the formulary features of such students' work confirm this to some extent: as is discussed below, he still makes use of prefabricated chunks. However, two factors combine to make a traditional approach difficult for him.

First, writing turns out not to be such a good device for "improving" oral transmission: in oral tradition, the pupil's unquestioning acceptance of his teacher's words is balanced by the fact that the process of transmission does not produce a fixed text but rather a complex of patterns, and homeostatic tendencies ensure that the knowledge acquired is not inviolable, whether the pupil is conscious of this or not. However, the problem with using writing in oral transmission is that when employed as the equivalent of a mnemonic device, it makes possible the preservation of every word, and this can cause the knowledge acquired by the student to become frozen. It is not, of course, writing itself which freezes knowledge. Indeed, as we have seen in traditional Malay literature, writing did not even ensure the fixity of a "work." It is rather that the possibilities offered by writing for preserving, reproducing, and even memorizing verbatim the teacher's words, when coupled with that same unquestioning acceptance of the teacher's words by the pupil, result in the student's acquiring an inflexible "text," which he may come to view as inviolable. In terms of the oral tradition, the fillers are all fixed in their slots, and such a development in oral transmission results in the demise of that tradition, or, at the very least, in the destruction of its dynamic quality.

The inclination of the orally oriented student to reproduce his teacher's words *in toto,* and for the purpose of operating under exam conditions even to memorize them, is reinforced by the second factor: that so much of what he learns is alien to him both culturally and also in the sense that what he receives is postulated for an audience which has interiorized the analytical thought processes of print literacy. Until he has mastered those processes, he has no option but to preserve the content of his instruction as wholes. Although he does not always reproduce a lecture *in toto,* he still works with prefabricated chunks of knowledge, which he endeavors to place in the equivalent of a "plot." However, before discussing the ways in which the orally oriented student attempts to overcome these problems of composition, it is first necessary to examine the nature of those problems: why, in fact, should the Malay student of his own literature find that so much of what he is taught and what he reads is alien to him?

In my *Authors and Audiences* (1980:6ff), I observed how Western colonial education defamiliarized traditional Malay literature for the Malays, and how the Malays have been taught to see their own literature from a Western viewpoint and to describe it using Western terms. The problem is threefold: first, what the student is taught often comes without context; second, he is unable to reconcile or synthesize what he is taught by different teachers; and third, what he is taught—which is what he learns to say—may not reflect what he *knows* about his own literature but cannot articulate, with the result that it does not occur to him to relate what he is taught to his own experience. The result is that the student does not acquire an integrated body of knowledge, nor does he have a frame of reference in which to place newly learned information. And so he must learn many things almost verbatim.

The problem is best illustrated by specific examples. During one semester, I examined the syllabi of the various courses attended by one batch of "Malay Studies" students. The courses included one on "oral literature" purporting to use a structuralist approach, one on literary criticism employing Wellek and Warren (1973) but also emphasizing Jungian archetypes, and one on "Classical" Malay literature using a traditional philological treatment. In none of these courses was the question of audience adequately considered. Even if we assume that the instructor himself had not merely learned his approach by rote, there was no indication that any adjustment or explanation of context had to be made for a non-Western audience. This is also very clear from translations of books in European languages into Malay. Many of these translations entertain the ludicrous notion that if a Malay term has been created to stand for a Western concept, that concept can simply be translated and immediately understood. The use of such a term in the Western language presupposes a knowledge of the context in which it appears. For example, the postulated audience of an introduction to structuralism is familiar with the ideas from which structuralism developed; and though the Western student (from a middle-class background) who reads such a book may have previously read little or nothing on such matters, many of those ideas are so pervasive in his culture that, be it unawares, and be it second- or third-hand, he will have at least some familiarity with them. Such a book, therefore, presupposes a very active role on the part of its reader, who is expected to bring to bear a large amount of prerequisite knowledge to the reading of the text. When such a work is handed to a Malay student from an oral background, he receives it in a cultural vacuum. He has absolutely no frame of reference in which to place it. The translated book does not translate its audience; the instructor's notes, furthermore, are often based upon books in Western languages or their translations, and thus pick up the audiences of those books. In the absence of any perspective in which to view what he is thus taught, the student's solution is to acquire the information as given, *in toto,* to seal it away and store it.

The problem becomes exacerbated when the student receives different approaches from different teachers. Unlike the pupils of the *dalang,* he is unable to reconcile or place in perspective the knowledge he receives from various sources. He does not appreciate the givens common to all these approaches. The approaches he is given are more often likely to conflict with one another than would the teachings of different oral specialists, which must conform to the relatively uniform level of expectation on the part of their audiences. But, far from being able to resolve those conflicting views, the student is rarely even made aware of the contradictions.

It might be observed that a common factor in what the student is taught is that it is all to be applied to the study of Malay literature, and here surely he is on firm ground. Often, however, what he is taught was, again, written for Western audiences, and though it may be given him in translation, the audience postulated is still Western. For example, one of the most widely used books on Malay literature is Hooykaas's *Perintis Sastra* (1961), which is a translation of his *Literatuur in Maleis en Indonesisch* (1952). Apart from the fact that the translation is often meaningless unless one has the Dutch original to hand, there has been no attempt to adjust the text to suit an Indonesian or Malaysian audience, so that analogies and illustrations from European culture are used to introduce the Malay to Malay literature! Thus, for example, on page 90, the student is expected to gain some insight into the language of the *penglipur lara* by being told that "In Europe, the words *charme* and *carmen* have the same origin"; on page 19, the remark that few composers are as free in the form of their poems as the priest Guido Gezelle from the district of Flanders is used to clarify a point on "sound values" (*nilai bunyi*). Although Hooykaas claims in the Dutch version (1952:4) that the book is specifically *intended* for Indonesians, the audience actually *postulated* turns out to be a European one.

If our concern were merely to emphasize the need to repostulate one's audience when one's work is translated into the language of a culture very different from one's own, there would be little more to be said on the matter. The significance here of these illustrations intended for a Western audience, however, lies in the fact that many of them have become "*topoi*" in Malay/Indonesian literary studies. Guido Gezelle, certainly, did not attract much attention, but generations of Indonesian students can attest to the necessity of memorizing what a "*carmina*" is in order to describe a *pantun*. A further example is Hooykaas's account of how Overbeck witnessed the creation of a *pantun* (1961:78). This again has often been used to teach Indonesian and Malaysian students about the composition of *pantun!*

It may seem strange that Malay students, most of whom can produce a *pantun* with great ease, will cheerfully trundle out the Overbeck episode when asked about *pantun* composition rather than attempt to draw upon their own knowledge. Yet this is no isolated instance: the student tends not to relate what he is taught to his own experience. As I have noted, the approach he is given may relate to nothing with which he is familiar. But even when the context is translated, he still tends to keep the knowledge purveyed separate from his own everyday existence. An example from my own experience also concerns the *pantun*. I gave a lecture on Lord's (*Singer of Tales*) oral-formulaic theory, related it to *pantun* composition, and gave many examples. The students appeared to grasp what I was saying, and demonstrated that they could spot formulas in written collections of *pantun*. A week later, I took the students to Perlis on a university bus to hear a professional storyteller. One of the students brought along his violin, and soon the students were singing *pantun* composed in performance, which described their projected activities in Perlis. When I pointed out to them that what they were doing was what Lord's theory was all about, their reaction was amused surprise that Lord should have spent his scholarly time on such an investigation. In subsequent essays, there was no evidence of a breakthrough; rather the discovery had become one more formula to the effect that Dr. Amin Sweeney had stated that *pantun* composition is *sesuai* ("in accord with") Lord's theory.

Another example from the same students' work concerns Propp's *Morphology of the Folktale*. The students absorbed everything I said, and learned to apply it to some Malay tales (although considerable difficulty was experienced in discerning functions or motifemes as opposed to their manifestations in specific acts). Subsequently, I conducted some experiments demonstrating their own expectations of certain motifemic patterns, and their ability to create new tales based upon those familiar patterns. It was clear that this was the first time they had considered Propp's approach in the light of their own use and expectation of patterns.

This tendency not to relate what they were taught to their own experience is due not merely to the fact that the approaches were alien, for here there had been an apparently effective attempt on my part to translate those approaches into the Malay context; nor is it due entirely to the fact that the student has difficulty articulating what he knows because the terms made available to him are not of his culture. We may refer again to the example of students' acceptance of Winstedt's (1958:19) statement that Malay folklore has three comic types embodied in five characters. The student knew these five characters well and understood Winstedt's contentions. At the Universiti Kebangsaan, as an experiment, I asked students to discuss this as an essay question. The result was, in many cases, a summary of Winstedt, with a generous amount of retelling of the five tales in the published *Cerita Jenaka,* which they accepted as the standard and "correct" version of the tales. However, outside the scholarly context, when these[2] students were in the circle of family or friends, they revealed by the tales they told and how they told them that there is considerable variety of character and type, that they were familiar with the schemata on which the tales are structured, and that they themselves were capable of using those schemata to create new tales. As part of my "folk literature" course at the Universiti Kebangsaan, I regularly took my students (as many as one hundred and fifty in one batch) on field trips collecting tales. Students were also sometimes assigned the vacation task of gathering such material. As a variation of the above experiment I asked students to discuss Winstedt's statement some time after these collecting trips. I noticed that if I pointed out, prior to their writing the essay, that their collecting activities—producing hundreds of farcical tales with many characters and types—clearly demonstrated that Winstedt was wrong, this would be reflected in the essays; often I would read that Dr. Amin Sweeney had stated. . . . However, if I did

2. Judging, at least, from those students whom I observed among family and friends, not to mention students related to my family.

not link Winstedt's statement with their own activities, many of the essays would follow the old pattern.

The problem experienced by the orally oriented person of relating what he is taught in school to what he knows, resulting often in the situation that what he says contradicts what he knows, stems, of course, from the traditionally almost sacred aura surrounding the written word in Malay society. The book carries with it authority. Power is in the hands of the literate. Prestige comes from book learning, and book learning is not part of the background of the orally oriented person. He does not expect to associate what he learns in books with that background. His aim is to acquire new knowledge, not to concern himself with the *dongeng* ("old wives' tales") of illiterates. It may, perhaps, seem strange that the student from an oral background who chooses to study "Malay literature" should study his own oral tradition from books; books which are for the most part, moreover, written by, derived from, influenced by, or—as in the case of texts until fairly recently—produced under the aegis of, foreigners. Yet were he to study *in* the oral tradition, he would become a *dalang,* storyteller, or folk practitioner. The study *of* oral tradition must be a literate activity, dependent upon the use of writing and books. Indeed, the very concept of "oral tradition" can arise only in a highly literate society. And even the idea of learning one's own language appears only with a high level of literacy. For example, in the nineteenth century, Munsyi Abdullah's (*Hikayat Abdullah,* 1953:46) excoriation of the Malays as "*bodoh*" (stupid) for not wanting to learn their own language reveals the attitude of the literate toward the oral person. Formally "learning one's own language" means learning the written dialect. People make "grammatical mistakes" only when they are using a learned dialect, a fact many linguists appear to ignore. "Orality" can be defined only in relation to "literacy." And though the Malays have had writing for centuries, and certainly possessed the concept of *cerita mulut* (tales [by word of] mouth), until the advent of print literacy, writing was so orally oriented and there were so few literate individuals that it was impossible for society to distance itself from the oral tradition far enough to become aware of it as an entity. The irony of the situation is that the modern scholar of language and oral tradition may spend his career trying to break through the barrier of his own literacy in order to understand the workings of a nonliterate tradition. The orally oriented university student, however, must discard his oral habits and acquire the analytical thought processes of the scholar. If he then decides to study his oral tradition, he, too, must attempt to break through the barrier that his literacy has created! Of course, the awareness even of the existence of such a barrier or the need to understand orality is a relatively new development in Western scholarship. As discussed in chapter 1, nineteenth-century scholars knew little of the nature of orality: an oral "text" was viewed as a sort of unwritten writing, and the sooner it was written down and the "shapeless colloquial language" turned into "grammatical prose" the better. The traditional respect of oral Malay tradition for the book was thus reinforced by the practices of colonial education. The "folk literature" read in Malay schools had little to do with oral tradition, and the student's own experience of hearing and telling tales seemed to have no bearing on what he did in school. Indeed, the aim was to eradicate those oral habits which produced that "shapeless colloquial language."

The term "folk literature" requires some comment here. It is important to recognize that this is a category created by Europeans to encompass tales and nonnarrative material which were not originally part of "Classical" Malay literature, but had been written down under the aegis of Europeans. It would be misleading, however, to imagine that the Malays who were presented with such texts as reading material in vernacular schools also saw them as a distinct category; and they would certainly not be seen to correspond to any of the genres of oral storytelling, such as *Selampit, Wayang, Jubang Linggang,* and the like. The Malay student would correctly classify them as *hikayat,* for that is what the published texts were: accounts produced in the written dialect of the palace scribe.

This, of course, is but one aspect of the process of defamiliarization of traditional Malay literature and oral tradition caused by colonial education. Put in broader terms, it may be seen as one manifestation of what turned out to be an inevitable transition from radical orality to mass literacy. On the one hand, the adoption of "Classical" Malay works for use in schools effectively reintroduced the Malays to their literature in a medium and a social context very different from the traditional ones. Literature had been an aural experience for most Malays, but now, although the same works were used, the experience was visual. On the other hand, it may be argued that the "classical" Malay literature to which the Malays were thus reintroduced was in a sense the creation of the colonial authorities. Thus, the works selected by the British for use in vernacular schools were those which most accorded with their taste rather than with that of the Malays. Indeed, this was realized and openly acknowledged: Wilkinson (1924:17), after mentioning several titles published "through European agency," cites a number of works "published, without European assistance, by Malay printing presses," which had recently been established, and remarks that, "The book-market indicates very decisively the difference between Malay and European taste." The *Hikayat Abdullah* is an example of a work favored by the British which did not appeal to the Malays (see Sweeney, 1980:6–7; 1980a:14 ff). Furthermore, the British actually initiated the creation of new works of "Classical Malay": oral tales—including both those which were originally performed in the stylized mode, and others usually told in the language of everyday conversation—were adapted into literary form, which employed the same style as traditional palace literature; and indeed these adaptations were published in the same textbook series as works of palace literature.[3] This raised the status of such material by affording it the dignity of print. However, it produced a change in Malays' perceptions of what kinds of materials constituted "old" literature, or indeed literature. Thus, for example, numskull tales—traditionally not considered worthy of literary treatment—were recomposed in palace Malay and bowdlerized to suit Victorian sensibilities.[4] The corpus of "vernacular" literature was further enlarged under colonial rule by translations, abridgments, and retellings.[5] The scholar of Malay literature who surveys this corpus may take it for granted that there are very clear distinctions to be observed between various categories such as folk literature, classical literature, classical tales retold or abridged, recent translations, and tales recomposed for children. The scholar who takes the existence of these categories to be self-evident, however, does not realize how arbitrary are the criteria he is employing, for the categories he perceives are those of the original forms, before they were adapted into *hikayat*. The Malay student who has not yet been trained to discern such categories will naturally tend to regard all of these writings as *sastra lama* ("old literature") or *sastra kelasik* ("clas-

3. Incidentally, this did not improve the standing of the old palace literature in the estimation of the Malays. In addition, this literature, once the prestigious literature of the palace, came to be associated with vernacular (i.e., peasant) education, and suffered a considerable loss of prestige (Sweeney, 1980:6).

4. See Sweeney, 1976.

5. In what is now Indonesia, the Dutch also produced similar materials through the *Commissie voor de Volkslectuur*. These were not, of course, confined to Malay, and were mainly based on written materials: oral Malay composition was not adapted into writing in this series.

sical literature"), the prose being *hikayat,* the poetry *syair.* In particular, there is no reason for him to see those tales originally from the oral tradition as a separate group.

This may be illustrated by the results of a survey I conducted among a class of students. The class consisted of fifty third and fourth (final) year undergraduate literature majors. They were asked to list the works of "older"/"Classical" Malay literature and "folk"/"oral" literature (*sastra lama/kelasik; sastra rakyat/lisan*) that they remembered ever having read. Apart from this cue, it was left to them to organize their lists and classify their material in the way they felt most suitable. Apart from three Chinese, the students were Malay, and the majority were elementary school teachers educated in the Malay medium. With five exceptions, there was no attempt at categorization; no distinction was even made between old/Classical and folk/oral, which had been my cue. The lists consisted of a mixture of:

1. "Classical" literature, mainly comprising texts romanized from *Jawi* manuscripts but also including a few texts published in *Jawi.* More than half the students listed *Hikayat Hang Tuah, Sejarah Melayu, Hikayat Merung Mahawangsa, Hikayat Raja-raja Pasai, Hikayat Saiful Lizan,* and *Syair Siti Zubaidah,* most of which had previously been required reading material in other courses or at school.

2. Retold and/or abridged versions of classical texts, such as *Hikayat Amir Hamzah, Hikayat Ganja Mara,* and *Hikayat Panji Semirang.*

3. *Penglipur lara* texts or "folk romances," including tales originally published in the Malay Literature Series, and texts subsequently published by the *Dewan Bahasa.*

4. Short folktales published as reading material for children, including *Bawang Merah Bawang Putih, Si Tenggang, Batu Belah Batu Bertangkup,* and the farcical tales included in the *Cerita Jenaka.*

5. Recently translated works, such as *Seribu Satu Malam (Thousand and One Nights).*

This fivefold classification—the criteria for which are mainly based upon external evidence of the provenance of the various texts—is of course my own. In the students' lists, tales such as *Si Tenggang* (in two instances upgraded to *Hikayat Si Tenggang*) rub shoulders with the *Hikayat Raja-raja Pasai; Cerita Pak Pandir* with the *Sejarah Melayu* (in one instance downgraded to *Cerita*). In some cases, students provided headings such as *Cerita* or *Sastra Rakyat, Sastra Lama* or *Sastra*

Kelasik, but no difference was found in the composition of their lists; everything was included under the one heading.

The aim of this digression has been to provide some illustration of the point made above: that European colonial interest in folk literature did not make the Malay conscious of his "oral tradition" as such, or even cause him to be aware of the category "folklore" as an entity distinct from other types of literature; rather, as observed above, by its endeavors to turn all manner of oral composition into literature, the colonial administration helped to reinforce the traditional Malay respect for the book. This belief in the supremacy of the book is often revealed by Malays who, asked by a researcher[6] about various tales they know, will refer him to the published versions of such tales, insisting that they are the standard or "correct" versions (Sweeney, 1973:1, 1976:15). The individual who expresses such opinions does not realize that these written texts came into existence through being dictated by people like himself. And, not infrequently, when my students were informed that a major focus of my course on oral tradition would be upon the tales they themselves had heard or told and not upon the published folklore texts, some of them would find it strange that scholarship should focus upon matters which to them were clearly nonscholarly. It was often difficult for students to appreciate that they themselves embodied Malay oral tradition. Even when I had hammered home the idea that oral tradition was *oral,* some students still perceived it as quite distanced from themselves.[7] This is illustrated by the efforts of two students who traveled over a hundred miles into a remote district of Kedah in search of "oral literature," because they did not know where to look for it near home. Eventually, I succeeded in getting them to tell stories to each other, and pointed out that they

6. The decisive factor is the ethos of researcher. Though he may be a friend or relative of the prospective informant, when he assumes the ethos of "scholarly inquirer," the friend or relative may feel he must assume the ethos of "informant." The resulting interview may turn out to be somewhat less than relaxing for both. (As I reread this note, I am unable to restrain myself further from voicing my frustration at the gender constrictions imposed by the English language. It might seem that all researchers and informants are male! In previous chapters, I have sometimes attempted to achieve a balance by referring to individuals as "she" as well as "he" where there is an option. But this can lead to confusion, and the use of "he or she" is no solution; it produces impossible sentences involving "he or she" speaking to "him or her." The use of a plural when a singular is needed merely leads to vagueness. In Malay, at least, the problem does not arise. A new pronoun is sorely needed.)

7. This may seem paradoxical. They were not so much distanced from orality, or their oral tradition, as from the concept of "oral tradition," which they had acquired in a literate and literary context.

need not even have left their house. Worthy of note, too, are the definitions of "oral tales" sometimes given by students which reveal the assumption that such tales are not really complete until printed in books; for example, *Cerita lisan adalah cerita yang disampaikan se-cara lisan sebelum ianya dibukukan* ("Oral tales are tales which are presented orally before they are made into books").

It was particularly difficult for students to appreciate the idea that they could possibly know more about their oral tradition than the scholars who had written the books. And, of course, their inability to express themselves on that tradition derived not from ignorance, but from the difficulty of articulating what they knew, and this in its turn is largely due to the fact that they were unaware of what questions should be asked. It is easy enough to say that the prerequisites for formulating such questions are a mastery of analytical thought and a familiarity with developments in the relevant field of scholarship. It should be noted, however, that in his efforts to fulfill these prerequisites and be accepted as a "serious" scholar, the Malay student—indeed most Third World students—labors under a handicap which is clearly unfair, but which is perhaps the inevitable outcome of histori-cal developments: the fact that "international scholarship" means, in effect, "Western scholarship" makes it necessary for the Third World scholar of the social sciences and humanities who would gain interna-tional recognition not merely to master an alien methodology but also to understand the nuances of Western culture to such an extent that he is able to speak to his Western audience in the terms they expect and to answer the questions they pose (Sweeney, 1980:8). In contrast, the Western scholar who understands the scholarly conventions, who can assume the correct ethos and has a penchant for theorizing, may be able to make do with a relatively rudimentary knowledge of the Third World culture about which he writes, perhaps even without being able to speak fluently and write in the language of that culture. The norms of the postulated audience of "international scholarship" are Western; even in a scholarly interchange between two Third World scholars from different countries the tendency is for the writer to postulate a Western reader and for the reader to identify with it.

I have discussed some of the problems faced by the student from an oral background who is required to acquire knowledge and a way of thinking that are basically alien, and for which he has difficulty creat-ing a frame of reference. I shall now examine some of the ways he uses to address these problems in his essays: ways which reveal an oral orientation. We have observed that the aim of the orally oriented student to make the sum total of his teacher's knowledge his own is no different from that of the pupil of the traditional oral specialist.[8] In the latter case, however, the mechanics of oral transmission ensured that the pupil did not acquire a fixed text, but rather a complex of patterns and a large amount of dynamic material to fit them. The situation of the orally oriented student of, say, literature differs considerably: For one still dominated by the oral insistence on uncritical acceptance of what he learns, writing, when used as an aid to oral transmission, may fossilize the knowledge he acquires. This tendency to adhere faithfully to a fixed text is reinforced by his unfamiliarity with many of the thought processes which have produced what he is taught. Though of course there are patterns in this material, too, they are the complex patterns of analytical thought; in other words, what he is taught is not *intended* to be processed or recomposed in traditional oral fashion. Yet until he becomes privy to the inner workings of what he is taught and learns to deal with it on its own terms, he appropriates, stores, and reproduces it in the only way he knows how: as wholes. And the use of writing enables him to preserve much larger chunks of knowledge than was traditionally possible, and to reproduce them verbatim. Though the student will endeavor to record his teacher's words faithfully, this does not mean that a courseful of lecture notes becomes for him merely an undifferentiated mass. He perceives that lectures are organized according to topics; he is well aware of certain points being emphasized. These, not surprisingly, become his headings, the basic units of knowledge with which he works. The problem is that what he learns is not seen as a complex of relationships; rather it becomes for him an accumulation of what might be termed *loci communes* or commonplaces. His approach is essentially conservative of wholes. When the statements and ideas which are to constitute a particular *topos* are acquired, they tend to be compartmentalized and sealed off to form an independent unit: the *topos*. The acquisition of new *topoi* thus does not tend to affect the integrity of those already in storage by leading to an examination of interrelationships and inconsistencies. When such *topoi* are detached from their original setting and placed in new combinations, the usual method, therefore, is to use an adding style.

8. A rather significant difference between pupils in the oral tradition and university students is that the former are much more able to choose their teachers than the latter.

It is, of course, often safer to preserve the original structure of what he receives, as when answering an examination question which is perceived to relate to a specific lecture; when a lecture or reading is particularly opaque to him, moreover, he will tend to reproduce it to the letter. Apart from these two instances, however, if the teacher's material provides the "correct" answers to a question, why should he attempt to change or improve it? An advantage of reproducing the words of the teacher, moreover, is that the "plot" is already supplied. On the other hand, he finds that a series of set answers to specific questions will obviously not serve all his requirements. The need to be original, or to discuss other aspects of a subject than those directly addressed by his teacher, means that he cannot simply rely on a text. It is here that his store of *topoi* is put to use, which entails bringing together all the *topoi* which appear to be relevant to his subject. The analogy made with the European commonplace tradition may perhaps be carried a step further: the relatively faithful reproduction of a particular treatise may be compared to the "cumulative commonplace," or disquisition on a set subject, while the smaller units more resemble "headings," or "seats of knowledge," in which are collected facts on a given subject.

It is worthy of note that certain scholarly procedures lend themselves particularly well to a paratactic, formulaic approach. The practice of providing quotations, for example, seems tailor-made for this purpose. The student is provided with a method of acquiring large, ready-made chunks of knowledge on a given subject, and at the same time the chance to credential himself in scholarly terms. Such chunks often become independent units having little bearing upon or connection with what precedes and follows them.

The material in a lecture or book which will become *topoi* for the student is that which he perceives as the "points" (indeed this English word is often used thus). Often, the signal to open a "compartment" for a new *topos* is provided by the use of a "term" (*istilah*), although what he perceives to be a "term" may not have been intended as such by the teacher or the book he is reading. Examples of terms which became *topoi* for many of my students were (in translation): "communal consumption," "postulated audience," "oral formulaic composition," "oral orientation," "stylized form," and "anaphora."[9] I would

9. The Malay terms: *konsumsi bersama; penonton yang dibayangkan; karangan rumus lisan; orientasi lisan; bentuk istimewa; anafora.*

explain these ideas in great detail, but found that the students were only really satisfied when I provided a short definition which could be learned by heart. These terms tend to be called "concepts" by the students. One may find that an unfamiliar word repeated in the course of a lecture or in an article may end up as a *topos*. I found, for example, that the word "catalyst," used by me as an analogy in an article in English, acquired the status of *topos*. On occasion, what is used by the teacher as an illustration of a point, an example, or an aside, becomes the *topos,* the original point to which the illustration referred being lost. For example, in discussing the secondary occupations of *dalang*s, I unwisely mentioned as an aside that one *dalang* kept a brothel. In subsequent essays, several students focused upon the *dalang*-as-brothel-owner concept, one of them even deciding that most *dalang*s kept brothels.

The processing of the material he studies into *topoi* is not always performed by the student. Often, it is presented to him already as *topoi,* for many of the lectures he hears and books he reads are already the result of schematic composition. A survey of books (particularly textbooks) on Malay literature produced in Indonesia and Malaysia reveals the existence of a literary commonplace tradition which has developed during the twentieth century: These books—especially those published in Indonesia—consist almost entirely of floating *topoi:* the same *topoi* float from book to book, so that it is possible to read forty such books in an afternoon. Examples of such works are: Simorangkir-Simandjuntak (vol. 1) (SS) (1951); Gazali Dunia (GD) (1959, 1969); Soeparlan D.S. (SDS) (1952); Usman Effendi (UE) (1953); Abdullah Ambary (AA) (1967). These books have been reprinted and/or re-edited many times; for example, Usman was reprinted for the twenty-first time in 1983; Abdullah was in use last year (1983) in high schools. In spite of the re-editing of these texts, however, there is no evidence of any development out of the commonplace tradition; on the contrary, the most recent reworkings are the most rigid, the most "topos-ized." Books published in Malaysia along similar lines include A. H. Edrus (AHE) (1960); Ariffin Nor (AN) (1957); Darus Ahmad (DA) (1957, 1957a, 1960); Harun (H) (1960); Tajul Kelantan (TK) (1958); Omardin (O) (1961).

Examples already referred to of *topoi* in such books are "*carmina*" and the "Overbeck-account-of-*pantun*-creation." The "*carmina*" is of particular interest in that it developed from a misunderstanding. The word is Latin, and, as used by Catullus or Horace, had the connotation of "song" or "lyric," but in its broadest usage covered even incantations and charms. As in the example of Hooykaas above, this was used by Western scholars to explain to their audiences the close connection in Malay between "magic" and "literature." This was mistaken by the Indonesian commonplace tradition to mean that the "*carmina*" was an old genre of Malay poetry, synonymous with *Pantun Kilat*. See, for example, SDS:23; SS:30; AA:28; TK:11; AN:37; H:16; AHE (2):39.

The example of *carmina* is typical of the dozens of *topoi* which have resulted from attempts to delineate literary genres, and categories such as figures of speech. Many of these categories are based upon entirely arbitrary distinctions, have no relevance in everyday usage, cannot be identified in a text by applying set criteria, and survive in the schoolroom only by being learned, together with their examples, by rote. The impetus for this categorizing activity was provided by Western colonial education, as were the sometimes rather shaky models for it. I have argued above that the perceived need for, and possibility of producing, formal definitions follows the advent of writing. This does not, of course, mean that an oral society does not possess "genres" or "categories" of performance which can be distinguished and defined by the application of formal criteria; rather it does not perceive the need to formulate those criteria and articulate a definition of something which everyone takes for granted. While this also applies to the orally oriented palace *hikayat* tradition, it would be quite erroneous to imagine that the formal definition is entirely the product of Western colonial education, for the writings of scholars in the *kitab* tradition clearly take for granted the need to define terms. Indeed, in the works of Hamzah Fansuri[10] and Raja Ali Haji of Riau,[11] we encounter definitions of poetic genres (respectively, *syair;* and *syair* and *gurindam*). In fact, it seems likely that in both cases new genres were being defined: the *syair* by Hamzah, and the *gurindam* by Raja Ali Haji. Both definitions articulated what was taken for granted in oral tradition: that the delineation of a genre is a process of making distinctions. A genre is what other perceived genres are not. For Hamzah, the context was Islamic poetry: unlike other genres of Islamic poetry, here was a *bait* with four "branches." For Raja Ali, here was a poem with two lines, not the usual four of Malay poetry. The appearance of

10. Doorenbos, 1933:120. See also Teeuw, 1966:437; al-Attas, 1968:2.
11. Who was very much a writer in the Islamic tradition. See, for example, his *Bustānu 'l-Kātibīn*. For his definitions, see Netscher, 1854.

a new genre, moreover, redefines the territory occupied by an existing form. In reference to the creation of the *syair*, for example, I have previously suggested (1971:68) that the already-existing form, the *pantun*, was thus designated only as a result of the emergence of the *syair* as a literary genre. In early texts, as remarked by Wilkinson (1924:43), the word *pantun* "was applied to any proverbial expression or simile and is not used in its specialized modern sense." Hamzah himself used "*pantun*" in this sense: *mithal dan pantun* (Doorenbos, 1933:49), and he insists (Doorenbos, 1933:34, 49) that he is not writing "*nyanyi*" ("songs") by which he appears to be referring to the genre we now term *pantun;* we note that the quatrains in the Raffles 18 version of the *Sejarah Melayu* are always referred to as *nyanyi,* while in later texts, the term *pantun* is also used to designate the poetic genre (Sweeney, 1971:68). It may be speculated that after the acceptance of the *syair,* which was sung, it was felt that the quatrain which had previously been sung, then generally referred to as *nyanyi,* required a specific designation, to wit, *pantun.*

Western culture was well aware that the delineation of genre results from the need to distinguish one form from others. That a genre owed its identity only to its position in a complex of relationships *in a specific culture* was not, however, always apparent: genres shared by or common to the various Western cultures acquired a seemingly universal significance and validity. When Western scholars came to study Malay literature, therefore, they projected these "universal" categories onto their subject of study; and their study had a tremendous impact, as it determined the content of colonial education, which was responsible for the spread of mass literacy. The result was that Malays were presented with myth, saga (*sage,* even in Malaysia, thanks to the Dutch influence of Indonesian commonplace collections), epos, parable, fable, and so on. These distinctions did not correspond to any delineations made by Malays themselves; nor did Western scholars attempt to demonstrate the validity of such labels by applying formal criteria to their material. The Malays were thus forced to learn the features of such so-called genres by rote, even though they were often quite meaningless in the Malay context. Occasionally, one heard a plaintive cry that these types are not easy to distinguish, but that, "Nevertheless, literary experts have divided them into five categories" (Edrus, 1960 [1]:84). This was good enough for the commonplace compilers, so that we frequently encounter these terms listed, "defined," and exemplified, even though any one of the terms might be applied to any one of the examples (AA:51–54; GD, 1969:11; SDS:50; UE:23–24; AHE [1]:84–129). The frequent inclusion of the Malay term *dongeng* into all this creates further confusion for the reader with some expectation of analytical classification. But of course there is none: each *topos* is sealed off by itself, to be learned with its examples. One is not expected to bring them into confrontation.

Western scholars were aware, of course, that not all Western societies shared exactly the same genres. Some indeed seemed universal; others were peculiar to specific cultures. Thus, while projecting the imagined universals onto Malay culture, they also endeavored to identify the various genres peculiar to Malay culture. It is in this area, particularly, that they had a hard time, and ended up giving the Malays an even harder time. Having identified *pantun* and *syair* correctly as poetic genres, they were encouraged to go on and identify more "genres," enabling them to come up with *gurindam, seloka,* and *nazam.* They also encountered *perumpamaan, peribahasa, bidalan, ibarat, tamthil, kiasan,* et cetera, and labored to provide formal distinctions between all these "genres" and "figures of speech." They failed to realize that not all these terms designate separate categories. This is not merely a feature of oral or orally oriented cultures, which tend to favor copious language, involving the use of strings of synonyms. In Western culture, too, there are many terms which do not designate distinct genres. If a foreigner who studied English culture superficially were to decide that the terms "ditty," "air," "number," "song," "chanson," "lay," "lied," "hit," and "verse" all refer to genres, and proceeded to define them by listing the formal features of an example they have heard described in such terms, his approach would be similar to that which sought to distinguish *seloka, gurindam,* and the like, on the basis of formal features. Thus, for example, the words *gurindam* and *seloka* were traditionally used to refer to a variety of stretches of utterance in fairly fixed wording. Only in the nineteenth century did Raja Ali Haji decide to use *gurindam* as a specific term for the two-line verses he composed. Scholars, however, have tended to define these terms as genres depending upon which example they were most familiar with, taking into account, of course, the etymologies of the words *gurindam* and *seloka,* respectively from Tamil and Sanskrit. Winstedt, for example, understands *gurindam* to be "rhythmical verse" (1958:145), a *seloka* to be a quatrain with all lines rhyming (1958:159). Yet in Malay tradition, the same rhythmical verse is often called *seloka,* and *pantun* are not uncommonly referred to as both *gurindam* and *seloka*. As with the comment from Edrus on parables, fables, et cetera, here, too, we sometimes hear a quiet sigh from Malay writers trying to make sense of all the definitions. For example, Harun (1960:70ff) quotes thirteen different definitions of *seloka,* and remarks that "it is indeed very difficult to recognize which is *seloka* and which *gurindam.*" However, it does not apparently cross his mind to question the need to have all these distinctions.

The practice of delineating categories which corresponded to no formal distinctions made in Malay tradition has provided a strange model for Malays. The results are clearly seen in the distinctions made by the commonplace writers between the many words referring to proverbs and similes. A problem was that many of these words were synonyms: on the one hand, not all these words hailed from the same written or oral dialect, and on the other, the oral orientation of traditional literature necessitated copiousness, resulting in the use of large numbers of synonyms. And it was only with the spread of literacy that collections of these terms came to be listed together. The vocabulary of a language is not a mere aggregation of words; but for the reasons just mentioned, such lists indeed became to a large extent mere aggregates, and the attempts to distinguish between the words often had little to do with how they were actually used. Many of them, moreover, did not pertain to formal categories. Again, we might imagine a collection of tunes classified into ditties, airs, numbers, and the like without any criteria to distinguish them. Typical examples of *topoi* dealing with *bidalan, perumpamaan, peribahasa, ibarat, tamthil, pepatah,* and *petitih* are found in SS:29; SDS:16ff; UE:7; AA:22ff; DA (1957):148ff; AN:29ff. Many of the distinctions made are quite arbitrary, particularly in the Indonesian collections; in UE, for example, an *ibarat* is said to be a "*perumpamaan* which is more emphatic than an ordinary *perumpamaan,*" though how is not made clear. The definitions often tell us nothing: A *peribahasa* is "a thing or situation expressed in language" (SS:29). Examples of one form may equally well apply to another. On occasion, disagreement may be encountered between various books. This tends not to be apparent from the definitions, which are so vague that almost any "figure of speech" would fit them, but from the examples. For instance, AA:22, SDS:17, and UE:7 all define *pepatah* in terms which would suit several other figures of speech, but the examples indicate that their conceptions of *pepatah* differ considerably, and it seems clear that the examples have been arbitrarily assigned to vaguely conceived categories. In general, how-

ever, the various books reveal great similarity. This is not because the
categorizations are any the less arbitrary; the reason is that, in typical
commonplace fashion, they have made use of exactly the same materials. Again and again, the same definitions and examples are reproduced verbatim, or with very minor changes of wording, as in: *Ibarat,
yaitu perumpamaan yang menyatakan sesuatu dengan sejelas-jelasnya
serta dengan mengambil perbandingan* (AA:23) and *Ibarat ialah perumpamaan yang mengatakan sesuatu dengan seterang-terangnya dengan mengambil perbandingan* (SDS:17). The translation in both cases
is: "An *ibarat* is a *perumpamaan* which expresses something with the
greatest clarity, making a comparison." Again, we hear the occasional
sigh from the Malay writers, as in Darus Ahmad (1960:39): "The
difference between *tamthil* and *ibarat* is very fuzzy indeed." It is, of
course, quite impossible for the student to use many of these definitions in order to distinguish and identify the various categories in a
text, and he learns these *topoi* merely by rote, their only function
being to clutter his mind uselessly.

In true *copie book* fashion, the compilers of these texts on literature
attempt to include everything.[12] Foreign terms are seized upon and
given the same treatment. For example, we have the "cynicism-sarcasm-irony" *topoi*, where the distinctions made distinguish nothing, and the
examples given are bizarre. Again these *topoi* tend to be reproduced
verbatim, as in SDS:68 and GD (1959):126, or in very similar form, as
in AA:127. Again, almost identical examples may illustrate different
forms: *Bagus benar gambarmu, dik* ("Your picture is really beautiful,
sis") for "irony," and *Harum benar badanmu, dik* ("Your body is really
fragrant, sis") for "cynicism" (AA:127)! AA, however, taking his cue
from SDS that "sarcasm" is stronger than "cynicism"/"irony," gives as
examples insults such as "Hei, monkeyface," "Hei, dog," "I don't care
even if you drop dead." (!)

Other popular *topoi* also based on foreign sources are the genres of
Arabic-Persian poetry. In his *Puisi Lama*, the highly erudite S. Takdir
Alisjahbana (1948:120ff)—no writer of commonplaces he—appended

12. For example, in SDS (148ff) we find lists of Indonesian singers, artists and
sculptors, etc.; Tajul Kelantan (1958), writing about *pantun*, commences with short
biographies of six literary figures, which include Shakespeare, Tagore, and Chair (*sic*)
Anwar, though what possible connection these have with the content of the book is not
made clear. AEH in his volume *Puisi of Persuratan Melayu*, also endeavors to include
everything he knows about all poets of the world, including two sections on "Indian
Poets," the latter being mainly devoted to a discussion of the world prize named the
"Noble Price."

a few pages of *Lain-lain* (others, i.e., other genres of poetry) for the sake of completeness. He pointed out that they were all from the *Tāju 's-Salāṭīn*, that there were very few of them, and that the distinctions between them were not very clear, so he would merely give a few examples. When this material was appropriated by the commonplace compilers, these genres acquired the same status as everything else. See, for example, SS:59 ff; SDS:32ff; GD (1959):40ff; UE:12–14; AN:68; DA (1957a):46ff; H:153ff; AHE (2):267ff. In UE, for example, Takdir's words are summarized, of course, but then the material in question is placed between "sonnet" and "poem" (*sanjak*) for learning by heart as *topoi* 41–46.

The same need for *topoi* is apparent in the compiler's treatment of modern Indonesian literature. There were no Malay/Indonesian terms available to apply to the variety of new poetry that arose in the twentieth century. A basic schema for the compiler, however, was the *topos* for *syair*, which stressed the four lines to a stanza (see, e.g., SS:70; H:123). The new poetry had stanzas of varying length. The obvious way to classify them was, therefore, by the number of lines to a stanza, particularly as a ready-made list existed in Western literary studies: distichon, terzina, sextet, septina, octavo, and so on. In the West, these terms served to distinguish but one formal feature of a poem. The compilers, however, appropriated these terms and used this one feature as the main criterion for classifying poetry. Thus, in English terms, for example (following this method), Shelley's "Ode to the West Wind" could be defined only as a terzina. There is no evidence, however, that these terms have ever actually been used outside the *topoi;* there is evidence on the contrary, that the compilers did not really understand the terms: for example, the "quintet," when it was first taken over by the commonplace tradition, must have been spelled in the abbreviated form "quint.," for all the compilers have used "quint" as their term, except when Malayized to "*quin*" or "*kwin*." The main attraction of these terms was that they provided the material for several more *topoi* which could be learned by heart. Again, the definitions and examples are reproduced well-nigh verbatim. See, for example, SS:68ff; SDS:34ff; GD (1959):54ff; UE:16ff; AA:38ff; AN:76ff; DA (1957a):51ff, (1960):59ff; H:123ff; AHE (2):284ff.

Two further examples will suffice to demonstrate how the learning by heart of a *topos* may be its only purpose. The first consists of a list of nine Western rhyme schemes such as *jambe* (= iamb), *troche* (= trochee), *dactylus* (= dactyl), *bacchius, amphybrachys* (= amphybrach), et cetera (e.g., SS:16ff; AA:13; UE:22ff), which have absolutely no relevance to Indonesian poetry, but which must be learned! The second example is typified by paragraph 204 of UE:57 (1983 printing). This concerns which books have been translated into Indonesian. The answer is a list of ten books. This is the only answer. An earlier edition had nine, only eight of which appear in the later edition. That was then the only answer. I know of several cases where students suggested other titles from the hundreds of translated works: they discovered that their answers were wrong; they were not in the list! Such students were thus quickly deterred from experimenting further with any attempt to relate what they were taught in school with their personal experience.

We may note that all the "floating *topoi*" cited above originated in Indonesia; during the fifties and early sixties, Malay-educated writers in Malaya looked to Indonesia for inspiration. Yet, although Indonesian literature and literary criticism had made great advances, the books used to teach "Indonesian literature" (i.e., traditional Malay and modern Indonesian literature) were much more in the nature of commonplace collections. Indonesian, a learned language for most Indonesians, acquired through the medium of writing, and "systemized" by Western grammarians, is very much a language of literacy. Yet this does not mean that all who speak it are highly literate. For many people from an oral background, those literate patterns become mere formulas, and the power of writing to freeze speech makes these formulas far more rigid than in the oral tradition. Thus, although writing may liberate the mind, it can also stultify it. When it becomes a mere device to codify schemata, and make inflexible what was flexible in the oral tradition, the mind can do little with the knowledge acquired, either in the oral or literate manner. The three references made above to the "difficulties" voiced by Malay-educated writers from (then) Malaya reveal clearly a feeling of dissatisfaction—though it is not articulated as such—with the rigidity of the materials presented to them. And this fossilization has certainly had a stultifying effect on the teaching of literature in Indonesian schools. Oral habits have been frozen; the writings of scholars both Indonesian and European have been "topos-ized"; and those *topoi* refer back only to themselves. This, unfortunately, is possible in a subject such as literature, which need have no practical application, and where people's lives do not depend on the outcome as in engineering or chemistry. Such an approach to teaching literature does not produce thinking people; it merely ensures the survival of what is taught. A comparison between what was taught in Indonesian schools twenty-five years ago and to-day reveals that exactly the same *topoi* still hold sway. This treatment of literature is particularly frustrating for students from a literate background, who find that what they have learned at home, and the way they have learned to think, is of little use to them in the study of literature, which merely entails learning God's truth *topoi*.

Another example of a scholarly practice which lends itself admira-bly to traditional habits is the etymology, which has become one of the most widely used *topoi*. The more traditional type of etymology was based upon the *sound* of the word. For instance, "Kelantan" was variously derived from *kilatan* (lightning) and *gelam hutan* (a jungle melaleuca tree), and tales were produced as evidence. Thus, for example, the Patani people saw a glow in the sky one night emanating from the area that is now Kelantan. The glow resembled lightning, so when Kelantan became a state, it was called "Kilatan," which eventually was turned into "Kelantan" (Asa'ad Syukri, *Sejarah Kelantan,* 1962:112). The Western philologist's concern with ety-mologies appeared to fit right into this pattern, and reinforced the Malay's partiality for the etymology. The spread of mass literacy, however, encouraged a shift of emphasis away from the sound of the spoken word to the form of the written word. For example, two of the most common floating *topoi* are those which purport to explain the *meaning* of *kebudayaan* ("culture") and *kesusasteraan* ("litera-ture"), both of which are modern terms. See, for example, SS:7; UE:5; Zuber Osman:8–9; GD (1969):10; AN:5; R. A. Selamat:1. The importance of the etymology is that it is felt to provide a key to the essence of a word's meaning. This, of course, accords with tradi-tional practice in the West, as will be attested to by all those who have been admonished by their teachers for using "awful," as the word "really" means "full of awe." Only with the development of modern linguistics has the arbitrary nature of the assignation of the word to its referent become apparent, and the fact that etymology sends us back only to itself (Jameson, 1972:6) become accepted. The notion in the Malay world that a knowledge of the etymology of a word will reveal its true meaning is not, however, merely a be-queathal of Western practice, although it has certainly received rein-forcement from it; nor is it merely a result of the fact that both Western and Malay society have been influenced by the doctrine of the Platonic forms. Becker (1979a:237) has observed that Javanese etymologizing tends to deal in proper names, and the same is true of Malay. We may add that, traditionally, a name is not assigned arbitrarily: it must accord with the nature of the person to be named. And sometimes, it is found that sickness is the result of a person's receiving the wrong name, which must then be changed. It is, therefore, essential to know the essence of a name. In the field of magic, the knowledge of the name is a key to gaining power over the bearer of that name. That power is further enhanced by an understanding of the meaning or essence of that name.

It is understandable, therefore, that for the orally oriented Malay student, a "term" is no mere label; it is a key to what the concept or thing really "is," and if one studies the word "deeply" enough, it will give up its hidden meaning. Etymologies are thus seen as an effective way of revealing the essence of the concept. That only by knowing the name can one understand the referent is often revealed in students' comments. For example, one elementary school teacher doubted that the Malays could ever have used anaphora, for they did not know the term "anaphora": "*Tak 'kan orang dulu tahu perkataan 'anafora'* " ("People in the past can't have known the word 'anaphora' "), so they must have merely used it "by accident." And in the example of "catalyst," a number of students did not see this as my attempt to draw a parallel; when they wrote: "*Ini disebut katalis*" ("This is called a 'catalyst' "), they did not mean "called" just by me; rather, that is what it *is,* in terms of absolute truth.

The student does not merely accumulate a large number of *topoi.* He also acquires fairly standard patterns which enable him to link and comment upon the *topoi* he includes in his writing.

The need to employ such patterns, and indeed to rely on the use of *topoi* is very much dependent on the approach required of the student. I regularly assigned students two projects per course. The first entailed recording, transcribing, and editing an oral tale,[13] or romanizing and editing a short *Jawi* text of *syair* or *hikayat.* The second project involved analyzing the texts they had produced. Here, the students were often allowed to choose their approach, which usually meant applying one of the "methods" they had learned, e.g., those based on Lord,

13. An example of the normative attitude which results from acquiring the written—thus standard—dialect is the tendency of students to refer to features of the dialects in which the tales they studied were told as *kesalahan* ("mistakes") when those features did not conform with the written dialect. Similarly, differences of pronunciation with the written dialect would always be spoken of as *perubahan* ("changes"), with the inference that the speakers had altered the correct pronunciation.

Propp, Bijleveld; or they might decide to employ what we may term
"free-style analysis." It is particularly in this latter type of "analysis,"
and in "introductions," that the need for patterns in which to arrange
their *topoi* became most apparent. In other tasks, the overall structure
was already supplied: editing or transcribing, for example, mainly
entailed filling a number of boxes—the text itself, notes, glossary,
description of storyteller and village or of the manuscript, et cetera. It
was noticeable, however, that those students who most relied on formulas elsewhere in their work revealed much more concern with form
than with content, with appearance than with significance or compre-
hension. For example, in transcribing a tape or manuscript, a student
might produce a text containing passages which were completely unintelligible. His explanation would often be, "but it sounded like that,"
or "that is what I read." It did not occur to him that the application of
the steps of the method he had been taught should produce something
which makes sense to him, and that if it does not, some explanation is
required. It is significant, moreover, that in transcribing the stylized
form, particularly, students from a rural background—originating
sometimes from the same village as the storyteller—might have more
difficulty than an urban speaker of the same dialect educated in the
English medium. For example, the filler *oleh kata* in *Tarik Selampit*
was consistently transcribed by one student as *olekator;* another transcribed the formula *murai membaca* ("the robin recited") as *mura
maisa;* in neither case was any comment supplied.

In this respect, it is often his glossary or list of "difficult" or unusual words which reveals the student's attention to form rather than
function. The glossary may become an independent entity serving as
an end in itself rather than clarifying the text. On the one hand,
unintelligible words in the text—many of which may have resulted
from his own transcription—may be passed over in silence. On the
other hand, glosses may be provided on what are extremely common
words. Many instances of this practice also occur in published material. In *Kesah Raja Marong Maha Wangsa* (1965:243) four consecutive entries of words which "have become rare or are no longer used
in our society" are the very common words *halal, hamba, hamil,* and
haram.

A similar situation arose with "approaches" which supply their
own structure, such as identifying formulas, formulaic expressions,
and various types of parallelisms, or recognizing the functions of a tale
in Proppian fashion. Many of the categories (e.g., formula, motifeme,

anaphora) presented themselves for processing into *topoi:* that is, to be learned by heart with examples and to acquire the status of "concepts." When the students were required to identify these forms in a body of material, it was noticeable that where the application was purely mechanical, as in spotting instances of repetition, which is the basic requirement for identifying parallelisms and Lordian formulas, most of the students eventually became quite proficient. Several of them, however, found the task quite daunting, and one should not underestimate the difficulties encountered by an orally oriented person in applying such a set of rules to written material. This became very apparent after the introduction in 1972 of the new spelling, which required that *é/o* and *a/e/i/u/* in a penultimate syllable should be followed respectively by *é/o or i/u* (or in either case by *a*) in the final syllable. The difficulty experienced by so many—manifested very frequently indeed in spellings such as *bolih, olih,* and *hurmat* (for *boleh, oleh, hormat,* which in fact remained unchanged) seemed quite puzzling to the more literate, who considered the new rules to require but minor adjustments.

However, when students were required to apply Propp's method, far more difficulties were encountered. Here, merely learning what a function or motifeme was did not enable immediate visual identification: an analytical leap was required from the specific act to the function it performed in the tale. Many of the students seeking similar functions in two tales would merely equate similar acts or motifs regardless of their very different significance for the tales in question.

The tendency of the orally oriented student to compartmentalize and conserve wholes often becomes apparent when, in his attempt to analyze a text, he employs two or more different "methods" on the same text without being aware that those methods are contradictory. In 1980 most of my students focused on plot patterns and character types. Several students, however, after discussing the characters and observing—as had been taught—that they were highly stereotyped, then started a new section on "character development," using material acquired in a course on "literary criticism," based on the Wellek and Warren approach. In this section, the characters of the folktales they were analyzing were given the standard *perwatakan tokoh* (characterization of *dramatis personae*) treatment they had been taught elsewhere to use on novels, which mainly involved summarizing the parts of the narrative in which a certain character appeared (thus the development of the tale, not of the character) and repeating the process for every character discussed, followed by praise and blame for good and bad characters, and concluded with remarks to the effect that the character development was of high quality and showed originality. Incidentally, the logic behind this is as follows: if what is said about a novel can also be applied to a simple oral tale, they must be of similar quality.

The students had made no attempt to reconcile the two approaches, nor were they aware of any need to relate them, and they had no idea that their comments were contradictory. A similar failure to reconcile two approaches was revealed in a number of essays which attempted a Proppian analysis and then, without comment, proceeded to add a section consisting of formulas concerning plot development taught in "literary criticism" and ultimately derived from Aristotle's *Poetics*. A graph indicating plot development, climax, et cetera, was usually appended.

From the above it is apparent that, although the "method" comes provided with a structure which determines to some extent the arrangement of the student's material, the various stages of the process or, indeed, the various methods and their application themselves may become self-contained wholes to be simply added one to another. Again, a framework for his study of plot development or characterization is supplied by the narrative itself, which frequently overpowers the analysis of it to the extent that the analysis lapses into a summary of the tale.

Thus, even when the student avails himself of such "methods," his inclination is still to conserve the wholes. This need to protect the integrity of whole units goes hand in hand with the adding style. And when he is not provided with a series of clearly defined steps, his tendency is simply to add one *topos* to another. Consequently, among the most commonly used linkages are phrases such as *Satu hal lagi* ("One more matter"), *Selain dari itu* ("Apart from that"), *Satu perkara lagi yang saya rasa menarik* ("One more matter which I feel is interesting"). Often, the adding style is disguised by the use of patterns of logical progression which provide the semblance of an argument, whereas in fact there may be but the most tenuous of connections between the points made; or points which are contradictory may appear to support each other, and vice versa. Examples of such linkages are *tambahan lagi* ("in addition"), *lagi pula* ("furthermore"), *namun demikian* ("however"), *walau bagaimanapun* ("nevertheless"), *tetapi* ("but"). The import of such phrases is often no more than "and," or "the next thing I am going to say," which is very reminiscent of the oral teller. This is best illustrated by the following example, taken from the introduction to an essay which sets out to compare two versions of a tale, one oral, one written.

1. "Oral literature is a type of culture which lives in society and is handed down from generation to generation in oral form. The features of this culture are not only found in societies which do not possess writing, but they are also found in societies which do not [*sic*] possess a tradition of writing.

2. "However [*namun demikian*], in the context of Malay culture, there are two patterns of storytelling, i.e., storytelling which is told by professional storytellers and amateur storytellers. The storytelling of professionals is rather more stylized compared with the amateur storyteller.

3. "Literary critics in general look at the literary values and analyse a folk story from the aspects of content, theme, and so forth. Psychologists will probably evaluate and interpret from the aspect of psychology, while historians will concentrate on historical perceptions, and linguists will concentrate on the aspects of linguistics.

4. "Nevertheless [*walaupun demikian*], in the process of development of folk tales which is unlimited and there is no social control over this practice has given birth [*sic*] to elements of improvization in their presentation.

5. "Furthermore [*lagi pula*], each folk tale is formulated into specific motifs as is done by Vladimir Propp. For stories such as the one I am studying here usually the pattern of the storytelling must begin with the birth of the prince, and then. . . ."

After this, there follows a summary of his tale, concluded with the observation (6) that communal consumption exercises constraints on the content of a tale. Before reaching his transcription, this student also managed to include the (7) "myth-fable-sage-parable" *topos,* and (8) the observation that the storyteller will move from house to house, from village to village, from district to district, and even from state to state.

It was a relatively simple task to trace the origin of these "points." Paragraph 1 was a rather fractured reproduction of a definition of "oral literature" given by another teacher; the student had not realized that the two clauses of the last sentence said the same thing. Indeed, the erasures and corrections seem to indicate that he wished to say "do not" in both cases. Points 3 and 4 also derived from the lectures of other teachers. Points 2, 5, 6 were appropriated from my lectures. I discovered that point 8 ultimately derived from Maxwell (1886:88), which had been quoted by another teacher (and was used by four other students). Point 7 had been acquired from readings of textbooks on literature.

The schematic nature of this student's essay is apparent not merely from the adding style and the lack of any attempt to integrate or even coordinate the various items presented; it is revealed also by comparative work with the essays and exams of the other students: each of those units of information also occurred in the work of several other students in a similar standardized form. It should be pointed out, however, that only approximately 20 percent of the students produced work so consistently schematic as the above.

Reliance upon the adding style is revealed by two other common practices: on the one hand, the use of words and phrases such as *jadi* ("so," "therefore") and *oleh itu, dari itu* ("due to this," "from this") may seem to indicate a deduction, when in fact there may be none. For example: "An anonymous source has laid down that oral literature differs somewhat from written literature. So, in oral literature there are found several types of tales such as animal tales, ghost stories. . . ." On the other hand, we encounter the use of conditional statements in which the conditional clause is a mere formula. I have referred to the habit of beginning a sentence with a clause to the effect that "If this be examined carefully. . . ." Often, this is merely placed before a statement such as "There is a connection between A and B" without actually creating a condition.[14]

A reliance upon *topoi* does not, however, preclude the expression of opinions. In chapter 2 I drew attention to Skinner's observations prompted by the concern with good and evil in the *Sya'ir Perang Mengkasar* (1963:11), and considered them in the context of Ong's arguments concerning the prevalence of praise and blame in oral (and residually oral) societies (1967:83ff). It is of some significance, therefore, that students from an oral background frequently concerned themselves with the distribution of praise and blame in their essays, and the indication is that this device is an important means of classifying experience. The recipients of praise and blame included scholars, the characters from literature, the works of literature, and even "concepts."

In lectures, I might compare various points of view offered by several scholars and point out what might be only minor disagreements I had with those views. I might present several theories on a certain

14. Such "false" arguments are common in the commonplace texts referred to above. See, for example, *Begitu juga* (SS:34); *Tetapi* (O:6, 22); *Kalau, Oleh sebab* (H:5, 123).

subject and express a preference for one of them. I would find that my remarks often underwent a polarizing transformation when they appeared in the students' essays. The scholars with whom I had agreed were often praised fulsomely; those with whom I had disagreed might be excoriated quite vituperatively; often the student seemed more concerned with attacking the scholar than his scholarship. Words such as *jahil* ("ignorant"), *bodoh* ("stupid"), and *tidak jujur* ("dishonest") might sometimes be bandied about.

The tendency to distribute praise and blame also reveals itself in the students' discussion of characters, and, of course, in evaluating the works themselves, be they written or oral; and here again, "literary criticism," particularly the variety which concerns itself exclusively with evaluating, lends itself to the traditional treatment.

Students also demonstrated a tendency to evaluate the "concepts." This usually meant stating that they are "important," "good," "interesting." For example, "The existence of the concept of communal consumption is very important in folk literature" and "Oral formulaic composition is of great interest in oral tradition." Sometimes a concept is said to hold another concept important. For example, "Folk literature places great importance upon its audience." Here we see the tendency to turn the concepts into actors, and what is then said about them acquires the form of an event. This development is noticeable in: "In order that communal consumption may take place, the storyteller will tell a tale which has a plot arrangement which is the same for each tale"; "Before oral literature is turned into book form, it emphasizes oral formulaic composition." We have already noted how definitions may assume the form of narrative. Here, too, we see a similar tendency with "analysis." Such statements, furthermore, achieve the purpose of linking what is said about two *topoi*. Another way of accomplishing this is to state that things are similar or closely connected. For example, "The concept of communal consumption is extremely closely connected with rhetoric"; "Between storyteller and audience possesses [*sic*] a very close connection"; "This [unclear what 'this' refers to] also has a connection with poetic justice [English term used]." It may be noted, however, that the reasons for these close relationships are not explained.

Finding similarities, of course, is seen as an effective way of bringing together disparate materials and views without fragmenting wholes. Thus, where two views differ, there is often an attempt at *muafakat* (compromise) by identifying areas of agreement, and passing over the differences in silence without any attempt to reconcile them. This is very common in students' essays, but perhaps the best illustration of this tendency is provided by Harun (1960) in his *Kajian Puisi Melayu*, where, as referred to above, he presumes to make pronouncements on *seloka, gurindam,* and the like, only after extracting the areas of agreement between his many sources.

Finally, it may be noted that when a student expressed an opinion, he often considered that merely to state how he *felt* was adequate. He clearly did not perceive any need to present evidence to support the reasons for his conviction; feeling tended to take the place of argument. For example, when an opinion was rejected by him, this might be in terms of *Rasanya kurang sesuai* ("felt to be less than suitable"). Among the commonest expressions are *Saya yakin bahwa* ("I am convinced that"), *Rasanya/Saya rasa bahwa* ("my feeling is that"), *Ini amat menarik* ("this is extremely interesting"), *Ini dapat diterima* ("this may be accepted"); the constant factor is that we are not told why. Perhaps the most extreme example of this tendency is the conclusion of one student to the effect that, "in carrying out our analysis, I feel that we can accept what was required and discussed by Propp." The only thing lacking was any analysis.

Conclusion

A book which commences with the perceptions of European Romanticists and ends with Malay students' essays may appear to be somewhat diffuse in its focus. I would contend, nevertheless, that the focus is quite sharp, and that the reader who starts out expecting a standard treatment which concentrates upon "Classical Malay" or "Malay folklore" is revealing evidence of prefocused vision. It was precisely in order to counteract this tendency to take as givens the perceptions of our predecessors and the categories identified by them that I decided to commence by examining their presuppositions. It became clear that an attempt to understand the interaction between oral and written Malay traditions could not rely upon the categories employed by our predecessors such as "folklore," "classical literature," and even "literature," for in the traditional Malay context these were imposed, prefabricated categories, resulting from the carving out by scholars of those areas of Malay discourse perceived to parallel Western forms. Little attempt was made to identify the delineations obtaining in Malay society. In carving out the "genres" of interest to him, the scholar would ignore what was left, or at best dismiss it as the concern of another discipline. The literary scholar, for example, would not see everyday conversation as falling within his purview; other areas of discourse would be left to the jurist. Yet Malay discourse was not organized along the lines of Western academic disciplines.

The categories imposed, moreover, were very much those of a print culture; little account was taken of the media of discourse and the interaction between the forms produced by the use of different media. Thus, while "Classical Malay literature" might at first seem to coincide with manuscript writings, we find that no contrast is possible with oral composition, for "folklore" was subsumed by scholars under the rubric of "classical literature." Again, although scholars included all types of written composition in "classical literature," any possibility of gaining a balanced insight into the shift from manuscript to print culture was negated by the practice of taking into consideration only that printed material which they perceived to be "Literature" with a capital "L," and thus including only that storytelling or poetry which reached for them a certain standard. This meant that a mere fraction of modern writing was compared to the sum total of traditional literature, and the new thus seemed truly remote from the old. Some scholars, who perceived modern literature to be the offspring of a marriage between the European literary spirit and the Malay language, apparently viewed that language as a *tabula rasa*. An understanding of the wider context of Malay discourse would have revealed to them how similar in its schematic structure to traditional literature and oral composition was and is so much of what the scholars would have regarded as "sub-literary" material. Such an understanding would have enabled them to throw much light upon the shift from manuscript to print culture. The modern, educated Indonesian who claims to know absolutely nothing of "old Malay literature" nevertheless often reveals in his speech an extensive familiarity with the traditional schemata employed to produce that literature. These come with the language. The scholar did not perhaps realize the extent of the battle with those traditional schemata that had to be waged by the Indonesian writers who succeeded in producing what the scholars welcomed as "modern literature." These writers did not begin with a neutral medium; they had to shear away the unwanted formulary features.

A similar problem was faced by scholars in understanding the shift from oral to written composition. The change undergone by rhythmical speech when adapted to the idiom of the *hikayat* was seen as a regressive step rather than an outcome of the change in medium: the mnemonic patterning so necessary for the retrieval and preservation of knowledge in an oral milieu could be dispensed with in direct proportion to the alleviation of the burden of memorization allowed by writing.

Clearly, an understanding of the workings of oral composition, both stylized and nonstylized, and written composition, be it in the form of manuscript or print, can result only from a study of the interaction between these forms in the context of Malay discourse as a whole. A comparison of material composed in these various forms reveals certain distinctive features attributable to the nature of the media employed.

In a society where the processing of information is an oral operation, knowledge must be woven into distinctive patterns if it is to survive. Mnemonic patterning is one aspect of this schematic structuring, and is employed when a specific word choice—or approximation thereof—is to be recalled, as in the retrieval of *adat* sayings and in stylized oral composition. However, schematic structuring is found not merely on the level of word choice, but operates on every level of composition up to that of the plot. Furthermore, the use of schematic composition is not restricted to the stylized form. Though specific word choice may be less important in nonstylized storytelling or in the recounting of experiences in the course of the daily round, it should not be thought that this everyday speech is somehow ephemeral. It, too, is schematically patterned. The use of schemata is not thus an artificial device peculiar to stylized performance. It reflects rather the general state of mind; indeed, the schematic features of stylized composition may be seen as an intensified form of the schematic features of everyday speech. Of course, in applying terms such as "schematic" or "formulaic" to the discourse of an oral milieu, we are not identifying some objective category. We are merely perceiving that, in comparison to our print-literate standards of what is normal, knowledge in Malay oral tradition was preserved and presented in larger units than those to which we are accustomed. There was much more of a need to preserve wholes, and thus a corresponding hesitation to fragment knowledge.

Of course, the advent of writing or print does not mean that people no longer speak or write, respectively. It may mean, however, that they learn to speak and write in ways not previously possible. On the other hand, it would be fatuous to insist that the intrinsic nature of literacy guarantees that the development of writing will everywhere follow inexorably one set pattern of development. For example, in traditional Malay manuscript literature, we see a much reduced use of mnemonic patterning. We also observe some attempt to adjust and adapt the traditional schemata. Nevertheless, the great bulk of manuscript literature was still highly schematic in structure. As long as the writer's audience experienced his work aurally, the advantages of literacy remained largely private to himself. By way of contrast, we observe that the contemporaneous *kitab* literature, which postulated a more literate and scholarly audience, reveals the presence of considerably more analytical and abstract thought patterns.

This leads us to consider the question of constraints, of possibilities, and of inevitabilities. Bearing in mind that a text or other composition constitutes a transaction between a composer and an audience, it is easy to appreciate how a specific medium and the nature of the audience may exercise constraints and preclude certain eventualities. In an oral milieu, for example, the evanescent nature of the spoken word makes it impossible for the speaker to detach himself from his speech and contemplate it as an object. An aurally consuming, nonliterate postulated audience, furthermore, places constraints on the level of complexity possible in a written text. And the widespread use of indexing could not develop in a manuscript culture.

Our awareness of such constraints derives, of course, from our knowledge of the possibilities offered by new media. For example, with writing and especially print, one is provided with new ways of classifying knowledge, and need no longer rely upon narrative, genealogies, or *adat* sayings to organize experience. The freedom from memorization is extended even further in the electronic age. Those of us who grew up in a pre-electronic, print culture are often amazed that the modern school child may find it unnecessary to learn multiplication tables by rote; he uses a calculator. It is paradoxical that the computer literate is often unable to spell the simplest words; he uses "Spelprogram."

My point is that our knowledge of the possibilities offered by new media derives entirely from possibilities realized. Thus, for example, when we say that alphabetic literacy leads to the development of analytical thought, we are merely saying that it did lead to what we now define as analytical thought.

That such developments are an inevitable outcome of the nature of literacy would seem to be an unprovable assertion in view of the fact that the alphabet in the strict sense was a nonce invention. The attainments of the Greeks, furthermore, were bequeathed not merely to Europe but also to the Islamic world, of which the Malay-speaking areas were a part. Yet in a sense, such developments may be said to have been inevitable in that they did indeed occur. We might think of

Batak writing—in the nineteenth century still largely an exercise in magic—as the most obvious exception to any rule which demands that writing produce certain predictable results. Yet if we examine Batak writing today, we see that those results have indeed been realized. And it is in the work of the Batak writer Iwan Simatupang writing in Indonesian that we observe some of the most abstract language of modern Indonesian literature.

However, the fact that such developments occurred is no indication that they occurred as an outcome of the nature of literacy *per se*. They resulted rather from Western expansionism, manifested here specifically in the introduction of mass education.

In light of these considerations, we see the problematic nature of any attempt to ascribe the developments of the past hundred years in the Malay world to the intrinsic quality of print literacy and its inevitable results. The transplanting of Western patterns of print literacy makes it impossible—and indeed irrelevant—to distinguish between what is the natural outcome of the introduction of print literacy and what was adopted from the West. Suffice it to say that the Malay/Indonesian language has undergone a radical transformation making it possible to express the most abstract and analytical thought patterns of Western culture. The proportion of the populace privy to such modes of thinking and expression is still relatively tiny in both Malaysia and Indonesia. The introduction of print literacy—which brought with it the possibilities already realized in the "donor" cultures—did not cause a clean break with the past. Even those highly literate in a Western language who rejected the old modes of expression found themselves in a battle with the past when they wrote in Malay, for the language brought with it the past, a past of radically oral manuscript culture. Though such groups as the Pujangga Baru may not have been aware that their battle was with orality, they clearly understood that a text is a transaction with an audience, and that merely translating their ideas into Malay would not suffice. For the mass of the population, who lacked the yardstick of an education in a Western language, old habits died much harder. The introduction of print literacy did not cause an immediate change in the general state of mind. The natural tendency was to perceive the new in terms of familiar schemata. The result was that even the educated sector of the populace continued to favor a paratactic, formulaic, copious, repetitive, narrative, and concrete mode of expression. Such a mode was necessary for effective communication in an oral or aurally consuming society; in a print culture, it is not: what became redundant in print now strikes us as mere verbosity.

It might be argued that the transition from the radical orality of manuscript culture to modern print literacy has been remarkably rapid in the Malay world, taking little more than a century, and that we must be patient, sitting back while further developments take their inevitable albeit tortuous course. Such a view is hardly very satisfying, however, for the teacher who wishes to see his students from an oral background develop into scholars equal in attainment to any in the West. And such a view is clearly defeatist.

To say that the society is still orally oriented is not to say that all its members are equally orally oriented. As we have seen, the experience of the individual need tell us little about the development of literacy in the society as a whole. Given the right conditions, the individual from an oral background may progress to the highest levels of literacy in a relatively short period of time. Evidence of this is provided by the work of numerous Malaysian and Indonesian scholars from radically oral backgrounds which is well able to hold its own in an international forum. However, the "right conditions" implies some form of special training, and in the past this has usually involved study abroad, which cut off the individual from his oral roots and militated against his being able to lapse into the orally oriented patterns of his usual speech. I am not at all suggesting that the way to analytical and abstract modes of thought and expression is therefore via the medium of a Western language and residence in a foreign country.

A far more economical and less roundabout approach would be to confront the problem directly, and it is here that we see the practical application of studying the interaction between orality and literacy in Malay society. We come to realize that the apparent woolly-mindedness of many students is in no way a reflection of any lack of intelligence. Rather, it is their strong oral orientation which hinders them from exploiting to the full the possibilities of print literacy. Only by identifying the student's oral habits as such can we help him overcome and discard them. There is no point in telling him to be critical. Rather he must be liberated from having to learn by rote; he must be trained to fragment his formulas, to free himself from the pull of narrative, and confront what he is taught with his own experience.

It is fitting that I should end by citing an example of a consummate lesson in critical thinking provided by the Indonesian author Pramoedya Ananta Toer in his tetralogy *Jejak Langkah di atas Lumpur*. In the first three novels of the series, the protagonist and narrator is Minke (R. M. Tirto Adhisoerjo). Although the reader is left in no doubt about the hero's quirks, he has no option but to depend upon this reliably unreliable narrator. The distance between implied author and narrator decreases appreciably after the first volume, and Adhisoerjo becomes the controlling consciousness. He represents the core of values, and his are the standards by which everything is measured. By the end of the third volume we do not think of questioning our narrator's assessment of his arch-enemy Pangemanann. Then, in the fourth volume, the controlling consciousness is split. We begin the first page expecting to be guided further by Adhisoerjo, and suddenly realize that Pangemanann is the narrator! The effect on the reader is quite devastating. He is forced to reconsider everything he has come to take for granted. Pramoedya has not attempted to lecture his audience on the importance of being critical; he has created a situation which demands it.

Glossary

adat	custom, correct mode of procedure
alim	learned, erudite, particularly in religious matters
Awang Batil	a genre of storytelling in Perlis and Kedah. The performer accompanies his rhythmical speech by strumming with his fingers on a brass bowl (*batil*)
bahasa	language, good breeding, discretion
bahasa berirama	rhythmical speech
bahwa	that, whereas
Bangsawan	Malay "opera." Urban-based popular drama
bilangan	a "run." A stretch of relatively fixed utterance
bomoh	folk practitioner, healer
cerita	tale
dalang	puppeteer, master of the shadow-play
fitnah	slander
gantang	a measure of weight equivalent to five *kati*s (1 *kati* = $1\frac{1}{3}$lbs.)
haji	one who has made the pilgrimage to Mecca
hikayat	written account, in prose
imam	prayer leader, mosque official
Jawi	traditionally "Malay" in a Muslim context. Now used mainly to refer to the Arabic script
jembalang	spirit, soul

Jubang Linggang	a genre of Kedah storytelling, in which the performer chants the tale without musical or rhythmical accompaniment
Kaba	traditional tale of the Minangkabau
kampung	village. The word "compound" is derived from *kampung*
kanun	administrative law
kata adat	customary saying, maxim
kitab	(Arabic: book.) In Malay, *kitab* has the connotation of book concerning matters of Muslim religion, philosophy, jurisprudence, etc. Although theoretically in Islam there is no distinction to be made between the sacred and the secular, in traditional Malay literature there is a clear distinction between the palace *hikayat* intended to be heard by a listening audience, and *kitab* literature, which was primarily intended to be read
konon	"It is said." Used as an opening formula in storytelling
latah	startle syndrome, paroxysmal neurosis. The person afflicted involuntarily imitates whatever startled him or her
lebai	pious individual
Main Puteri	spirit mediumship, involving drama and music, performed to diagnose and cure
Mak Yong	traditional Malay dramatic genre, found on the east coast of the Malay Peninsula, Kedah, and parts of eastern Sumatra
masa adat	the era of the *adat,* q.v.
Mek Mulung	traditional Malay drama found in Kedah. All the roles are performed by males
merisik	discreet inquiries, sounding out
minduk	the spike fiddle player in *Main Puteri.* Acts as control of the performer in trance
mulut masin	lit. salty-mouthed. Refers to someone whose words always come true
nazam	literary composition, usually in metrical form. A variety of verse types have been labeled "*nazam*"
negeri	homeland, state, settlement
nyanyi	song, sing

pandan	screwpine
pantun	quatrain, rhyming *a b a b*
pawang	specialist in skill requiring magic
penglipur lara	"soother of cares." A term applied to various types of traditional storytelling. Has acquired a more specific connotation, now designating mainly tales collected from professional storytellers under British auspices
pepatah	adage, maxim, customary saying
petua	directive, advice, framed as a maxim
pidato	ceremonial speech
pontianak	birth demon. Appears in form of beautiful woman
Pujangga Baru	"the new poets." A group of Indonesian writers of the thirties of this century
rojak	mixed salad
sajak	modern poem, rhyme
sastra	literature. Traditionally, the term referred to divination, astrology
sastra lisan	"oral literature"
sejarah	account of the past. Now equivalent to "history"
Selampit	a genre of traditional storytelling in Kedah and Perlis. See also *Tarik Selampit*
serati	a breed of domesticated duck
Sijobang	sung narrative of Minangkabau concerning the hero Anggun nan Tungga
silsilah	genealogy, chronicle
sombong	proud and haughty
songkok	black velvet fez
Srivijaya	maritime state based on Southeast Sumatra which emerged at least as early as the seventh century A.D.
syair	traditional poem written to be sung, with four-line stanzas rhyming *a ;a ;a ;a, b ;b ;b ;b,* etc.
tabik	greeting, salutation
Tambo	traditional annals of Minangkabau
Tarik Selampit	a genre of traditional storytelling found in Kelantan and Patani. The performer accompanies his chant on a spike fiddle
tashdid	a sign indicating that a consonant is to be doubled, or, in Arabic, "strengthened"

tukang pidato	ceremonial speech maker of Minangkabau
undang-undang	legal digest
wayang, wayang kulit	shadow-play
Wayang Siam	the Malay shadow-play, featuring characters drawn mainly from the tale of Rama

Bibliography

ABBREVIATIONS

BKI   *Bijdragen tot de Taal-, Land- en Volkenkunde van het*
           Koninklijk Instituut
JMBRAS   *Journal of the Malayan/Malaysian Branch of the Royal Asiatic*
           Society
JSBRAS   *Journal of the Straits Branch of the Royal Asiatic Society*
TBG   *Tijdschrift voor Indische Taal-, Land- en Volkenkunde van het*
           Bataviaasch Genootschap van Kunsten en Wetenschappen

WORKS CITED

Abdullah Ambary. 1967. *Intisari Sastra Indonesia.* Bandung: Djatnika. (3rd
    printing: 1974.)
Adat Raja-raja Melayu. 1929. Ph. S. van Ronkel, ed. *Adat Radja Radja Mela-*
    joe, naar drie Londensche Handschriften. Leiden: Brill.
Alisjahbana, Sutan Takdir. 1937. *Lajar Terkembang.* Djakarta: Balai Pustaka.
———. 1948. *Puisi Lama.* Djakarta: Pustaka Rakjat. (5th printing: 1961.)
Anderson, John. 1826. *Mission to the East Coast of Sumatra in 1823.* Edin-
    burgh and London. (Reprinted by Oxford: 1971.)
Anderson, Walter. 1923. *Kaiser und Abt.* FF Communications 42. Helsinki.
Ariffin Nor. 1957. *Rangkaian Sastera Melayu; Puisi.* Penang: Sinaran.
Asa'ad Shukri Haji Muda. 1962. *Sejarah Kelantan.* Kelantan: PAP (Pustaka
    Aman).
Asmah Haji Omar. 1968. "Word Classes in Malay." *Anthropological Linguis-*
    tics 10 (5): 12–21.
Asmah Haji Omar and Rama Subbiah. 1968. *An Introduction to Malay*
    Grammar. Kuala Lumpur: Dewan Bahasa dan Pustaka.

al-Attas, Syed Naguib. 1968. *The Origin of the Malay Sha'ir*. Kuala Lumpur: Dewan Bahasa dan Pustaka.

——. 1970. *The Mysticism of Hamzah Fansuri*. Kuala Lumpur: University of Malaya Press.

——. 1972. *Islam Dalam Sejarah dan Kebudayaan Melayu*. Kuala Lumpur: Universiti Kebangsaan Malaysia.

Barzun, Jacques. 1974. *Clio and the Doctors*. Chicago: University of Chicago Press.

——. 1975. *Classic, Romantic and Modern*. Chicago: University of Chicago. (This edition first published 1961.)

Becker, A. L. 1979. "The Figure a Sentence Makes: An Interpretation of a Classical Malay Sentence." *Syntax and Semantics* 12:243–59.

——. 1979a. "Text-building, Epistemology, and Aesthetics in Javanese Shadow Theatre." In A. L. Becker and A. Yengoyan, eds. *The Imagination of Reality: Essays in Southeast Asian Coherence Systems*. Norwood, N.J.: Ablex.

Bijleveld, B. J. 1943. *Herhalingsfiguren in het Maleisch, Javaansch en Soendaasch*. Groningen/Batavia: J. B. Wolters.

Booth, Wayne C. 1961. *The Rhetoric of Fiction*. Chicago: University of Chicago Press.

Braginsky, V. I. 1975. *Evolyutsiya Malayskogo Klassicheskogo Stikha*. Moscow: Nauka.

Brakel, L. F. 1980. "Postscript" in Jones, 1980:128–31.

Brown, C. C. 1956. *A Guide to English-Malay Translation*. London: Longmans, Green & Co.

de Casparis, J. G. 1956. *Selected Inscriptions from the 7th to the 9th Century A.D. Prasasti Indonesia II*. Bandung: Masa Baru.

Cherita Jenaka. 1941. R. O. Winstedt and A. J. Sturrock, eds. Singapore: Malaya Publishing House. (First published 1908.)

Clifford, Hugh. 1899. *In a Corner of Asia*. London: T. Fisher Unwin.

——. 1925. *In a Corner of Asia*. (Revised version.) New York: Robert M. McBride & Co.

Coedes, G. 1930. "Les Inscriptions Malaises de Çrivijaya." *Bulletin de l'École Française d'Extrême-Orient* 30:29–80.

Collins, William. 1979. "Besemah Concepts: A Study of the Culture of a People of South Sumatra." Ph.D. dissertation. University of California, Berkeley.

Coster-Wijsman, L. M. 1929. *Uilespiegel-Verhalen in Indonesie*. Dissertatie, Leiden. Santpoort: C. A. Mees.

Curtius, Ernst Robert. 1973. *European Literature and the Latin Middle Ages*. Princeton: Princeton University Press. (First published in German in 1948.)

Darus Ahmad. 1957. *Kesusasteraan Tua Melayu*. Penang: Sinaran.

——. 1957a. *Alam Puisi Melayu*. Penang: Sinaran.

——. 1960. *Persuratan Melayu, Lama-Baru*. Penang: Sinaran.

Day, Anthony. 1978. "*Babad Kandha, Babad Kraton* and Variation in Modern Javanese Literature." *BKI* 134 (4):433–50.

Day, Clive. 1904. *The Policy and the Administration of the Dutch in Java*. New York: Macmillan.

Djojopoespito, Soewarsih. 1940. *Buiten het Gareel*. Amsterdam: Vrij Nederland.

Doorenbos, J. 1933. *De Geschriften van Hamzah Pansoeri*. Dissertatie, Leiden.

Drewes, G. W. J. 1950. "De Herkomst van het Voegwoord Bahwasanja." *Bingkisan Budi*. Leiden: Sijthoff, 104–16.

———. 1961. *De Biografie van een Minangkabausen Peperhandelaar in de Lampongs*. Verhandelingen van het Koninklijk Instituut, 36.

Dundes, Alan, ed. 1965. *The Study of Folklore*. Englewood Cliffs, N.J.: Prentice-Hall.

Dundes, Alan, and Carl R. Pagter. 1975. *Urban Folklore from the Paperwork Empire*. Austin, Tex.: American Folklore Society.

Edrus, A. H. 1960. *Persuratan Melayu. I. Prosa* (and) *II. Puisi*. Singapore: Qalam.

Errington, Shelly. 1979a. "Some Comments on Style in the Meanings of the Past." In Anthony Reid and David Marr, eds. *Perceptions of the Past in Southeast Asia*. Singapore: Heinemann.

———. 1979b. "Some Comments on Style in the Meanings of the Past." *Journal of Asian Studies* 38 (2):231–44.

Fatimah Busu. 1980. *Kepulangan*. Penang: Teks Publishing.

Finnegan, Ruth. 1977. *Oral Poetry*. Cambridge: Cambridge University Press.

Gazali Dunia. 1959. *Sedjarah dan Tela'ah Seni Sastra*. Djakarta: Widjaja. (3rd printing: 1971.)

———. 1969. *Langgam Sastera Lama*. Kuala Lumpur: Oxford University Press.

Gibson, Walter M. 1855. *The Prison of Weltevreden*. New York: Riker.

Gombrich, E. H. 1969. *Art and Illusion: A Study in the Psychology of Pictorial Representation*. Princeton: Princeton University Press. (First published 1960.)

Gonda, J. 1940. "Een Zeventiende-eeuwse Stem over het Maleis." *BKI* 99 (1):101–10.

Gonggryp, G. F. E. 1934. *Geïllustreerde Encyclopaedie van Nederlandsch-Indië*. Leiden.

Goody, Jack. 1968. *Literacy in Traditional Societies*. Cambridge: Cambridge University Press.

———. 1977. *The Domestication of the Savage Mind*. Cambridge: Cambridge University Press.

Haiman, J. 1980. "The Iconicity of Grammar: Isomorphism and Motivation." *Language* 56 (3).

Harun Aminurrashid. 1960. *Kajian Puisi Melayu*. Singapore: Pustaka Melayu. (3rd printing: 1962.)

Havelock, Eric A. 1963. *Preface to Plato*. Cambridge, Mass.: Harvard University Press.

———. 1971. *Prologue to Greek Literacy*. Cincinnati, Ohio: University of Cincinnati.

———. 1982. *The Literate Revolution in Greece and Its Cultural Consequences*. Princeton: Princeton University Press.

Hervey, D. F. A. 1884. "Valentyn's Description of Malacca." *JSBRAS* 13:49–74.

Hikayat Abdullah. N.d. Reprint of original lithograph. Djakarta: Perdana.
————. 1953. R. A. Datoek Besar and R. Roolvink, eds. Djakarta: Djambatan.
Hikayat Aceh. See Iskandar, 1959.
Hikayat Andaken Penurat. See Robson, 1969.
Hikayat Hang Tuah. 1949. Malay Literature Series. Singapore: Malaya Publishing House.
————. 1964. Kassim Ahmad, ed. Kuala Lumpur: Dewan Bahasa dan Pustaka.
Hikayat Indera Bangsawan. 1915. Betawi: Commissie voor de Volkslectuur.
Hikayat Marsekalek. Cod. 2276d in Leiden University Library. Wan Mat Seman, ed. Unpublished B.A. thesis. Universiti Kebangsaan Malaysia, 1974.
Hikayat Merung Mahawangsa. See Siti Hawa Saleh, 1970.
Hikayat Nakhoda Muda. See Drewes, 1961.
Hikayat Pandawa Lima. 1964. Khalid Hussein, ed. Kuala Lumpur: Dewan Bahasa dan Pustaka.
Hikayat Raja-raja Pasai. Raffles Manuscript 67, Royal Asiatic Society, London.
————. 1960. A. H. Hill, ed. *JMBRAS* 33 (2):1–214.
Hikayat Seri Rama. 1915. W. G. Shellabear, ed. *JSBRAS* 71:1–285.
————. 1980. See Achadiati Ikram, 1980.
Hill, A. H. 1960. See *Hikayat Raja-raja Pasai.*
Hirsch, E. D., Jr. 1967. *Validity in Interpretation.* New Haven: Yale University Press.
de Hollander, J. J. 1882. *Handleiding bij de Beoefening der Maleische Taal en Letterkunde.* Breda. (1st edition: 1845.)
————. 1856. See *Syair Ken Tambuhan.*
Hooykaas, C. 1939. "Modern Maleisch, zijn Verspreiding, Bruikbaarheid en Toekomst." *Koloniale Studiën* 23:405–38.
————. 1947. *Over Maleise Literatuur.* Leiden: Brill. (1st edition: 1937.)
————. 1952. *Literatuur in Maleis en Indonesisch.* Groningen: J. B. Wolters.
————. 1961. *Perintis Sastra.* Groningen: J. B. Wolters. (1st published 1951.)
Ikram, Achadiati. 1980. *Hikayat Sri Rama; Suntingan Naskah disertai Telaah Amanat dan Struktur.* Jakarta: Universitas Indonesia.
Innes, Emily. 1885. *The Chersonese with the Gilding Off.* 2 vols. London. (Reprinted in 1974 by Oxford in Asia.)
Iskandar, Teuku. 1959. *De Hikajat Atjeh.* Dissertatie, Leiden.
————. 1967. "Three Malay Historical Writings in the First Half of the 17th Century." *JMBRAS* 40 (2):38–53.
Ismail Hussein. 1966. *Sejarah Pertumbuhan Bahasa Kebangsaan Kita.* Kuala Lumpur: Dewan Bahasa dan Pustaka.
————. 1970. "Masalah Pensejarahan Sastra Melayu Baru." *Penulis* 4 (1–2):220–28.
————. 1974. *The Study of Traditional Malay Literature with a Selected Bibliography.* Kuala Lumpur: Dewan Bahasa dan Pustaka.
————. 1976. "Kesusasteraan Nasional Malaysia." In Anwar Ridhwan, ed. *Di Sekitar Pemikiran Kesusasteraan Malaysia.* Kuala Lumpur: Dewan Bahasa dan Pustaka.
Jameson, Frederic. 1972. *The Prison-House of Language.* Princeton: Princeton University Press.

Jaspan, M. A. 1964. *Folk Literature of South Sumatra; Redjang Ka-Ga-Nga Texts*. Canberra: Australian National University.

Jones, Russell. 1980. "Review Article: Problems of Editing Malay Texts." *Archipel* 20:121–27.

de Josselin de Jong, P. E. 1964. "The Character of the Malay Annals." In J. Bastin and R. Roolvink, eds. *Malayan and Indonesian Studies*. Oxford: Clarendon. 235–41.

Kassim Ahmad. 1964. See *Hikayat Hang Tuah*.

de Kat Angelino, A. D. A. 1930. *Staatkundig Beleid en Bestuurzorg in Nederlandsch-Indië. Tweede Deel; De Overheidzorg in Ned.-Indië*. The Hague: Martinus Nijhoff.

Kern, H. 1910. *Itinerario, Voyage ofte Schipvaert van Jan Huygen van Linschoten naer Oost ofte Portugaels Indien 1579–1592*. (2nd edition revised by H. Terpstra, 1955.) The Hague: Martinus Nijhoff.

Kern, W. 1956. *Commentaar op de Salasilah van Koetai*. Verhandelingen van het Koninklijk Instituut, 19. The Hague: Martinus Nijhoff.

Kesah Raja Marong Maha Wangsa. 1965. Abdullah Hj. Musa Lubis, ed. Kuala Lumpur: Pustaka Antara.

Kratz, E. U. 1981. "The Editing of Malay Manuscripts and Textual Criticism." *BKI* 137 (2 & 3):229–43.

Kuda Semirang Seri Panji Pandai Rupa. 1931. Kota Baru, Kelantan: Perkitapan Press.

Kwee Tek Hoay. 1930. *Boenga Roos Dari Tjikembang*. Batavia: Panorama. (First published 1927.)

Lewis, M. B. 1947. *Teach Yourself Malay*. London: Hodder & Stoughton.

Liaw Yock Fang. 1975. *Sejarah Kesusasteraan Melayu Klassik*. Singapore: Pustaka Nasional.

Lord, Albert B. 1976. *The Singer of Tales*. New York: Atheneum. (First published 1960.)

Luria, A. R. 1976. *Cognitive Development: Its Cultural and Social Foundations*. Cambridge, Mass.: Harvard University Press. (First published in 1974 in Russian)

Macknight, C. C. 1981. "The Oral Transmission of a Written Tradition: Bugis Chronicles from Sulawesi, Indonesia." Paper presented at Conference on Transmission in Oral and Written Traditions, Australian National University, Canberra.

Maier, H. J. M., and A. Teeuw, eds. 1976. *Honderd Jaar Studie van Indonesië 1850–1950*. The Hague: Smits.

Marsden, William. 1811. *The History of Sumatra*. London. 3rd edition. (1st edition: 1783.)

———. 1812. *A Grammar of the Malayan Language*. London.

Maxwell, W. E. 1886. "Sri Rama, a Malay Fairy Tale Founded on the Ramayana." *JSBRAS* 17:86–115.

Mees, C. A. 1935. *De Kroniek van Koetai*. Dissertatie, Leiden. Santpoort: C. A. Mees.

Memoranda Angkatan Sasterawan '50. 1962. Kuala Lumpur: Oxford University Press.

Milner, A. C. 1982. *Kerajaan: Malay Political Culture on the Eve of Colonial Rule*. Association for Asian Studies Monograph, 40. Tucson: University of Arizona Press.

Misa Melayu. 1919. R. O. Winstedt, ed. Malay Literature Series 15. Singapore.

Netscher, E. 1854. "De Twaalf Spreukgedichten door Radja Ali Hadji van Riouw." *TBG* 2:11–32.

Newbold, T. J. 1839. *Political and Statistical Account of the British Settlements in the Straits of Malacca*. 2 vols. London. (Reprinted in 1971 by Oxford in Asia.)

van Nieuwenhuijze, C. A. O. 1945. *Šamsu 'l-Din van Pasai; Bijdrage tot de Kennis der Sumatraansche Mystiek*. Leiden: Brill.

Omardin Haji Asha'ari. 1961. *Kajian Pantun Melayu*. Singapore: Malaya Publishing House.

Ong, Walter J. 1967. *The Presence of the Word*. New Haven: Yale University Press. (Reprinted in 1981 by University of Minnesota Press.)

———. 1971. *Rhetoric, Romance, and Technology*. Ithaca: Cornell University Press.

———. 1977. *Interfaces of the Word*. Ithaca: Cornell University Press.

———. 1982. *Orality and Literacy: The Technologizing of the Word*. London and New York: Methuen.

Overbeck, Hans. 1925. *Malaiische Erzählungen*. Jena: Diederichs.

———. 1938. Review article: "Over Maleische Literatuur, door Dr. C. Hooykaas." *TBG* 78 (2):292–333.

Pane, Armijn. 1940. *Belenggu*. Pudjangga Baru, 7. Djakarta.

Paterson, H. S. 1924. "An Early Malay Inscription from Trengganu." *JMBRAS* 2 (3):252–58.

Phillips, N. G. 1981. *Sijobang: Sung Narrative Poetry of West Sumatra*. Cambridge: Cambridge University Press.

———. 1981a. "Further Thoughts on the Metre of Sijobang." Paper presented at the Third European Colloquium on Malay and Indonesian Studies, Naples.

Pijnappel, J. 1870. "De Maleische Handschriften der Leidsche Bibliotheek." *BKI* 3 (5):142–48.

Pramoedya Ananta Toer. 1980–. *Jejak Langkah di atas Lumpur*. A tetralogy in the *Seri Bumi Manusia*. (At the time of writing this book, only the first two parts [*Bumi Manusia* and *Anak Semua Bangsa*] have been published.) Jakarta: Hasta Mitra.

Propp, Vladimir. 1968. *Morphology of the Folktale*. Austin: University of Texas Press. (First published in 1928 in Russian.)

Raffles, Thomas S. 1817. *The History of Java*. 2 vols. London.

Raja Ali Haji. 1857. *Bustānu 'l-Kātibīn*. Penyengat.

Richards, I. A., and C. M. Gibson. 1952. *English through Pictures*. New York: Pocket Books.

Robson, S. O. 1969. *Hikajat Andaken Penurat*. Bibliotheca Indonesica, 2. The Hague.

Rockwell, Joan. 1974. *Fact in Fiction*. London: Routledge & Kegan Paul.

Roff, W. R. 1974. *The Origins of Malay Nationalism*. Kuala Lumpur: University of Malaya Press. (First published by Yale University Press in 1967.)

――――. 1974a. "The Mystery of the First Malay Novel (and Who Was Rokambul?)." *BKI* 130 (4): 450–64.

van Ronkel, Ph. S. 1899. "Over Invloed der Arabische Syntaxis op de Maleische." *TBG* 41:498–528.

――――. 1900. "Over eene Oude Lijst van Maleische Handschriften." *TBG* 42: 309–22.

――――. 1909. *Catalogus der Maleische Handschriften*. Verhandelingen van het Bataviaasch Genootschap, 57.

Roolvink, R. 1967. "The Variant Versions of the Malay Annals." *BKI* 123:301–24.

――――. 1975. *Bahasa Jawi; de Taal van Sumatra*. Rede. Leiden: Universitaire Pers Leiden.

Roorda van Eysinga, P. P. 1827. *De Kroon aller Koningen van Bocharie van Djohor*. Batavia.

――――. 1838. *Radin Mantri. Eene Romance naar een Indisch Handschrift van Ali Musthathier*. Breda.

Saintsbury, George. 1898. *A Short History of English Literature*. London: Macmillan. (16th printing: 1944.)

Scholes, Robert, and Robert Kellogg. 1966. *The Nature of Narrative*. London: Oxford University Press.

Sejarah Melayu. Raffles Manuscript 18 of the Royal Asiatic Society, London.

――――. 1938. R. O. Winstedt, ed. "The Malay Annals or Sejarah Melayu." *JMBRAS* 16 (3):1–226.

――――. 1952. T. D. Situmorang and A. Teeuw, eds. *Sedjarah Melaju, menurut Terbitan Abdullah*. Djakarta: Djambatan.

Selamat, R. O. 1963. *Bunga Rampai Kajian Sastera Melayu*. Penang: Sinaran.

Shellabear, W. G. 1901. "The Evolution of Malay Spelling." *JSBRAS* 36:75–135.

――――. 1915. See *Hikayat Seri Rama*.

Silsilah Raja-raja Berunai. 1968. Amin Sweeney, ed. *JMBRAS* 41:1–82.

Simatupang, Iwan. 1982. *Tegak Lurus dengan Langit*. Jakarta: Sinar Harapan.

Simorangkir-Simandjuntak, B. 1951. *Kesusasteraan Indonesia*. In 3 vols. Djakarta: Pembangunan. (14th printing: 1962.)

Siti Hawa Saleh. 1970. *Hikayat Merong Mahawangsa*. Kuala Lumpur: University of Malaya Press.

Situmorang and Teeuw. See *Sejarah Melayu*.

Skeat, W. W. 1953. "The Cambridge University Expedition to the Northeastern Malay States and to Upper Perak, 1899–1900." *JMBRAS* 26 (4):3–147.

Skinner, C. 1963. *Sja'ir Perang Mengkasar*. Verhandelingen van het Koninklijk Instituut, 40. The Hague.

――――. 1965. *The Civil War in Kelantan in 1839*. Monographs of the Malaysian Branch of the Royal Asiatic Society, 2.

――――. 1978. "Transitional Malay Literature. Part I." *BKI* 134 (4):466–87.

Snouck Hurgronje, C. 1888 & 1889. *Mekka*. 2 vols. Leiden.
————. 1900. "Islam und Phonograph." *TBG* 42:393–427.
Soeparlan D. S. 1952. *Rangkuman Kesusasteraan Indonesia*. Djakarta: Pustaka Dewata.
Sweeney, Amin. 1967. "The Connection between the Hikayat Raja-raja Pasai and the Sejarah Melayu." *JMBRAS* 40 (2):93–105.
————. 1971. "Some Observations on the Malay Sha'ir." *JMBRAS* 44 (1):52–70.
————. 1972. *The Ramayana and the Malay Shadow-play*. Kuala Lumpur: National University of Malaysia Press.
————. 1972a. *Malay Shadow Puppets*. London: British Museum.
————. 1973. "Professional Malay Storytelling: Some Questions of Style and Presentation." *JMBRAS* 46 (2):1–53. (Reprinted in Michigan Papers on South and Southeast Asia, no. 8, 1974.)
————. 1976. "The Pak Pandir Cycle of Tales." *JMBRAS* 49 (1):15–88.
————. 1979. "Rakugo, Professional Japanese Storytelling." *Asian Folklore Studies* 38 (1):25–80.
————. 1980. *Authors and Audiences in Traditional Malay Literature*. Monograph no. 20, Center for South and Southeast Asia Studies. Berkeley: University of California.
————. 1980a. *Reputations Live On: An Early Malay Autobiography*. Berkeley: University of California Press.
————. 1983. "The 'Literary' Study of Malay-Indonesian Literature." *JMBRAS* 56 (1):33–46.
Sweeney, Amin, and Sylvia Tiwon. 1986. "The Views of Valentijn and Werndly on Malay Literature." Forthcoming.
Syair Ceritera Bijaksana. circa 1923. (The foreword is dated 1923. The work was probably published in Kelantan. Printed by The United Press, Penang.)
Syair Ken Tambuhan. 1856. J. J. de Hollander, ed. *Sjair Ken Tamboehan*. Leiden: Brill.
Syair Perang Mengkasar. See Skinner, 1963.
Syair Siti Zubaidah Perang Cina. 1924 (Rejab, A.H. 1343). Singapore: Sulaiman Mari'e.
Taju 'l-Salatin. See Roorda van Eysinga, 1827.
Tajul Kelantan. 1958. *Perinchis Pantun*. Penang: Sinaran.
Taufik Abdullah. 1966. "Adat and Islam: An Examination of Conflict in Minangkabau." *Indonesia* 2:1–24.
————. 1970. "Some Notes on the Kaba Tjindua Mato: An Example of Minangkabau Traditional Literature." *Indonesia* 9:1–22.
Taylor, Archer. 1965. "Folklore and the Student of Literature." In Dundes, 1965. (Reprinted from *Pacific Spectator*, 2, 1948.)
Teeuw, A. 1955. *De Bahasa Indonesia, de Wereld en Nederland*. Rede. Amsterdam: Djambatan.
————. 1961. *A Critical Survey of Studies on Malay and Bahasa Indonesia*. The Hague: Martinus Nijhoff.
————. 1964. "Hikayat Raja-Raja Pasai and Sejarah Melayu." In J. Bastin

and R. Roolvink, eds. *Malayan and Indonesian Studies*. Oxford: Clarendon Press, 222–34.

———. 1966. "The Malay Sha'ir: Problems of Origin and Tradition." *BKI* 122:429–46.

———. 1967. *Modern Indonesian Literature*. The Hague: Martinus Nijhoff.

Tiwon, Sylvia. 1985. "Breaking the Spell: Tradition and Indonesian Poets of the 1930's." Ph.D. dissertation. University of California, Berkeley.

Usman Effendi. 1953. *200 Tanja Jawab Tentang Sastra Indonesia*. Djakarta: Gunung Agung. (21st printing: 1983.)

Valentijn, F. 1724. *Oud en Nieuw Oost-Indien*. 5 vols. Dordrecht-Amsterdam.

Voorhoeve, P. 1927. *Overzicht van de Volksverhalen der Bataks*. Dissertatie, Leiden.

———. 1940. "Uit de Letterkunde van Zuid-Sumatra." *Supplement op het Triwindoe-Gedenkboek Mangkoe Nagoro VII*. 132–44.

———. 1951. "Van en Over Nuruddin Ar-Raniri." *BKI* 107:353–68.

———. 1964. "A Malay Scriptorium." In J. Bastin and R. Roolvink, eds. *Malayan and Indonesian Studies*. Oxford: Clarendon. 256–66.

———. 1971. *Sudsumatranische Handschriften*. Verzeichnis der Orientalischen Handschriften in Deutschland, vol. 29. Wiesbaden.

———. 1978. "Some Notes on South Sumatran Epics." In S. Udin, ed. *Spectrum*. Jakarta: Dian Rakyat. 92–102.

de Vries, Jan. 1925 & 1928. *Volksverhalen uit Oost-Indië*. 2 vols. Zutphen.

Wellek, R., and A. Warren. 1973. *Theory of Literature*. Middlesex: Penguin. (First published 1949.)

Werndly, G. H. 1736. *Maleische Spraakkunst*. Amsterdam.

Wilkinson, R. J. 1922. *Law. Part I*. Papers on Malay Subjects. Kuala Lumpur.

———. 1924. *Malay Literature. Part I. Romance, History, Poetry*. Papers on Malay Subjects. Kuala Lumpur. (First published 1907.)

———. 1925. *Malay Literature. Part III. Malay Proverbs on Malay Character*. Papers on Malay Subjects. Kuala Lumpur.

———. 1932. *A Malay-English Dictionary*. 2 vols. Mytilene.

Willinck, G. D. 1909. *Het Rechtsleven bij de Minangkabausche Maleiërs*. Leiden: Brill.

Winstedt, R. O. 1913. *Malay Grammar*. Oxford: Clarendon. (Revised edition: 1927.)

———. 1923. *Malay Literature. Part II. Literature of Malay Folklore*. Papers on Malay Subjects. Kuala Lumpur. (First published 1907.)

———. 1927. See Winstedt, 1913.

———. 1938. See *Sejarah Melayu*, 1938.

———. 1939. "A History of Malay Literature." *JMBRAS* 17 (3):1–243.

———. 1950. *The Malays: A Cultural History*. London: Routledge & Kegan Paul. (1st edition: 1947.)

———. 1957a. "Note" in *Malim Deman*. Edited with A. J. Sturrock. Singapore. (First published 1908.)

———. 1957b. "Note" in *Awang Sulong Merah Muda*. Edited with A. J. Sturrock. Singapore. (First published 1908.)

———. 1958. "A History of Classical Malay Literature." *JMBRAS* 31 (3):1–
261. (Revised version of Winstedt, 1939.)

Winstedt, R. O. and R. J. Wilkinson. 1974. *A History of Perak.* Malaysian
Branch of the Royal Asiatic Society Reprints, no. 3. (First published in
JMBRAS 12 (1), 1934.)

Worsley, P. J. 1972. *Babad Buleleng.* Bibliotheca Indonesica 8. The Hague:
Martinus Nijhoff.

Yakof bin Kasim. 1975. "Adat Mendirikan Rumah Baru di Kawasan Masjid
Tanah, Melaka." B.A. thesis. Universiti Kebangsaan Malaysia.

Za'ba [Zainal-'Abidin bin Ahmad]. 1948. *Pelita Bahasa Melayu.* In 3 vols.:
1940, 1948, 1957. Malay School Series, no. 30.

Zieseniss, A. 1963. *The Rama Saga in Malaysia.* Singapore: MSRI. (Translation of *Die Rama Sage unter Malaien, ihre Herkunft und Gestaltung,*
Hamburg, 1928.)

Zuber Osman. 1957. *Kesusasteraan Lama Indonesia.* Djakarta: Gunung
Agung.

Zurbuchen, M. 1976. *Introduction to Old Javanese Language and Literature:
A Kawi Prose Anthology.* Michigan Series in South and Southeast Asian
Languages and Literatures, no. 3.

Index

Compositor:	Huron Valley Graphics
Text:	10/13 Sabon
Display:	Sabon
Printer:	Malloy Lithographing, Inc.
Binder:	John H. Dekker & Sons